ColdFusion Web Development with Macromedia Dreamweaver MX 2004

JEN AND PETER DEHAAN
with
Simon Horwith,
Curtis Hermann,
Massimo Foti,
and Eduardo Zubler

APress Media, LLC

ColdFusion Web Development with Macromedia Dreamweaver MX 2004
Copyright © 2004 by Apress
Originally published by Apress in 2004

ISBN 978-1-59059-237-3   ISBN 978-1-4302-0685-9 (eBook)
DOI 10.1007/978-1-4302-0685-9

Trademarked names may appear in this book. Rather than use a trademark symbol with every occurrence of a trademarked name, we use the names only in an editorial fashion and to the benefit of the trademark owner, with no intention of infringement of the trademark.

Lead Editor: Chris Mills

Technical Reviewers: Simon Horwith, Curtis Hermann

Editorial Board: Steve Anglin, Dan Appleman, Gary Cornell, James Cox, Tony Davis, John Franklin, Chris Mills, Steve Rycroft, Dominic Shakeshaft, Julian Skinner, Jim Sumser, Karen Watterson, Gavin Wray, John Zukowski

Project Manager: Kylie Johnston

Copy Manager: Nicole LeClerc

Copy Editor: Scott Carter

Production Manager: Kari Brooks

Production Editor: Janet Vail

Compositor: Kinetic Publishing Services, LLC

Proofreader: Greg Teague

Indexer: Nancy Guenther

Cover Designer: Kurt Krames

Manufacturing Manager: Tom Debolski

Distributed to the book trade in the United States by Springer-Verlag New York, Inc., 175 Fifth Avenue, New York, NY 10010 and outside the United States by Springer-Verlag GmbH & Co. KG, Tiergartenstr. 17, 69112 Heidelberg, Germany.

In the United States: phone 1-800-SPRINGER, e-mail orders@springer-ny.com, or visit http://www.springer-ny.com. Outside the United States: fax +49 6221 345229, e-mail orders@springer.de, or visit http://www.springer.de.

For information on translations, please contact Apress directly at 2560 Ninth Street, Suite 219, Berkeley, CA 94710. Phone 510-549-5930, fax 510-549-5939, e-mail info@apress.com, or visit http://www.apress.com.

The information in this book is distributed on an "as is" basis, without warranty. Although every precaution has been taken in the preparation of this work, neither the author(s) nor Apress shall have any liability to any person or entity with respect to any loss or damage caused or alleged to be caused directly or indirectly by the information contained in this work.

The source code for this book is available to readers at http://www.apress.com in the Downloads section.

Contents at a Glance

Contents

About the Authors

Jen deHaan

Jen deHaan is a freelance "deseloper" (designer/developer) and has been involved in writing, contributing to, or editing 15 computer books on Flash, ActionScript, digital video, and ColdFusion between 2002 and 2004. Jen contributes her help and expertise through the busy and top-ranked community web sites www.flash-mx.com and www.flashmx2004.com and enjoys writing articles for other leading web sites on Flash, including Macromedia.com. Jen spent five years in university and graduated with a BFA in Art Education, and following this graduated with top honors in New Media. Jen, also an experienced teacher and entrepreneur, manages the local Macromedia user group. Jen's company is based in Calgary, Alberta, and she regularly develops web sites for clients in Canada, the United States, and Australia.

Peter deHaan

Peter deHaan comes from a computer science background and has been building web sites since 1995. He began working with ColdFusion in 1997, and has since built several sites using barcode scanners, e-commerce, and dynamic Flash. He has coauthored several books and articles with his wife, Jen.

Simon Horwith

Simon Horwith has been using ColdFusion since version 1.5. He's a member of Team Macromedia, a Macromedia certified instructor, and is an advanced certified ColdFusion and Flash Developer. For the past four years Simon has regularly spoken at the DevCon, MAX, CFUN, MXDC, CF Underground, and CF Europe conferences and has presented at countless CFUG meetings. In addition to writing code, teaching, and presenting at conferences and user groups, Simon tech edits and writes a monthly column for *ColdFusion Developers Journal*, has written and edited several ColdFusion books, and has written several whitepapers and Dev Net articles that can be found online. Simon is a private contractor who also works as Chief Technology Officer at eTRILOGY ltd., a small software development company in London.

For the past several years, Simon's professional focus has been toward software architecture theory and methodology and its implementation in CFML development. In early 2004 he launched cfstandards.org, a site devoted to defining CFML architecture and coding best practices and standards, as well as the development of free modules that allow common functionality to be easily integrated with existing CFML applications. When not writing code, Simon likes to play chess and three-cushion billiards, and he reads books on classical strategy and game theory.

Simon would like to thank Forest, Olivia, Ayesha, Mom, Dad, and Aimee for being who they are—which is what's made him who he is.

Curtis Hermann

Curtis P. Hermann is a seasoned senior Internet application developer specializing in Flash and ColdFusion development. He focuses on cutting-edge web technologies, is a certified Macromedia Flash MX developer, and an experienced Java and ColdFusion developer. Along with his dedication to software development, Curtis focuses on how quality assurance integrates with the software development process to ensure the best possible products. He has established a leadership role in the Flash development community by authoring articles published through the *ColdFusion Developer's Journal* (http://www.sys-con.com/coldfusion/). Curtis's articles include topics such as Flash development guidelines, such as Ramping Up On Flash MX 2004 (December 2003) and ActionScript 2.0 (January 2004) and Flash MX 2004 / ColdFusion MX Web Services Integration (March 2004). He owns and operates a web development consulting firm, iindwell, inc. (www.iindwell.com), heads the Flash MX development and quality-assurance department for WisdomTools.com (www.wisdomtools.com), and is the Internet outreach developer for Friends United Meeting (www.fum.org).

Massimo Foti

Massimo Foti began using Dreamweaver on the day the first beta was available, and has used Dreamweaver ever since.

Massimo has been a prolific extension developer since the pioneering days of Dreamweaver 1. He is the creator of massimocorner.com, and is winner of the Macromedia Best Extension Developer award in 2000 and Top New Extension award for Dreamweaver MX. He also cofounded dwteam.com. His extensions are featured on the Macromedia Exchange for Dreamweaver and have been featured in many books and magazines. A Team Macromedia Member for Dreamweaver, he is a certified Dreamweaver developer and certified advanced ColdFusion developer.

Edoardo Zubler

Edoardo Zubler is a multimedia developer who specializes in creating rich media applications for a wide range of devices and platforms. He has produced both front-end and back-end solutions for Tablet PCs, set top boxes, and handheld PDAs. Throughout his career, Edoardo has been involved in pioneering projects such as the development and implementation of a content repurposing system based on Macromedia Generator for the first regular digital terrestrial (DVB-t) data broadcasting service in Europe. He has developed many Flash-based rich client applications for fixed and mobile devices. As a Team Macromedia Volunteer, Edoardo has written several articles and developed a number of extensions for many Macromedia products including, FlashBang! with Joseph Lowery. He also runs Aftershape.com, his personal web site, where he showcases his "digital oddities."

Introduction

THIS BOOK EXPLORES the great partnership between ColdFusion, a fantastically powerful but easy to learn server-side scripting language originally released by the Allaire corporation in 1995, and Dreamweaver, Macromedia's world-class visual web-authoring tool, the original version of which first surfaced around 1997.

The product versions supported by this book are Dreamweaver MX 2004, which was released in late 2003, and ColdFusion MX 6.1 (the 6.1 release is a minor upgrade to the main ColdFusion MX version, available for free to those who already have MX, at http://www.macromedia.com/software/coldfusion/productinfo/upgrade/).

ColdFusion is one of the five server models available to Dreamweaver MX 2004 users (the others being ASP, ASP.NET, PHP, and JSP), so much integrated support it is provided fro ColdFusion in Dreamweaver MX 2004, especially because Macromedia now owns both products. By using Dreamweaver MX 2004, you can set up your ColdFusion web site, connect it to your database, put together all the code for the pages—and style them too—with very little hassle. The only other place you'll probably visit often is the ColdFusion Administrator, which provides even more power over your web sites.

In this book, we aim to do just one thing: teach you how to build great ColdFusion-based web applications using Dreamweaver MX 2004! We won't take you through an exhaustive tour of *every* tiny little Dreamweaver feature and obscure ColdFusion function; instead, we cover just the stuff you need to know in a concise, clear, and enjoyable manner.

It won't be long before you have mastered ColdFusion, so read on.

What's Inside?

Here is an overview of what each of this book's 13 chapters covers.

Chapter 1: Welcome to ColdFusion MX 6.1

This chapter provides a detailed introduction to the technology, including notes on ColdFusion's history and architecture, how to install it, and how to use the ColdFusion Administrator and set up a ColdFusion site in Dreamweaver MX 2004. Here we also take a very brief look at some basic CFML to give you a taste of the following chapters.

Chapter 2: Databases and Dreamweaver MX 2004

Now we look at one of the most important pieces in the ColdFusion puzzle: databases. Here we focus on what databases are and what different types are available (going on to examine the inner workings of a Microsoft Access database), using the Structured Query Language (SQL) to query databases, setting up data sources, and building queries and Recordsets in Dreamweaver MX.

Chapter 3: Introduction to ColdFusion Markup Language

The object of this chapter is to give you a detailed overview of how to start coding with ColdFusion Markup Language (CFML). Here we look at the most common CFML tags and their functionality, and we discuss what Application.cfm files are and how to use them.

Chapter 4: ColdFusion Variables and Logic

This chapter first looks at the different types of variable scope available for use in ColdFusion before going on to examine the available ColdFusion data types and functions in detail.

Chapter 5: Form Processing

Here we begin applying some of the base knowledge introduced in previous chapters, looking at building forms in ColdFusion and client- and server-side form validation (including some complete adaptable examples: an e-mail feedback form and a file upload form). We then go on to look at using checkboxes and multiple submit buttons in forms before rounding off the chapter by building some examples that make use of Dreamweaver MX's form-enhancing server behaviors.

Chapter 6: Database Manipulation

Databases are the order of the day again here. Building on the basic knowledge of Chapter 2, we explore using Recordsets with advanced queries and dynamic tables to display, update, and delete data from a database (incorporating a master/detail page set and Recordset paging). We then go on to build up a dynamic image gallery that includes image uploading functionality, and round off the chapter with a look at some advanced database features: stored procedures, views, query of queries, caching queries, and query parameters.

Chapter 7: Maintaining State

This chapter looks at how we can use the Application, Client, Cookie, and Session scopes to maintain state across pages in a ColdFusion application, including creating cookies, Session variables and locks, using the Application scope within a content-management system, and enabling and deleting Client variables. This chapter finishes off by looking at using WDDX to display complex values within the Client scope, and understanding Cookie-less sessions.

Chapter 8: Exception Handling with CFML

Here we look at the mechanisms available to ColdFusion for handling errors and exceptions. We start with error handling at the server level via the ColdFusion Administrator, then look at handling errors at the application level with <cferror>. Next we show how to build more robust error-handling code by using <cfcatch>, <cftry>, <cfthrow>, and <cfrethrow>, and describe best practices for structured exception handling. Lastly, we cover debugging by using the ColdFusion Administrator, <cfdump>, and <cftrace>, protecting data integrity by using <cftransaction>, and the impact of Flash Web Services on application exception handling.

Chapter 9: Dreamweaver MX 2004 Extensions

We look at how to install and manage Dreamweaver MX Extensions by using the extension manager, how to use a couple of the more popular publicly available extensions, and how to build our own extensions (using the Server Behavior Builder) and distribute them.

Chapter 10: Code and Component Reuse

This chapter looks at the mechanisms available to Dreamweaver and ColdFusion for reusing code and components, including the <cfinclude> tag, ColdFusion user-defined functions (UDFs), ColdFusion custom tags, ColdFusion Components (CFCs), Dreamweaver Snippets, the Dreamweaver library, Dreamweaver templates, and Dreamweaver tag libraries.

Chapter 11: Working with XML in ColdFusion MX 6.1

Now it's time to explore ColdFusion's native XML-handling abilities. Here we take a quick look at what XML is, then go on to look at how ColdFusion can create XML dynamically and access and manipulate XML from external sources. We then examine how XPath can be used to parse and retrieve specific data from an XML document, and how XSLT can be used to transform XML into other markup.

Chapter 12: Flash MX 2004, Web Services, and ColdFusion MX 6.1

Chapter 12 delves deep into the world of Flash web services, specifically looking at how it can be used in conjunction with ColdFusion to dynamically transfer data to and from Flash applications. We start with a brief review of Flash and Flash web services and how they work, then go on to look at some increasingly complicated ColdFusion Flash web services examples.

Chapter 13: A Complete ColdFusion-Based Web Site

This last chapter is a case study that looks at the planning, design, and implementation of a complete ColdFusion-based web site, revisiting many of the techniques we have discussed over the course of the book.

Who's This Book For?

This book is for web professionals with some Dreamweaver knowledge who want to gain a solid understanding of the ColdFusion MX language, and learn to use Dreamweaver MX to create powerful, dynamic web applications with ColdFusion by using Dreamweaver's extensive built-in ColdFusion support.

What Do I Need to Begin?

To use this book, you primarily need a copy of Dreamweaver MX 2004 and a copy of ColdFusion server. If you have bought Studio MX 2004, you are in luck; this comes with a limited version of ColdFusion MX 6.1 Server, which can be used by only one user at a time. Although this would be no good for a production environment, it is perfect for developmental and testing purposes. You can also download the version 6.1 upgrade free from http://www.macromedia.com/software/coldfusion/productinfo/upgrade/, if you don't have it.

Secondarily, you need a copy of Microsoft Access (preferably XP or 2000) or another database of choice, a web server to run your examples through (see Chapter 1 for more details), and a web browser to view your examples. You also need a copy of Flash MX to work through the examples in Chapter 12, "Flash Web Services." A few more minor downloads are required over the course of the book, but we'll refer to these when required.

You'll also want to download the example code for this book, available from http://www.apress.com. This contains all the examples discussed in the book, making your job even easier.

Welcome to ColdFusion MX 6.1

BECAUSE YOU HAVE PICKED UP this book, you're probably interested in planning and developing dynamic web sites using ColdFusion MX and Dreamweaver MX (latest versions—ColdFusion 6.1 and Dreamweaver MX 2004). Luckily, using ColdFusion MX 6.1 together with Dreamweaver MX 2004 has never been easier! ColdFusion MX 6.1 is aimed at developers who want to make dynamic web sites or applications by introducing interactivity between the user and a server.

ColdFusion MX 6.1 is a powerful server-side technology that essentially combines an application server and a specialized scripting language called ColdFusion Markup Language (CFML). ColdFusion MX 6.1 Application Server has its own web server, but it can work with a wide range of web servers. When the end-user requests a ColdFusion MX 6.1 page, the server processes the page and returns it to the user. Because the code executes on the server, the users cannot see the source code, and the server-side code works the same way regardless of what browser the end-user employs.

CFML is perhaps the easiest server-side scripting language to learn. Despite ColdFusion MX 6.1's simplicity, it can be used to create large-scale enterprise applications on its own, or it can be integrated with JavaServer Pages (JSP). You can use it to create anything from a content management system to a fully featured e-commerce site!

A Brief History of ColdFusion

At the time of writing, the ColdFusion Application Server has been with us for nearly eight years. In fact, ColdFusion was the first web application server released. Since its early days, there have been some remarkable changes in how the software works and how developers use it to develop content-rich and interactive web sites. Let's look at the history of ColdFusion.

In early 1995, Jeremy and J. J. Allaire formed Allaire Corporation. Only a couple of months later, ColdFusion 1.0 was launched. In 1996, ColdFusion 1.5 was released, by which time it had already generated a sizeable following.

In March 1997, Allaire bought HomeSite from Bradbury Software. (HomeSite is a popular HTML editor now bundled with Dreamweaver MX 2004, and is currently known as HomeSite+.) Three months later, ColdFusion 3.0 started shipping to a user-base of 30,000 developers.

ColdFusion 3.1 was introduced in January 1998, with greater support for Windows NT and Solaris platforms. This version was released with ColdFusion Studio, an enhanced version of HomeSite with specific tools to aid the development of dynamic ColdFusion applications.

In November 1998, Allaire shipped HomeSite 4 and ColdFusion 4.0, and exactly one year later they announced the launch of ColdFusion 4.5. In 1999, Allaire acquired Live Software's JRun engine, and for some time the two were completely separate standalone products. This would not be the case forever.

Much later, in March 2001, Macromedia announced the completion of a merger between it and Allaire Corporation. Just three months later, Macromedia ColdFusion Server 5 was launched and made available to developers. Though this release of ColdFusion did not leverage much of the power of JRun, certain features and functionality that shipped with the server made use of an underlying feature-limited JRun engine.

In May 2002, Macromedia ColdFusion MX was released to the public. It was included in the Macromedia MX family of products, and the Developer version was also bundled with the Windows version of Macromedia Studio MX. ColdFusion MX was the most significant release of ColdFusion to date, because it was a complete rewrite of the server code. Completely rewritten in Java, it featured a more significant integration across a broad spectrum of technologies, including Macromedia Flash and Dreamweaver, and introduced many significant features to the CFML language and the server's underlying engine. ColdFusion MX, being a complete rewrite, was essentially a version 1 release—it just happened to have a history of predecessors. In fall 2003, Macromedia released ColdFusion MX 6.1 as a free upgrade dot-release for anyone with a CFMX license. MX 6.1 addressed the vast majority of reported bugs and server behavior "issues," including an amazing compiler performance improvement. For lack of a better way to put it, MX 6.1 has been the most significant and flat-out best version of ColdFusion released to date.

Integration with Studio MX

As you already know, the Developer Version of ColdFusion MX 6.1 is bundled with Studio MX 2004. The Developer version is fully functional and free, but restricted to requests from a single IP address. You will find support for CFML and for ColdFusion MX 6.1 in most of these products, some more than others. For example, there is not much integration with FreeHand MX and Fireworks MX, but they are primarily graphics-based products used to design web site front-ends, so this is to be expected. On the other hand, you can use Flash MX 2004 (standard or professional), Dreamweaver MX 2004, and HomeSite+ in conjunction with ColdFusion MX 6.1 to create dynamic web sites more efficiently than ever because of their integration with the server. Other new products, such as Flex, also integrate with ColdFusion MX 6.1 very well. Flex is Macromedia's new server product that generates Rich Internet Application (RIA) interfaces from XML (see www.macromedia.com for more information about Flex).

This section outlines some of the key points regarding the integration of ColdFusion MX 6.1 with other products in the Studio MX suite.

Flash Integration

Since Flash 4, developers have been able to integrate server-side languages with Flash movies. With the introduction of Flash Remoting in Flash MX, ColdFusion MX and Flash have been brought together in an entirely new way. This is still true for ColdFusion MX 6.1. Flash Remoting offers an efficient, lightweight, and easy-to-use method for integrating ColdFusion MX 6.1 with Flash movies. Flash MX 2004 also has improved support for consuming web services and XML data—and it should come as no surprise that ColdFusion MX 6.1 has excellent support for XML and for web services. These technologies make it easy to share data between Flash applications and ColdFusion applications without having to write more than a couple lines of code!

Macromedia's support for integrating ColdFusion MX 6.1 with Flash is certainly the strongest when it comes to server-side support. Flex, a server-side Flash generation server, is one such example. Who knows what might be next? Expect to see further advancements in the near future.

For more information on Flash integration with ColdFusion MX 6.1, refer to Chapter 12.

HomeSite+

HomeSite+ is an enhanced version of Macromedia's HomeSite 5 and ColdFusion Studio 5. It is an advanced code editor for several languages, including ColdFusion MX 6.1. It fully supports ColdFusion MX 6.1 tags for code completion and hinting. You can find HomeSite+ in the Dreamweaver folder on the Studio MX 2004 CD-ROM. It must be installed separately.

Integration with Dreamweaver

Macromedia has made it easier than ever to develop rich ColdFusion MX 6.1 applications with Dreamweaver MX 2004. For example, Dreamweaver MX 2004 allows you to create Recordsets using a simple wizard interface and add server behaviors that can page through those Recordsets with a few mouse clicks.

> **TIP** *A Recordset is a specific group of records selected from a database and defined as a single object, thus enabling you to easily manipulate the data via your server-side language.*

Dreamweaver MX 2004 also offers code hinting for ColdFusion MX 6.1 tags, which brings up a list of available tag attributes and suggested values where appropriate. Also available is a complete tag editor that allows you to right-click on ColdFusion MX 6.1 tags and fill in attributes by using a wizard-style interface that uses text boxes and drop-down menus, and support for CFML functions, keyboard shortcuts (including snippet keyboard shortcuts), and more.

You can also receive ColdFusion MX 6.1 server debugging information from within Dreamweaver MX 2004, which helps you debug your applications. Macromedia has also made it very simple to use web services and ColdFusion Components (a powerful new tool in CFMX 6.1) within Dreamweaver MX 2004. Tell Dreamweaver MX 2004 the URL of any web service, select Insert Code, and Dreamweaver MX 2004 generates all the necessary code and embeds it into your ColdFusion MX 6.1 template.

The ColdFusion MX 6.1 Server and CFML

The ColdFusion MX 6.1 Server and CFML have a good deal of competition in the world of server-side languages and web application servers. Before working with ColdFusion MX 6.1 (or any language, for that matter), it is always wise to weigh the pros and cons.

Advantages of ColdFusion MX 6.1

ColdFusion MX 6.1 provides several advantages. Foremost is its simplicity and ease of use. This means that it is easy to learn (as you will find out soon) and fast to develop in, which can—and almost always does—make it cheaper for your clients in the long run. ColdFusion MX 6.1 makes it easy to perform queries, send e-mails, search your site or collect documents, grab remote web pages or files, or force users to log in to an application, all by providing standard tags to perform these actions instead of requiring you to write custom code.

Despite its simplicity, CFML is a powerful server-side language. You can use custom tags, use a number of network protocols, have full database access, and integrate with enterprise-level solutions (such as Enterprise JavaBeans [EJB], Component Object Model [COM], and Common Object Request Broker Architecture [CORBA]). The ColdFusion Component Architecture, introduced to CFML in ColdFusion MX and refined in MX 6.1, allows developers to take advantage of many of the powerful Object Oriented Language benefits such as inheritance, instance-based development, and encapsulation.

ColdFusion MX 6.1 almost always pays for itself tenfold because of the amount of development time it saves compared to its competitors.

Disadvantages of ColdFusion MX 6.1

Many server-side programming language alternatives to ColdFusion, such as ASP, PHP, JSP, and Perl, are free to use. However, none comes with the technical and community support, variety of supported OS platforms, and out-of-the-box features ColdFusion MX 6.1 has. Sure, ColdFusion MX 6.1 does cost a little bit of money initially, but this is compensated by other savings as we already mentioned, and it is free for development purposes. You can run a fully featured copy of ColdFusion MX 6.1 Enterprise Edition for free to develop your applications—the only catch is that it will not allow other browsers to visit your applications (obviously—it's only for development until you purchase a license or arrange for a host).

Installing the ColdFusion MX 6.1 Server

You can install ColdFusion MX 6.1 MX on several different operating systems: Windows, Mac OS X, Linux, Solaris, and HP-UX. It also has the advantage of having a built-in web server, so you can test and develop on a system that does not have a server already installed. In this section, we explain how to install ColdFusion MX 6.1 server onto a Windows-based system.

Before you begin the installation, we strongly recommend that you make sure that your computer system meets the minimum hardware requirements as specified by Macromedia. You can find these system requirements at http://livedocs.macromedia.com/coldfusion/6.1/htmldocs/part_ins.htm.

How to Install ColdFusion MX 6.1

1. Start the install procedure. After agreeing to the end-user license agreement, you will be taken to the Customer Information dialog box. This is where you enter details like your name and organization name. You can also enter a serial number if you have purchased a license for ColdFusion

MX or ColdFusion MX 6.1. If you leave the serial number text field blank, you will install the 30-day trial version. There is a bullet for opting to immediately install the developer version, which is a single-IP address fully-functional version (if you install the 30-day trial and let the trial expire, it becomes a developer edition anyway). In addition to the license type, you choose the install type. Several options are available. In this book we focus on the standalone version, but be aware that ColdFusion MX 6.1 is a Java 2 Platform Enterprise Edition (J2EE) application, and as such it runs on top of a J2EE server. There are options to install ColdFusion MX 6.1 on top of JRun 4, or to deploy it on an existing J2EE application server as either a .ear or .war file. If you don't know what all of that means, don't worry about it right now. Just know that ColdFusion runs as a Java application and that there are many options for how ColdFusion MX 6.1 can be configured and deployed. You can read more about installing the J2EE version of CFMX 6.1 at http://livedocs.macromedia.com/coldfusion/6.1/htmldocs/installj.htm#wp109411.

2. Next, the installer detects which web servers you currently have installed and gives you the option of using any of these or Macromedia's standalone web server. Macromedia recommends that you use the standalone server only for developmental purposes and not on production systems. Note that by default the standalone server runs on port 8500. So, if you are connecting to your local machine, you must always append :8500 onto the domain in the URL. For example, to access the ColdFusion MX 6.1 Administrator, you would need to enter http://localhost:8500/CFIDE/administrator/ in the address bar of your web browser. If you are using Internet Information Server (IIS) or Apache (or any other web server) with the default HTTP port (80), you will connect to the local machine as http://localhost/CFIDE/administrator/. Choose one of these options and click the Next button.

3. Now you define the paths to which you want to install the program files and web files. By default, ColdFusion MX 6.1 installs to the C:\CFusionMX\ directory. When finished, click the Next button.

4. The next step of the install procedure allows you to choose what components are installed. The first component is the application server itself, which must be installed. The second component is the Documentation and sample applications, and these are optional.

In a production environment, do not install the documentation or sample applications, because they may be exploited by malicious Web users. When you have finished making your decision, click on the Next button.

> **TIP** *You can access the most recent documentation at* `http://livedocs.macromedia.com/`, *and users can actually add comments and notes to most pages for other people to read. These comments often contain useful tips or workarounds for bugs.*

5. Next, you choose passwords for the administration web site and for users connecting through Remote Development Services (RDS). RDS is one way that HomeSite and Dreamweaver MX 2004 can connect remotely to the ColdFusion MX 6.1 server and edit files. If you wish to use the same password for both, simply click the "Use the same password as above" checkbox and enter a password into both of the upper text fields. Click the Next button after you are finished.

6. The final step is a confirmation screen. This allows you to check all settings before actually installing the files. You can go back and make changes before returning and clicking on the Install button. ColdFusion MX 6.1 will then take several minutes to install before the wizard completes.

7. Once the installation wizard has successfully completed, it will launch the ColdFusion MX 6.1 Administration web site, which we walk you through later in this chapter. Once you log in to the Administrator, click on Version Information near the top right, and you will see a brief summary of the server details and the Java Virtual Machine (JVM) details.

   A text field near the top of this page lets you enter a new serial number. If you installed the Developer or 30-day trial edition of ColdFusion MX 6.1 and later want to upgrade to the Professional or Enterprise edition, simply return to this page and enter your serial number. ColdFusion MX 6.1 will remove the connection limitations of the Developer edition.

Before getting started with ColdFusion MX 6.1, update your software to the latest version. At the time of writing, the latest update offered by Macromedia is ColdFusion MX 6.1. As new bug fixes and features are released, hotpatches and sometimes even updaters are made available for download. You can check for new patches and updates at `http://www.macromedia.com/support/coldfusion/`.

Changing the Port Number for ColdFusion MX 6.1

If using the Macromedia standalone web server with ColdFusion MX 6.1, you can also change the port from 8500 to 80 or any other available port.

Simply open the install directory: `\CFusionMX\runtime\servers\default\SERVER-INF\jrun.xml` file and search for `<attribute name="port">8500</attribute>`, which is near the bottom of the document. Change the port number from 8500 to the available port you wish to use, such as port 80, and save this file. Stop and restart the ColdFusion MX 6.1 MX Application server service from the Services window at the Control Panel➤ Administrative Tools➤Services interface. You will now be able to access your ColdFusion MX 6.1 Administrator and pages on the new port that you specified. More information about configuring the built-in web server appears at `http://www.macromedia.com/support/coldfusion/adv_development/config_builtin_webserver/`.

The ColdFusion MX 6.1 Administrator

ColdFusion MX 6.1 settings are defined in two places: the Web-based ColdFusion MX 6.1 Administrator (also known as the *Admin*), and within XML files in the ColdFusion MX 6.1 program directory.

Most of the changes you'll ever need to make can be done through the ColdFusion MX 6.1 Administrator, found at `http://localhost:8500/CFIDE/administrator/` if you are using ColdFusion MX 6.1's built-in web server by default. If using IIS, Apache, or have configured ColdFusion MX 6.1 to respond to a different port, then you must modify the port (and any other URLs in this book) accordingly. We assume that you are running the server on port 8500.

When you first connect to the Administrator, it will provide you with a login screen. This is where you enter your ColdFusion MX 6.1 Administrator password (which you selected while installing the ColdFusion MX 6.1 Server). Enter the password and click on the Login button. You will be taken to the administration homepage.

The Administrator has five major sections down the left side of the interface:

- Server Settings

- Data & Services

- Debugging & Logging

- Extensions

- Security

All these sections have areas of their own you must consider while working with this tool. We describe all these areas next. However, we provide only a brief overview of Extensions and Security, two highly advanced areas of ColdFusion MX 6.1 development beyond the scope of this book.

Server Settings

The Server Settings area has ten different areas (nine if you're using the J2EE version) primarily used to control server-wide settings, such as enabling and disabling certain variable scopes, and mail server and caching settings.

Settings

These are general server settings that control behavior and performance. You can set the number of seconds that a user request is allowed to run before it times out (if at all), and also limit the number of simultaneous requests a user can run. You can define which template will be called if ColdFusion MX 6.1 cannot find the requested template, and can also specify which template is called if an error occurs and is not handled in the ColdFusion MX 6.1 code. We cover error handling in detail in Chapter 8.

Caching

This is where you define how many ColdFusion MX 6.1 templates (.cfm files) and database queries can be cached in the server memory at one time. You can also specify if the server should check whether the file currently being served by ColdFusion MX 6.1 is the most recent version of the file. This last setting, called Trusted Cache, is an option you would enable only if your files never changed after you upload them to the server.

When ColdFusion MX 6.1 runs a template for the first time, it compiles the template into a .class file and caches the file on the server. The next time the file is requested, ColdFusion MX 6.1 checks whether the requested file is newer then the one in the cache; if so, it recompiles the template and returns it to the visitor. If the file in the cache is the latest version, then the file is returned immediately to the visitor, and ColdFusion MX 6.1 doesn't need to recompile the file. This enables ColdFusion MX 6.1 to recompile files only when they have changed, greatly improving server performance.

Client Variables

ColdFusion MX 6.1 allows you to store persistent data for users. At a shopping site, for example, if a user were to leave the site and return later, you could save the contents of the visitor's shopping cart. ColdFusion MX 6.1 does this by issuing the visitor a unique key and storing the visitor's data in a database, cookie, or the system registry. This section is where you define which databases should store the persistent data, how long it is stored before being purged from the database, and whether ColdFusion MX 6.1 should store the data in the registry, in cookies, or in a particular database by default. We cover client variables in detail in Chapter 7.

Memory Variables

ColdFusion MX 6.1 also allows developers to store data in server memory instead of saving it as session variables in a database, cookie, or registry. Memory variables and persistent data are covered in Chapter 7.

Mappings

ColdFusion MX 6.1 mappings are aliases to directories, even those outside the Web-root, and are similar to the virtual directories that you would define in your web server. We mainly use them when creating custom tags in ColdFusion MX 6.1 or include files. Instead of including a file by specifying the path `../../includes/header.cfm`, you could create a mapping named SiteA that points to the root of the SiteA.com web site. Then you could include this file in the following way: `/SiteA/includes/header.cfm`. This mapping will work no matter how deeply `header.cfm` is located within the site's directory structure.

How to include external files by using the `<cfinclude>` tag is covered in Chapter 10.

Mail Server

This is where you enter your mail server settings into ColdFusion MX 6.1; this enables us to use the `<cfmail>` tag to send e-mails through ColdFusion MX 6.1. We cover `<cfmail>` in Chapter 5.

Charting

ColdFusion MX 6.1 lets you dynamically create bar charts, pie charts, line graphs, and several other types of charts in two or three dimensions. This is where you specify whether to cache charts to the hard drive or the server memory. You also choose where to save any charts that are cached to the disk, and also the maximum number of charts in either cache. You can also specify the maximum number of thread requests (between one and five) that can be processed at the same time.

Java and JVM

This is where you define settings relating to the JVM by specifying the location where the JVM is installed, and any initialization arguments that you need to pass to the JVM. Typically, you don't ever need to change these settings. You can specify any additional class paths for the JVM that are sometimes needed when adding Java custom tags. Note that in the J2EE version of ColdFusion MX 6.1, this section is omitted (the J2EE application server settings are used instead).

Archives and Deployment

ColdFusion MX 6.1 allows you to save your web server's (or a specific application's) configuration information to an archive and migrate the archive to a different computer, or back up the archive and restore it later on the current machine.

Settings Summary

This is just a report of the current configuration. The page makes it easy for you to see all your configuration settings in one place and print a record. You can also click on the different sections of the report, which takes you to the corresponding page in the Administrator.

Data and Services

The next major section, Data and Services, has four different areas. You use these to create data sources, assign aliases to web services, and set up the Verity search engine (described shortly).

Data Sources

This is where you define your data sources for each database for this server. A data source is essentially an alias (that you define on your server) that allows you to communicate with your database.

Verity Collections

ColdFusion MX 6.1 ships with an indexing engine called Verity, which allows you to build a search engine for your web site. Verity lets you index MS Word documents, Adobe PDFs, databases, and most other document types. For more information on Verity, check out Macromedia's online documentation at `http://livedocs.macromedia.com/coldfusion/6.1/htmldocs/indexseb.htm#wp1160419`.

Verity K2 Server

Macromedia ships with a limited version of Verity's K2 Server, which is used to index and search documents within a site. Using Verity K2 Server, you can create "collections" of documents (such as MS Word documents or Adobe PDFs), search the collection(s) for a combination of words, and display the results within your ColdFusion MX 6.1 pages sorted by a ranking generated by Verity, and much more. You can find more information on Verity and the K2 Server at `www.verity.com`.

Web Services

This is where you can set up aliases for your commonly used web services. Instead of always typing the URL to the web service you want to use, you can simply register it in this section. For example, you can set up an alias called GoogleSearch for the URL `http://api.google.com/GoogleSearch.wsdl`. We cover web services in detail in Chapter 10.

Debugging and Logging

ColdFusion MX 6.1 includes a robust debugging environment that allows developers to debug applications easily during development. We cover the debugging options in detail here, including how to set which IP addresses are able to view debugging output, and which variable scopes and debugging output will be displayed.

Debugging Settings

This section is where you decide whether to enable debugging, and in which layout you want to display the debugging information (at the bottom of each template, or in a popup window with an expandable/collapsible tree). By defining what information should be shown in the debug output, developers can get detailed information on variables, queries, execution times, which pages were processed for the current request, and all sorts of valuable error/exception information. You can also define whether to show database query information and which variables and their corresponding values should show up in the debugging output. This debugging output can also be used within Dreamweaver MX 2004 and HomeSite+ in addition to being displayed at the bottom of each template.

Debugging IP Addresses

This is where you enter the IP addresses that will receive the debugging information. It is important to note that if you don't define IP addresses in this section, all users will receive the debugging output. For this reason, it is advisable to enter at least the IP address of the ColdFusion MX 6.1 Server, or simply the IP address 127.0.0.1, which will always point to the local machine, or in this case the server running ColdFusion MX 6.1.

Logging Settings

When ColdFusion MX 6.1 encounters errors in the code, it will typically log the error to a file, which administrators and developers can peruse later. This helps developers figure out which part of their application is encountering problems and needs attention. In this section, you tell ColdFusion MX 6.1 which directory to save the log files in, the maximum allowed size of the log files before ColdFusion MX 6.1 archives them, and how many archived files to keep before deleting the older error logs. You can also tell ColdFusion MX 6.1 to log any template that takes more than a certain number of seconds to execute. This helps track templates that are performing badly and are perhaps inefficient and/or experiencing problems.

Log Files

This is where you view the log files ColdFusion MX 6.1 has produced. You can also go to the log directory that you defined in the Logging Settings section and open the files in Notepad or any other text editor. Log files can be downloaded, viewed, archived, or deleted.

Scheduled Tasks

ColdFusion MX 6.1 provides developers with an easy way to schedule templates to run at a specific day and time. Using this Web interface, you can create a new task that will execute once or recur every few hours. For example, you could schedule a ColdFusion MX 6.1 template to fetch new data from a remote newsfeed every 8 hours, or delete customers' shopping carts if they haven't made any changes in the past 24 hours.

System Probes

You can use system probes to check whether your web site is running and functioning properly. Simply create a new probe, enter the URL to check, along with a string or regular expression to check for, and if the probe fails, it can either send an e-mail to a specified address or execute a script or program that could be used to restart the ColdFusion MX 6.1 service.

Code Analyzer

The code analyzer is useful when migrating from an earlier version of ColdFusion MX 6.1. It examines existing code and reports any potential issues that may arise because of deprecated ColdFusion MX 6.1 tags or features.

Extensions

This section is mainly for advanced development. It lets you extend ColdFusion MX 6.1 by registering new Java Applets that you want to use in your applications. You can also define new ColdFusion Extension (CFX) tags (custom tags written in Java or C++) that usually add features beyond those you could build using just CFML. For example, some CFX tags can resize images or convert them to different formats, or just tell you the width and height of an existing image.

Security

In this final section, you can define/disable a password for connecting to the ColdFusion MX 6.1 Administrator or for users to connect to ColdFusion MX 6.1 servers using Dreamweaver MX 2004 or ColdFusion Studio/HomeSite+. The final section, Sandbox Security, is used to restrict which sites can have access to which ColdFusion MX 6.1 elements, functions, and resources. You could prohibit certain sites from using elements such as <cffile>, <cfdirectory>, <cfhttp>, <cfftp>, or <cfmail>. You could even limit which servers or IP addresses the web site can connect to. Sandbox security is primarily used for servers employed in a shared hosting environment, where you want to lock down access to tags and data sources.

Setting Up a Site in Dreamweaver MX 2004

Dreamweaver MX 2004 is the recommended IDE for developing CFML applications, and it does everything in the context of a site. Fortunately, setting up a ColdFusion

MX 6.1–based site in Dreamweaver MX 2004 is extremely easy. Follow the simple steps listed here, and you will be ready to start developing your web site. Because we required only the basic features for setting up my site, and the site definition wizard nicely steps through each required piece of information, we use it in the following section. If you need any additional features, simply click on the Advanced tab at any time and enter your custom settings along with the following ones.

1. In Dreamweaver MX 2004, open the Files panel and select the Site tab. In the site menu at the top, click Manage Sites➤New➤Site, and the site definition wizard dialog box will open. If the Basic tab is not already selected at the top of your screen, select it.

2. You must give your site a name (Figure 1-1). For the purpose of this example, call it "cfbook" and click Next. (This name needs to be a unique identifier for Dreamweaver MX 2004.)

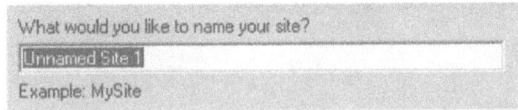

Figure 1-1. Enter the name of your site into this box.

3. You want to use a server technology to build your web site, so make sure the "Yes, I want to use a server technology" option is selected here. For the server technology, select ColdFusion from the drop-down menu as shown in Figure 1-2. Click on the Next button.

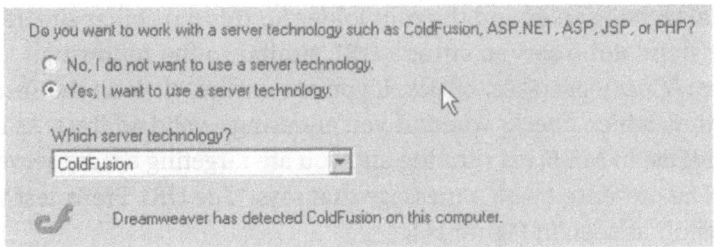

Figure 1-2. Select ColdFusion as the server technology you want to use.

4. You will be working with your files locally during development, so in the Editing Files, Part 3 section of the Site Definition dialog box, choose the first option and enter the path to a folder to store your ColdFusion MX 6.1 files in (see Figure 1-3). If you want or need to edit your files on a remote server (or edit them locally then upload them) using FTP, enter the location of the remote server at this point.

   Here, you will be using the default location specified by Dreamweaver MX 2004. This will be the install location of ColdFusion MX 6.1, typically C:\CFusionMX. The Web-root directory for ColdFusion MX 6.1 is wwwroot—within this, create a new folder for this site. You will probably want to use the site name, but this can be changed by using the browse button (the folder icon to the right) or by typing in a new name. When finished, press the Next button.

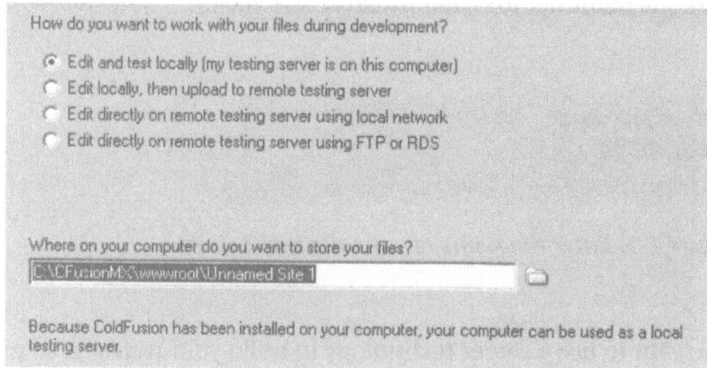

Figure 1-3. Choose where to edit and store files.

5. For the Testing Files section of the Site Definition dialog box, enter your local testing server and the root folder for this particular site. If using the standalone server, enter a URL similar to the following: http://localhost:8500/cfbook. If you are unsure, click on the Test URL button, which checks whether you are using a valid address. As long as ColdFusion MX 6.1 is running and you are targeting a valid server, you will be presented with a message that says "The URL Prefix test was successful" as seen in Figure 1-4.

   If you get an error message, make sure your server is running and that you are using the correct port number. If you were running a server such as IIS, your URL would be http://localhost/cfbook. If you were using a remote server running ColdFusion MX 6.1, this would be the location provided by the company hosting your site. When finished, click Next.

Figure 1-4. Successful URL prefix dialog

6. Finally, in the Site Definition dialog box, select the No radio button if you do not want to upload your files to another machine (see Figure 1-5).

   We will not be using this feature in this book. However, you may want to use this for testing if your ColdFusion MX 6.1 server is on another machine or on your hosting provider's server. Click the Next button.

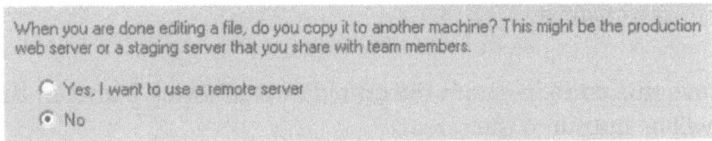

Figure 1-5. If you are not using a remote server, click the No option.

7. When finished, you will see a summary screen showing all your settings. To further configure these settings, select the Advanced tab at this time and make the desired modifications. Otherwise, click on the Done button.

Now you are back in Dreamweaver MX 2004, and you should notice a few changes in the authoring environment. First, there are certain additions specific to ColdFusion MX 6.1 in the Application panel group (Database, Bindings, Server Behaviors, and Components). You can define RDS logins (the RDS password is the one you defined earlier during installation), create data sources, and select Recordsets using these new features. The Insert bar now has tabs for CFML (and are labeled appropriately).

Getting Started with CFML

One of ColdFusion MX 6.1's greatest strengths is the simplicity of its tag-based language, CFML. If you have experience with coding HTML, the migration to

ColdFusion MX 6.1 should be very easy. Like HTML, CFML is not case-sensitive, so it doesn't matter if you type a tag in uppercase, lowercase, or mixed case. In this section, we are going to run through a few CFML tags. For developers used to a JavaScript-like syntax, CFML supports CFScript, which allows access to most ColdFusion MX 6.1 functionality through a more traditional coding style. We provide several more in-depth examples in Chapter 3.

Setting a Variable

To set a variable in a page, type

```
<cfset myVar = "myValue">
```

To output this variable, type

```
<cfoutput>#myVar#</cfoutput>
```

If you save this code in a `.cfm` file and view it in a web browser, the text "myValue" will be output to the screen.

When you output variables in ColdFusion MX 6.1, remember that they must be enclosed in pound signs (#). Without pound signs, ColdFusion MX 6.1 assumes that you want to output a string, so typing `<cfoutput>myVar</cfoutput>` would simply output myVar to the window. Likewise, if we forget the `<cfoutput>` tags, ColdFusion MX 6.1 won't parse the variables, and #myVar# will show up as the output! One place where ColdFusion MX 6.1 differs from other programming languages is that it doesn't require you to declare a data type for a variable before setting a value. ColdFusion MX 6.1 automatically converts variables and determines their data type for you.

Functions

ColdFusion MX 6.1 also has a very extensive list of functions available, including the ability to create your own user-defined functions (UDFs). For example, you could simply add `<cfoutput>#Now( )#</cfoutput>` to a web page to have it display the current server date and time on the screen. #Now( )# is a built-in ColdFusion MX 6.1 function that takes no arguments and returns the current date and time of the server. Several other date and time functions allow you to extract just the year, month, hour, second, or any component of a date, along with numerous other formatting options to choose for displaying dates.

Looping with <cfloop>

This tag has a few different parameters and performs different tasks depending on which attributes you specify, but one of the easiest ways to call this tag is like this:

```
<cfloop from="1" to="3" index="i">

  ...
</cfloop>
```

This example loops from 1 to 3. This is similar to a for...next loop structure in other languages. Using other attributes of the <cfloop> tag, do...while and other types of loops can be used. For each time you go through the loop, you set a variable called "i" that holds the current value. If you changed the code to:

```
<cfloop from="1" to="3" index="i">

  <cfoutput>#i#</cfoutput>
</cfloop>
```

It would generate the following output:

```
1 2 3
```

Sending Mail with <cfmail>

ColdFusion MX 6.1 allows you to send e-mails quickly and easily by using the <cfmail> tag, as shown in the following snippet:

```
<cfmail from = "admin@yourdomain.com" to = "info@yourdomain.com"

  subject = "your subject here">

  this is the body of the e-mail.
</cfmail>
```

As long as you have entered a valid mail server in the ColdFusion MX 6.1 Administrator, you will be able to send e-mails from ColdFusion MX 6.1. You could easily modify this example to allow you to send e-mails to a variable that a user typed into a web form; this would enable you to build a simple form that allows visitors to e-mail questions and feedback to the webmaster.

Summary

In this chapter, we described many different areas of the ColdFusion MX 6.1 environment, such as the CFML language, ColdFusion MX 6.1 application server, and how these interact with Dreamweaver MX 2004. We covered:

- The background and history of ColdFusion and how it integrates with the Web today

- The advantages and disadvantages of ColdFusion MX 6.1

- How to install and set up the standalone version of ColdFusion MX 6.1 server on the Windows platform

- How to set up a ColdFusion MX 6.1 web site in Dreamweaver MX 2004

- How to get started with CFML

The next chapter focuses on using databases and SQL, which is used to select, insert, update, and delete data from databases. We will also take a look at how to create a data source in the ColdFusion MX 6.1 Administrator, which allows ColdFusion MX 6.1 to talk to databases.

CHAPTER 2

Databases and Dreamweaver MX 2004

DATABASES ALLOW US TO serve dynamic content to our web sites. They are integral to building applications such as image galleries, content management systems, news systems, and so on. Usually, larger web sites use databases to help them organize and manage large amounts of data, because data stored in databases can be easily retrieved and manipulated. Although we discuss the basics of databases in this chapter, you may want to explore the topic further: an excellent book dedicated to the topic is *Practical Web Database Design* by Chris Auld et al. (Apress, 2003).

Whether or not you have ever actually seen a database, you have almost certainly used one. Every time you make a deposit or a withdrawal from the bank, your account balance is updated in a central database. However, not all databases are the same, as you will see shortly.

Most dynamic web sites, whether large corporate intranets or small personal sites with a simple "blog" system or gallery, involve the use of a database. Databases are arguably the most common way to add dynamic content to a web site. Other common methods of creating dynamic content include XML (see Chapter 11), ActiveX controls, Java applets, and DHTML.

Before jumping into databases and building full-blown dynamic sites, it is important to understand how to communicate with the data in the database. Databases have their own language called Structured Query Language (SQL), which is used to select, insert, update, and delete data stored within databases. The SQL language syntax used within each database application (be it Microsoft Access, MySQL, or Oracle) is pretty much the same, but there will be some differences in keywords, functions, and data types. We use Access for our sample databases throughout this book, but don't worry, because most of the SQL and Dreamweaver MX 2004 functionality will be the same no matter what database product you use.

In this chapter, we first look at the different database applications available for use with ColdFusion. We then explain how to use Microsoft Access with ColdFusion MX 6.1 and Dreamweaver MX 2004, and finish up with an introduction to using SQL queries and Dreamweaver's features that facilitate this. Let's get started!

Different Kinds of Databases

You can choose from several database systems. Although some swear by Microsoft SQL Server, others praise MySQL or Oracle. There seems to be no consensus on what database system is the best, but we hope to shed light on the differences between the various products.

Databases fall into two main categories: file-based and server-based. File-based databases (such as Microsoft Access) reside in a single file and are easy to distribute, but often suffer from inferior performance compared to their server-based counterparts. Server-based databases (such as Microsoft SQL Server) offer better performance and can handle more concurrent users, but are often more difficult to set up and export and distribute to other servers.

Perhaps the most widely distributed and available product around is Microsoft Access, which ships with the Microsoft Office suite. This database is a great product for setting up a nice, quick database for test environments and for small sites, but for large-scale production environments with many concurrent users, we would recommend something a bit more robust, such as Microsoft SQL Server, Microsoft SQL Server 2000 Desktop Engine (MSDE 2000), MySQL, or Oracle. All have strengths and weaknesses. MySQL tends to be popular because it is inexpensive.

Microsoft Access

Microsoft Access comes bundled with the Microsoft Office Suite. Microsoft has made many improvements to Access in the XP version. The most notable improvements include XML support, a new SQL Server 2000 desktop engine that is compatible with SQL Server 2000, and the ability to link Access database tables to tables in SQL Server. One of the downsides to Access, however, is that it was *not* designed to be used with web sites. It cannot handle several concurrent connections efficiently, and database file sizes can get large very quickly. As we said earlier, you should really use Access databases only for small web sites and test environments, but not for large-scale production environments.

You can find more information on Microsoft Access at http://www.microsoft.com/office/access/.

Microsoft SQL Server

SQL Server (pronounced "Sequel Server"), is an enterprise-level product with a very impressive feature set. Some of its more notable features include XML support, stored procedures, views, triggers, and wizards that help you optimize indexes and primary keys. SQL Server is also highly scaleable for high-end servers—it allows multiple ways of performing multiserver replication, integrated backup and restore, and other useful management functions. Several different versions are available, including Enterprise, Standard, Personal, Developer, and even a version for Windows CE.

The main drawback of using SQL Server is the cost. Depending on your licensing needs, the price can get very high. For a pricing comparison between SQL Server and Oracle, check out http://www.microsoft.com/sql/evaluation/compare/pricecomparison.asp. Another drawback is that SQL Server has very limited platform support; it is available only for Windows platforms at this time.

You can find more information on SQL Server at http://www.microsoft.com/sql/.

Microsoft SQL Server 2000 Desktop Engine

The Microsoft SQL Server 2000 Desktop Engine (MSDE 2000) is similar to Microsoft SQL Server in many aspects, but it is a low-cost alternative. If you meet licensing requirements, you are able to redistribute the royalty-free database engine without paying any royalties. MSDE 2000 supports various Microsoft operating systems ranging from Windows 98 to Windows XP. Find out more at http://www.microsoft.com/sql/techinfo/development/2000/MSDE2000.asp.

MySQL

MySQL is a very good *open source* package that runs on a variety of platforms. It is an excellent alternative to Access, but it can be a little trickier to install and configure. In addition to this, you must have a greater knowledge of SQL in order to create tables and view data. MySQL lacks a graphical user interface, and administration is typically done through a console window similar to DOS or Telnet. However, many third-party applications exist to add a graphical front-end to MySQL.

MySQL is a powerful database product, and it is free only as long as you meet certain licensing requirements. Although it is not as feature-rich as SQL Server or Oracle, future versions promise to incorporate stored procedures, triggers, and views (all of which we discuss in Chapter 6). Overall, MySQL is a very popular package because of its low cost, speed, and power, and it is an excellent multiplatform product. Visit http://www.mysql.com/products/mysql/ for more product and download information.

Oracle

Oracle is another extremely powerful large-scale enterprise solution. Like SQL Server, Oracle offers stored procedures, XML support, and is a secure and stable platform. Oracle also offers additional features not intrinsic to SQL Server, such as the ability to cluster a database across several computers and the ability to run on both Windows and Linux operating systems. Oracle's most significant detracting factor would have to be the price, which is prohibitively high for many development houses. Find out more about Oracle at http://www.oracle.com.

> **TIP** *A solid knowledge of SQL and databases is essential for building larger sites with dynamic content. Poorly designed databases tend to perform slowly and make it much more difficult to retrieve data easily later.*

Using an Access Database

Let's open up an Access database and look at its inner workings. When you installed ColdFusion, several databases were automatically copied into the install directory. Go to the folder where you installed ColdFusion (by default, this would be C:\CFusionMX\ on a Windows machine) and open the db folder. You should see three Microsoft Access Databases: cfexamples.mdb, cfsnippets.mdb, and company.mdb. We are interested only in company.mdb right now, so double-click on it to open it.

> **NOTE** *If you get a warning about the version of the database being created in an earlier version of Access, simply click on OK to open the database. Be aware that you will be able to edit table content, but you won't be able add additional objects, such as other tables, to the database.*
>
> *To have full control over the database, you must convert it to a version usable by the version of Access you have. To do this, close the database and select Tools ➤ Database Utilities ➤ Convert Database, and choose the format you want to convert to. You then must browse to the database location and select it. The format conversion process is explained in further detail in this Microsoft Knowledge Base Article:* http://support.microsoft.com/ default.aspx?scid=kb;en-us;324702.

The company.mdb database is broken down into three separate tables: Departmt, Employee, and LoginInfo. Let's begin by double-clicking on the LoginInfo table to open it.

You can see from Figure 2-1 that the table is broken down into three separate columns: UserID, Roles, and Password. This allows us to build an authentication system where users can enter their login credentials (UserID and Password) through form fields on a web page and the action page can run a query to compare the entered details against the values stored in the database.

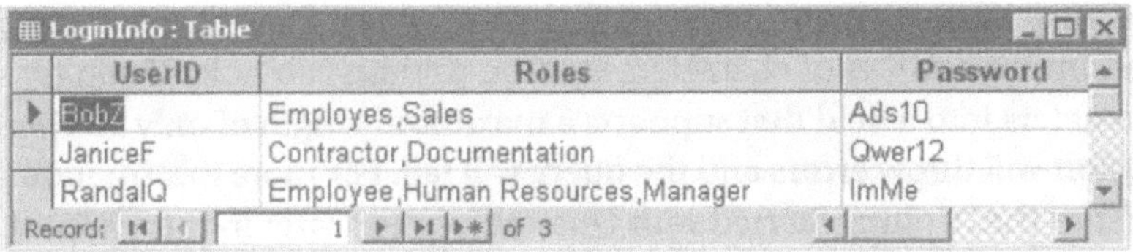

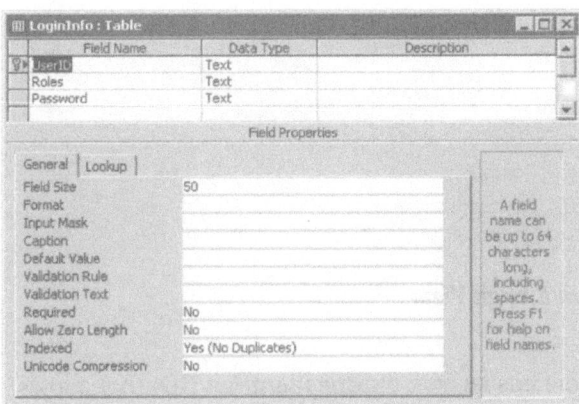

Figure 2-1. User details stored in the LoginInfo table

If this query returns a matching record, then you know that the UserID and Password supplied are correct. The roles that belong to the person logging in are also available in the one record that had both a matching UserID and Password. If you cannot find a match in the database, it means that the user may have entered an incorrect UserID and Password combination, or that the user is not in the database.

Let's close this window and right-click the LoginInfo table. Select Design View from the context menu, and you will see the names of the three columns under the heading Field Name. You will also see their respective data types under a column called Data Type, as shown in Figure 2-2.

Figure 2-2. The LoginInfo table in Design View

Note that all three columns have the same data type: Text. This means that the column will accept any sort of textual input (numbers, dates, or Booleans), although it is considered bad form to store anything but strings in a text data type column. You should always choose the "native" data types for numbers, dates, and yes/no values whenever possible to avoid having your database convert data types automatically and making it difficult to retrieve the data at a later date. Try clicking on one of the columns in this database, such as UserID. Look at the attributes of this column in Field Properties (shown in Figure 2-2).

One of the most important attributes for Text data types is Field Size, which dictates the maximum number of characters that the column can hold. If you try to enter 60 characters into a field that supports a maximum length of only 50 characters, ColdFusion will throw errors and the query will fail. For more information on queries, refer to the "Getting Started with Queries" section later in this chapter.

Other important attributes in Access include:

• Required: Controls whether a value is required for this field or not

• Allow Zero Length: Controls whether you can enter an empty string for this field

Now close the LoginInfo table and look at the Departmt table instead. Right-click the table name and select Design View. You should see the table shown in Figure 2-3. This table also has three fields: Dept_ID, Dept_Name, and Location.

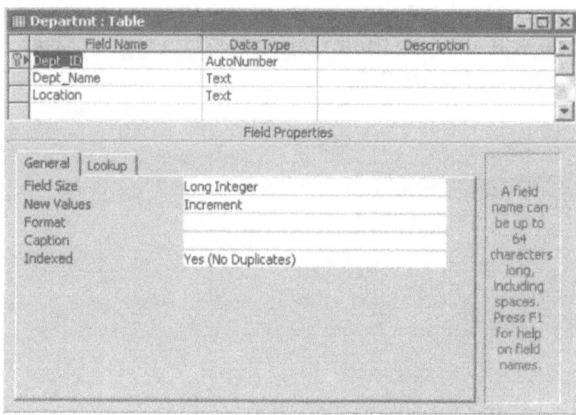

Figure 2-3. The Departmt table in Design View

Each department in this table has its own unique identifier (ID) that allows you to point to that row. Notice that this table has a different Data Type (that you haven't seen before) called AutoNumber. AutoNumber is a sequential number inserted automatically by Access; every time you enter a new record into the database, Access will generate a unique Dept_ID for you. You should also notice a small "key" icon beside the Dept_ID field, as shown in Figure 2-4.

Figure 2-4. The Access primary key icon

This icon represents a *primary key*. Primary keys make sure that you cannot insert null values into that column, and that no two values in that column are ever the same. For instance, in this example, no two users can have the same UserID in the Departmt table. Each table must have a primary key that uniquely identifies each single row in the database table. If another unique identifier is not available for a record (such as a product ID or employee number), it is common to use an AutoNumber field as the primary key.

Close this table and look at the final table, Employee. Once again, you have a column called Emp_ID, which is both an AutoNumber data type and a primary key. You also have columns called FirstName, LastName, Dept_ID, StartDate, Salary, and Contract. FirstName, LastName, and Contract share a Text data type, and Dept_ID is a Number data type, which means it accepts only numeric input.

NOTE *By default, numeric columns have a field size of long integer, which supports a range of roughly —2.1 billion to +2.1 billion.*

The Dept_ID column in the Employee table holds the same values as the Dept_ID column from the Departmt table you looked at earlier. When a primary key in one table is found in a different table, we refer to it as a *foreign key*. So, we say that Dept_ID is a foreign key in the Employee table. If you store only the Dept_ID foreign key in the Employee table, you don't need to save both a department name and location for each employee as well. This means that you are reducing the duplication of data, which minimizes the size of the database. Another benefit of breaking down tables this way is that if you change the value of a Dept_Name in the Departmt table, you don't need to update the tens or hundreds of corresponding records in the Employee table. So, data would need to be changed in only one place. This process of organizing data to minimize redundancy by breaking it into several tables that use primary key–foreign key relationships is known as "normalization."

A relational database stores data in tables and allows you to define relationships between the tables. The link between the tables is based on one or more fields/columns common to the tables, as shown in Figure 2-5.

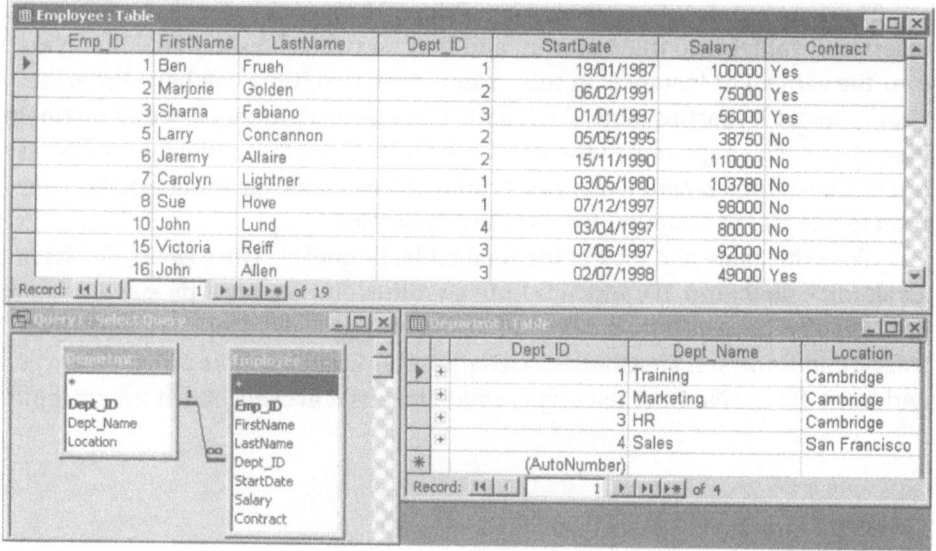

Figure 2-5. A simple illustration of a relationship between two tables in the company.mdb database

You can see in Figure 2-5 that each employee in the Employee table at the top has a value for Dept_ID. That value corresponds to the Dept_ID on the Departmt table on the bottom. The Relationships window allows you to see which tables have relationships with one another.

The remaining columns in the Employee table are StartDate (which is a Date/Time data type), Salary, and Contract. In this database, Contract is a Text data type, although, because it stores a Boolean value (yes or no), the Access Yes/No data type might have been a better choice for it.

Getting Started with SQL Queries

Typically, incorporating a database with ColdFusion requires the following:

- A database

- A data source

- SQL queries

SQL queries allow you to select, insert, update, and delete data from a database. A *data source* is a name that you assign to a database in the ColdFusion Administrator. It is probably easiest to think of a data source as being an alias pointing to the database file. You will use this alias when you create Recordsets in Dreamweaver or write your own queries using CFML. To learn how to set up a data source, refer to the "Setting Up a Data Source" section later in this chapter.

You will use SQL to talk to the database. The four most common SQL statements are SELECT, INSERT, UPDATE, and DELETE. Each type of database application has its own "extensions" to SQL, but these are the four basic SQL commands that are commonly supported. Let's look at these four actions in more detail.

> **TIP** *It is usually good practice to terminate each SQL statement with a semi-colon (;). Although not required, it makes SQL statements a bit easier to read, and you are able to separate multiple SQL statements within a single* <cfquery> *block. You will also see in the SQL examples in this chapter that SQL keywords are commonly written in uppercase. Although the SQL language isn't case-sensitive, it makes the code a little more readable.*

SELECT

SELECT queries retrieve data from your database, and this type makes up the majority of queries you will encounter in CFML development. You can return data from a single table, multiple tables, all columns in a table, or only rows in a table that match a certain criteria.

The generic syntax for SELECT statements is:

```
SELECT [list of columns]
FROM [table name]
WHERE [column] = [value]
ORDER BY [column] [order];
```

The WHERE and ORDER BY clauses in the SELECT statement are optional, and it is worth mentioning that you can have as many WHERE clauses as you need, as long as each one is separated by AND or OR keywords (or some other Boolean operator). You will look at a series of SELECT clauses later in this chapter.

The simplest form of the SELECT statement would be:

```
SELECT [list of columns]
FROM [table name];
```

This will return all the data in the listed columns from the specified table.

The following is a sample SELECT query that retrieves a single record from the Employee table:

```
SELECT Emp_ID, FirstName, LastName, Dept_ID
FROM Employee
WHERE Emp_ID = 24;
```

To view all of the data in a table, use "*" as the column name.

INSERT

INSERT queries are responsible for adding new records into a table. For example, you could use them to allow new members to register on the web site. You could also post new news articles to a web site. Typically, an INSERT query will add only a single record into a database, but in Chapter 6 you will learn how to use a single INSERT query to add multiple records into a table.

The generic syntax for INSERT statements is:

```
INSERT INTO [table name] ( [list of columns] )
VALUES ( [corresponding list of values] );
```

A single record is inserted into the table, and the columns are set to the corresponding values. You can see an example of this here:

```
INSERT INTO Employee( FirstName, LastName, Dept_ID, StartDate, Salary, Contract )
VALUES ( 'test', 'employee', 2, '2-28-2003', 1000, 'No' );
```

You can see in the preceding code that you must enclose all alphanumeric strings in single quotes; numeric values do not need quotes.

UPDATE

UPDATE queries are similar to INSERT queries, except that they update existing records in a table. UPDATE queries can be very dangerous unless you exercise caution, because by default they update *all* records in a table unless you explicitly specify which records you wish to update (by using a WHERE clause).

The generic syntax for UPDATE statements is:

```
UPDATE [table name]
SET [column] = [value]
WHERE [column] = [value];
```

Records in the table are updated to the values specified in the SET line WHERE the column has a particular value. You can use this behavior a couple of ways. You can update a single record where the table's primary key has a particular value, like so:

```
UPDATE Employee
SET Dept_ID = 3
WHERE Emp_ID = 21;
```

You can also update all records within a table where a column has a particular value. For example, say you wanted to move all employees from one department to another, as follows:

```
UPDATE Employee
SET Dept_ID = 4
WHERE Dept_ID = 2;
```

The UPDATE statement can update multiple columns at the same time as well. Using the following code, you can modify both the salary and department of an employee in a single UPDATE statement:

```
UPDATE Employee
SET Dept_ID = 4,
        Salary = 100000
WHERE Emp_ID = 20;
```

If you accidentally forget the WHERE clause in an UPDATE statement, SQL assumes that you want to update every record in the table, which usually produces undesirable results. For this reason, always keep backups of your current data; it is all too easy to make a simple mistake in your SQL statement and lose a large amount of data.

DELETE

DELETE queries remove records from a table. DELETE will remove *all* records from a table unless you explicitly specify which records to delete, so be very careful when writing these queries.

The generic syntax for DELETE statements is:

```
DELETE FROM [table name]
WHERE [column] = [value];
```

Every row is deleted from the specified table WHERE a column contains a certain value. There are a few different ways to use this tag. You could delete every record from the Employee table where the Emp_ID equals 6 (where 6 is the value of the primary key), causing one row to be deleted from the database:

```
DELETE FROM Employee
WHERE Emp_ID = 6;
```

You could also use the preceding DELETE statement to delete all records from the Employee table where the employees belong to a certain department. An example of this is shown here:

```
DELETE FROM Employee
WHERE Dept_ID = 1;
```

Exercise caution here, just as you did when using the UPDATE statement; if you accidentally forget the WHERE clause in a DELETE statement, SQL will assume that you want to delete every record in the table. It is also worth mentioning that SQL is not deleting columns or fields in the table, but entire records! To clear the contents of a column or field, you must use an UPDATE statement and specify the particular columns you are interested in.

We discuss SQL in more detail later in this chapter and in Chapter 6.

Setting Up a Data Source

As mentioned before, when you installed ColdFusion, some databases were also installed by default. ColdFusion usually sets up data sources automatically for these databases. However, in case you don't have a data source set up, we will briefly explain how to use the ColdFusion Administrator to set up data sources for Access databases. The procedure for other databases is similar but may require additional information (such as a database username and password in the case of Microsoft SQL Server and Oracle databases).

1. Open a web browser and direct it to http://localhost:8500/CFIDE/ administrator/. If you've set up your ColdFusion server on a port other than 8500, you will need to modify this URL accordingly.

2.   Once you've logged into the Administrator, click on Data Sources under the Data & Services section of the menu on the left-hand side. If CompanyInfo shows up in the Connected Data Source area with a Microsoft Access driver, click on it. Otherwise, enter **CompanyInfo** in the Data Source Name field in the Add New Data Source area near the top of the window. (We will reference this name later in Dreamweaver and in the <cfquery> CFML tag.) Next select Microsoft Access from the Driver drop-down menu, and then click on the Add button. You will now see the dialog box shown in Figure 2-6.

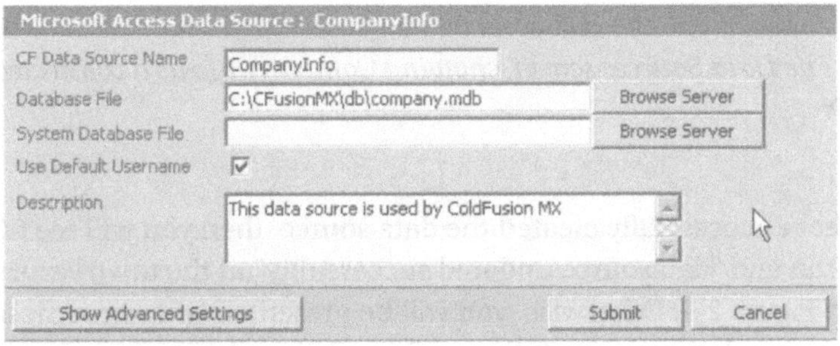

Figure 2-6. The Microsoft Access Data Source dialog box

3.   Next click on the Browse Server button beside the Database File field and navigate to the directory where you installed ColdFusion server (typically, C:\CFusionMX\). From here, navigate into the db folder, select company.mdb, and click on Apply.

You'll be taken back to the previous screen with the path to the database file filled in. Make sure that Use Default Username is checked, and click on Submit.

The Administrator window will now list all of your data sources, as shown in Figure 2-7.

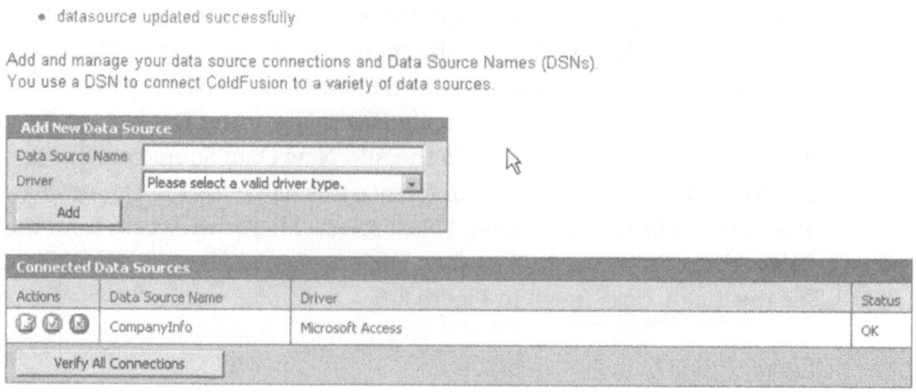

- datasource updated successfully

Add and manage your data source connections and Data Source Names (DSNs).
You use a DSN to connect ColdFusion to a variety of data sources.

*Figure 2-7. The Data Sources screen, showing CompanyInfo as a connected
Data Source*

If you have successfully created the data source, then you will see OK in the
Status column and "datasource updated successfully" at the top of your screen,
as shown in Figure 2-7. Otherwise, you will be presented with error messages.

Now that you have successfully configured your database, let's create
some queries!

Using Dreamweaver MX 2004 to Create Queries

Let's start by opening Dreamweaver and trying out some simple queries to pull
data from our sample database. Open the site you defined in Chapter 1 and you
can begin to create some Recordsets. Before proceeding, make sure you have
a data source set up, as detailed previously.

1. Open the Application panel, and then select Bindings➤+➤Recordset
    (Query). The dialog box shown in Figure 2-8 will open:

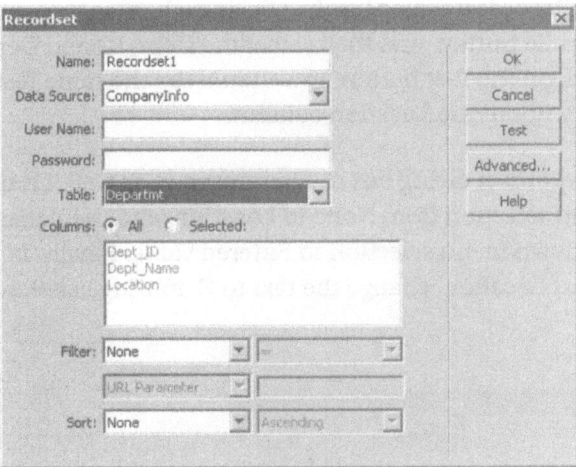

Figure 2-8. The Recordset dialog box

2. Now select our CompanyInfo Data Source from the Data Source drop-down menu. Leave the User Name and Password fields blank, and select Departmt from the Table drop-down menu. For this example, the name of the Recordset is not relevant, so use the default Name, Recordset1. Later, this will be used as a reference name for the code that Dreamweaver will create.

3. Leave the other fields at their default values and click the Test button. The Test SQL Statement pops up, displaying the search results, as shown in Figure 2-9.

   Our query simply selects all the columns from the Departmt table. If you want to select only certain columns from a table, simply click the Selected radio button next to Columns in the Recordset dialog box, then click on the columns that you wish to select. To select multiple columns, hold Ctrl while clicking on them.

Record	Dept_ID	Dept_Name	Location
1	1	Training	Cambridge
2	2	Marketing	Cambridge
3	3	HR	Cambridge
4	4	Sales	San Francisco

Figure 2-9. The results of testing our Recordset

4. Return to the Recordset dialog box by clicking OK. This time, click on the Selected radio button, and then select the Dept_ID and Dept_Name columns. Click on the Test button. You should see the same results as last time, but without the Location column.

You can use the Recordset dialog box to filter out rows as well. Change the Filter drop-down menu selection from None to Location, and then change the URL Parameter drop-down menu selection to Entered Value. Finally, in the text field containing the text Location, change the text to Cambridge as shown in Figure 2-10.

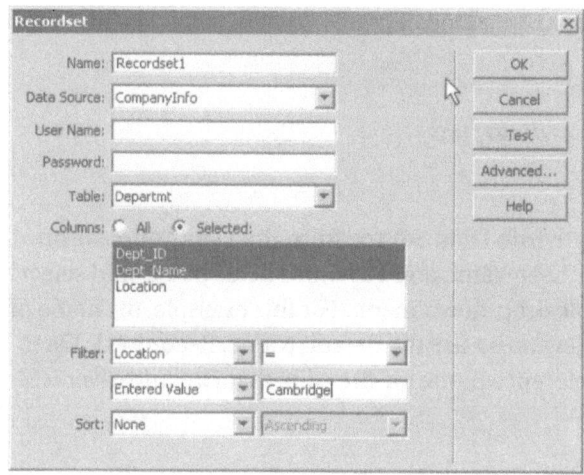

Figure 2-10. The Recordset dialog box with the filter applied

You will see only three records instead of four. This is because the fourth record was for the location San Francisco, so it wasn't selected by the filter that we set up.

If you want to sort the records by a particular criterion, such as department name, you simply need to change the value in the Sort drop-down menu from None to Dept_Name. Click on Test again, and you will see the three departments in Cambridge sorted by department name in ascending (A to Z) order, as shown in Figure 2-11.

Record	Dept_ID	Dept_Name	Location
1	3	HR	Cambridge
2	2	Marketing	Cambridge
3	1	Training	Cambridge

Figure 2-11. The three departments in Cambridge, sorted in ascending order

To sort the results in reverse order (Z-A), simply change the value in the Sort drop-down menu from Ascending to Descending.

By now, you must have noticed that Dreamweaver allows you to create simple queries without having to write any SQL. Unfortunately, you are limited to simple queries. If you want to write anything more complicated, for example, to order the search results by more than one column, you must switch to the Advanced interface and write some SQL, or manually tweak our SQL code in Code View.

You may have also noticed that you can do only SELECT queries in the basic Recordset dialog box, not INSERT, UPDATE, or DELETE statements. If you want to create any of these statements, you must write your own SQL.

Now let's look at creating advanced queries by switching to the Advanced Recordset interface.

> **NOTE** *We will look at* INSERT, UPDATE, *and* DELETE *queries later in Chapter 6.*

Using Dreamweaver MX 2004's Advanced Recordset Interface

The advanced mode in Dreamweaver allows you to customize SQL syntax and write complex queries that can select data from more than one table. To switch to advanced mode, simply click on the Advanced button in the top right of the Recordset dialog box. The advanced layout of the Recordset dialog box is shown in Figure 2-12.

Recordset

Name:	Recordset1		OK
Data Source:	CompanyInfo		Cancel
User Name:			Test
Password:			Simple...

SQL:
```
SELECT *
FROM Departmt
WHERE Location = 'Cambridge'
ORDER BY Dept_Name ASC
```

Help

Page Parameters: + −

Name:
Default:
Edit...

Database Items:
⊞ 📇 Tables
⊞ 🔍 Views
⊞ 🐾 Stored Procedures

Add to SQL:
SELECT
WHERE
ORDER BY

Figure 2-12. The Advanced Recordset dialog box

At the bottom of the window is the Database Items tree, which shows any existing tables, views, and stored procedures for the selected data source.

We cover views and stored procedures in Chapter 6, but for now just expand the Tables tree by clicking on its plus symbol. You should see three database tables. You can expand these as well, as shown in Figure 2-13, to see the columns for each of these tables.

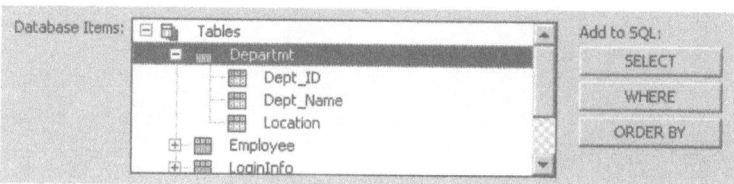

Figure 2-13. You can expand the Database Items tree to view the structure of the database.

If you followed the previous example and clicked Advanced, you would see the following SQL code, which Dreamweaver generated when you selected your options in the simple Recordset dialog, as shown in Figure 2-14.

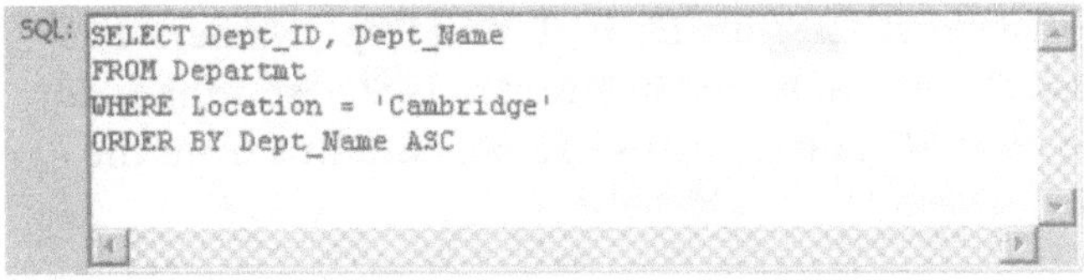

```
SQL: SELECT Dept_ID, Dept_Name
     FROM Departmt
     WHERE Location = 'Cambridge'
     ORDER BY Dept_Name ASC
```

Figure 2-14. Dreamweaver automatically generates this SQL code.

The SQL statements shown SELECT the Dept_ID and Dept_Name from the Departmt table for all records where the location equals Cambridge, and then sort any matching records by department name in ascending order.

> **TIP** *It is important to note that SQL uses single quotation marks around strings. If you accidentally use double quotation marks, SQL will throw an error. Numbers and Booleans do not need single quotation marks around them.*

Notice that in the ORDER BY statement, department name in ascending order is specified. By default, SQL orders all columns in ascending order, so you could shorten this line to ORDER BY Dept_Name and produce exactly the same results. You can verify this by clicking on Test. To reverse the sort order, add the DESC (descending) keyword after the column name.

Let's create a few queries in advanced mode before moving on to writing SQL from scratch.

Writing a SELECT Query in Advanced Mode

SELECT queries are the most common type you will encounter in CFML applications. While developing your applications, often you will need to create more complex queries than is possible in the Basic Mode, so a good knowledge of SQL is essential to building a robust application. By using Advanced Mode you can write custom queries to handle your specific needs.

1. Clear the SQL code from the SQL text field. Now highlight the Departmt table in the Database Items tree and click the SELECT button to the right of the tree. You should now see the following code added into the SQL text field:

    ```
    SELECT *
    FROM Departmt
    ```

You can see that instead of selecting Dept_ID and Dept_Name, it has entered an asterisk (*). As mentioned before, this is SQL shorthand for "all columns," so your SQL query will select all columns from the Departmt table.

2. If you want to select only a few columns, expand the Departmt table, click on a specific column, and click the SELECT button. You can select only one column at a time through this interface. Let's select both the Dept_ID and Dept_Name. Highlight Dept_ID and click SELECT, then highlight Dept_Name and click SELECT again. Click on Test to view the output. As you can see from Figure 2-15, it is slightly different from the previous example.

   Notice that it has attached the table name before each of the column names. While this isn't necessary when you are selecting values from a single table, it will be important later on when you start joining data from separate tables.

   Removing the Departmt from the columns in the SELECT list will not affect the query results if you are only dealing with a single table.

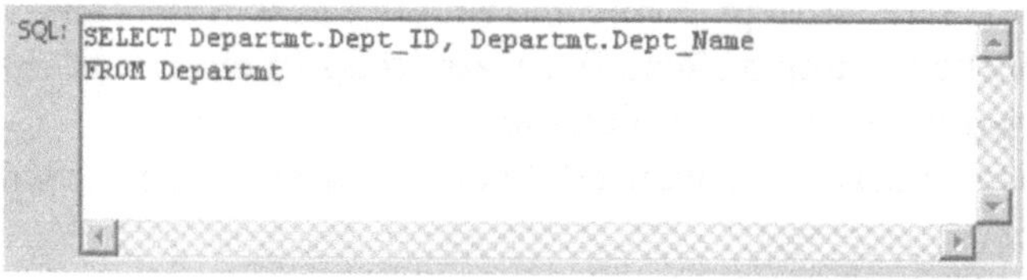

```
SQL: SELECT Departmt.Dept_ID, Departmt.Dept_Name
     FROM Departmt
```

Figure 2-15. The table name is attached to the column name.

3. To filter the records according to location, highlight the Location column from the Database Items tree and click WHERE. Dreamweaver adds WHERE Departmt.Location to the end of the previous query, but you must finish the rest of the statement. To select only departments in Cambridge, you must modify the WHERE clause to say:

```
WHERE Departmt.Location = 'Cambridge'
```

> **TIP** *You could use "Cambridge" or "cambridge" here, because most databases aren't case-sensitive by default. Both spellings would return the same query results. Check your specific database configuration before making this assumption in the real world.*

4. Click the Test button. Notice that you now have only three results, as shown in Figure 2-16. The fourth record is hidden because its location is San Francisco, and so it did not meet the requirements of the WHERE clause.

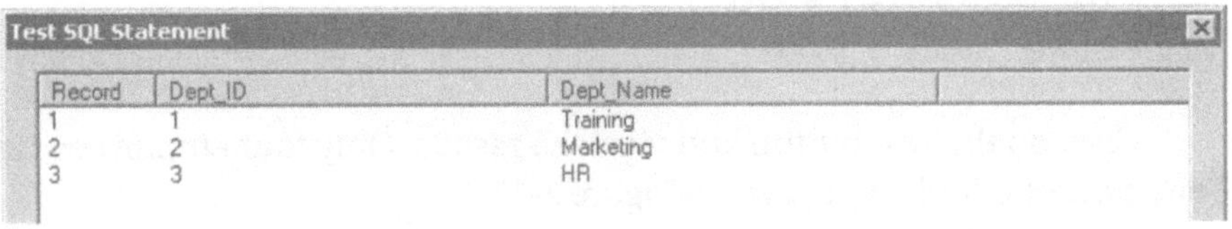

Figure 2-16. Records filtered according to the location Cambridge

Ordering the Query

Ordering the results is quite straightforward. You simply highlight the column you want to sort the results by and click ORDER BY. If you click the Dept_Name column, you will see the following code in the SQL text field:

```
SELECT Departmt.Dept_ID, Departmt.Dept_Name
FROM Departmt
WHERE Departmt.Location = 'Cambridge'
ORDER BY Departmt.Dept_Name
```

We have managed to recreate the functionality of the original query we wrote in simple mode. Clear the SQL text field. You will now generate some queries with more complexity using the Employee table.

Filtering by Multiple Parameters

Highlight the Employee table from the Database Items tree and click SELECT to select all columns for this table. Test the query, and you will see all the employee records returned. Now change the query to select only employees who are on contract. Highlight the Contract column in the Employee tree, click on WHERE, and change the WHERE clause to say:

```
WHERE Employee.Contract = 'Yes'
```

Because the Contract column is a Text data type, you need to enclose its value in single quotation marks. Test the query, and you will see the seven employees who matched our search criteria.

Now let's say you want to see only employees who are on contract and make more than $50,000 salary. Highlight Salary within the Employee tree and click the WHERE button. Now you must manually type a condition for Salary into the SQL text field to select for the condition where Salary is greater than 50,000. Add >50000 to the end of the AND clause line. Your final SQL code should look like this:

```
SELECT *
FROM Employee
WHERE Employee.Contract = 'Yes'
AND Employee.Salary > 50000
```

Click on the Test button and view the results. Only four employees match our current criteria, as shown in Figure 2-17.

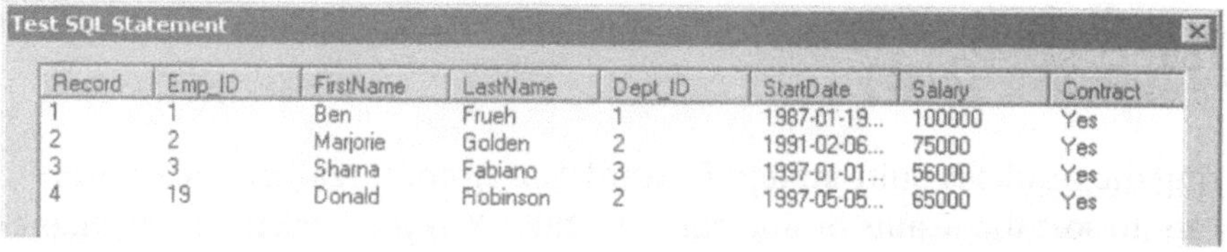

Record	Emp_ID	FirstName	LastName	Dept_ID	StartDate	Salary	Contract
1	1	Ben	Frueh	1	1987-01-19...	100000	Yes
2	2	Marjorie	Golden	2	1991-02-06...	75000	Yes
3	3	Sharna	Fabiano	3	1997-01-01...	56000	Yes
4	19	Donald	Robinson	2	1997-05-05...	65000	Yes

Figure 2-17. The search results for contract employees who earn more than $50,000

Creating a Simple Join

You can also select data from multiple tables at once. The data in the separate tables is linked by using primary and foreign keys.

In the following example, we join the Departmt and Employee tables and display the name of each employee, and each employee's department name and location. Because the Employee table has only a Dept_ID column, you must join it with the Departmt table to get the values for Dept_Name and Location.

Let's get started. Again clear the SQL code from the text field. Now expand both the Departmt and Employee tables and select the following columns (the order is unimportant): Departmt.Dept_ID, Departmt.Dept_Name, Departmt.Location, Employee.Emp_ID, Employee.FirstName, and Employee.LastName.

Your query should now look similar to the following:

```
SELECT Departmt.Dept_ID, Departmt.Dept_Name, Departmt.Location,
            Employee.Emp_ID, Employee.FirstName, Employee.LastName
FROM Departmt, Employee
```

If you test this query, you will see that something has definitely gone wrong! (See Figure 2-18.)

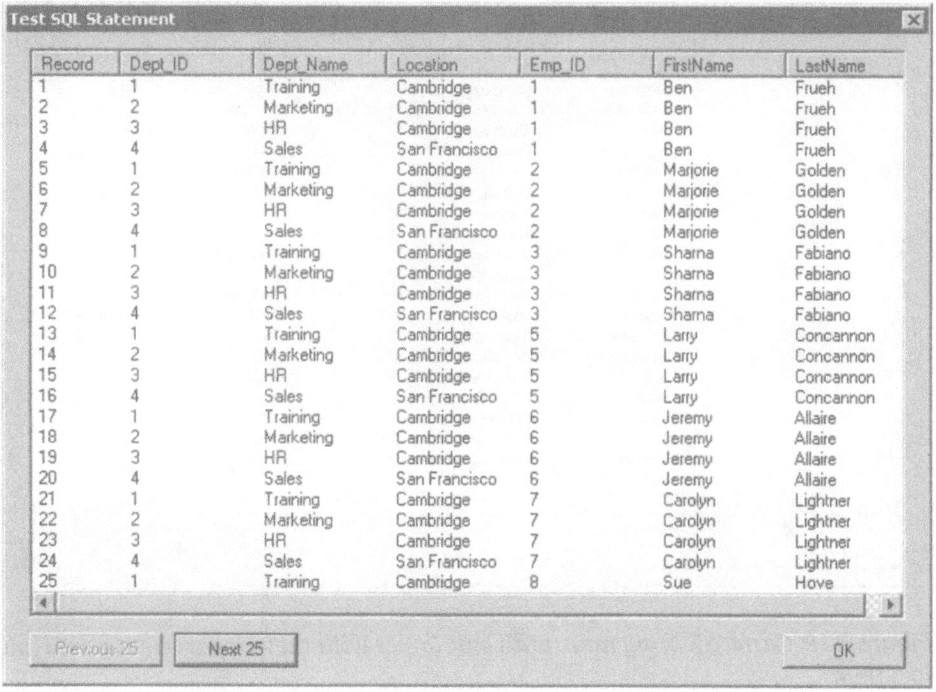

Test SQL Statement

Record	Dept_ID	Dept_Name	Location	Emp_ID	FirstName	LastName
1	1	Training	Cambridge	1	Ben	Frueh
2	2	Marketing	Cambridge	1	Ben	Frueh
3	3	HR	Cambridge	1	Ben	Frueh
4	4	Sales	San Francisco	1	Ben	Frueh
5	1	Training	Cambridge	2	Marjorie	Golden
6	2	Marketing	Cambridge	2	Marjorie	Golden
7	3	HR	Cambridge	2	Marjorie	Golden
8	4	Sales	San Francisco	2	Marjorie	Golden
9	1	Training	Cambridge	3	Sharna	Fabiano
10	2	Marketing	Cambridge	3	Sharna	Fabiano
11	3	HR	Cambridge	3	Sharna	Fabiano
12	4	Sales	San Francisco	3	Sharna	Fabiano
13	1	Training	Cambridge	5	Larry	Concannon
14	2	Marketing	Cambridge	5	Larry	Concannon
15	3	HR	Cambridge	5	Larry	Concannon
16	4	Sales	San Francisco	5	Larry	Concannon
17	1	Training	Cambridge	6	Jeremy	Allaire
18	2	Marketing	Cambridge	6	Jeremy	Allaire
19	3	HR	Cambridge	6	Jeremy	Allaire
20	4	Sales	San Francisco	6	Jeremy	Allaire
21	1	Training	Cambridge	7	Carolyn	Lightner
22	2	Marketing	Cambridge	7	Carolyn	Lightner
23	3	HR	Cambridge	7	Carolyn	Lightner
24	4	Sales	San Francisco	7	Carolyn	Lightner
25	1	Training	Cambridge	8	Sue	Hove

Previous 25 | Next 25 | OK

Figure 2-18. Incorrect joining returns all possible employee-department combinations.

For every employee, it has returned every employee and department combination possible! So, even though only 19 employees (and four departments) exist, it has returned 76 (19*4) records. The problem is that SQL still doesn't know how to join these two tables. You must explicitly specify which columns you want to join these two tables on by using the `WHERE` statement.

Highlight the Employee.Dept_ID column in the Database Items tree. Click on WHERE, then update the `WHERE` statement so that your final code looks like this:

```
SELECT Departmt.Dept_ID, Departmt.Dept_Name, Departmt.Location,
            Employee.Emp_ID, Employee.FirstName, Employee.LastName
FROM Departmt, Employee
WHERE Employee.Dept_ID = Departmt.Dept_ID
```

Press the Test button, and you'll see that you now have the correct results, and that each record returned has the employee's first and last name, department, and location, as shown in Figure 2-19. The preceding snippet works because the `WHERE` clause joins the two tables via the common Dept_ID column.

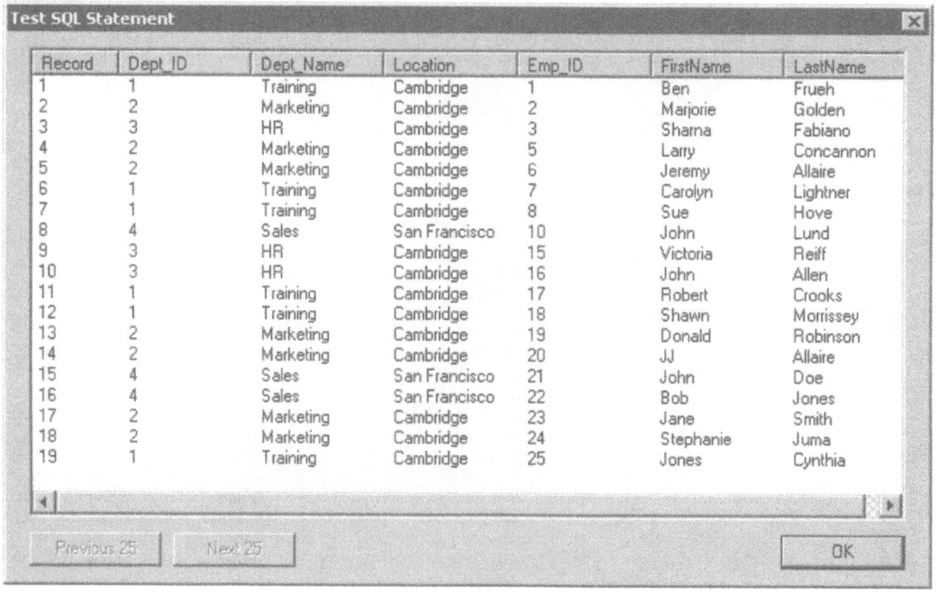

Record	Dept_ID	Dept_Name	Location	Emp_ID	FirstName	LastName
1	1	Training	Cambridge	1	Ben	Frueh
2	2	Marketing	Cambridge	2	Marjorie	Golden
3	3	HR	Cambridge	3	Sharna	Fabiano
4	2	Marketing	Cambridge	5	Larry	Concannon
5	2	Marketing	Cambridge	6	Jeremy	Allaire
6	1	Training	Cambridge	7	Carolyn	Lightner
7	1	Training	Cambridge	8	Sue	Hove
8	4	Sales	San Francisco	10	John	Lund
9	3	HR	Cambridge	15	Victoria	Reiff
10	3	HR	Cambridge	16	John	Allen
11	1	Training	Cambridge	17	Robert	Crooks
12	1	Training	Cambridge	18	Shawn	Morrissey
13	2	Marketing	Cambridge	19	Donald	Robinson
14	2	Marketing	Cambridge	20	JJ	Allaire
15	4	Sales	San Francisco	21	John	Doe
16	4	Sales	San Francisco	22	Bob	Jones
17	2	Marketing	Cambridge	23	Jane	Smith
18	2	Marketing	Cambridge	24	Stephanie	Juma
19	1	Training	Cambridge	25	Jones	Cynthia

Figure 2-19. Correct joining returns all employees with their department name and location.

We mentioned earlier that you don't need to prefix the name of the table onto each column when you are working with only one query. However, if you don't prefix columns when dealing with multiple tables, SQL throws an error, stating that a specified field could refer to more than one table in the `FROM` clause of the query. For this reason, it is important to prefix the table name for any column that may appear in more than one table. In this case, it is the Dept_ID column that appears in both the Departmt and Employee tables. SQL allows you to assign aliases to table names, which helps reduce the amount of typing necessary if you are hand-coding SQL. You could rewrite the last query to use table aliases, as seen here:

```
SELECT D.Dept_ID, D.Dept_Name, D.Location,
               E.Emp_ID, E.FirstName, E.LastName
FROM Departmt D, Employee E
WHERE E.Dept_ID = D.Dept_ID
```

We assign the table's alias after the table name in the `FROM` line. Notice that the table names have been replaced by their aliases in all the SQL statements. It is important to note that if you create aliases for a table, you must always use that alias and not switch back and forth between aliases and table names; otherwise, errors will be thrown when executing queries.

The LIKE *Operator*

A useful operator in SQL is the LIKE operator, which allows you to search columns for the occurrence of a character or string. For example, you can search for all employees whose last names start with the letter A. You can easily achieve this by modifying the preceding query, highlighting the Employee.LastName in the Database Items tree, and clicking on the WHERE button. Dreamweaver will append AND Employee.LastName to the query.

Now you need to add LIKE 'A%' to the query. You should also change the Employee prefix to the alias E, or SQL will throw an error. Your final query should look something like this:

```
SELECT D.Dept_ID, D.Dept_Name, D.Location,
            E.Emp_ID, E.FirstName, E.LastName
FROM Departmt D, Employee E
WHERE E.Dept_ID = D.Dept_ID
 AND E.LastName LIKE 'A%'
```

If you click the Test button, you will see the three records that match the search criteria. The SQL statement now basically says "Select all records where employee's last name begins with the letter 'A' and return their Dept_ID, Dept_Name, Location, Emp_ID, FirstName, and LastName." The % character is a special wildcard character in SQL; A%, means "A, then anything after it." Multiple wildcards can be used; a statement such as LIKE '%A%' will return all records that have an "A" anywhere in the column.

Summary

This has been a fairly quick introduction to databases and SQL. You should now be able to:

- Create an Access data source by using the ColdFusion Administrator

- Create some basic SQL SELECT statements using the simple and advanced Recordset interface in Dreamweaver

- Perform a simple join

You should also be a little more familiar with the Microsoft Access interface, know how to browse tables using Design View and view the data, and have a better understanding of the different data types used in Access.

We revisit databases later in Chapter 6, where we look at creating and utilizing Recordsets with Dreamweaver in more detail; creating some INSERT, UPDATE, and DELETE statements by writing our own SQL from scratch; creating queries with CFML; and more.

Introduction to ColdFusion Markup Language

COLDFUSION MARKUP LANGUAGE (CFML) is ColdFusion's own set of tags that makes up the bulk of the dynamic functionality found on ColdFusion pages. CFML has two different parts that make ColdFusion work: *tags* and *functions*. In this chapter we cover a whole bunch of CFML tags and also some basic functions. Chapter 4 shows you how to use some of the more advanced functions and teaches you about variable scopes and different data types.

Tags are used to carry out operations, such as looping over Recordsets, uploading files to a web server by way of a web form, dumping the contents of a variable to the screen for debugging, and grabbing the contents of a remote page on the Web. Functions within ColdFusion are used to manipulate data or perform calculations. For example, ColdFusion has a function called #ArrayAvg()#, which calculates the average of the numeric values within an array. You often must use tags and functions together to build a completely functional site.

Introducing CFML

HTML and ColdFusion tags can exist together within a document that is requested from a web server. All ColdFusion tags start with <cf. The ColdFusion server will process anything within these tags, ignoring any plain HTML tags. The server will return any HTML generated by processing your ColdFusion tags, and then the entire page is returned to the user's browser. Other things to note about CFML include:

- Whenever using ColdFusion tags within a document, you must save it as a .cfm file for it to be recognized and interpreted by the ColdFusion server.

- In text strings, all text is considered literal unless it is within a set of pound/hash (#) signs.

- ColdFusion elements (the opening and closing tags, and everything in between) are called *blocks*. For example, if you were using a `<cfif>` element in your code, it would be called the `<cfif>` block.

- To add comments inside ColdFusion tags, you must use CFML comment delimiters: `<!--- CFML comment --->`. Notice that these are similar to HTML comments, but have three dashes instead of two. If you use HTML comments inside your CFML, they will not be ignored by the ColdFusion server as expected, and you will either get errors or will dynamically create HTML comments. Also, CFML comments will not send text back to the user's browser like HTML comments do.

Now we provide a general overview of the many categories of tags, and the most common ones you will be likely to use in your work. We then go through some of these tags in detail, along with the functions that help these tags work and make your applications run.

> **TIP** *You can also extend ColdFusion by writing your own custom tags using CFML, or even Java or C++. Writing custom tags is covered in more detail in Chapter 10. Custom tags written in ColdFusion are prepended with CF_, whereas any custom tags written in Java or C++ are prepended by CFX_.*

Tags Used in CFML

Let's look at some of the tags that make up CFML. This section provides a quick overview of some of the most common tags and their use. This should give you a general idea of what ColdFusion MX 6.1 is capable of. Following later are descriptions and code snippets detailing how to use some of these tags in a ColdFusion page.

ColdFusion MX 6.1 has more than 100 CFML tags, which Macromedia's documentation breaks down into the following categories:

- Application framework

- Database manipulation

- Data output

- Debugging

- Exception handling

- Extensibility

- File management

- Flow-control

- Forms

- Internet protocol

- Page processing

- Variable manipulation

However, what's more important are the specific tags that you will discover you use every day in ColdFusion. Some of the more useful tags are:

- `<cfchart>`: Generates charts on the fly in a variety of formats, including `.jpeg`, `.png`, and `.swf` (Flash).

- `<cfdirectory>`: Performs directory management tasks and allows you to create, delete, rename, or list the contents of a directory.

- `<cfdump>`: Displays the contents of a variable to the screen for debugging purposes. Variables can contain simple values such as strings and numbers, or complex data such as Recordsets and structures.

- `<cferror>`: Tells ColdFusion how to handle errors that occur in your application.

- `<cffile>`: Performs file-management tasks and allows you to read, write, delete, move, rename, or append data to files on the server.

- `<cfform>`: Similar to HTML forms, except that it allows developers to take advantage of automatically generated JavaScript validation provided by the ColdFusion server.

- `<cfftp>`: Allows ColdFusion to FTP files to and from remote FTP sites.

- `<cffunction>`: Allows you to write your own custom functions using CFML tags.

- `<cfhttp>`: Allows you to post variables to remote sites, or grab the contents of a file on a different server.

- `<cfif>`: Performs if ... then ... else logic in ColdFusion, running code only if certain conditions are met.

- `<cfinclude>`: Embeds other HTML or CFML code into the current document. This allows developers to break up larger files and reuse certain code/functions throughout the site.

- `<cfinput>`: Used in conjunction with the `<cfform>` tag to take advantage of built-in JavaScript validation.

- `<cflocation>`: Redirects the currently running page to a different page, or redirects users to a different site altogether.

- `<cfloop>`: Allows you to loop over Recordsets and structures a defined number of times, or while a certain condition is true.

- `<cfmail>`: Sends an e-mail to a single user or group of users.

- `<cfmodule>`: Allows you to call your own custom tags with ColdFusion.

- `<cfoutput>`: Used to output the value of a variable, or loop over a Recordset.

- `<cfparam>`: Checks to see if a certain variable exists; if not, it creates the variable and assigns a default value. It can also be used to validate the data type of a variable.

- `<cfquery>`: Used to pass SQL statements to a database.

- `<cfqueryparam>`: Used within `<cfquery>` to insert dynamic values into a SQL statement.

- `<cfset>`: Define the value of a variable.

- `<cfstoredproc>`: Execute a stored procedure (if supported by your database of choice).

- `<cfswitch>`: Passes control to a matching `<cfcase>` tag and evaluates passed expressions. This could be performed using a series of `<cfif>` tags, but this method saves space and simplifies things.

- `<cftry>`: Monitors a block of ColdFusion code and tries to catch any errors that may occur. It is used in conjunction with the `<cfcatch>` tag.

ColdFusion also has a couple of special files that are triggered before or after every user request and can be used to hold site-wide variables or settings; we will look at these now.

The `Application.cfm` *File*

The first file is called `Application.cfm`. If it exists, it is called before any other ColdFusion code is executed. If we request a file called `index.cfm`, ColdFusion first checks for a file called `Application.cfm` in the same directory as the requested `index.cfm` file. If `Application.cfm` is not found, ColdFusion checks the current directory's parent directory for the file. This process continues until a file called `Application.cfm` is found or there are no more parent directories to check. If no `Application.cfm` file is found, ColdFusion simply continues processing the requested document.

If an `Application.cfm` is found, ColdFusion processes this file and then goes on to process the requested file, which in our example was `index.cfm`. You can think of it as an implicit include file—an "on request start" if you will. The `Application.cfm` file is used as a container for global content that developers want to be available to every page, such as site-wide variables (like data source names) and for code that should be executed on every page request, although it is possible to have many `Application.cfm` files within a single web site.

A similar file called `OnRequestEnd.cfm` executes after the `Application.cfm` and the requested file have finished executing, but it executes only if an `Application.cfm` file exists inside the same folder. The `OnRequestEnd.cfm` file is useful for controlling debugging output that would be sent to the screen or for writing a footer to the screen.

It is important to remember the proper spelling and casing of these file names: `Application.cfm` and `OnRequestEnd.cfm`. Although Windows environments are not case-sensitive and will treat `application.cfm` and `Application.cfm` as the same file, Linux and UNIX environments are case-sensitive, and will treat the two files differently. Make sure you name them exactly as we did previously, so that if you migrate from a Windows environment to a Linux/Unix environment in the future, you don't have to worry about renaming several files.

Now let's look at `Application.cfm` in action to illustrate how and in which order the files are processed.

1. Open the cfbook site again in Dreamweaver MX 2004. Let's begin by creating a simple `Application.cfm` file in the cfbook folder. Create the new file and enter the following ColdFusion code:

    ```
    <cfset numCats = 2>
    ```

2. Now create another new file called `index.cfm` in the cfbook folder and enter this code:

    ```
    <cfoutput>#numCats#</cfoutput>
    ```

3. Open index.cfm in a web browser by choosing File►Preview in Browser and selecting your default browser (in Dreamweaver MX 2004). When viewing ColdFusion pages in your web browser, it is important that the file is placed within the Web-root and that you type in the URL to the file (such as http://localhost:8500/index.cfm), not the physical path (C:\CFusionMX\ wwwroot\index.cfm, for example). Otherwise, you will receive unexpected results, because the code will not be put through to the ColdFusion server. When the browser opens, you will simply see the number 2 in the window. This works because Application.cfm is being executed before the index.cfm page. In fact, the #numCats# variable should be available to all pages in the same directory, and any other child directories, as long as no other Application.cfm files are found in the directory tree.

   Once ColdFusion locates an Application.cfm file, it stops looking for other Application.cfm files. If we have a subfolder under the cfbook folder that also contains an Application.cfm file, any files within that subfolder will not be able to access variables or functions defined in the /cfbook/Application.cfm file.

4. Let's create another variable in the Application.cfm file. Add another line, as follows:

```
<cfset numCats = 2>
<cfset Today = "Saturday">
```

5. Because the value of #numCats# is numeric, you do not have to enclose it in quotes while setting it. However, when working with strings, it is very important to make sure that they are enclosed in either single quotes or double quotes as shown in the <cfset> tag. Without the quotes around "Saturday" in the second <cfset>, ColdFusion will assume you are setting the "Today" variable equal to the value of a "Saturday" variable and will throw an error if said variable does not exist. In the case of numeric values, ColdFusion simply uses the value with or without quotes (this makes sense, because CFML variable names cannot begin with a numeric character). We can also set variables equal to the result of a function. ColdFusion MX 6.1 has hundreds of built-in functions available to developers, and we cover several throughout this chapter. One useful function is the #Now()# function covered briefly in Chapter 1. This function does not take any parameters and simply returns the current date/time of the server.

   Back in index.cfm, delete the existing code, type in the following and save it:

```
<cfset datetime = Now()>
<cfoutput>#datetime#</cfoutput>
```

Because you aren't outputting the value of #Now()# to the screen and it is used within a tag and not inside quotes, it is not necessary to enclose the function in pound/hash signs while setting it. A good rule of thumb is that any time you are not inside quotes and are inside of function parentheses or a tag (not between opening and closing tags, but inside a tag), you do not need the hash marks. If you view this page in a web browser, you should see an output similar to Figure 3-1.

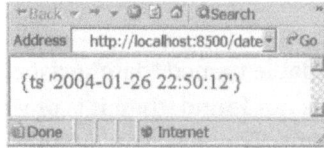

Figure 3-1. Outputting the value of a variable with <cfoutput>

Although this isn't the most user-friendly date/time format, ColdFusion does offer some excellent formatting options. Two useful formatting functions are #DateFormat()# and #TimeFormat()#. Both functions take in a date as the first parameter and an optional formatting mask. Change the index.cfm code to the following:

```
<cfset currDateTime = Now()>
<cfoutput>#DateFormat(currDateTime)#</cfoutput>
```

If you test this code, it yields an output similar to the following in the browser window, depending on the date the code is executed:

```
30-Jan-03
```

We cover the formatting options of #DateFormat()# and #TimeFormat()# in Chapter 4. Now let's look at some more of the common CFML tags that you will encounter on a regular basis.

Understanding Common ColdFusion Tags

In this section we look at some more common CFML tags that you'll use in everyday ColdFusion development. The functions these tags have range from setting variables and interacting with the operating system on the server, to sending e-mails to users or administrators.

<cfparam>

The <cfparam> tag is similar to the <cfset> tag used in the previous section, but with one important difference: <cfparam> will set the variable only if it does not yet exist. This is useful when you want to set default values or need to make sure that a variable exists before trying to use it.

The syntax is as follows:

```
<cfparam name="Url.date" default="#Now()#">
```

What this snippet does is check to see if a URL variable named "date" exists; if it does, then <cfparam> does nothing. If the variable is not found, then it is created and given a value equal to the current date and time. This way, you are not overwriting variables if they are already defined, and you can always be sure that variables exist and have values. Note that if the value of the "name" attribute (the variable name) does not have a prefix, the server will assume you are setting a variable in the local "variables" scope.

With the simple addition of a type attribute, this tag can also check to make sure that a variable is of a certain data type. Here's an example:

```
<cfparam name="Url.date" default="#Now()#" type="date">
```

In this case, if the value of the #Url.date# variable is not a valid date, ColdFusion will throw an error, as shown in Figure 3-2.

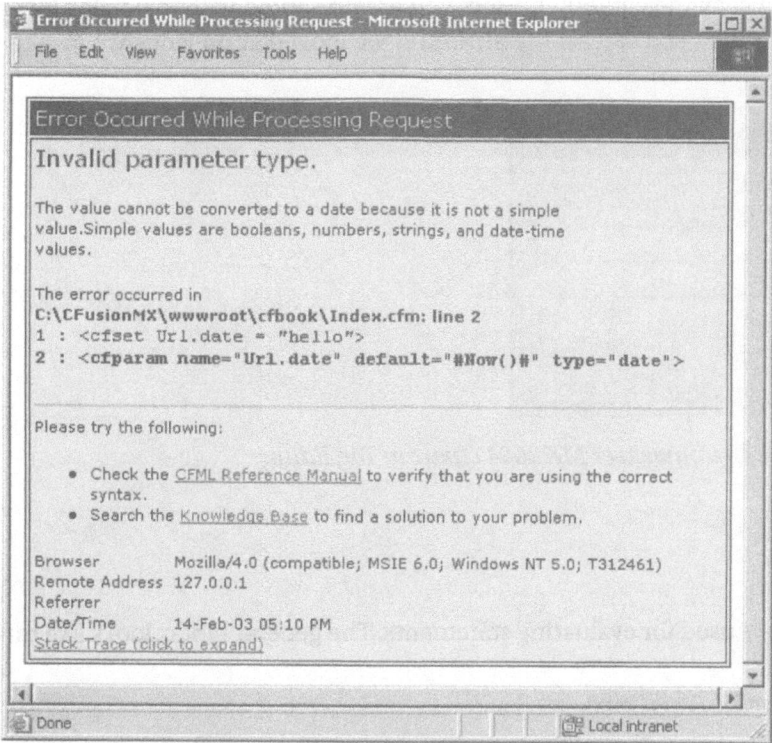

Figure 3-2. An error is thrown if the data type specified in the <cfparam> type attribute is not the same as the data type of the variable being set.

We cover error handling in more detail in Chapter 8.

If you provide only a name and type attribute for the <cfparam> tag, ColdFusion makes sure that the variable already exists and is of the correct data type. If either of these conditions fail, ColdFusion will throw an error.

We can view the supported types in Dreamweaver MX 2004. Click on the CFML Basic tab on the Insert bar in Dreamweaver, then click on the cfparam button, which looks like an exclamation mark and is ninth from the left, as shown in Figure 3-3.

Figure 3-3. The Dreamweaver MX 2004 Insert bar, with the basic CFML functions shown and the cfparam button illustrated

When you click the cfparam button, you are presented with the dialog box in Figure 3-4, in which you can set the attributes we looked at previously.

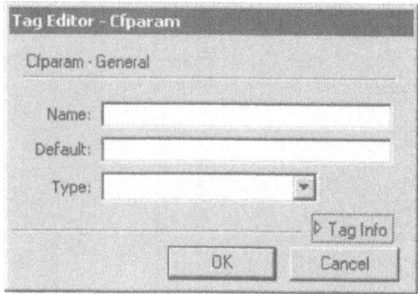

Figure 3-4. The Dreamweaver MX 2004 cfparam Tag Editor

`<cfif>`

The `<cfif>` tag is used for evaluating statements. The general syntax looks like this:

```
<cfif [statement]> ... </cfif>
```

If the statement in the opening `<cfif [statement]>` tag evaluates to True, then the code between `<cfif>` and `</cfif>` is executed. It is important to note that in CFML, "true" (case-insensitive), "yes" (also case-insensitive), and any number not 0, evaluate to a Boolean true. "False," "No," and the number 0 all evaluate to a Boolean false. For example, we can also use `<cfif>` to check whether variables exist. Consider the following code:

```
<cfif IsDefined( "Url.date" )>
   ...
</cfif>
```

In the preceding snippet, we are using the `IsDefined()` function to programmatically check whether a variable already exists. If the variable #Url.date# is already defined, then the block of code between the opening and closing `<cfif>` tag is executed. Otherwise, the block of code will evaluate to False and be skipped entirely. Note that `IsDefined()` accepts the name of a variable, not the variable itself, as it's only argument—you do not put pound signs around the variable name, and you must use quotes.

We can also add a `<cfelse>` tag between the opening and closing `<cfif>` tags, which then executes a block of code if the statement in the `<cfif>` evaluates to False. Let's look at this in action. Delete the code in index.cfm file and enter the following code into the Dreamweaver Document window:

```
<cfif IsDefined( "Url.date" )>
  I would be executed if the variable was defined.
  <cfelse>
  I would be executed if the variable was NOT defined.
</cfif>
```

If #Url.date# was defined previous to this code block, the first block between the <cfif> and <cfelse> tag would be executed. If the variable was not defined, then the code between the <cfelse> and </cfif> would be executed instead. In Dreamweaver MX 2004, either test the code in a browser window (press F12) or turn on Live Data view to see the results, as shown in Figure 3-5.

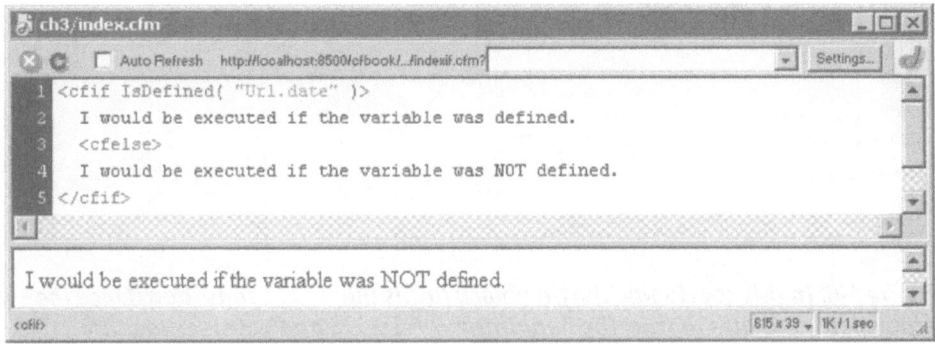

Figure 3-5. The result of running the preceding code. The second code block is executed, because the Url.date variable was not defined.

We can also add one or more <cfelseif> tags—these are placed between the <cfif> and <cfelse> tags. This allows us to chain together a series of if statements together. Take a look at this example (see cfif.cfm in the book's downloadable code, which is available from the Downloads section of the Apress web site at www.apress.com):

```
<cfset thisMonth = 1>
<cfif thisMonth EQ 1>
    It is January.
  <cfelseif thisMonth EQ 2>
    It is February.
  <cfelseif thisMonth EQ 3>
    It is March.
  <cfelse>
    It is some other month.
</cfif>
```

This code tests to see if the value of the #thisMonth# variable equals 1, which in this case evaluates to True. Therefore, you will see It is January. output when we test the code, as shown in Figure 3-6.

Figure 3-6. In this <cfif> *tag, the first block fulfils the* if ... *condition. Once the expression evaluates to true, the remaining* <cfelseif> *and* <cfelse> *tags are skipped.*

> **TIP** *If you try changing the value of the* #thisMonth# *variable in the* <cfset> *tag to 3, you will see* It is March. *as output.*

Though not a recommended practice unless unavoidable, you can nest if statements inside of each other as well. The following code is exactly like the previous example, only it has a special message when the "thisMonth" variable does not exist.

```
<cfif not isDefined("thisMonth")>
  Month is not defined.
  <cfelse>
    <cfif thisMonth EQ 1>
      It is January.
    <cfelseif thisMonth EQ 2>
      It is February.
    <cfelseif thisMonth EQ 3>
      It is March.
```

```
    <cfelse>
      It is some other month.
  </cfif>
</cfif>
```

<cfswitch>

ColdFusion also has another conditional logic mechanism that is usually more efficient and results in more modular and easy-to-read code: the <cfswitch> tag. We could change the series of if ... statements in the first "thisMonth" <cfif> example into the following switch statement (see cfswitch.cfm in the book's downloadable code):

```
<cfset thisMonth = 1>
<cfswitch expression="#thisMonth#">
  <cfcase value="1">
    It is January.
  </cfcase>
  <cfcase value="2">
    It is February.
  </cfcase>
  <cfcase value="3">
    It is March.
  </cfcase>
  <cfdefaultcase>
    It is some other month.
  </cfdefaultcase>
</cfswitch>
```

If you replace the code from the previous example with this, then you will also see It is January. in the browser window.

The expression in the <cfswitch> tag is executed only once, and ColdFusion tries to match the expression to a case. If ColdFusion finds no cases that match, it executes the optional <cfdefaultcase> block if it is present. The <cfdefaultcase> acts as the <cfelse> statement did previously. Once ColdFusion finds a matching <cfcase> statement, it skips over the remaining <cfcase> and <cfdefaultcase> blocks. The case statement also accepts a list of comma-separated values, which allows us to say "If the value is X, Y, or Z, then do this."

Here's an example of this (defaultcase.cfm):

```
<cfset thisMonth = 1>
<cfswitch expression="#thisMonth#">
  <cfcase value="1,2,3">
    It is January, February or March.
```

```
    </cfcase>
    <cfcase value="4,5,6">
      It is April, May or June.
    </cfcase>
    <cfdefaultcase>
      It is something else.
    </cfdefaultcase>
</cfswitch>
```

The preceding code block does the following: if #thisMonth# is 1, 2, or 3, then the first case will match and the code block will be executed. Otherwise, the <cfswitch> keeps trying to match the value of #thisMonth# to the values listed within the <cfcase> tags until it finds a match or encounters the <cfdefaultcase> tag.

There is one important difference between using a series of <cfif> statements and a <cfswitch> statement. We can test for multiple expressions by using a <cfif> statement by separating them with an AND or OR keyword.

```
<cfif (IsDefined("Url.Name")) AND (Url.Name EQ "Larry")>
   ...
<cfelseif (IsDefined("Url.Number")) AND (Url.Number EQ 7)>
   ...
</cfif>
```

This behavior isn't possible using <cfswitch>, which can evaluate only a single expression and match a value or series of values, so it isn't always possible to rewrite a <cfif> block as a <cfswitch>. You can also see that, because you are comparing the value of Url.Name to a string, you do need to enclose the string in a pair of quotes.

<cflocation>

You can use the <cflocation> tag to stop processing the current page and redirect to a new URL. It is very similar to using a meta refresh or a JavaScript redirection. No output is sent to the user's screen prior to the redirection, though any CFML code up to the <cflocation> is executed.

Try entering the following code into a new Document window in Dreamweaver:

```
<cflocation url="http://www.apress.com">
```

When you test the page in a browser window, you will notice it bounce automatically to whatever URL you specify. The <cflocation> tag is very useful in situations where you want to insert a record into a database and then redirect the user to a confirmation page, or else redirect the user to the next step in a wizard. It is also useful after inserting a new record into a database, because it can prevent the user from refreshing the action page and submitting duplicate data.

<cfinclude>

The <cfinclude> tag is a very useful tag because it allows you to include the contents of another file in the current page (essentially serving the same function as classic HTML server-side includes). For example, you could build header and footer files and then dynamically include them in each page of your site.

Using <cfinclude> eliminates having to copy and paste the HTML and/or CFML for the header and footer into every page; instead, you can centralize the code and make modifications in only one place. Let's look at an example.

1. Create two new ColdFusion files, one named header.cfm and the other called footer.cfm, in the cfbook site using Dreamweaver. Make sure that you save these two files in the same directory as the Application.cfm and index.cfm files that you created in the earlier examples.

2. In the header.cfm file, enter the following code:

    ```
    <html>
    <head>
      <title>Welcome</title>
    </head>
    <body>
      This is our header.<br />
      ----------<br />
    ```

3. Then enter the following code in the footer.cfm file:

    ```
      ----------<br />
      this is our footer.<br />
    </body>
    </html>
    ```

4. Clear the contents of the index.cfm and type in the following code:

    ```
    I am the original page.<br />
    ```

5. Create a new line at the beginning of the index.cfm page. The code you entered in step 4 should be on line 2 now. Next, select the CFML Basic tab in the Insert bar and click on the cfinclude button, as shown in Figure 3-7.

After clicking on the button, the Tag Editor – Cfinclude dialog box will open with a text field named Template and a Browse button to the right, as shown in Figure 3-8.

Click on the Browse button and select the header.cfm page that we just created. After completing this step, click OK and OK again to insert this tag into the index.cfm page.

Figure 3-7. Using Dreameaver MX 2004 to insert a <cfinclude> *tag into a web page*

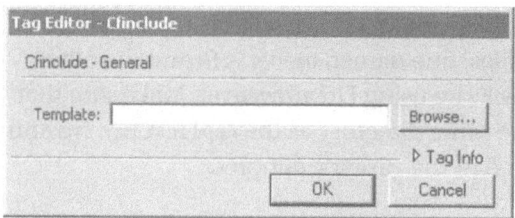

Figure 3-8. The <cfinclude> *Tag Editor*

6. Now use the same procedure to include footer.cfm at the bottom of the page. The index.cfm file should now look like the following:

```
<cfinclude template="header.cfm">
I am the original page.<br />
<cfinclude template="footer.cfm">
```

When you run index.cfm in a web browser, you will see the output in Figure 3-9.

Figure 3-9. Our page output, as seen in Internet Explorer 6

You can see that the header.cfm and footer.cfm files are included in the index.cfm page, processed, and then output into the browser. You can use this technique to embed headers, footers, counters, menus, Flash movies, or pretty much any sort of web content you wish. Be aware that any code in an included file will be executed in the file doing the include as if it were coded right there in the file doing the include, which means that variable-name conflicts could result in undesirable behavior. It is also important to become familiar with relative paths if you aren't already familiar with them. "../" goes up one directory level and "directoryname/" goes down. Just like HTML <img>, <a>, and other tags, relative paths are a good way to specify files in other directories for inclusion. Later in this book, you will learn about CFMappings, which are another way to specify the location of files for inclusion.

<cfloop>

Loops are typically used to iterate through a Recordset one record at a time, or when you need to execute a block of code a certain number of times. There are five different kinds of <cfloop>s: index loops, conditional loops, query loops, list loops, and collection loops. We cover all five in this section.

Index Loops

Index loops (also known as for ... next loops in other languages) are used to loop from a starting value to a predefined end value. The following snippet loops from 1 to 12:

```
<cfloop index="counter" from="1" to="12">
   ...
</cfloop>
```

For each iteration of the loop, a variable (in this case #counter#) is set to the value between 1 and 12. For example, by using this kind of loop you can loop from 1 to the number of days in a specific month and build a simple calendar, as you will see in the next chapter. This loop is useful when you know exactly how many times you need to loop through a block of code.

You can also specify an optional step attribute that controls how much the counter is incremented or decremented for each iteration of the loop, as you can see in the following code. By default, the step is 1, which means that the loop increments by 1 each time. For the next iteration, the #counter# variable equals 2, then 3, and so on. If we set a step of –1 or –2, then we will loop backwards by 1 or 2 on each iteration. To test this, type the following code into a new ColdFusion file (indexloop.cfm):

```
<cfloop index="counter" from="12" to="1" step="-2">
  <cfoutput>#counter#<br /></cfoutput>
</cfloop>
```

If you run this code in a web browser, you'll get the output shown in Figure 3-10.

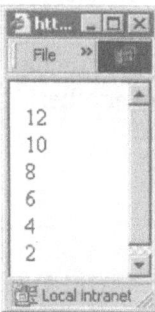

Figure 3-10. The numbers output by the index loop

Conditional Loops

Conditional loops (also known as do ... while loops) loop just as long as a condition is true. An example of a conditional loop is as follows (condloop.cfm):

```
<cfset i = 18>
<cfloop condition="i GTE 10">
  <cfoutput>#i#<br /></cfoutput>
  <cfset i = i - 1>
</cfloop>
```

Here we are setting an initial value of #i# to 18 and creating a conditional loop that will loop as long as #i# is greater than or equal to (GTE) 10. For each iteration of the loop, we are displaying the current value of #i# and then decrementing the value of #i#. This loop will display the numbers 18 to 10 to the screen in descending order.

> **CAUTION** *Conditional loops can be dangerous! If the end condition cannot be met, the loop does not stop, thus causing what is known as an* infinite *loop. An infinite loop can cause system instability and eat up a lot of system resources.*

Because conditional loops will loop as long as the condition evaluates to true, you can use this behavior to create a controlled infinite loop. This is useful if you don't know exactly how many times you need to loop, or need to exit the loop based on a complex condition. Let's look at an example (condloop2.cfm):

```
<cfloop condition="TRUE">
  <cfset i = RandRange( 1, 10 )>
  <cfoutput>#i#<br /></cfoutput>
  <cfif i EQ 10>
    <cfbreak>
  </cfif>
</cfloop>
```

By setting the loop condition to TRUE, you are essentially creating an infinite loop. This means that you must manually exit the loop because the end condition is always true. You can exit the loop by using the <cfbreak> tag.

In this example, you are also using a function that you haven't seen yet: #RandRange()#. This function generates a random integer between two specified values. So, you're setting #i# to a random integer between 1 and 10 and outputting the value of #i# to the browser. If #i# is equal to 10, you exit the loop.

You will find out more about #RandRange()# in Chapter 4.

Query Loop

This kind of loop will iterate over a Recordset (covered in Chapter 2). However, in this example we will create a simple query, loop over the query, and then output each employee in the database. Create a new file in the cfbook site and enter the following code (queryloop.cfm):

```
<cfquery name="getEmployees" datasource="CompanyInfo">
  SELECT
    *
  FROM
    Employee
</cfquery>
<cfloop query="getEmployees">
  <cfoutput># getEmployees.FirstName# # getEmployees.LastName#<br /></cfoutput>
</cfloop>
```

In this code, you begin by creating a query using the <cfquery> element, which contains SQL code between the opening and closing tags. Then you call the <cfloop> tag and pass it the name of the query from the <cfquery> tag.

When looping over a query, each iteration of the loop returns the next record from the Recordset. So, the preceding code grabs all employees from the CompanyInfo database and outputs each employee's name in the browser window, as shown in Figure 3-11. When looping over queries, ColdFusion automatically exits the loop once the end of the records is reached. Using <cfloop> rather than <cfoutput> to loop over a query can be very advantageous—especially when you want to loop over one recordset inside of a loop over another recordset. You cannot nest <cfoutput> query loops over different queries inside each other, but you can do this with <cfloop>.

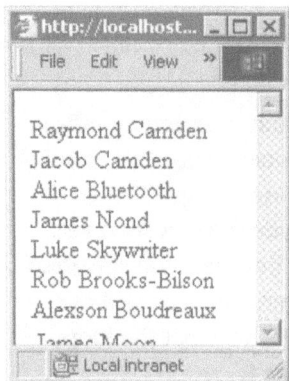

Figure 3-11. The result of using a query loop to output each employee name from the Employee table

List Loop

Looping over a list can be very useful in many circumstances. A list is nothing more than a string containing one or more items delimited by a set character, usually a comma. For example, you could loop over a list of menu links to create a dynamic menu. Enter the following code into a new ColdFusion document in Dreamweaver (listloop.cfm):

```
<cfloop list="home,tutorials,forum,articles,contact" index="currentLink">
  <cfoutput><a href="#currentLink#.cfm">#currentLink#</a><br /></cfoutput>
</cfloop>
```

Test the code. For each item in the list, you are outputting a link to the browser window, as you can see in Figure 3-12.

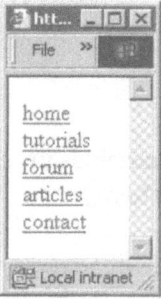

Figure 3-12. Using a list loop to create a simple list menu

> **TIP**   *When building lists, don't put a space after the comma. Doing so will insert a space before each item in the list.*

Also note that the <cfloop> "delimiter" attribute will allow you to specify some character other than a comma to use as the list entry separator.

Collection Loop

The final loop type loops over a collection, or *structure*. Structures (sometimes referred to as "associative arrays" in other programming languages) are containers for data, and that data is accessed by using what is called a *key*. In the following example demonstrates looping over a structure named #CGI# and accessing its contents by providing the key to the structure. The CGI structure is a special structure containing run-time information created by the ColdFusion Server. In fact, every "scope" (variable prefix) is exposed to your page as a structure. You can loop over "form," "url," "variables," and so on. For each iteration through the loop, we are setting a variable called #item# that is used to hold the current key. We cover structures in more detail in Chapter 4.

Enter the following code block into a new Dreamweaver document (colloop.cfm):

```
<table>
  <cfloop collection="#CGI#" item="item">
    <cfoutput>
      <tr>
        <td>#item#</td>
        <td>#CGI[ item ]#</td>
      </tr>
```

```
      </cfoutput>
    </cfloop>
</table>
```

Test the document in a browser, and you will see all of the CGI variables in the window, as shown in Figure 3-13. (Only a small sample is shown here.)

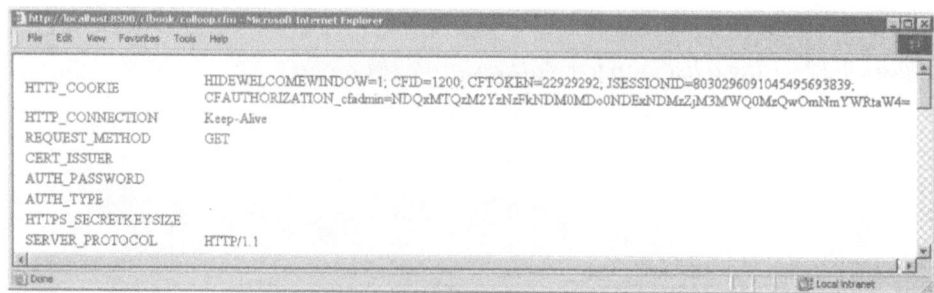

Figure 3-13. Using a collection loop to output all the CGI variables

<cfmail>

We briefly touched on <cfmail> in Chapter 1. This tag is responsible for sending e-mails from within ColdFusion applications to a designated e-mail address. Unlike mailto: links in HTML, the mail is sent via an SMTP mail server and not the user's mail client and mail server. Typically, <cfmail> is used to send news-letters and reminders to users, or error messages to administrators.

The basic syntax for the <cfmail> tag is as follows (cfmail.cfm):

```
<cfmail to="admin@yoursite.com" from="name@visitor.com"
        subject="This is the subject">
  The message of the e-mail goes here.
</cfmail>
```

Several other options for the <cfmail> tag allow you to attach files to the e-mail or specify whether you want to send an e-mail with HTML formatting, and so on. However, we go through only the basic options here. Follow these steps to use this tag in Dreamweaver.

1. Create a new ColdFusion file in Dreamweaver MX, click on the CFML Advanced tab, and click on the CFMAIL icon, which is the little envelope icon ninth from the left on the toolbar, as shown in Figure 3-14. This will cause the Tag Editor – Cfmail dialog box to open.

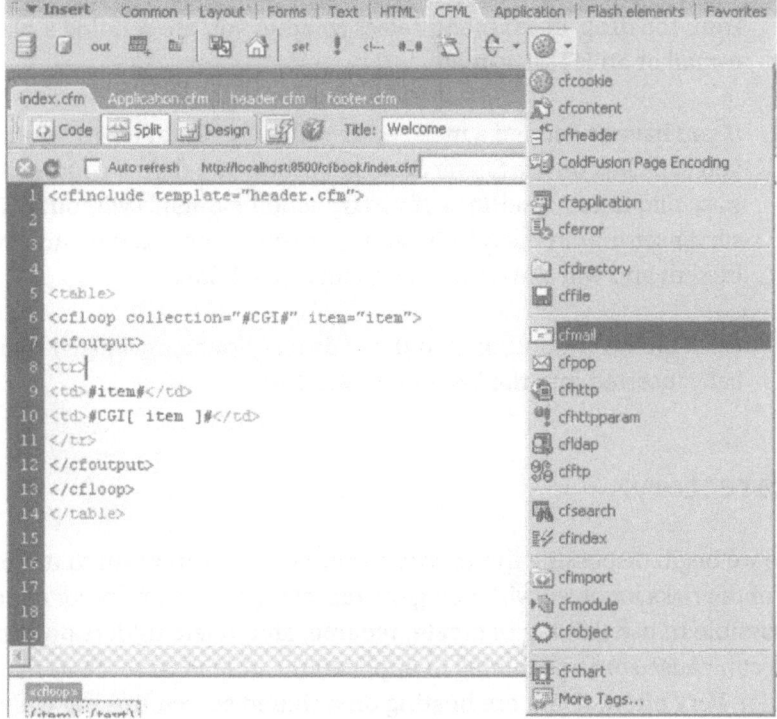

Figure 3-14. The Dreamweaver MX 2004 Insert bar with the advanced CFML functions shown and the cfmail button illustrated

2. In the dialog box General tab, you can set the values of the To, From, and Subject attributes by using the appropriate text fields, as shown in Figure 3-15. You can also set CC and BCC addresses.

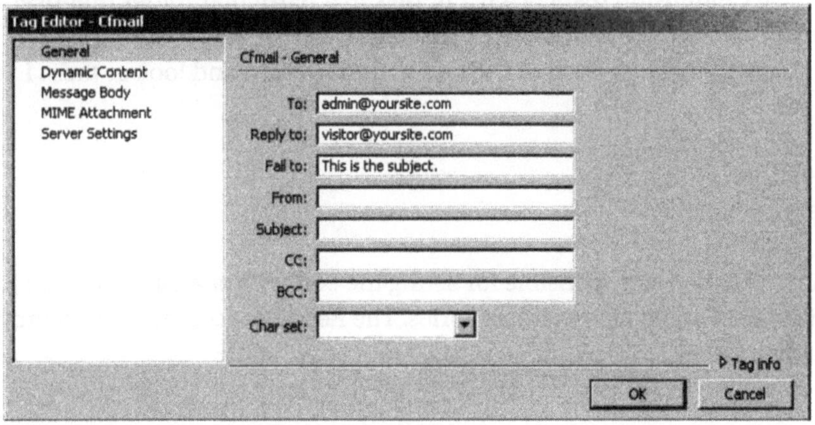

Figure 3-15. The Tag Editor – Cfmail dialog box's General tab

3. Next, click on the Message Body tab, fill in the body of the e-mail, and from the drop-down menu select whether you are sending a plain text e-mail or an HTML e-mail.

4. If you haven't defined a mail server within the ColdFusion Administrator, you can click on the Server Settings section and define your mail server, port, and timeout settings. If you try sending e-mails without defining server settings in the Administrator or within the tag, the e-mail will not be sent and will end up in an undeliverable folder.

5. Click on the OK button, and the code (as shown previously) is automatically inserted into the Document window.

<cfdirectory>

Before we begin discussing the <cfdirectory> tag, it is important to understand a few of the risks involved with using the tag, along with a few other concerns. It is possible to use this tag to create, rename, and delete folders on the server, which can cause some problems in applications or lead to some destructive behavior. Very often, if you are hosting on a shared server, this tag will be disabled to prevent people from looking through system folders or doing anything malicious to other directories. If this tag hasn't been disabled, you should always exercise extreme care so you don't delete or modify the wrong directory.

The <cfdirectory> tag has four different actions: list, create, delete, and rename. You can use this tag to make ColdFusion create new directories on the server on the fly, which can be useful if you want to upload images and keep them in separate folders based on which galleries they belong to. We can also use this tag to list the contents of directories on the server, which makes it easy to have ColdFusion display a list of files in a particular folder that users can download via their web browser instead of FTP.

Let's go through each of the four actions in turn and look at them in more detail.

list

The list action is responsible for listing the contents of a directory, and it returns a Recordset of the files and directories. The Recordset contains six columns as follows:

- Name: The file or directory's name. In ColdFusion MX and above, it does not include "." or "..".

- Size: Size of the file in bytes. Directories return 0.

- Type: Either File or Dir.

- DateLastModified: Date and time the file/directory was last modified.

- Attributes: Tells you whether the directory is read-only (R) or hidden (H), if applicable.

- Mode: Tells you the file permissions of the file/directory (UNIX and Linux only).

There is one new function in the following example that we haven't seen yet called #ExpandPath()#: it takes a single parameter, a relative path (for example, "."), and returns an absolute path. <cfdirectory action="list"> requires an absolute path, such as "C:\CFusionMX\wwwroot\cfbook\", and a name, which ColdFusion assigns to the Recordset it creates.

Type the following code into a new ColdFusion file (listdirectory.cfm):

```
<cfdirectory directory="#ExpandPath( '.' )#" action="list" name="currentDir">
<table>
  <cfloop query="currentDir">
    <cfoutput>
      <tr>
        <td>#currentDir.Name#</td>
        <td>#currentDir.Size#</td>
        <td>#currentDir.DateLastModified#</td>
        <td>#currentDir.Type#</td>
      </tr>
    </cfoutput>
  </cfloop>
</table>
```

When you test the page, you will see a browser output similar to that shown in Figure 3-16.

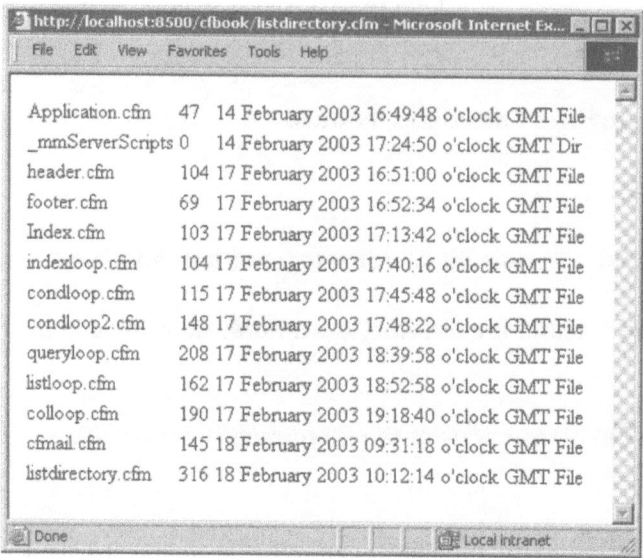

Figure 3-16. Using the list action of <cfdirectory> to output the current directory contents

As you can see, this code outputs a list of all the files and subfolders of the current working directory. If you wanted ColdFusion to display recursively all files and the content of each folder as well, you would need to create your own function or custom tag to handle it. Read more about custom functions and tags in Chapter 10.

create

The create action simply creates a new directory. The syntax for this action is as follows:

```
<cfdirectory directory="#ExpandPath( '.\NewFolder\' )#" action="create">
```

Again, use the #ExpandPath()# function to expand the path of the current directory. Then append the name of the new folder that you want to create onto the path, which in this case is NewFolder. If the directory already exists, ColdFusion will throw an error.

We can programmatically check to see if a directory exists by using a ColdFusion function named #DirectoryExists()#. The #DirectoryExists()# function takes a single parameter, which is the fully qualified path of the directory that we want to check for.

The syntax is as follows (createdirectory.cfm):

```
<cfif DirectoryExists( ExpandPath( ".\NewFolder\" ) )>
  Directory already existed.
  <cfelse>
  <cfdirectory directory="#ExpandPath( '.\NewFolder\' )#" action="create">
  Directory was created.
</cfif>
```

If we save this file in our cfbook directory and test it in a browser, a NewFolder folder will be created in our cfbook folder, and we will see the following message in the browser window:

```
Directory was created.
```

The first thing you'll notice in the preceding code is the #DirectoryExists()# function call. However, there are a couple other new things you haven't seen yet. Inside the #DirectoryExists()# function, the current directory path is expanded and appended with "\NewFolder\". If the directory already exists, the #DirectoryExists()# function returns True, and the <cfif> statement block executes. If the directory doesn't exist yet, then the <cfelse> block executes, and the desired folder is created.

You could modify the preceding snippet as follows (createdirectory2.cfm):

```
<cfif NOT DirectoryExists( ExpandPath( ".\NewFolder\" ) )>
  <cfdirectory directory="#ExpandPath( '.\NewFolder\' )#" action="create">
  Directory was created.
</cfif>
```

In this case, if the directory doesn't already exist, ColdFusion will create the new directory and output a message saying that the directory was created successfully. If it does exist, then nothing happens, which is more pleasant than having a nasty error message returned to the user.

Notice the use of the NOT keyword. Because the #DirectoryExists()# function returns True if the directory exists, adding the NOT keyword to the <cfif> tag causes it to trigger only when the directory does not already exist. This is because if the directory doesn't exist, the #DirectoryExists()# function call returns False. Therefore, by adding NOT to the statement, you are saying NOT False, which evaluates to True, causing the <cfif> block to be executed.

delete

The delete action deletes an existing directory. It is called in much the same way you call the create action. However, there is one important thing to note: you cannot delete a directory if it contains any files or subfolders. An example of the delete action syntax is shown here:

```
<cfdirectory directory="#ExpandPath( '.\NewFolder\' )#" action="delete">
```

As with the Create example we presented previously, make sure that the directory exists (and that it is empty) before trying to delete it.

1. Open Dreamweaver, create a new file named deletedirectory.cfm in your cfbook directory, and enter the following code into it:

```
<cfset targetFolder = ExpandPath( ".\NewFolder\" )>
<cfif DirectoryExists( targetFolder )>
  <cfdirectory directory="#targetFolder#" action="list"
name="CheckEmpty">
    <cfif CheckEmpty.RecordCount EQ 0>
      <cfdirectory directory="#targetFolder#" action="delete">
      Directory deleted.
    <cfelse>
      Directory was not empty.
    </cfif>
  <cfelse>
  Directory was not found.
</cfif>
```

2. Delete the NewFolder folder we created in the previous example. Now test our deletedirectory.cfm file in a web browser or in Live Data View. You should see a message on the screen saying "Directory was not found."

3. Recreate the NewFolder folder under the current working directory. Within this folder create a new file or subfolder. Now rerun the deletedirectory.cfm file, and you should see the message "Directory was not empty" as output.

4. Now delete all files and subfolders within the NewFolder directory (but do not delete the directory itself) and run the deletedirectory.cfm code one last time. Now you should see the message "Directory deleted" on your screen, and the folder should have been deleted from inside cfbook.

Now let's look at how this code works.

In this code, you begin by creating a variable to hold the complete path of the directory that you want to delete. Next check to see if the directory exists on the server. If it does, proceed to check if the directory is empty. Call <cfdirectory action="list">, which in turn returns a Recordset of any files or subfolders that may be in the folder you are trying to delete.

For any Recordset created by ColdFusion, a few other variables are created automatically. The three main variables created are RecordCount, CurrentRow, and ColumnList. These three variables work in the following way:

- `RecordCount` tells you how many records are in the Recordset.

- `CurrentRow` tells you which record you are currently on within the Recordset.

- `ColumnList` tells you the name of the columns in the Recordset.

So, when you check the value of #CheckEmpty.RecordCount#, you are checking if any records are present in the Recordset. If the `recordcount` is equal to 0, then you can be sure that no files or subfolders are in the folder you are trying to delete. Therefore, it is safe to go ahead and delete the target directory.

rename

The final action, `rename`, simply renames a folder. It is used as follows:

```
<cfdirectory directory="#ExpandPath( '.\NewFolder\' )#" action="rename"
      newdirectory="#ExpandPath( '.\archive\' )#">
```

Unlike the delete action, a folder does not have to be empty to use the `rename` action. You can safely rename a directory with files and subfolders inside. One important point to remember is that you must make sure that the new directory name, specified in the `newdirectory` attribute, is not already in use as a directory name in the current directory; ColdFusion will throw errors if this is the case. Because of this, it is advisable to use the #DirectoryExists()# function to verify that you don't already have a folder with that particular name.

<cffile>

Like <cfdirectory>, this tag is often disabled in shared hosting environments because of its potentially destructive effects. Exercise caution when working with this tag, because it is all too easy to delete the wrong file in the wrong directory if you are not careful.

ColdFusion offers a <cffile> tag that works in a way similar to <cfdirectory>, providing similar functionality for files within directories. <cffile> manipulates files on the server by using nine distinct actions: upload, copy, move, rename, delete, append, write, read, and readbinary. Let's go through each of these now.

upload

ColdFusion allows users to upload files to the server easily by using the HTML form element <input type="file">. When a user submits the form, the file is sent to the server, and you are able to upload the file using code like the following snippet:

```
<cffile action="upload" filefield="MyFile"
        destination="#ExpandPath( '.' )#"
        nameconflict="makeunique">
```

This will upload the file that was passed to this page in an `<input type="file" name="MyFile">` form field, and will upload the file to the same directory as the `.cfm` file with the `<cffile action="upload">` code in it.

The final attribute, `nameconflict`, tells ColdFusion how to deal with the file upload if there is already a file with that name. There are four possible values:

- `Error`: ColdFusion throws an error if a file with this name already exists in the directory.

- `Skip`: The file will not be uploaded. ColdFusion just ignores it.

- `Overwrite`: The older file is overwritten by the newer file.

- `Makeunique`: If a file already exists with this name, ColdFusion creates a unique filename for the newer file.

We'll cover this action in more detail in Chapter 5.

copy

This action allows us to copy an existing file and assign it a new name. You can see an example of the copy action here:

```
<cffile action="copy"
        destination="#ExpandPath( '.\index_copy.cfm' )#"
        source="#ExpandPath( '.\index.cfm' )#">
```

This code snippet makes a copy of the `index.cfm` file in the current folder and names the new file `index_copy.cfm`. The file is then saved to the same folder. If there is already a file with the same name and path as the destination file, it will be overwritten.

To check to see if a file already exists, we can use a function called `#FileExists()#`. `#FileExists()#` takes a single parameter, which is a fully qualified path to the file. Here's an example of this (`filecopy.cfm`):

```
<cfif NOT FileExists( ExpandPath( '.\index_copy.cfm' ) )>
  <cffile action="copy" destination="#ExpandPath( '.\index_copy.cfm' )#"
          source="#ExpandPath( '.\index.cfm' )#">
</cfif>
```

If you create this file inside your cfbook directory, a copy of the index.cfm file, index_copy.cfm, will be created in the same directory.

move

The move action simply moves a file, either within the same directory or to a different folder on the server. The most basic usage of this action is shown here (filemove.cfm):

```
<cffile action="move"
       destination="#ExpandPath( '.\archive\' )#"
       source="#ExpandPath( '.\index.cfm' )#">
```

This snippet takes the file defined in the source attribute and moves it to the location defined in the destination attribute. In this example, we copy the index.cfm in the current directory into a subfolder named archive. This file will keep the same name in the new folder. If there is already a file named index.cfm in the destination directory, it will be overwritten by the file we move.

You can rename files while moving them by simply adding a filename to the end of the destination attribute (filemove2.cfm):

```
<cffile action="move"
       destination="#ExpandPath( '.\archive\old_index.cfm' )#"
       source="#ExpandPath( '.\index.cfm' )#">
```

The preceding code takes the index.cfm file from the current directory, moves it to a subfolder called archive, and renames the file old_index.cfm.

It is important to note that the destination folder must exist prior to calling this action. If you don't already have a subfolder named archive in the current directory, then ColdFusion will throw an error.

rename

You have already seen how to rename files using the move action, but you can also use the rename action. The way that you use this action is almost exactly the same, as shown here (filerename.cfm):

```
<cffile action="rename"
       destination="#ExpandPath( '.\old_index.cfm' )#"
       source="#ExpandPath( '.\index.cfm' )#">
```

This code renames the current index.cfm file to old_index.cfm.

delete

The delete action simply deletes the file specified in the file attribute. The basic usage is shown here (filedelete.cfm):

```
<cffile action="delete"
        file="#ExpandPath( '.\old_index.cfm' )#">
```

Like the other tags, it requires a full path to the target file. If the file doesn't exist, ColdFusion will throw an error. Therefore, it is best to make sure that the file exists prior to calling this tag by using the #FileExists()# function outlined in the copy action earlier in this section.

append

Not surprisingly, the append action appends text to an existing file. Let's make use of it now.

1. Create a new file named createlog.cfm in our cfbook directory, and enter the following code into the Document window:

   ```
   <cffile action="append"
           file="#ExpandPath( '.\log.cfm' )#"
           output="Hello World" addnewline="Yes">
   ```

2. Open createlog.cfm file in a web browser and reload the page a couple of times.

3. If you then open the log.cfm file that is created, you will see that it contains text similar to the following:

   ```
   Hello World
   Hello World
   ```

You'll notice that each time you refresh the createlog.cfm page, a new line is added to the log.cfm file. This technique can be useful if you want to create your own log files and record whenever a user performs a certain action. Or you might use this if you encounter an error and want to create a log file for an administrator to browse through to better understand how and why the error occurred.

If the file specified in the file attribute doesn't exist prior to calling this tag, ColdFusion will create the file for you. If the file does exist, ColdFusion will append the text in the output attribute to the end of the file. The final attribute in the preceding listing, addnewline, controls whether ColdFusion should add a line break after writing the output to the file. In the preceding example, the addnewline attribute is set to Yes, so you only need to append Hello World to the log.cfm file, and a line break is added to the end of the output.

If we set the addnewline attribute to No and run the code again a couple times, we will observe that ColdFusion just appends the Hello World onto the end of the previous line, so our output will look similar to this:

```
Hello WorldHello WorldHello World
```

write

The write action is very similar to the append action, but with one important difference. This action will overwrite the file if it already exists, rather than adding to the same file. The basic usage is shown here (createlog2.cfm):

```
<cffile action="write"
        file="#ExpandPath( '.\log.cfm' )#"
        output="Hello World" addnewline="yes">
```

If there is an existing log.cfm file in the current directory, calling this tag will destroy the contents of that file and simply write Hello World to the file. If the file does not exist prior to calling this tag, ColdFusion will automatically create the file for you.

read

The read action reads a file and saves the content to a variable. Here's how you use it (readlog.cfm):

```
<cffile action="read"
        file="#ExpandPath( '.\log.cfm' )#"
        variable="logfile">
<cfoutput><pre>#logfile#</pre></cfoutput>
```

This code reads the contents of the log.cfm file located in the current directory, saves its contents to a variable called #logfile#, and finally outputs the contents of the file to the browser window. If the file does not exist prior to calling this tag, ColdFusion will throw an error. It is best to check that the file exists prior to using this tag, which can be done by using code such as the following (readlog2.cfm):

```
<cfset targetFile = ExpandPath( ".\filedoesntexist.cfm" )>
<cfif FileExists( targetFile )>
  <cffile action="read" file="#targetFile#" variable="logfile">
  <cfoutput><pre>#logfile#</pre></cfoutput>
  <cfelse>
  Unable to find file.
</cfif>
```

readbinary

The final action, readbinary, is used to read the contents of binary files, such as images and executables, and store their contents in a ColdFusion variable. This action enables you to do such useful things as storing images in a database. An example of using this tag is as follows (readbinary.cfm):

```
<cffile action="readbinary"
        file="#ExpandPath( '.\gn_mm_logo.gif' )#"
        variable="myImage">
<cfoutput>#ToBase64( myImage )#</cfoutput>
```

The preceding code snippet opens the GIF image, stores the binary information into a variable, and outputs a string representation to the screen. If you want to database the image file, you would need to write a query that stores the string in Base64 format using the #ToBase64()# function shown in the preceding code. To retrieve the image, you would need to write a query that selects the data from the database and then writes it to a temporary file before using <img src=""> to display the newly created image. The #toString()# function is used to convert a Base64 representation to a string.

<cfform>

ColdFusion's <cfform> tags are quite similar to their HTML counterparts, but they do have a few impressive features that go beyond what HTML is capable of doing. HTML's <input> tag has been replaced with CFML's <cfinput> tag, which adds a few attributes allowing you to add JavaScript validation to forms easily.

We will now look at a brief comparison to demonstrate the advantages of ColdFusion forms over their HTML counterparts.

Enter the following code into a new file and save it as forms.cfm:

```
<!-- HTML -->
<form action="action.cfm" method="post">
  UserName: <input type="Text" name="UserName"><br />
  Password: <input type="Password" name="Password"><br />
  <input type="Submit" value="Login">
</form>
<!-- CFML -->
<cfform action="action.cfm" method="post">
  UserName:
  <cfinput type="Text" name="UserName"
          required="Yes" message="Please Enter your user name."><br />
  Password:
  <cfinput type="Password" name="Password"
          required="Yes" message="Please enter your password."><br />
  <input type="Submit" value="Login">
</cfform>
```

The preceding code creates two forms, as you can see in Figure 3-17.

Figure 3-17. Two identical-looking forms, but one is a standard HTML form and one is a ColdFusion form

The topmost form is a simple HTML form without validation. If we wanted to verify that the user had entered a UserName and Password, we would need to create our own JavaScript functions and validate the data using an OnClick or OnSubmit handler. The bottom ColdFusion form allows us simply to add required='Yes' to the <cfinput> tag, and if the user tries to submit the form without entering a value, a JavaScript pop-up message will prompt the user to enter a value, as shown in Figure 3-18.

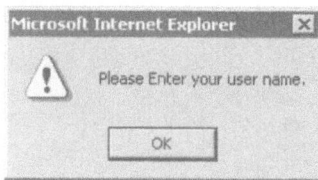

Figure 3-18. Form validation is really simple to add to ColdFusion forms.

By adding the message attribute to the <cfinput>, you can customize the JavaScript message produced by ColdFusion to be more user-friendly. When using the <cfinput> tag, ColdFusion provides you with the validation code. This allows you to develop applications much faster.

ColdFusion also allows you to specify the data type for the <cfinput>. Now let's take a look at another example. Create a new .cfm file, enter the following code into it, and save it as ageform.cfm:

```
<cfform action="action.cfm" method="post">
  <cfinput name="Age" type="text" size="2" maxlength="3"
           range="0,100" required="yes"
           message="Please enter a valid integer"
           validate="integer">
  <input type="submit" value="Go">
</cfform>
```

Test this in a browser, and you will see something similar to Figure 3-19.

Figure 3-19. Our ColdFusion age form

ColdFusion will allow users to enter only integers in this text field, and will make sure that the users' age is between 0 and 100. A JavaScript pop-up containing the custom error message will appear if the user does any of these things:

- Does not enter a value

- Enters a non-integer

- Enters a number that is out of the allowed range

The user is not allowed to submit the form until the field passes the validation, as shown in Figure 3-20.

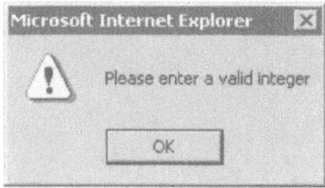

Figure 3-20. If the user does not enter a valid integer, the custom error message appears.

It is important to note that all of this JavaScript validation will work only if users have JavaScript enabled in their browsers. If the users have JavaScript disabled, they will be able to enter whatever values they wish and submit the form to the server. For this reason, you should also perform server-side validation on user-entered data before entering it into a data store. We explain validation in more detail in Chapter 4 and Chapter 5. <cfform> also enables you to use Java-based controls not available in native HTML, such as trees and grids. We also cover <cfform> in more detail in Chapter 5.

Summary

This has been a fairly quick introduction to some of the more common CFML tags. You should now have a better understanding of the CFML syntax and have a very basic knowledge of the difference between ColdFusion tags and ColdFusion functions.

There are certainly a lot of tags that we don't have the space to explain in detail; you can find a complete list of tags and functions (and detailed explanations) at http://livedocs.macromedia.com/. Before proceeding, you should also understand the difference between the <cfset> and <cfparam> tag, and understand and be familiar with basic <cfif> syntax; these will be used heavily throughout the rest of the book.

You should now be relatively familiar with the following CFML tags (remember that practice makes perfect):

- `<cfset>`

- `<cfparam>`

- `<cfif>`, `<cfelseif>`, and `<cfelse>`

- `<cfswitch>`, `<cfcase>`, and `<cfdefaultcase>`

- `<cflocation>`

- `<cfinclude>`

- `<cfmail>`

- `<cfdirectory>`

- `<cffile>`

- `<cfform>`

ColdFusion Variables and Logic

Variables are the cornerstone of ColdFusion. Without a proper understanding of how variables work, it is impossible to write scaleable and efficient code. Therefore, you must have a clear understanding of which data types should hold what kind of information, and which variable scopes are the best solutions for your particular needs.

Throughout this chapter we explain the different types of variable scopes (URL, Form, Cookie, and so on) and how the data types differ from one another. We finish this chapter with a look at ColdFusion's most commonly used functions.

Variable Scopes

Before you get too far into programming ColdFusion, it is important to look at some of the different variable scopes. A *variable scope* tells you where the variable in question came from, and how and when it can be used. For example, if the variable was passed from a form, then the variable would be prefixed by "#Form.".

We briefly looked at the Client scope in Chapter 1 while we were going through the ColdFusion Administrator. Some of ColdFusion's common scopes are: Variables, Form, URL, Client, Session, Application, Server, Request, CGI, Cookie, Arguments, and Attributes. Each scope has its own strengths and weaknesses depending on what you are trying to accomplish, and each behaves slightly differently. Some variables expire after a user request is made, whereas other variables can persist for hours or even days. In this section, we take a look at some of these scopes in more detail.

One problem with the Web is that it is a "stateless" environment. This means that the Web generally has no concept of a "user" and doesn't know which requests you have made already. As far as the Web is concerned, it is just another request. This is because on any given HTTP request, variable scopes are created, populated, manipulated and used, then destroyed. These variables must be recreated on every subsequent request. Usually this is OK, but sometimes you will wish to track certain users as they use your Web site so, for example, you can always tell who is logged in and which specific user posted comments to a certain article or message board. Using certain variable scopes, ColdFusion makes tracking individual users easy by handling all the hard work behind the scenes, as you will see shortly.

When a user requests a template, certain variables last only for the duration of that single page request. Once the ColdFusion server has successfully parsed the CFML and returned the final result to the user, any local, Request, Form, and URL variables expire and are cleared from ColdFusion's memory. This is done because it is part of HTTP's nature and also saves system resources for the next user request.

Other types of variables, called persistent variables, are able to last across multiple user requests. That means that you can set a persistent variable with the users' names and login IDs, track specific users throughout the site, and know who they are and when they are logged in. Persistent variables are stored in one of three ways:

- As cookies on the user's computer

- In the server's memory

- In a database or in the server's registry

Each option has its own drawbacks, as you will see later. First we will explore the different variable scopes available.

Variables *Scope*

The Variables scope is where all local variables are stored. When we used the <cfset> tag in earlier chapters, the tag stored the variables in the Variables scope by default. The Variables scope is only available to the file requested by the user and any files included in that file. It is important to note here that the following two lines of code do the exact same thing; the only difference is that the second line of code explicitly sets the variable within the Variables scope, whereas the first line doesn't.

```
<cfset testvar = "testing 1234">
<cfset Variables.testvar = "testing 1234">
```

More often than not you will see people simply set a variable and not explicitly use the Variables scope, but if you establish the habit of always explicitly adding the Variables scope to your variables, it can help avoid confusion when you go back through your code in the future.

> **TIP** *All variables in the* Variables *scope expire at the end of the user request (after the requested file has been parsed and sent back to the user) and don't persist throughout multiple requests. Local variables are also not shared between custom tags and components; each can use the* Variables *scope locally.*

Form *Scope*

Form variables are present when a user submits a form that uses the POST method. We briefly looked at the <cfform> tag in the previous chapter. When you submit the form by using the POST method, all field names are prepended by #Form.<field name>#. Let's look at a code snippet that uses the Form scope (this will be familiar if you have read Chapter 3):

```
<!-- HTML -->
<form action="action.cfm" method="post">
  UserName: <input type="Text" name="UserName"><br />
  Password: <input type="Password" name="Password"><br />
  <input type="Submit" value="Login">
</form>
```

When you submit this form, ColdFusion creates two variables called #Form.UserName# and #Form.Password# within the action.cfm template in the Form scope (if the submit button had a name attribute, a variable would be created in the Form scope with the same name, if that button were clicked to submit the form). For each form submission, ColdFusion also creates a special variable called #Form.FieldNames#, which contains a comma-separated list of the field names on the form. This is useful when creating and working with dynamic forms.

Form-scoped variables do not persist; they expire after each page request. Also, they are unable to store complex data types such as arrays and structures.

URL *Scope*

URL-scoped variables are similar to Form-scoped variables, except they are passed along in the query string (which is the part of the URL after the "?") or in forms where the method is GET. In the preceding example, if you changed the method from POST to GET, the variables would be passed as #Url.UserName# and #Url.Password#, respectively, and you would see a query string similar to the following on the action.cfm template:

```
http://localhost:8500/action.cfm?UserName=test&Password=1234
```

In the preceding code, two variables would be created: #URL.UserName#, which would have a value of test, and #URL.Password#, which would have a value of 1234.

This is the same as with Form-scoped variables; the variables expire after each page request. URL variables are nice because users can bookmark a page that uses URL variables in their web browsers and come back later, and the variables will be recreated. Form action pages cannot be bookmarked if the form must be submitted in order for the page to work. One disadvantage of URL-scoped variables is that the values are exposed in the address bar. You are also limited by the number of characters you can pass in the address bar (although the exact number can vary from browser to browser). URL variables are limited to simple data types such as strings, numbers, and dates. Their values cannot contain special characters such as ", ', /, ?, :, ., etc. Fortunately, the CFML language has a #urlEncodedFormat()# function to transform illegal URL characters into allowed equivalents.

Client *Variables*

Client variables are persistent, lasting longer than a single request. Client variables persist for each page request that a particular client (web browser) makes. We covered Client variables briefly in Chapter 1, when we defined where Client variables would be stored by default (either in the registry, client cookies, or a data source).

Usually, the best place to store Client variables is in a database, although before you can do that, you must enable Client variable storage for that database by using the ColdFusion Administrator. First you must set up a data source for the particular database you want to use.

For directions on setting up a data source, refer to the section "Setting Up a Data Source" in Chapter 2. It is important to know that you would never really want to store Client variables within the system registry, because doing this can degrade server performance. At the very minimum you would want to store the Client variables in an Access database, but ideally you would use an enterprise database server such as SQL Server or Oracle, because they are better designed to handle large loads and multiple concurrent users.

Now click on the Client Variables link in the ColdFusion Administrator menu. You are presented with a screen where you can highlight the Data Source you wish to enable Client variable storage for, which looks like Figure 4-1.

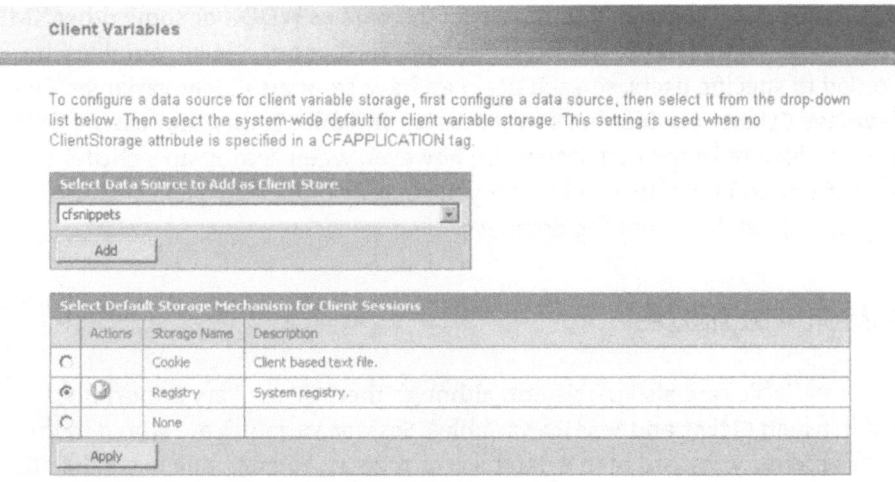

Figure 4-1. Highlighting the data sources to enable Client variable storage

After choosing a Data Source and clicking Add, you are brought to the page shown in Figure 4-2, where we define how long the Client variables are kept before they expire.

Add/Edit Client Store: cfsnippets

◀ Click arrow on left to return without submitting changes   Submit Changes

Description

Your data source requires you to manually create the necessary database tables to store your client variables. See the Online Help for details.

☑ **Purge data for clients that remain unvisited for** 90 **days**
Enable this option if you want ColdFusion to periodically purge client data that has not been accessed in the specified number of days.

If this data source is being used by more than one ColdFusion server, as in the case of clustered servers, make sure that only one server in the cluster is configured to purge client data.

☐ **Disable global client variable updates**
This option controls how ColdFusion updates global client variables, such as HITCOUNT and LASTVISIT. If updates are disabled, ColdFusion updates these variables only when they are set or modified. If updates are enabled, ColdFusion updates global client variables for each page request.

Figure 4-2. Choosing how long the Client variables are kept before expiration

ColdFusion automatically expires client data after that visitor has not visited within a certain number of days. Because data is stored in the database, you are unable to store complex objects such as structures and Recordsets; you are limited to strings and simple values. If complex data must be written to the client scope, a common practice is to represent the data as WDDX or some other XML string (more on this under the "XML" section further on). Client variables are also tied to specific users, so each user can have separate Client variables. One advantage Client variables have over Session variables is that they can be used within a clustered server environment; however, when setting up a cluster of web servers, you must be careful that you set only one ColdFusion server to purge the client data from the database.

Session *Variables*

Session variables are also persistent, although there is one very important difference between Client and Session variables. Session variables are stored in the server's memory instead of in a database or registry. You are able to set default timeout values for Session variables in the ColdFusion Administrator or even on a site-by-site basis by using the <cfapplication> tag, which is covered in greater detail in Chapter 7.

Because Session variables are stored in system memory, you are able to store Recordsets and complex data, but you are limited by the amount of available system memory, which can impact server performance. Session variables are tied to a specific user, and no two users should be able to access the same data. Session variables are typically set to expire in minutes or hours rather than days, like Client variables. We cover these issues in Chapter 7 as well.

Application *Variables*

Application variables are similar to Session variables in that they are stored in system memory and persist across multiple requests. However, unlike Session variables, Application variables are available to, and have the same value for, all users of an application, so all users are able to access to this information. This allows us to cache content or save common queries into an application scope so we don't have to constantly query the database.

Application variables expire when the ColdFusion web server is restarted or at the preset time specified in the ColdFusion administrator or <cfapplication> tag.

Server *Variables*

Server variables are similar to Application variables except that they are available to all sites on a server.

> **NOTE** Server *scope is also a persistent variable scope.*

Request *Variables*

Request variables are not persistent, but are available to all pages within a single user request. When creating your own custom tags in CFML, the custom tag will run in its own memory space, so it is a little trickier to access local variables created on the calling pages. This is where the Request scope becomes useful. For example, if you have a variable called Request.Datasource, you can access that variable whether you are within the requested page, an included page, a custom tag, or a user-defined function. Request variables are therefore similar to "global" variables in other languages.

Request variables are specific to a single user request and are not persistent.

CGI *Variables*

CGI variables typically are produced by the server and browser. Some examples of CGI variables are:

- #CGI.CF_TEMPLATE_PATH#: the complete path to the template requested by the user (this will look something like C:\CFusionMX\wwwroot\cfbook\index.cfm)

- #CGI.HTTP_REFERER#: the page the user last came from

- #CGI.QUERY_STRING#: what came after the "?" in the address bar

- #CGI.REMOTE_ADDR#: the IP address of the user's computer

- #CGI.SERVER_PORT_SECURE#: if you are viewing this page using HTTP or HTTPS

- #CGI.HTTP_USER_AGENT#: contains the browser software's unique identifier to determine what browser is being used

For a full list of the CGI variables for your server, you can run the following snippet on a ColdFusion page: <cfdump var="#CGI#">. CGI variables are not persistent and are unique to each user request. These variables are generally considered read-only and shouldn't be changed.

Cookie *Scope*

The Cookie scope holds all cookies for a user. Cookies are pieces of data stored on a user's computer that can hold simple values such as strings, numbers, dates, Booleans, etc.

Cookies are an excellent way to store data on a user's computer for a short time or persist indefinitely, although cookies do have a few drawbacks. The first drawback is that they are able to hold only simple values as discussed previously. Other drawbacks are the limit to how many cookies you can store per domain on a user's computer is limited, and limited size of the cookie. Another drawback is that because cookies are stored on users' machines, the users can decide to disable any cookies from being set on their computers, which could cause problems in your application if you are relying on cookies.

You can access only the cookies that you've created, and cookies can be set either by using <cfset Cookie.UserID = 1> or <cfcookie name="UserID" value="1">. Cookies are persistent and can expire when a user closes the browser, after a certain amount of time, or never.

Arguments *Scope*

The Arguments scope is used when you create your own functions. We cover how to create your own custom functions (often referred to as *user-defined functions* [UDFs]) in Chapter 10. Basically, you use the Arguments scope when using a UDF or writing a function within a *ColdFusion Component* (CFC). This scope allows us to refer to the values that have been passed into our function by name, as shown here:

```
<cffunction name="DateTimeFormat" returntype="string">
  <cfargument name="thisDate" type="date" default="#Now( )#">
  <cfargument name="dateFmt" type="string" default="mmm d, yyyy">
  <cfargument name="timeFmt" type="string" default="h:mm tt">
  <cfreturn DateFormat( Arguments.thisDate, Arguments.dateFmt ) &➡
" " & TimeFormat( Arguments.thisDate, Arguments.timeFmt ) >
</cffunction>
<cfoutput>#DateTimeFormat( Now( ) )#</cfoutput>
```

In the preceding function, we are creating a custom function with three arguments. Each argument has a default value. This function takes in a date, applies a date format, and a time format to the supplied date. If a date is not passed in, the current server date/time is used. In the <cfreturn> tag, you can see a reference to the arguments passed to the function in the Arguments scope, such as #Arguments.thisDate# and #Arguments.dateFmt#.

Attributes *Scope*

The Attributes scope is used when creating custom tags. (We cover creating custom tags in Chapter 10.) Custom tags can access the calling page's local variables by using the Caller scope.

If you converted the previous example from the "Arguments Scope" section into a ColdFusion custom tag, you could call the custom tag by using this code snippet:

```
<cfmodule template="dtformat.cfm" thisDate="#Now( )#"➥
dateFmt="mm/dd/yyyy" timeFmt="h:mm TT">
```

or this one:

```
<cf_dtformat thisDate="#Now( )#" dateFmt="mm/dd/yyyy"➥
timeFmt="h:mm TT">
```

Within the same directory as the preceding listing, you also would need to have a file named dtformat.cfm containing the following code:

```
<cfparam name="Attributes.thisDate" type="date" default="#Now( )#">
<cfparam name="Attributes.dateFmt" type="string" default="mmm d, yyyy">
<cfparam name="Attributes.timeFmt" type="string" default="h:mm tt">
<cfoutput>#DateFormat( Attributes.thisDate, Attributes.dateFmt )#
  #TimeFormat( Attributes.thisDate, Attributes.timeFmt )#
</cfoutput>
```

The preceding code listing creates three default values for the attributes if the attribute was not defined. This is similar to the code you saw in the "Arguments Scope" section. Next you output the date and time to the screen by using ColdFusion's #DateFormat()# and #TimeFormat()# functions, and you can see references to the values in the <cfparam> tag and #DateFormat()# and #TimeFormat()# functions within the Attributes scope.

It is important always to refer to variables by using both the variable's name *and* its scope. When you don't scope your variables in CFML, ColdFusion has to check many scopes to try to find a variable that matches your particular variable names. This in turn can lead to code that is inefficient and much harder to debug.

If you know that a variable is going to be submitted by way of a form, then you should always explicitly use #Form.UserName# instead of simply #UserName#. There are two reasons for this:

- It is much more readable and easier for you and other developers to understand.

- It can help reduce possible variable conflicts, such as if you have both a form variable and a local variable named UserName, and ColdFusion is forced to guess which you want.

Now that we've gone through the different variable scopes, let's briefly look at ColdFusion's different data types.

Data Types

Unlike other languages, CFML does not require you to declare a variable's type prior to using it. ColdFusion often is referred to as a "typeless environment"; it stores values in a variable with disregard for what data type the value is. In other words, there is no difference between the number 5 and the string character "5" until you use the value in a string or mathematical function. ColdFusion variables can be "cast" into several different data types. The simplest data types are strings, numbers, Booleans, and dates. Complex data types include arrays, structures, Recordsets, and XML documents. Because ColdFusion is "typless," and because you do not declare a data type when creating a variable, you can "repurpose" data (use it as any data type you want) in a single variable. Let's look at some of these data types in more detail.

- *Strings* hold any sort of string data as well as numbers and dates. You can create strings in ColdFusion by simply typing the following:

```
<cfset UserName = "Scott">
```

- *Lists* are technically not a separate data type, but are a string. They are listed here because of ColdFusion's extensive support for treating strings as a delimiter-separated list of values. By default, list items in ColdFusion are separated by a comma, but you can change the default delimiter to almost any character.

- *Numbers* can hold floating point numbers and integers. Again, you use a simple `<cfset>` to set a numerical value, as shown here:

```
<cfset Age = 21>
```

- *Booleans* are simple values of true or false, yes or no, or 1 or 0. These are set like so:

```
<cfset IsActive = true>
```

- *Dates* in ColdFusion can be created in the following ways:

```
<cfset myDate = parseDateTime("9/14/2002")>
<cfset myDate = CreateDate( 2002, 9, 14 )>
```

ColdFusion has a very comprehensive set of date and time manipulation functions to allow you to format dates and extract years, months, and days very easily.

- *Arrays* are like numbered containers for data. They can contain simple or complex values, so it is possible to create arrays of arrays or arrays of structures very easily. Arrays in ColdFusion differ from those in most other programming languages. ColdFusion arrays start at 1 instead of 0, so always account for this when coding. Another difference is that you must always define whether it is a one-dimensional or two-dimensional array. Here is an example of creating a simple one-dimensional array:

```
<cfset myArray = ArrayNew( 1 )>
```

Let's look at the Array data type in closer detail. We will cover dimensions in later in this section, but first let's cover how to add data to an array. You can add items to an array by using the following method:

```
<cfset myArray[ 1 ] = "one">
<cfset myArray[ 2 ] = "two">
```

Now you can see what is meant by a numbered container. Each item in the array has a numerical index that lets you retrieve it later. A handful of functions also let us get the number of items in an array or append (or prepend) values in an array. We'll cover array-specific functions later in this chapter. For now, think of a one-dimensional array as a single row in a database. Every item within the array is a column within that database.

The preceding example was a one-dimensional array. If you created a two-dimensional array, the code would look similar to the following:

```
<cfset my2dArray = ArrayNew( 2 )>
<cfset my2dArray[ 1 ][ 1 ] = "one-a">
<cfset my2dArray[ 1 ][ 2 ] = "one-b">
<cfset my2dArray[ 2 ][ 1 ] = "two-a">
<cfset my2dArray[ 2 ][ 2 ] = "two-b">
```

Continuing our database analogy, a two-dimensional array would be similar to a database with multiple rows but only one table. The first dimension is the row number, and the second dimension is the specific column.

A three-dimensional array would simply have another pair of square brackets, and you would have to create the array by using `<cfset my3dArray = ArrayNew( 3 )>`. Strictly speaking, the maximum number of dimensions an array can have is three, although it is possible to create arrays of arrays and overcome this limit.

Think of a three-dimensional array as a database with multiple tables and multiple rows in each table. Three-dimensional arrays are the most difficult to manage because the numerical indexes can become very confusing to keep straight and reference properly. Many developers find it easier to think of multi-dimensional arrays as an array of arrays.

Structures

Structures are very similar to arrays, except instead of having numerical indexes, they use strings. To create a structure we use code similar to the following:

```
<cfset myStructure = StructNew( )>
<cfset myStructure[ "cats" ] = 2>
```

In the preceding code, our structure is called myStructure, and you have a *key* named cats, which has a value of 2. There are two coding styles for creating and retrieving data from a structure; the first method (shown in the preceding code) is called *array syntax*, and the other method is referred to as *dot syntax* and is shown here:

```
<cfset myStructure = StructNew( )>
<cfset myStructure.cats = 2>
```

You can see that here, instead of putting square brackets and quotes around the key, a simple dot (.) separates the structure name from the key.

Structures can also store other structures to create nested objects. Structures can also contain Recordsets and arrays.

Recordsets (Queries)

You can create Recordsets a couple different ways. The most common method is by using the <cfquery> tag, which would execute an SQL statement and return a Recordset. An example of this would be:

```
<cfquery name="getEmployees" datasource="CompanyInfo">
  SELECT *
  FROM Employee
</cfquery>
```

The preceding code selects all columns and rows from the Employee table and returns the results as a Recordset named getEmployees.

Another way to create queries is manually through CFML. Although not very common, it is possible to create a Recordset manually with a few select CFML functions, as shown here:

```
<cfset getEmployees = QueryNew( "Emp_ID,FirstName" )>
<cfset QueryAddRow( getEmployees )>
<cfset QuerySetCell( getEmployees, "Emp_ID", 1 )>
<cfset QuerySetCell( getEmployees, "FirstName", "Scott" )>
<cfset QueryAddRow( getEmployees)>
<cfset QuerySetCell( getEmployees, "Emp_ID", 2 )>
<cfset QuerySetCell( getEmployees, "FirstName", "Kate" )>
```

The preceding code creates a Recordset named getEmployees. You tell ColdFusion that you are creating a new query with two columns: Emp_ID and FirstName. Next you add a new row to your getEmployees query, set the Emp_ID column of your new row to 1, and finally set the FirstName column to Scott. You can now create another new row containing the values 2 and Kate.

As seen in the previous chapter, some ColdFusion tags also create Recordsets. An example of this was the <cfdirectory> tag, which grabbed the names of files and subfolders in a directory and returned the results as a Recordset. Another cool feature of ColdFusion is its ability to query an existing Recordset. This feature is referred to as "Query of Queries," and it can be used to filter records of an existing Recordset instead of having to query the database again.

XML

ColdFusion MX was the first version with built-in full XML support. Previous versions of ColdFusion provided a set of tools for working with Web Distributed Data Exchange (WDDX), an XML-based format for transferring data between systems (covered in Chapter 7). ColdFusion developers can now easily create, read, search, and transform almost any XML document without the need for third-party custom tags or by using COM objects, and without having to worry about complicated document type definitions (DTDs). Here's an example of how to create XML objects:

```
<cfset myXml = XmlNew()>
<cfset myXml.XmlRoot = XmlElemNew( myXml, "message" )>
<cfset myXml.message.XmlText = "Hello World">
<cfdump var="#myXml#">
```

We cover XML in great detail later in Chapter 11.

Functions

Now that you have a better understanding of ColdFusion data types and variable scopes, let's look at some of the more common functions built into ColdFusion.

As you learned in Chapter 3, functions are often used in conjunction with ColdFusion tags to provide a well-rounded application. Functions are typically used to format data and check to see if data is of a certain data type. They are also used to convert values, round numbers, search strings for occurrences of a certain substring, and a large number of other tasks.

Roughly 265 functions are broken down into 18 categories. These categories are:

- Array

- Authentication

- Conversion

- Date and time

- Decision

- Display and formatting

- Dynamic evaluation

- Extensibility

- Full-text search

- International

- List

- Mathematical

- Other miscellaneous

- Query

- String

- Structure

- System

- XML

You saw several of these functions in the previous chapter, and we will explore many new functions in this chapter and throughout the rest of the book. In the following sections, we cover `Array`, `Date` and `Time`, and `String` functions.

Array Functions

Arrays can be used almost anywhere to hold a collection of items, such as states, countries, or names. Arrays have some useful functions, such as #ArrayMin()#, #ArrayMax()#, #ArraySum()#. This makes them ideal for storing numerical data on which you may need to perform some mathematical calculations. ColdFusion also provides functions allowing you to easily convert arrays to and from a list, which makes it easy to turn a simple comma-separated list of values into an array on which you can perform calculations.

#ArrayNew(dimension)#

As discussed earlier in this chapter, #ArrayNew()# is used to create new arrays. Remember that arrays in ColdFusion are one-based instead of zero-based. This means that if you try to add a value at an index of 0, ColdFusion will generate an error as shown in the following example. Type the following two lines into a new file in Dreamweaver (badarray.cfm):

```
<cfset myArray = ArrayNew(1)>
<cfset myArray[0] = "blah">
```

Test this code in a browser, and you should generate the error shown in Figure 4-3.

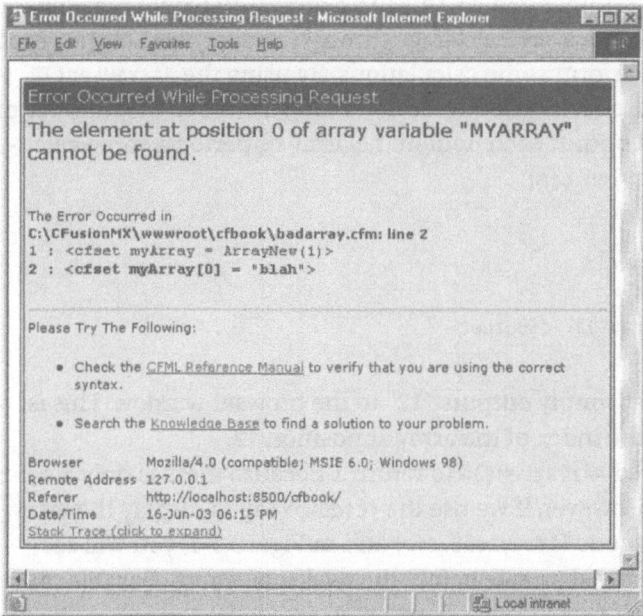

Figure 4-3. Trying to add a value to an array at an index of 0 generates an error

For this reason, it is important to make sure that you use only positive integers as array indexes.

#ArrayIsEmpty(array)#

This function is used to test whether an array contains any elements. This function could be used to test if an array is populated before trying to determine whether you can use any functions such as #ArraySum()# on it. If the array is empty, the function returns True, and if the array is populated, the function returns False. You can see an example of this here (arrayempty.cfm):

```
<cfset myArray = ArrayNew(1)>
<cfset myArray[1] = "blah">
<cfoutput>#ArrayIsEmpty( myArray )#</cfoutput>
```

This script outputs "NO" to the browser window because the array has an element in it. This function is typically used when you want to test if an array has any values before trying to calculate the minimum and maximum values in an array.

#ArrayLen(array)#

This function returns the number of elements in an array. You would typically use this when you want to use a <cfloop> to go through an array and output each item within the array or perform some calculations. By using the #ArrayLen()# function, you can easily use an indexed <cfloop> to loop from 1 to the number of elements in the array and output each item in the array or perform some calculations. For example (arraylen.cfm):

```
<cfset myArray = ArrayNew(1)>
<cfset myArray[12] = "blah">
<cfoutput>#ArrayLen( myArray )#</cfoutput>
```

The preceding snippet simply outputs "12" to the browser window. This is because we have started the index of the array at position 12.

You may have expected #ArrayLen()# to return 1 because there is only a single element in our array. However, if we use the <cfdump> tag to display the array, as shown in the following code (arraylen2.cfm) and in Figure 4-4, you will see that there are 11 empty array elements before the twelfth element. For this reason you should be careful if using high indexes in an array; if you must start arrays at a high index or need to use noncontiguous indexes, consider using a structure instead.

```
<cfset myArray = ArrayNew(1)>
<cfset myArray[12] = "blah">
<cfdump var="#myArray#">
```

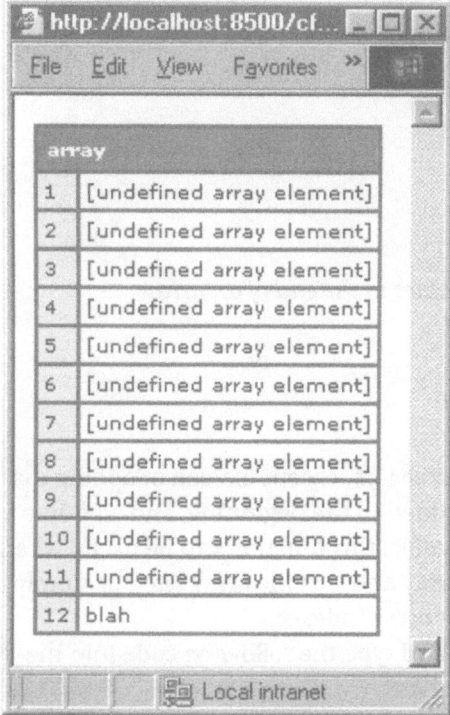

Figure 4-4. Using `<cfdump>` *to display our array on the screen*

#ArrayAppend(array, value)#

`#ArrayAppend()#` simply adds a value to the end of an array. This can be useful if you just want to enter data into an array and either sort the data later using `#ArraySort()#` or simply perform calculations and not worry about indexes. Using the following code (`arrayappend.cfm`), you can enter two elements into an array and output the array object to the browser window.

Enter the following code into a new file in Dreamweaver:

```
<cfset myArray = ArrayNew(1)>
<cfset ArrayAppend( myArray, "one" )>
<cfset ArrayAppend( myArray, "two" )>
<cfdump var="#myArray#">
```

When testing your file, you will see the array depicted in the browser, as shown in Figure 4-5.

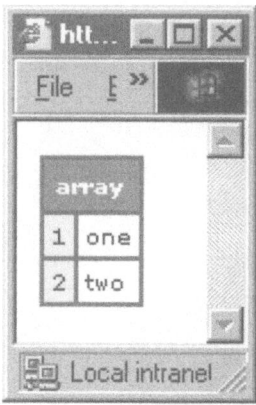

Figure 4-5. Using #ArrayAppend()# *to add values to the end of an array*

#ArrayPrepend(array, value)#

#ArrayPrepend()# is very similar to #ArrayAppend()#, except instead of adding the value to the end of the array, the value is added to the beginning, and all other elements are shifted. Much like #ArrayAppend()#, this function can be useful when you simply want to insert a value into an array and sort the array later, or simply perform a calculation and not worry about array indexes.

Open a new .cfm file in Dreamweaver and type the following code into the Document window (arrayprepend.cfm):

```
<cfset myArray = ArrayNew(1)>
<cfset ArrayPrepend( myArray, "a" )>
<cfset ArrayPrepend( myArray, "b" )>
<cfset ArrayPrepend( myArray, "c" )>
<cfdump var="#myArray#">
```

Now test your file in a browser window, and you should see the output shown in Figure 4-6.

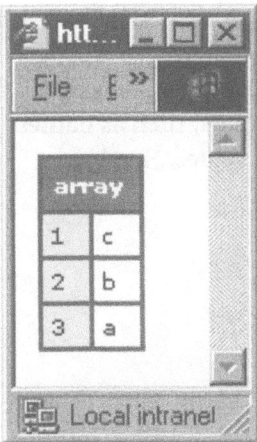

Figure 4-6. Using #ArrayAppend()# *to add values to the start of an array*

#ArrayClear(array)#

To remove the contents of an array, simply call #ArrayClear()# and pass the name of the array to clear. The following code creates a new array, populates it, clears the contents, and then outputs the empty array to the screen. This is useful if you are creating a new array for each iteration of a loop and want to clear the contents after each loop has finished.

For example, if you were looping over a Recordset and needed to perform calculations for each record in the database, but didn't want to create a unique array for each record, you could simply create one array and delete its contents at the end of each iteration. The following code presents an example of this function (arrayclear.cfm). Calling the <cfdump> tag displays the array and all its elements, showing us that the array is in fact empty.

```
<cfset myArray = ArrayNew(1)>
<cfset ArrayPrepend( myArray, "a" )>
<cfset ArrayPrepend( myArray, "b" )>
<cfset ArrayClear( myArray )>
<cfdump var="#myArray#">
```

When you test this code in a browser window, you will simply see an empty array.

#ArraySort(array, sort_type, sort_order)#

#ArraySort()# lets you sort the elements of an array either alphabetically or numerically. This is useful when you have an array full of items, such as names or states, that must be ordered before looping through the values. Here's an example of this function (arraysort.cfm):

```
<cfset myArray = ArrayNew(1)>
<cfset ArrayAppend(myArray, 'p')>
<cfset ArrayAppend(myArray, 'a')>
<cfset ArrayAppend(myArray, 'n')>
<cfset ArrayAppend(myArray, 't')>
<cfset ArrayAppend(myArray, 's')>
<cfset ArraySort(myArray, "textnocase", "ASC")>
<cfloop from="1" to="#ArrayLen(myArray)#" index="i">
  <cfoutput>#myArray[i]# </cfoutput>
</cfloop>
```

This code produces the following output:

```
a n p s t
```

#ArraySum(array)#

#ArraySum()# simply calculates the sum of the elements in a numeric array. This function is useful if you have an array of numbers and must calculate the total sum of the array. An example of this might be if you were building a dynamic array of statistics and needed to grab the total number of visitors to your site by storing the number of daily visitors in an array. By using this function, you can easily sum the entire array to calculate the total number of visitors over a long period of time.

Here's a sample of this tag's usage (arraysum.cfm):

```
<cfset myArray = ArrayNew(1)>
<cfset ArrayAppend( myArray, 7.6 )>
<cfset ArrayAppend( myArray, 7.7)>
<cfset ArrayAppend( myArray, 8.1)>
<cfoutput>Sum: #ArraySum( myArray )#</cfoutput>
```

The preceding listing simply outputs the following to the screen:

```
Sum: 23.4
```

If the array contains any nonnumeric data, ColdFusion generates an error message.

```
#ArrayMin( array )#, #ArrayMax( array )#, and
#ArrayAvg( array )#
```

The final three functions described in this section are all mathematical functions that can be used on arrays. #ArrayMin()# and #ArrayMax()# return the lowest and highest numbers in an array, whereas #ArrayAvg()# simply calculates the mean average value within an array.

Each of these functions would be used when working with numeric arrays on which you need to perform mathematical calculations. For example, if you're logging statistics for news articles and want to track which articles have been clicked the most frequently, and whether each article is below or above the average number of clicks, you would use these functions.

You can see an example of each of these three functions in action in the following code (arraymath.cfm):

```
<cfset myArray = ArrayNew(1)>
<cfset ArrayAppend( myArray, 7.6 )>
<cfset ArrayAppend( myArray, 7.7)>
<cfset ArrayAppend( myArray, 8.1)>
<cfoutput>
  Min: #ArrayMin( myArray )#<br />
  Max: #ArrayMax( myArray )#<br />
  Avg: #ArrayAvg( myArray )#<br />
</cfoutput>
```

The preceding code displays the following output in the browser window:

```
Min: 7.6
Max: 8.1
Avg: 7.8
```

If any items in the array are nonnumeric, ColdFusion generates an error.

String Manipulation Functions

You've seen how to create simple strings in ColdFusion. Now it is time to move onto something a bit more challenging. In this section, you'll learn how to use some of the more powerful string functions in the everyday CFML coding arsenal. We'll revisit these functions throughout the book to show you how to encrypt and decrypt data before inserting it into a database and formatting it.

#Compare(string, string)# *and* #CompareNoCase(string, string)#

The first function we'll look at is #Compare()#, which takes two string values as arguments to compare. If both strings are equal, then the #Compare()# function returns 0. If the first string is greater than the second string, a value of 1 is returned. Otherwise, #Compare()# returns the value -1. The only difference between these two functions is that #Compare()# does a case-sensitive comparison, whereas #CompareNoCase()# obviously does not.

Let's look at a brief example:

```
<cfoutput>#Compare( "Scott", "Kate" )#</cfoutput>
```

The preceding code outputs the value "1" because the first string is "greater than" the second string. If you were to reverse the strings in the preceding example so "Kate" came first, ColdFusion would output the value -1.

Let's briefly look at another example. Enter the following code into a file:

```
<cfoutput>#Compare( "Scott", "scott" )#</cfoutput>
```

The preceding code outputs the value "-1" because the second string has a higher ASCII value than the first string. If you wanted to treat strings the same regardless of case, you would use the #CompareNoCase()# function, which is case-insensitive. In that case, it would have returned a value of 0 in the preceding code snippet.

If you want to check out the ASCII values of a character to see how it would be sorted, ColdFusion gives us a function called #Asc()#, which takes a character or string as a parameter and returns the numerical ASCII value of that string. Here's an example of this (asciivalues.cfm):

```
<cfoutput>
  #Compare( "Scott", "Kate" )#<br />
  The ASCII value of "S" is: #Asc("S")#<br />
  The ASCII value of "K" is: #Asc("K")#<br />
</cfoutput>
```

This code generates the output shown in Figure 4-7.

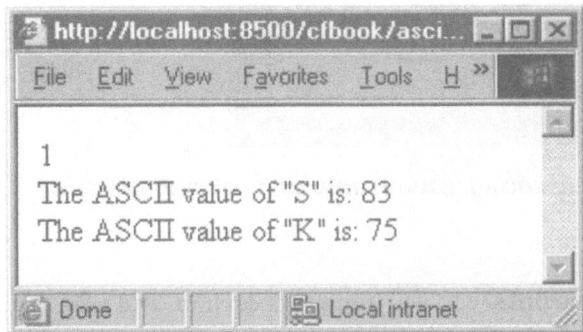

Figure 4-7. Outputting character ASCII values by using the Asc function

There is also a function called #Chr()#, which takes in a numerical ASCII value and returns the character value. Here's an example of this (chr.cfm):

```
<cfoutput>
  #Chr(97)#<br />
  #Chr(84)#<br />
</cfoutput>
```

This code generates the following output:

```
a
T
```

This has some very useful possibilities; by using a combination of <cfloop>, #Asc()#, and #Chr()#, you can output each letter of the alphabet and create a simple navigation for browsing records. Because using an index loop in CFML requires numeric values for the from and to attributes, you can simply use #Asc()# to return the ASCII value for A and Z. Then when you need to output the current letter, you can use #Chr()# to convert the numeric value back to a character. You can see a simple example of this in the following code (alphabetlinks.cfm). Enter this code into a new file:

```
<cfoutput>
  <cfloop from="#Asc('A')#" to="#Asc('Z')#" index="temp">
    <cfset currentLetter = Chr(temp)>
    <a href="index.cfm?letter=#currentLetter#">#currentLetter#</a>
      
  </cfloop>
</cfoutput>
```

Test this code in a browser, and you will see the output shown in Figure 4-8.

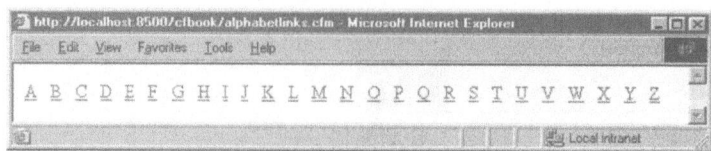

Figure 4-8. Creating simple alphabetic navigation links using a combination of ColdFusion functions

When you click on any of the links, you will jump to index.cfm, and a URL variable called letter will be passed, which has the value of whichever letter you happened to click on. Using this code, it is easy to create a query that will grab only records where the last name begins with a specific letter.

#Find(substring, string)# *and* #FindNoCase(substring, string)#

These very powerful functions can be used to find an occurrence of a particular substring within a string. If the substring is found in the string, these two functions return the position in which the substring has been found. If the substring isn't present within the string, then the function returns a value of 0. Let's look at an example and try to get a better understanding:

```
<cfset sentence = "Industry layoffs are at an all-time high.">
<cfoutput>#Find( "lay", sentence )#</cfoutput>
```

The preceding code outputs "10" to the window. The first occurrence of the substring lay appears in the word "layoffs" in the sentence, so the #Find()# function returns the start position of the first character. If you modify the substring in the previous example to search for a series of letters that do not exist, the function will return 0.

These two tags can be very powerful if you are trying to search strings for occurrences of substrings, or want to test to see if a desired character is within a string. For example, using the <cffile action="read"> tag and the #Find()# function, we could read in a file from our hard drive, save the contents to a variable, and then search the file for a single tag or even find the entire contents of the <body> tag. We would also need to use one new function we haven't looked at yet, called #Mid()#.

The #Mid()# function simply extracts a certain amount of characters from a string. It takes three arguments: the string that we want to extract a substring from, a starting index, and the number of characters to extract. Let's try an example of this.

1. First create a new HTML file called `appointments.html` and enter the following code into it:

```html
<html>
<head>
  <title>My Appointments</title>
</head>
<body>
  <table border="1">
    <tr>
      <td>Monday</td>
      <td>Watch TV.</td>
    </tr>
    <tr>
      <td>Tuesday</td>
      <td>Play Xbox.</td>
    </tr>
  </table>
</body>
</html>
```

2. Next, create a new ColdFusion file called `getAppointments.cfm` and type in the following code:

```cfml
<cffile action="read" file="#ExpandPath( 'appointments.html' )#"
        variable="myAppointments">
<cfset startBody = FindNoCase( "<body>", myAppointments )>
<cfset endBody = FindNoCase( "</body>", myAppointments )>
<cfset contents = Mid( myAppointments, startBody+6,➥
endBody-startBody-6 )>
<cfoutput>#contents#</cfoutput>
```

3. When you test this file in a browser, you will see the output shown in Figure 4-9.

Figure 4-9. Using <cffile> *to read in the contents of a file and display them as part of the contents of another*

Although you would definitely want to add in some error checking to make sure that #startBody# and #endBody# are greater than 0, we are trying to keep it simple here for demonstration purposes. You can use the #FileExists()# function outlined in the previous chapter to first test for the existence of the file before trying to read its contents. We cover more advanced error checking methods in Chapter 8.

In the preceding example, you begin by reading the file in and saving its contents to a variable called #myAppointments#. You then use #FindNoCase()# to locate the opening and closing <body> tags within the file. Following this, you use the #Mid()# function to extract the substring between the opening and closing <body> tags.

You will probably notice that you are doing a slight bit of math within the #Mid()# function. This is because the #Find()# and #FindNoCase()# functions return the index of the first character in the substring. Therefore, you need to add six to the #startBody# variable so that you don't include the actual opening <body> tag. For the same reason, you must subtract six from the final argument in the #Mid()# function; otherwise, you'll return a portion of the </body> tag. It is important to note that the final argument in the #Mid()# function is the actual number of characters that you want to extract, and not the index of the </body> tag.

Although we were only reading in a local file from our own site when we created this code, it would be possible to apply this same concept to HTML pages on remote web sites as well, assuming it falls within proper Web etiquette and is allowed by the remote site. You can even fine-tune the #Find()# function and extract only small portions of a web page. ColdFusion has several other string functions that make it very easy to extract portions of strings, determine the length of a string, or even trim out any excessive spaces from the beginning or end of a string.

#Left(string, count)# *and* #Right(string, count)#

Similar to the #Mid()# function used in the previous subsection, these two functions are used to extract substrings from a string. #Left()# extracts a certain number of characters from the left of the string, and #Right()# extracts characters a certain number of characters beginning from the right of a string. Let's look at a simple example.

Enter the following code into a new file (leftright.cfm):

```
<cfset myString = "The rain in Seattle is cold and wet.">
<cfoutput>#Left( myString, 12 )#</cfoutput><br />
<cfoutput>#Right( myString, 4 )#</cfoutput><br />
```

Test this code in a browser window. You will find that this listing outputs the following text:

```
The rain in
wet.
```

This code simply extracts substrings from the original sentence. These functions come in handy when you want to grab the contents of a file from a remote server, but need to parse out some of the formatting before integrating the data into your site.

For example, say you wanted to show the first 1,000 characters of a Web-based article as a "teaser" on another web page, or trim data before entering it into a database to reduce the possibility of errors. If you try inserting 5,000 characters of text into a database text field that accepts a maximum of 4,000 characters, ColdFusion will generate an error, and you will not be able to insert the record. You would be better off truncating the data before inserting it into the database, then notifying the user about the exceeded maximum number of characters for that particular column.

#Len(string)#

This function takes only one argument and returns the length of the string. This can be used to test the length of a string and see if it needs to be cropped before inserting it into a database, or to check if a user filled in a field before submitting a form, as shown in the following code (stringlength.cfm):

```
<cfif Len( Form.UserName ) EQ 0>
  <cfset Variables.errorMessage = "Please enter your user name.">
</cfif>
```

In a full form example, the preceding listing would simply check that the user had entered at least one character into the UserName form field before clicking the Submit button. If not, it sets a variable called #Variables.errorMessage#, which contains a useful message to display to the user. This can be a very useful technique for verifying user data before inserting it into a database, although the user could still enter white space into the field. Luckily, ColdFusion allows you to easily trim empty space from the beginning and/or end of a string by using the #LTrim()#, #RTrim()#, or #Trim()# functions.

#LTrim(string)#, #RTrim(string)#, and #Trim(string)#

As mentioned in the previous section, these functions remove leading and/or trailing space from a string. The #LTrim()# function trims any white space from the left side of a string, #RTrim()# trims white space from the right side, and #Trim()# removes excess white space from both ends of a string. Let's look at an example.

Enter the following code into a new .cfm file in Dreamweaver (trim.cfm):

```
<cfset myString = "        this is a sentence with no social significance        ">
<cfset LTrim_String = LTrim( myString )>
<cfset RTrim_String = RTrim( myString )>
<cfset Trim_String = Trim( myString )>
<cfoutput>
<pre>
[#LTrim_String#]
[#RTrim_String#]
[#Trim_String#]
</pre>
</cfoutput>
```

This code generates the following output:

```
[this is a sentence with no social significance        ]
[        this is a sentence with no social significance]
[this is a sentence with no social significance]
```

As you can see, the #LTrim()# function removed the excess spaces from only the beginning of the string. In most cases you'll want to use #Trim()# to remove safely any excess white space from a string before inserting it into a database. These functions are very useful when uploading files by using the <cffile action="upload"> tag we used in the previous chapter.

Certain versions of Microsoft Internet Explorer for the Mac platform have a bug where the browser is unable to append spaces onto the end of form fields when a user clicks on the Submit button. This can lead to problems when uploading files to the server, or if we are using the #Len()# function to test if a user has properly filled in a form field.

Therefore, let's revise the stringlength.cfm example we saw previously to check that the user doesn't simply enter a space into a form field and send it to the server (trim2.cfm):

```
<cfif Len( Trim( Form.UserName ) ) EQ 0>
  <cfset Variables.errorMessage = "Please enter your user name.">
</cfif>
```

This code snippet begins by trimming the excessive white space from #Form.UserName# and then calculates the length of the string. The user will no longer be able to bypass the JavaScript validation by simply entering a space into the form field.

> **TIP** *Never rely only on simple JavaScript validation. All validation should be backed up by using ColdFusion as well as JavaScript where possible to ensure that data is in a valid format.*

#UCase(string)# *and* #LCase(string)#

These two functions are useful when you need to convert a string to either uppercase or lowercase. These functions are mainly just used for formatting. Let's look at a simple example.

Open a new document in Dreamweaver and type in the following code (case.cfm):

```
<cfset myString = "ColdFusion MX 6.1 is the most powerful version➥
of ColdFusion to date.">
<cfoutput>#UCase( myString )#<br /></cfoutput>
<cfoutput>#LCase( myString )#<br /></cfoutput>
```

This will generate the following output:

```
COLDFUSION MX 6.1 IS THE MOST POWERFUL VERSION OF COLDFUSION TO DATE.
coldfusion mx 6.1 is the most powerful version of coldfusion to date.
```

This tag could also be used in conjunction with the #Left()# and #Right()# functions described earlier in this chapter to uppercase just the first character in a string. Take a look at a simple example of this (uppercase.cfm):

```
<cfset myName = "jen">
<cfset newName = UCase(Left( myName, 1 )) & LCase(Right(myName, Len(myName)-1))>
<cfoutput>#newName#</cfoutput>
```

Viewing the preceding snippet simply outputs "Jen" to the screen. This is just a simple example. Typically, you would want to check for spaces in a name and uppercase the first character of middle or last names in addition to using the other string functions.

#ParagraphFormat(string)#

This is a very useful formatting function that takes in a single string and replaces a pair of line breaks with a <p> tag. Without the <p> tags, the text would be hard to read, because HTML ignores spaces and carriage returns otherwise. This can be handy when displaying blocks of text in an article or press release. By using this function, you can add line breaks into our code. For example (paragraph.cfm):

```
<cfquery name="getNews" datasource="myCompanyDsn">
  SELECT
    PressReleaseID,
    PressReleaseTitle,
    PressReleaseText
  FROM
    PressReleases
  WHERE
    PressReleaseID = #Url.prid#
</cfquery>
<cfoutput query="getPressReleases">
  #PressReleaseTitle#<br />
  #ParagraphFormat( PressReleaseText )#<br />
</cfoutput>
```

This code snippet grabs a single press release from a database and displays the title and text in the browser window. This press release text should now be nicely formatted with <p> tags inserted automatically by ColdFusion. You could also easily write a simple script to do this and have much greater control over the display. By using a tag called #Replace()#, you can replace any occurrence of a substring with a different substring, within a specified string.

#Replace(string, substring1, substring2)# and #ReplaceNoCase(string, substring1, substring2)#

These two tags let you replace the occurrence of substring1 with substring2 within a given string. There is also an optional fourth attribute, scope, which is covered later in this section. First let's look at a simple example. Create a file in Dreamweaver called replace.cfm and enter the following code:

```
<form action="replace.cfm" method="post">
  <textarea cols="40" rows="5" name="myString"></textarea>
  <input type="Submit" value="Replace()">
</form>
<cfif IsDefined( "Form.myString" )>
  <cfset crlf = Chr(13) & Chr(10)>
  <cfset newString = Replace(Form.myString, crlf, "<br />")>
  <cfoutput>#newString#</cfoutput>
</cfif>
```

The preceding code displays a simple HTML textarea with a Submit button. Following this, some ColdFusion code begins by testing to see if a variable called #Form.myString# is defined. If the user has submitted the form, the variable will exist and the <cfif> block will be executed.

Inside the <cfif> block, a variable, #crlf#, that holds #Chr(13)# and #Chr(10)# is set. You've already looked at the #Chr()# function, but what you may not know is that #Chr(13)# is a carriage return, and that #Chr(10)# is a line feed. Furthermore, the ampersand (&) is ColdFusion's way of concatenating two strings. So, you're creating a variable that holds a carriage return and line feed (cr/lf).

The next line of code sets a variable #newString# to the string returned by the #Replace()# function. The #Replace()# function replaces any cr/lf it finds with the substring <br />.

Test this code by entering a couple of small paragraphs in the text area and clicking the Submit button. You should see each cr/lf replaced with a <br /> tag. What you may also notice is that it replaces only the first occurrence of the cr/lf. This is where the fourth optional scope argument comes in. Scope has two possible values: one and all. If scope isn't specified, the default value is one. This is why only the first occurrence of cr/lf was replaced.

If you specify ALL as the scope, then ColdFusion will replace all of the cr/lfs in the string with the <br /> tag. Test this by changing the third line from the bottom of the preceding snippet to this:

```
<cfset newString = Replace(Form.myString, crlf, "<br />", "ALL")>
```

Save the file and rerun the code. Now every cr/lf is replaced with a <br /> tag, so the formatting remains intact. Using this code allows you to customize the output a lot more than if you use the #ParagraphFormat()# tag.

Finally, #ReplaceNoCase()# is the same as #Replace()# except that it is case-insensitive, so it doesn't care if you are trying to find <br />, <BR />, or <Br />.

#Val(string)#

#Val()# is a function very useful for testing data before inserting it into a database. This function takes a string and tries to convert it into a number; if the number cannot be converted, it returns 0 (zero). This function cannot convert the string one into the number 1, but if a user passes a string of 123four; the #Val()# function will convert that to the number 123. Let's look at a simple example. Create a file named val.cfm and type in the following code:

```
<form action="val.cfm" method="post">
  <input type="Text" name="myString">
  <input type="Submit" value="Val()">
</form>
<cfif IsDefined( "Form.myString" )>
  <cfoutput>
  You entered: '#Form.myString#'<br />
  Val() returns: '#Val( Form.myString )#'<br />
  </cfoutput>
</cfif>
```

This is a simple form that has a single text input box and a Submit button. Fill in some text and hit the Submit button, and you should now see the exact text that you entered and how #Val()# interprets that string. If you enter a numeric value, #Val()# returns the exact value that you entered, but if you enter a string, #Val()# will return 0.

Before inserting any data that you expect to be numeric into a database or using it in a query, it is always a good idea to use #Val()# to convert that data. If you are getting a value from a URL variable, it is possible that the user has manually changed the value of that variable in the query string in an attempt to corrupt data in your database. If you don't test that the value you are trying to insert is numeric, you may find that ColdFusion or SQL generates an error message and the query fails.

#UrlEncodedFormat(string)# *and* #UrlDecode(string)#

These two functions are used to encode and decode strings for use with a query string. Whenever passing data along the query string, which is any URL variable, you should encode the data to be sure that you can safely read the data on the following page. Encoding variables involves replacing any spaces with %20, question marks (?) with %3F, ampersands (&) with %26, and other nonalphanumeric characters with equivalent hexadecimal escape sequences. This can be essential if you are passing values in a query string and a user enters a ? or &. ColdFusion may not be able to parse out the values in the query string properly if they aren't properly encoded. Before going any further, let's look at some sample code. Create a new file called urlencode.cfm and enter the following code:

```
<form action="urlencode.cfm" method="post">
  <input type="text" name="myString">
  <input type="submit" value="UrlEncodedFormat()">
</form>
<cfif IsDefined( "Form.myString" )>
  <cflocation url="urlencode.cfm?myString=#Form.myString#">
<cfelseif IsDefined( "Url.myString" )>
  <cfoutput>#Url.myString#</cfoutput>
</cfif>
```

View the code in a web browser and enter some text into the text box. Click on the Submit button, and the code will be passed as a form variable. Then the first <cfif> statement will relocate the browser and pass the string you entered as a URL variable.

If you simply changed the form's method to get instead of post, ColdFusion would automatically encode the values. However, the get method truncates the value, so the value that you are trying to pass is changed. You can fix this problem quite simply by adding #UrlEncodedFormat()# around the #Form.myString# variable, as shown here:

```
<cflocation url="urlencode.cfm?myString=#UrlEncodedFormat( Form.myString )#">
```

This will convert any special characters and preserve the value that you originally entered.

#Encrypt(string, key)# *and* #Decrypt(string, key)#

Another strategy for passing values along query strings is to encrypt the data so that it cannot be read easily in that form. To decrypt the value and put it back into a readable form, simply use the #Decrypt()# function. It is important to note that both functions take a string to encrypt/decrypt, as well as a key. The key is needed so that after encrypting the data, you are able to decrypt it at the other end. If the same key is not used, you will be unable to decrypt the encrypted string. Let's look at an example (encrypt.cfm):

```
<cfset myPassword = "taintedbeef">
<cfset myKey = "arbitrary string">
<cfset encryptedPassword = Encrypt( myPassword, myKey )>
```

```
<cfoutput>
  original password: #myPassword#<br />
  encrypted password: #encryptedPassword#<br />
  decrypted password: #Decrypt( encryptedPassword, myKey )#<br />
</cfoutput>
```

The preceding snippet generates the following output:

```
original password: taintedbeef
encrypted password: +4M>44H<"BP6#NJ@
decrypted password: taintedbeef
```

Note that when decrypting the password, you must pass the encrypted string and key to properly retrieve the original string. Typically, you would not need to encrypt and decrypt a string on the same page; you would encrypt the value and pass it along the URL or within a form, and then decrypt the value on the action page. It should be noted that if you pass data along the query string, you still need to URL encode the value in case the string contains any special characters. An example of this would be:

```
<cfoutput><a href="action.cfm?#URLEncodedFormat(encryptedPassword)#">➥
click here</a></cfoutput>
```

If using a single key to encrypt and decrypt data for all users in a site, you can just save the key in your Application.cfm page, and every template within your site would have access to that key. If each user were to have a personal key to encrypt and decrypt data, then you would need to save that key to a persistent scope unique to a particular user, such as Session, Client, or Cookie.

The Application or Server scope would not be ideal in this situation, because those scopes are shared across all users of the server or particular session. It also wouldn't be too useful to pass the encrypted string and the key used to decrypt that key in the URL, because any hacker would be able to easily decrypt the key and view your data. If you must store sensitive information in a database, such as a user's credit card number or password, you could encrypt those before inserting them into the database. That way, if a malicious user hacks your site and accesses your database, the data would be more difficult for the hacker to view. Ideally, however, you would never store any credit card information on your servers at all.

#CreateUUID()#

ColdFusion has a function called #CreateUUID()# that creates a unique 35-character string used to assign unique keys to each user. A Universally Unique Identifier (UUID) is a 35-character string made up of hexadecimal values (0–9, A–F) and is created based on the system time, the HostID of the server, and a highly random number. In theory, you guarantee that a random number generated by your system will not exist on any other servers, or be created more than once on your server. To assign each user a random UUID, you could simply use the following code (createUUID.cfm):

```
<cfif NOT IsDefined( "Cookie.UUID" )>
  <cfcookie name="UUID" value="#CreateUUID( )#">
</cfif>
```

This code will check to see if users already has a UUID assigned, and if so, it doesn't do anything. If users doesn't have a #Cookie.UUID# assigned, it creates a temporary cookie that will stay with those particular users until they close their browsers. If you want to create a cookie that will never expire (unless the users delete their cookies, whichever comes first), you can simply change the <cfcookie> code to:

```
<cfcookie name="UUID" value="#CreateUUID( )#" expires="NEVER">
```

You can also use the expires attribute to specify a particular date and time at which you want the cookie to expire. If you want to delete that user's UUID programmatically at any point, you can use this:

```
<cfcookie name="UUID" value="0" expires="NOW">
```

#Hash(string)#

The final function we examine in this section is #Hash()#, which takes a string as an argument and returns a 32-byte hexadecimal (A–Z, 1–9) string using the MD5 algorithm. It is important to note that there is no way to *unhash* a string once hashed; it is a one-way conversion. This tag can be very useful for tasks such as encoding a password before inserting it into a database. If we store hashed passwords in the database, it is very difficult (if not impossible) for a hacker to decrypt the original value, and we can still check the password even though it is hashed.

Open Dreamweaver and enter the following code into a new file named loginform.cfm:

```
<cfform action="dologin.cfm" method="post">
  User Name:
  <cfinput type="text" name="UserName" required="yes"➡
          message="Please enter your user name."><br />
```

```
    Password:
    <cfinput type="password" name="Password" required="yes"➥
            message="Please enter your password."><br />
    <input type="submit" value="Login">
</cfform>
```

Save this file and create another new file called `dologin.cfm` containing the following code:

```
<cfset Variables.UserName = "admin">
<cfset Variables.Password = Hash("socks")>
<cfparam name="Form.UserName" type="string">
<cfparam name="Form.Password" type="string">
<cfif Form.UserName EQ Variables.UserName AND
Hash( Form.Password ) EQ Variables.Password>
    Login successful.<br />
    the correct hashed password is:
    <cfoutput>#Variables.Password#</cfoutput>.
    <cfelse>
    Invalid UserName/Password. Please try again.
    <cfinclude template="loginform.cfm">
</cfif>
```

Browse to `loginForm.cfm` in a web browser and experiment with some fake usernames and passwords. Next, try the correct username (admin) and the correct password (socks).

This is just sample code, and you'd probably never want to store usernames and passwords in the page like this. Typically, you'd want to store this information in a database so everybody can have distinct usernames and passwords. We'll expand upon this example in Chapter 6, where we take an in-depth look at integrating ColdFusion with a database.

Date and Time Functions

ColdFusion has an excellent group of functions to allow developers to work easily with dates and times. They range from functions that can format dates and get the name of a month to functions that compare two dates—all the functions are there. If you need a function that ColdFusion doesn't provide, you can easily create your own custom function, as you will see in Chapter 10.

```
#Now()#
```

We briefly looked at this function in Chapter 1. #Now()# doesn't take any arguments and simply returns the current ColdFusion server date and time. You'll see examples of #Now()# throughout the rest of this section.

```
#CreateDate( year, month, day )#, #CreateTime( hour,
minute, second )#, and #CreateDateTime( year, month, day,
hour, minute, second )#
```

These functions are useful for manually creating a date and/or time. You can use #CreateDate()# to help build a calendar, or when you need to build a date based on a user's input. Let's begin by looking at some sample code (createdate.cfm):

```
<cfset Christmas = CreateDate( 2003, 12, 25 )>
<cfoutput>This year Christmas is on day #DayOfWeek(Christmas)#➥
of the week.</cfoutput>
```

The preceding code outputs "5" to the browser window. #DayOfWeek()# takes a date as an argument and returns a number between 1 (Sunday) and 7 (Saturday) representing the day of the week. If you want to display the day of the week as a string instead of a number, ColdFusion has a function called #DayOfWeekAsString()#, which takes a integer from 1 to 7 as an attribute and returns the day of the week, for example, "Sunday" or "Saturday." You can see an example of this in the following code (dayofweek.cfm):

```
<cfoutput>#DayOfWeekAsString( DayOfWeek( Now() ) )#</cfoutput>
```

This code outputs "Thursday" to the screen (assuming it is Thursday, of course).

The #CreateTime()# function is similar to #CreateDate()#, except that it deals strictly with time values. When using #CreateTime()#, it creates a default date of December 30, 1899. We can see an example of this function (createtime.cfm):

```
<cfset myDate = createTime( 18,17,0 )>
<cfoutput>#myDate#</cfoutput>
```

which outputs the following:

```
{ts '1899-12-30 18:17:00'}
```

#CreateDateTime()# is a combination of the #CreateDate()# and #CreateTime()# functions and allows you to create full dates and times using one function. Three similar functions, called #CreateODBCDate()#, #CreateODBCTime()#, and #CreateODBCDateTime()#, format the date-time object so that it is safe to use in an SQL query. This may not work on all database products, however, so be sure to consult your database documentation if you encounter problems. Whenever inserting dates into a database, you should always use #CreateODBCDate()# or one of the other functions to make sure that Access (or whichever database product) can safely read the date. You'll see examples of this in Chapter 6.

Extracting Dateparts

Next we examine extracting certain portions of a date, as well as how to format dates and times so that they are more readable.

If we want to extract part of a date, a number of functions isolate dateparts:

- #Year(date)# returns the year from a date as a four-digit integer, such as 2003.

- #Month(date)# returns an integer from 1 to 12.

- #Day(date)# returns an integer from 1 to 31.

- #Hour(date)# returns an integer from 0 to 23.

- #Minute(date)# returns an integer from 0 to 59.

- #Second(date)# returns an integer from 0 to 59.

- #Week(date)# returns an integer from 1 to 53 representing a week of the year.

- #Quarter(date)# returns an integer from 1 to 4 representing the quarter of the year.

- #DatePart(datepart, date)# is similar to the preceding functions, except with a bit of added functionality we describe later.

Most of the preceding functions are fairly self-explanatory, but we'll look at #DatePart()# in more detail in the next section.

#DatePart(datepart, date)#

#DatePart()# extracts portions of a date and returns integers similar to the preceding functions listed. Valid dateparts are as follows:

- yyyy: year, same as the #Year()# function

- q: quarter, same as the #Quarter()# function

- m: month, same as the #Month()# function

- y: day of year, same as the #DayOfYear()# function

- d: day, same as the #Day()# function

- w: weekday, same as the #DayOfWeek()# function

- ww: week, same as the #Week()# function

- h: hour, same as the #Hour()# function

- n: minute, same as the #Minute()# function

- s: second, same as the #Second()# function

Before going any further, let's look at an example. The following example creates a date and then loops through each datepart option and outputs an entry for our sample day (dateparts.cfm):

```
<cfset Christmas = CreateDateTime( 2003, 12, 25, 7, 15, 0)>
<cfoutput>
  <strong>#Christmas#</strong><br />
  <cfloop list="yyyy,q,m,y,d,w,ww,h,n,s" index="thisDatePart">
    #thisDatePart#: #DatePart( thisDatePart, Christmas )#<br />
  </cfloop>
</cfoutput>
```

This code generates the following output:

```
{ts '2003-12-25 07:15:00'}
yyyy: 2003
q: 4
m: 12
y: 359
d: 25
w: 5
ww: 52
h: 7
n: 15
s: 0
```

You start by creating a new date/time and displaying it to the screen. Next you loop over a list of each possible datepart and output the results of the #DatePart()# function. You can see that Christmas day 2003 occurs in the 4th quarter, 359th day of the year, 5th day of the week (Thursday), 52nd week, and 2003rd year, along with the month, day, hour, minute, and second values.

A couple other functions also are useful for building calendar applications or other systems that depend on dates, such as message boards and so on:

- #DaysInMonth()# returns the number of days in a particular month.

- #DaysInYear()# returns the total number of days in a particular year.

- #FirstDayOfMonth()# returns the day of the year that the first day of the given month falls on.

- #DayOfWeek()# returns the numerical day of the week from 1 (Sunday) to 7 (Saturday).

We will look at the first of these in more detail in the following section.

#DaysInMonth(date)#

This function returns an integer from 28 to 31. Using this function, we can easily loop from 1 to the number of days in the month to create a simple calendar, as seen here (calendar.cfm):

```
<cfparam name="Url.date" default="#Now()#" type="date">
<cfoutput>
  <table border="1">
    <tr>
      <td colspan="2" nowrap>
        #MonthAsString( Month(Url.date) )# #Year(Url.date)#
      </td>
    </tr>
    <cfloop from="1" to="#DaysInMonth( Url.date )#" index="thisDay">
      <cfset tempDate = CreateDate( Year(Url.date), Month(Url.date), thisDay )>
      <tr>
        <td>#DayOfWeekAsString(DayOfWeek(tempDate))#</td>
        <td>#thisDay#</td>
      </tr>
    </cfloop>
  </table>
</cfoutput>
```

Figure 4-10 shows the output from this code.

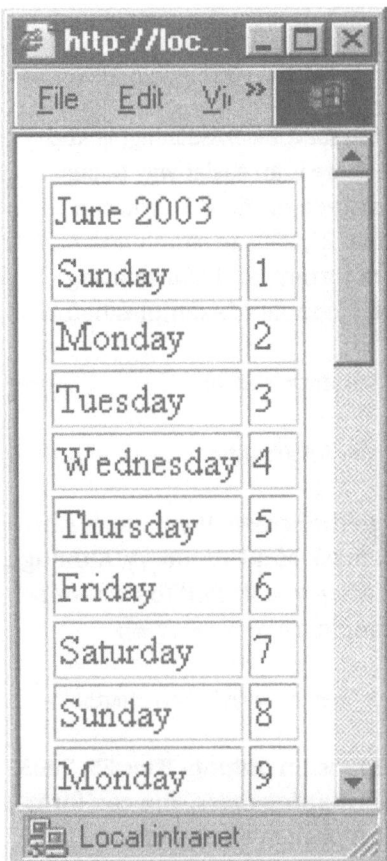

Figure 4-10. A simple ColdFusion calendar display

As you can see in the preceding code, sometimes it is necessary to nest functions to get the results we want. We will revisit this example later in this chapter to see how the same results could be achieved by using the #DateFormat()# and #DateAdd()# functions.

The code first calls #Month(Url.date)#, which returns the value 1 (in our example), to the #MonthAsString()# function. #MonthAsString()# takes an integer from 1 to 12 and outputs the month name to the browser window, in this case January. Similarly, #DayOfWeekAsString(DayOfWeek(tempDate))# is nested to get the name of the current day of the month. Another useful trick is to set the #tempDate# variable each time through the loop. #CreateDate()# is used and passed in the current year and current month, as is a variable for the day of the month.

In the previous example, all you have to do is pass a new #Url.date# value to the page, and you can see a calendar for any month. If we wanted to show appointments/news/blog entries, all you would need to do is run a query inside the <cfloop> and select all records where the date matches the #tempDate#.

#DateFormat(date, mask)#

Although it's possible to format the dates by using the #DayOfWeekAsString()# and #MonthAsString()# functions in the earlier example, there is an easier way to customize dates. #DateFormat()# allows you to apply a style to the date, so you can choose between formats such as Thursday, December 25, 2003 or simply 2003/12/25.

#DateFormat()# takes two arguments: a date to format, and a formatting mask to apply to the date. Let's start by looking at a couple of examples before going through each of the mask options.

Enter the following code into Dreamweaver (christmas.cfm):

```
<cfoutput>#DateFormat( CreateDate( 2003, 12, 25) )#</cfoutput>
```

The preceding snippet outputs "25-Dec-03" to the screen. If you don't supply any mask at all, ColdFusion will use a default mask of dd-mmm-yy. Although this works, it isn't the most readable format, and often you'll want to customize the output a little more. Let's look at another example (christmas2.cfm):

```
<cfoutput>#DateFormat( CreateDate( 2003, 12, 25), "mmm d, yyyy" )#</cfoutput>
```

This time you are specifying a mask, and ColdFusion outputs "Dec 25, 2003" to the browser window. By specifying your own formatting mask, you can format dates in any number of ways. The following is a list of each type of mask option. As you can see from the preceding example, you can group as many masks together as you want to customize your display.

- d: day of month as number; days less than 10 do not have a leading 0 (for example, 7)

- dd: day of month as number; days less than 10 have a leading 0 (for example, 07)

- ddd: abbreviated day of week as three-character string (for example, Sat)

- dddd: full day of week as string (for example, Saturday)

- m: month as number; months less than 10 do not have a leaving 0 (for example, 8)

- mm: month as number; months less than 10 have a leading 0 (for example, 08)

- mmm: abbreviated month name as three-character string (for example, Aug)

- mmmm: full month as string (for example, August)

- y: last two numbers of year; years less than 10 do not have a leading 0 (for example, 3 for 2003)

- yy: last two numbers of year; years less than 10 have a leading 0 (for example, 03 for 2003)

- yyyy: full four digits of year (for example, 2003)

- Short: uses the mask m/d/yy

- Medium: uses the mask mmm d, yyyy

- Long: uses the mask mmmm d, yyyy

- Full: uses the mask dddd, mmmm d, yyyy

You can see from this list that instead of specifying mmm d, yyyy, as did the mask in the previous example, you could simply have put in Medium and achieved the same result.

ColdFusion includes four of these prebuilt masks along with the default mask of dd-mmm-yy. If you want any other formats, you must create our own custom masks from the preceding list. For example, if you want to format a date similar to 02/28/2003, you would simply create the mask "mm/dd/yyyy" and pass it to the #DateFormat()# function as follows:

```
<cfoutput>#DateFormat( CreateDate( 2003, 2, 28 ), "mm/dd/yyyy" )#</cfoutput>
```

#TimeFormat(time, mask)#

In a fashion very similar to the preceding #DateFormat()# function, this function is responsible for formatting a time according to a certain mask.

- h: hours without a leading zero, based on 12-hour clock

- hh: hours with a leading zero, based on 12-hour clock

- H: hours without a leading zero, based on 24-hour clock

- HH: hours without a leading zero, based on 24-hour clock

- m: minutes without a leading zero

- mm: minutes with leading zero

- s: seconds without a leading zero

- ss: seconds with a leading zero

- t: one-character time marker (A or P)

- tt: two-character time marker (AM or PM)

- short: uses the mask h:mm tt

- medium: uses the mask h:mm:ss tt

- long: uses the mask h:mm:ss tt, but appends time zone information

- full: uses the mask h:mm:ss tt, but appends time zone information

#DateCompare(date, date)#

Much like the #Compare()# function we looked at earlier, ColdFusion offers a similar function that allows you to compare two dates. #DateCompare()# takes two arguments and returns –1 if the first date is less than the second date, 0 if both dates are equal, and 1 if the first date is greater than the second date.

There is also a third and optional parameter that tells ColdFusion the precision it should check to. By default it compares the two dates down to the second. If the dates aren't exactly the same, it will return –1 or 1. However, by specifying precision, you can tell it to check only the precision down to the minute, hour, day, or month.

Let's look at some sample code (datecompare.cfm):

```
<cfloop from="1" to="#DaysInMonth(Now())#" index="thisDay">
  <cfset tempDate = CreateDate( Year(Now()), Month(Now()), thisDay)>
  <cfoutput>#thisDay#: #DateCompare( tempDate, Now(), "d")#<br></cfoutput>
</cfloop>
```

This listing loops from 1 through the number of days in the current month. For each day, it checks to see how that particular day compares to the current day. If the current day of the month is greater than the #tempDate#, the page will display −1. If the two days match, the code will display 0, and if the current day is less than #tempDate#, it outputs "1."

#DateAdd(datepart, number, date)#

This function is responsible for adding time to an existing date. The datepart attribute tells ColdFusion whether you want to add seconds, minutes, hours, days, etc. to the specified date. The number argument tells ColdFusion how many seconds/minutes/hours of time you want to add (or subtract) from the specified date. If you specify a positive number, ColdFusion will add time. If you specify a negative number, ColdFusion will subtract time from the specified date.

Type the following code into Dreamweaver (dateadd.cfm):

```
<cfset nextMonth = DateAdd("m", 1, Now() )>
<cfoutput>#DateFormat( nextMonth, "mmmm yyyy" )#</cfoutput>
```

Save the file and view it in a web browser, and you should see an output similar to "February 2003," which will be one month in the future. The possible datepart options are similar to those found in #DatePart()#:

- yyyy: year

- q: quarter

- m: month

- y: day of year

- d: day

- w: weekday

- ww: week

- h: hour

- n: minute

- s: second

Now let's look at a more complicated example. Open Dreamweaver and enter the following code into a new file (dateadd2.cfm):

```
<cfparam name="Url.date" default="#Now()#" type="date">
<cfset firstOfMonth = CreateDate( Year(Url.date), Month(Url.date), 1)>
<cfoutput>
  <table>
    <tr>
      <td colspan="2" nowrap>#DateFormat( Url.date, "mmmm yyyy" )#</td>
    </tr>
    <cfloop from="1" to="#DaysInMonth( Url.date )#" index="thisDay">
      <cfset tempDate = DateAdd("d", thisDay-1, firstOfMonth)>
      <tr>
        <td>#DateFormat(tempDate, "dddd")#</td>
        <td>#thisDay#</td>
      </tr>
    </cfloop>
  </table>
</cfoutput>
```

This listing is a revised version of a previous example, calendar.cfm. We're now using #DateAdd()# instead of #CreateDate()#, and #DateFormat()# instead of #MonthAsString()#. The #DateFormat()# function makes it much easier to format dates, and we no longer have to nest as many functions to achieve the same result.

#DateDiff(datepart, date, date)#

The final function we're going to look at in this category is #DateDiff()#, which takes three arguments (a datepart, and two dates to compare). #DateDiff()# returns an integer representing the number of units that the dates differ by. Refer to the following list for valid datepart values:

- yyyy: year

- q: quarter

- m: month

- y: day of year

- d: day

- w: weekday

- ww: week

- h: hour

- n: minute

- s: second

Create a new file in Dreamweaver and type in the following code (datediff.cfm):

```
<cfset Christmas = CreateDate(2003, 12, 25)>
<cfoutput>#DateFormat( Christmas, "mmm d, yyyy" )# is➥
#DateDiff("d", Now(), Christmas)# days away.</cfoutput>
```

The preceding example creates a new date, #Christmas#, then calculates the number of days between today and #Christmas#. When you test the code, you should see an output similar to "Dec 25, 2003 is 306 days away."

This function is very useful when creating an accounting system or a project management system and you need to calculate how many days it is until (or since) your deadlines.

Summary

We have covered many tags in this chapter. You should now understand the difference between CFML tags and functions. You should also have an understanding of the differences between the different variable scopes and what a "persistent" variable is. You should also be familiar with the different data types and how each differs.

Although this list of ColdFusion functions is by no means exhaustive, it covers a fair number of common functions. We'll cover more functions in the upcoming chapters, as well as how to write custom UDFs. Here we covered:

- Array functions

- String manipulation functions

- Date and time functions

The next chapter focuses on form processing, how to effectively use the various ColdFusion form tags, and writing code to validate user input before inserting data into a database.

CHAPTER 5

Form Processing

IN THIS CHAPTER we explore and explain how to build and use forms within ColdFusion. We also cover how to upload files to the server, send e-mails using ColdFusion, add security to applications, and use basic data validation (along with Dreamweaver server behaviors) to generate applications quickly and easily.

This chapter and Chapter 6 are closely linked; here, we focus on the basics of forms and how to use them. In Chapter 6, we expand on this knowledge and explain how to take data from these forms and use them with databases so you can insert, update, delete, and search data.

Building forms to collect user data is fine, but CFML and web programming become much more powerful when you use SQL to store that collected data. The data is inserted into a database and can be retrieved later so that users can log in to a web site, create articles or news updates, or upload files to an image gallery.

Getting Started with Form Processing

Let's begin the discussion on form processing with a simple example. In this exercise, we explain how to refer to form variables and loop over all fields within a form.

To start, create a new file in Dreamweaver called form.cfm and enter the following code into the document window:

```
<form action="submit.cfm" method="post">
  <input type="text" name="EmailAddress">
  <input type="submit" value="send">
</form>
```

After entering this code, create a new document called submit.cfm and save it in the same directory as form.cfm. Enter the following code into this document:

```
<cfoutput>#Form.EmailAddress#</cfoutput>
```

View the form.cfm template in a web browser and enter an e-mail address into the text field. After you click the Submit button, you will see the e-mail address you entered as output in the browser window, as shown in Figure 5-1.

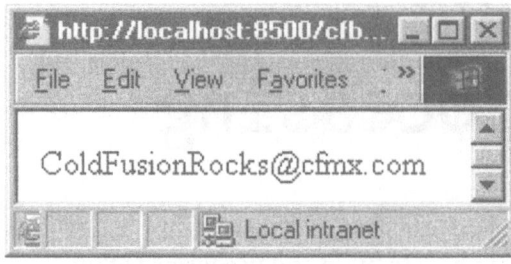

Figure 5-1. Form submission output in the target page

Although this is a very simple demonstration of forms, it would be quite easy to extend this example and add form validation and database interaction on the action page. If you don't know exactly which form variables will be passed to the ColdFusion template, you can use the <cfdump> tag to output the entire form structure. The <cfdump> tag is covered in more detail in Chapter 8.

Return to the submit.cfm template created in the previous example and add the following line of code:

```
<cfdump var="#Form#">
```

View the form.cfm template again, and enter some text into the text input field. Click the Submit button, and now you will see the output shown in Figure 5-2 in the browser window.

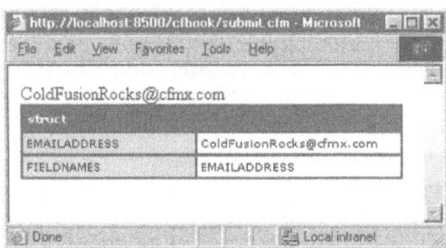

Figure 5-2. Displaying the variables passed to the target page and the text submitted

Notice that two form variables are present even though only a single form field was passed. ColdFusion automatically creates a second variable called #Form.FieldNames#, which is a comma-separated list of field names.

Also notice that #Form.FieldNames# has a value of EMAILADDRESS. If you passed two form variables, called #Form.EmailAddress# and #Form.Password#, then the value of #Form.FieldNames# would be EMAILADDRESS, PASSWORD. You can use this variable to loop through each field in the form.

Clear the contents of submit.cfm and enter the following code:

```
<cfoutput>
  <cfloop list = "#Form.FieldNames#" index = "thisField">
    #thisField#: #Form[ thisField ]#<br />
  </cfloop>
</cfoutput>
```

This code will generate the following output shown in Figure 5-3.

Figure 5-3. Looping through and outputting the field names and values in the form

The previous script loops through each of the fields passed to that template. For each field, it simply outputs the field name and then the value of that field. Instead of typing #Form.EmailAddress#, use array notation to get the value of that form field. #Form.EmailAddress# is the same as referring to it as #Form['EmailAddress']#, although using array notation allows you to get the values of dynamic variables.

You could have looped over the #Form# structure, using a collection loop as discussed in Chapter 3. Here's an example of this code (collectionloop.cfm):

```
<cfoutput>
  <cfloop collection = "#Form#" item = "thisField">
    #thisField#: #Form[ thisField ]#<br />
  </cfloop>
</cfoutput>
```

Notice that this code is almost identical to the list loop shown earlier. The only difference in the code is the syntax of the <cfloop> tag. The collection loop example gives a slightly different output, as shown in Figure 5-4.

Figure 5-4. Outputting form field information via a collection loop gives slightly different results.

When you use the collection loop, it also displays the #Form.FieldNames# variable in the output.

Probably the most important aspect of working with forms is to validate the data and make sure that the proper fields are filled with the expected data types. If a user enters text into a field where you expected a number, ColdFusion will generate an error when you try to perform a calculation or insert the data into a database. Unless you check that the user is providing valid data, you will become frustrated when the application frequently generates errors and the database is filled with bad records.

We will now look at implementing server-side form validation using hidden form fields (we first looked at validation using <cfform> back in Chapter 3).

Server-Side Validation

Open the form.cfm file and change the contents of this file to the following:

```
<form action="submit.cfm" method="post">
  <input type="text" name="EmailAddress">
  <input type="hidden" name="EmailAddress_required">
  <input type="submit" value="send">
</form>
```

Notice that now you have a second form field called EmailAddress_required, which is a hidden form field. If you view this file in the browser, it will look the same as it did before, but now when you submit the form without entering a value in the text field, you will see the error message shown in Figure 5-5.

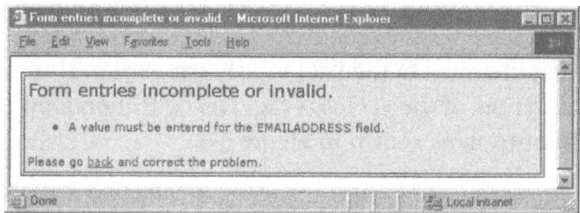

Figure 5-5. Now an error message appears if you don't enter a value into the form before submission; you have made the form field "required."

By simply adding this hidden form field, you prevent users from proceeding to the next page unless they have filled out the required field. The one bonus that this code has over the <cfform> tag is that it doesn't use JavaScript, which can be disabled on the client's browser. Perhaps the biggest drawback of this code is that sometimes, when users click on the Back button after not filling out the fields properly, they will lose any data that they have typed in. For this reason, hidden form fields can be a cumbersome solution if you have long registration forms and don't want to risk having users lose any information that they've already entered.

Let's look at how this code works and what other types of validation exist. Looking at the preceding code, you can see that the text field is EmailAddress, and the hidden field is EmailAddress_required. ColdFusion can tell which field is mandatory by looking for _required at the end of the field name. We also set the input type to hidden, so that adding the validation does not spoil the look of our form.

If you omit the value attribute in the hidden field, ColdFusion creates a default error message that says a value must be entered for the EMAILADDRESS field. By entering a value in the EmailAddress_required field, you can customize the text in the error message and make it more user-friendly, as follows:

```
<form action="submit.cfm" method="post">
  <input type="text" name="EmailAddress">
  <input type="hidden" name="EmailAddress_required"➥
          value="Please enter an e-mail address.">
  <input type="submit" value="send">
</form>
```

Validation types other than _required are available, as you can see in the following complete list:

- _date: Verifies that the user has entered a date. Most date formats are recognized by ColdFusion, such as mm/dd/yyyy.

- _eurodate: Same as validation for _date, except that it allows the user to enter a number in the European format, dd/mm/yyyy.

- _float: If the user does not enter a numerical value, ColdFusion displays a message prompting the user to return to the previous page and enter a number for that field.

- _integer: Same as the validation for _float, except that if the user enters a number with decimal places, the number automatically will be rounded to an integer.

- _range: Verifies that a number falls within a certain minimum and maximum range.

- _required: If a user does not enter a value for this field, ColdFusion displays a message after the form is submitted, prompting the user to return to the previous page and fill out that field.

- _time: Similar to the validation for _date, except that the user must enter a valid time in the text field; examples of valid time formats include 4:30, 16:40, or even 5:17 PM.

Let's quickly open Dreamweaver and look at another example. Begin by creating a new file called age.cfm, and enter in the following:

```
<form action="submitage.cfm" method="post">
  Age:
  <input type="text" name="age">
  <input type="hidden" name="age_required"➥
    value="Please enter your age.">
  <input type="hidden" name="age_integer"➥
    value="Age must be an integer between 18 and 75">
  <input type="hidden" name="age_range" value="Min = 18, Max = 75">
  <input type="submit" value="send">
</form>
```

This example demonstrates usage of _required, _integer, and _range; if you were to submit this form without entering an integer from 18 to 75, an error would be thrown.

Using this type of server-side validation is quick and easy, although you usually would want to do client-side validation using JavaScript as well. Using client-side validation means that (as long as the user has JavaScript enabled) the data is validated using JavaScript before the form is even submitted to the server. This is good: any submission errors you can catch on the client-side are a bonus, because server-side validation requires round-trips to the server, which is time- and resource-intensive.

Back in Chapter 3, we explained how to add JavaScript validation to forms by using the <cfform> tag. Adding validation was as simple as changing the <form> tag into a <cfform> tag, and the <input> tags into <cfinput> tags. Everything else was pretty much identical.

Adding Client and Server-Side Validation

In the following exercise, we explain how to add server-side and client-side validation by using <cfform> and hidden _required fields. Open Dreamweaver, create a new page named register.cfm, and enter the following code:

```
<cfform action="doRegister.cfm" method="post">
  <table>
    <tr>
      <td>Name</td>
      <td>
        <cfinput type="text" name="Name" required="yes"➡
          message="Please enter your name.">
      </td>
    </tr>
    <tr>
      <td>Email</td>
      <td>
        <cfinput type="text" name="Email" required="yes"➡
          message="Please enter your e-mail address.">
      </td>
    </tr>
    <tr>
      <td>Birthdate</td>
      <td>
        <cfinput type="text" name="Birthdate" required="yes"➡
          validate="date" message="Please enter your birth date.">
      </td>
    </tr>
    <tr>
      <td colspan="2">
        <input type="submit" value="Register">
        <input type="hidden" name="Name_required"➡
          value="Please enter your name.">
        <input type="hidden" name="Email_required"➡
          value="Please enter your email address.">
        <input type="hidden" name="Birthdate_required"➡
          value="Please enter your birthdate.">
        <input type="hidden" name="Birthdate_date"➡
          value="Birth date must be a valid date."></td>
    </tr>
  </table>
</cfform>
```

Notice that this time you are using the <cfform> and <cfinput> tags, which allow you to incorporate client-side validation easily by using JavaScript. By simply setting an attribute to required and setting the error message text in the <cfinput> tag, ColdFusion automatically creates all the required JavaScript to make sure the field is filled out correctly.

Next, create a template called doRegister.cfm to output all the form variables by using the following code:

```
<cfdump var="#Form#">
```

Run the register.cfm page in a web browser and enter some information into the Name, Email, and Birthdate fields. Note that the birthdate value must be formatted this way: MM/DD/YYYY. If you filled in all three fields properly, the output will be similar to Figure 5-6.

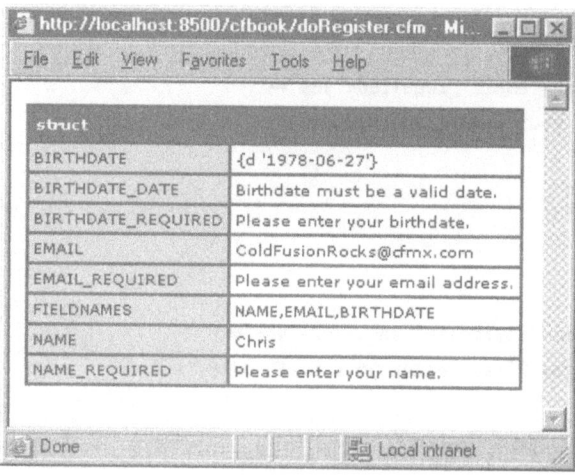

Figure 5-6. The screen dump of all our form variables from register.cfm

Click the browser's Back button and enter some bad data by either leaving one of the fields blank or by entering a name in the Birthdate field. If you have JavaScript enabled, you will see a JavaScript alert box prompting you to enter valid data. As long as JavaScript is enabled, users will not be able to submit the form until the data is of the correct data type and the required fields are filled. If they have disabled JavaScript, they will be able to submit the form at any point. However, if the data is invalid, a server-side error message saying "Form entries incomplete or invalid" is displayed.

To test this, disable JavaScript in your browser and try filling out the form. For example, in Internet Explorer 6, click Tools ➤ Internet Options, which is at the bottom of the menu. In the Internet Options dialog box, click on the Security tab. Select the Local intranet icon from the top and click on the Custom Level button near the bottom of the panel. You will now see the Security Settings dialog box. Scroll almost all the way to the bottom of this window to find a section called Scripting, and disable Active scripting.

Apply the changes, and close the Security Settings and Internet Options dialog boxes. Close all open browser windows and view the registration form in a browser again. This time, you will be able to submit the form without the JavaScript alerts, but if you fill the form fields improperly, you will see the server-side validation and will not be able to proceed until each field is filled out properly.

> **TIP** *After you are finished experimenting with this code and example, don't forget to re-enable your JavaScript!*

You should also provide some data validation on the CFML page to which you are submitting data. This should be done for a few different reasons, the most important of which are security and data integrity. For example, you cannot always be sure that a user has submitted data from the template you created. It is possible to post form variables to another page by using the <cfhtml> tag, or by passing different variables along the Querystring. If you do not validate the data before inserting it into the database, you could allow users to enter invalid data that could be harmful or cause potential errors. Before using any form variables on the doRegister.cfm page, check that they are defined, are not blank, and are of the correct type (strings, numbers, or dates).

To do this, open doRegister.cfm in Dreamweaver and change the existing code to the following:

```
<cfset ErrorMessage = "">
<cfset invalidForm = FALSE>
<cfif (NOT IsDefined("Form.Name")) OR (Len(Trim(Form.Name)) EQ 0) >
  <cfset invalidForm = TRUE>
  <cfset ErrorMessage = ErrorMessage & "Name was not defined, or was blank.<br>">
</cfif>
<cfif (NOT IsDefined("Form.Email")) OR (Len(Trim(Form.Email)) EQ 0) >
  <cfset invalidForm = TRUE>
  <cfset ErrorMessage = ErrorMessage & "Email was not➥
defined, or was blank.<br />">
</cfif>
<cfif (NOT IsDefined("Form.Birthdate")) OR (NOT IsDate(Form.Birthdate)) >
  <cfset invalidForm = TRUE>
  <cfset ErrorMessage = ErrorMessage & "Birthdate was not➥
defined, or was invalid date.<br />">
</cfif>
```

```
<cfif invalidForm>
  <!-- The form is invalid. Display error message here. -->
  <cfoutput>#ErrorMessage#</cfoutput>
<cfelse>
  <!-- The form is valid, begin processing data. -->
  <cfdump var="#Form#">
</cfif>
```

This code goes through the three form fields and makes sure that the variable is defined for each. If the text field is a string, it checks its length. If it is expecting a date, it checks that the variable is a valid date by using the #IsDate()# function. If any of the <cfif> blocks fail, ColdFusion sets a variable called #invalidForm# to TRUE and appends an error message onto the existing #ErrorMessage# variable.

In this code, remember to set the #invalidForm# variable to TRUE without quotes. If you set the variable to TRUE, it would be a string instead of a Boolean value. Acceptable Boolean values are 0 or 1, TRUE or FALSE, and YES or NO.

Finally, check to see if the form's contents were invalid. If so, an error message is displayed in the browser window. If the data is valid, we dump the contents of the #Form# variable to the browser.

To properly test the preceding code, it would be necessary to remove the required, validate, and message attributes from the input fields, then temporarily comment out the validation rules on register.cfm. To do this, simply comment out all the hidden form fields at the bottom of the file.

Creating an E-mail Feedback Form

In this section, we explain how to create an e-mail feedback form. The form is quite similar to the previous examples, and will have input boxes for name, e-mail, and user comments. Let's start creating the form.

1. Create a new file called feedbackForm.cfm and enter the following code:

```
<cfform action = "sendFeedback.cfm" method = "post">
  <table>
    <tr>
      <td colspan = "2"><h1>Feedback Form</h1></td>
    </tr>
    <tr>
      <td>Name:</td>
      <td>
        <cfinput name="Name" type="text" size="32" maxlength="48"➥
          required="yes" message="Please enter your name.">
      </td>
    </tr>
```

```
  <tr>
    <td>Email:</td>
    <td>
      <cfinput type="text" name="Email" size="32"➥
        maxlength="128" required="yes"➥
        message="Please enter your email address.">
    </td>
  </tr>
  <tr>
    <td>Comments:</td>
    <td>
      <textarea name="Comments" cols="24" rows="4" wrap="virtual">
      </textarea>
    </td>
  </tr>
  <tr align="center">
    <td colspan="2"><input type="submit" value="Send Comments"></td>
  </tr>
</table>
</cfform>
```

2. Create another file called sendFeedback.cfm and enter the following code. You may fill in your e-mail address in the <cfmail to="you@yoursite.com" ... > tag.

```
<cfmail to="you@yoursite.com" from="#Form.Email#"
subject="Feedback from the site">
#Form.Name# sent the following comments at #DateFormat( Now(),➥
"mmm d, yyyy")# #TimeFormat( Now(), "h:mm tt")#;
#Form.Comments#
</cfmail>
<cflocation url="thankYou.cfm">
```

3. Create a third file called thankYou.cfm and enter the following code:

```
<p>Thank you for your comments.</p>
```

Now that you've finished typing in the code for the three files, let's point a browser to the feedbackForm.cfm file to view the form.

Fill out the form, and with any luck you should see the message: "Thank you for your comments." This usually means that ColdFusion has sent the e-mail you just created and everything worked perfectly. However, ColdFusion does not throw error messages if the user's e-mail address doesn't exist. Nor does it always throw errors if it was unable to find the outgoing SMTP mail server. The users are just directed to the thankYou.cfm page, and they think that the whole process completed without incident.

This process may have failed in a few places, however. If you changed the To address in the <cfmail> tag of the sendFeedback.cfm page to your own e-mail address, but haven't received the e-mail even after a couple minutes, the mail may have been marked "undeliverable" by the ColdFusion Server. This could be because you entered a bad e-mail address in the Email text input field, or else ColdFusion was unable to locate the SMTP server. Also, the SMTP server could be experiencing delays. In this case, you may see the error message in Figure 5-7.

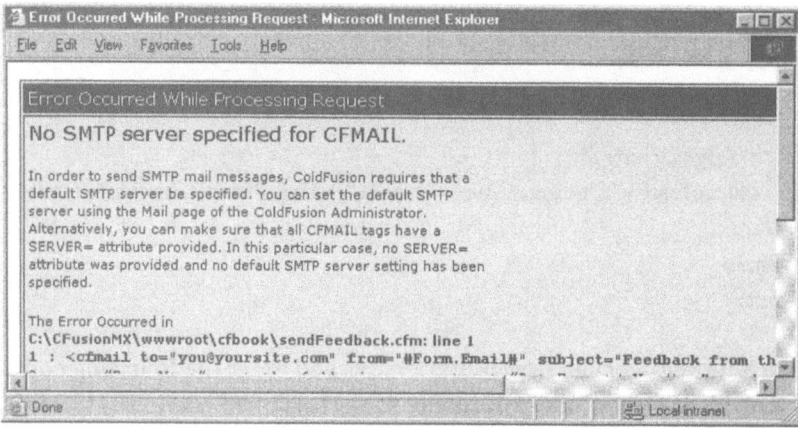

Figure 5-7. The error message generated if ColdFusion has difficulties locating the SMTP server

This means that we haven't provided an SMTP server in the <cfmail> tag or in the ColdFusion Administrator. It is best to set this variable in the ColdFusion Administrator web site. Even though it is quicker and easier, in the short term, to set the attribute in the <cfmail> tag, you would have to explicitly set it every time you wanted to send an e-mail by using <cfmail>. More importantly, if your server changed in the future, you would need to change the server details in every page that uses the <cfmail> tag.

Open a web browser and go to http://localhost:8500/CFIDE/administrator/. You may need to modify this URL based on your specific installation settings (such as a different port number) and whether you're running ColdFusion on your local machine or on a remote machine. Once the admin login page appears, enter your password and click on Login. Under the SERVER SETTINGS section on the left, click on Mail to get the screen shown in Figure 5-8 (for brevity, not all is shown here).

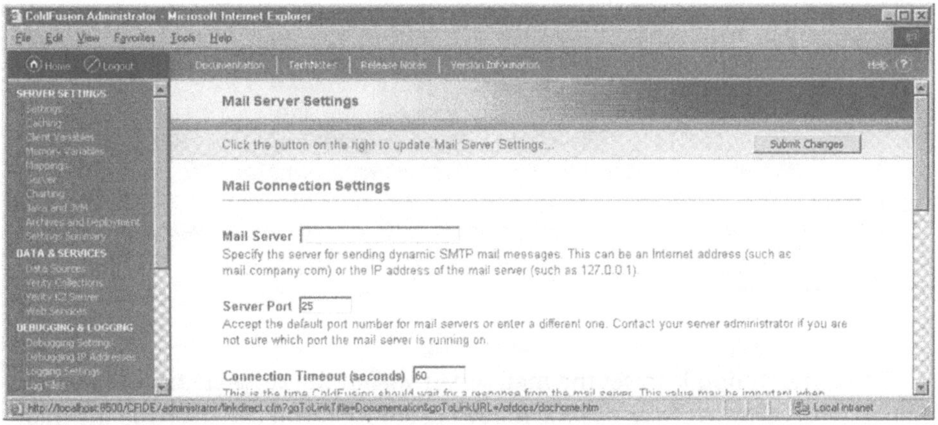

Figure 5-8. The ColdFusion Administrator Mail Server Settings screen

Defining the mail server is as simple as entering a value in the Mail Server text input box—enter your mail server now, if you have one. You can enter either an IP address for the mail server, or a domain name such as mail.yoursite.com. It's useful to check the Verify Mail Server Connection checkbox. Now submit this form by clicking the Submit Changes button, and ColdFusion will verify that it can connect to the mail server you specified.

> **TIP** *If you are not sure what to enter for your mail server address, try using the SMTP server for your mail account in Outlook Express, Eudora, Netscape Mail, etc. If none of these settings works, try entering **127.0.0.1**. This will work if an SMTP mail server is installed on your ColdFusion server machine. As a last option, you could ask your network administrator or ISP. If you are running IIS, you can also install the built-in IIS SMTP server.*

If you checked the Verify Mail Server Connection checkbox, ColdFusion will display "Connection Verification Successful" at the top of the page if it was able to connect to your mail server. Otherwise, it will display "Connection Verification Failed!" in red text at the top of the page.

NOTE   *If you want to install IIS and the SMTP service, simply go to Windows Control Panel ➤ Add/Remove Programs. Within the Add/Remove Programs dialog box, click on the Add/Remove Windows Components icon from the left side. A new window called the Windows Components Wizard will open. Click on Internet Information Services (IIS) in the Components pane and click the Details button. Make sure that the SMTP Service is checked in the Subcomponents of Internet Information Services (IIS) panel. Finally, click the OK button to return to the previous window, and click on Next to begin the installation.*

The other option is to set the mail server within the `<cfmail>` tag itself. If you change `sendFeedback.cfm` to use the following snippet, you can override the mail server setting in the Administrator. To do this, use this value instead:

```
<cfmail to="you@yoursite.com" from="#Form.Email#"➥
  subject="Feedback from the site" server="mail.yoursite.com">
```

Remember to set the To address to your actual e-mail address so you can test whether the mail server is relaying messages properly.

Try using the feedback form a couple times to see if you receive an e-mail. If you don't, look for the messages within the ColdFusion directories and see if they were undeliverable or are still in the mail queue. This is discussed in the next section.

If you are using your ISP's mail server, it is important to note that not all ISPs allow you to relay messages if the sending address is not one they recognize.

Debugging `<cfmail>`

To check the mail folder for unsent messages, navigate to the ColdFusion installation directory (the default is `C:\CFusionMX\`) and open the Mail folder. You should now see two subfolders: Spool and Undelivr.

- Spool: Similar to the "Outbox" in an e-mail client, this folder holds the messages not yet sent by ColdFusion. Messages are temporarily spooled and sent out at a regular interval (default is 15 seconds, but this value can be changed in the Mail Server page in the ColdFusion Administrator).

- Undelivr: This folder holds messages unsuccessfully sent from the Spool folder. If you see a message in the Undelivr folder, then it is just that: undelivered. ColdFusion will not try to resend the message once it reaches the Undelivr folder.

If you manually move a file from the Undelivr folder into the Spool folder, ColdFusion will try to resend it. You can view e-mails in the Undelivr folder by opening them in a simple text editor, such as Notepad. Here, you can view the mail server through which you are trying to send; the From and To addresses; the subject and body; and whether it was a text or HTML e-mail.

This helps you debug the application because you can check which e-mails are not being sent because of possibly invalid From or To addresses, or because of an invalid mail server. Or, perhaps the e-mail simply timed out and will be sent if you move it back into the Spool folder.

Another way to debug <cfmail> in your application is to look in the logs folder in the CFusionMX directory. There should be a file in this directory called mail.log, which logs any errors that occurred when trying to send e-mails via ColdFusion. Some of the most common errors are as follows:

- *550 relaying mail to* <domain> *is not allowed*: This error is saying that you are trying to send e-mail via an SMTP server that does not recognize you as an authorized user. You must double-check your mail server settings and make sure you have permission to send mail using this server

- *...was missing server information*: This error message says that you did not provide a server. Typically, you would get this message in the log file if you have not defined a mail server in the ColdFusion Administrator or in the server attribute of the <cfmail> tag.

There is another setting in the Mail section of the ColdFusion Administrator that says "Log all e-mail messages sent by ColdFusion." Enabling this saves the From, To, and Subject to a log file named mailsent.log in the logs folder. You can view these logs in any text editor, such as Notepad.

You can also view the file through the ColdFusion Administrator by using the Log Viewer. This is particularly useful if you are not developing on the same computer that is running ColdFusion, or if you want to sort and filter the data being shown. Log into the ColdFusion Administrator and click on Log Files under the Debugging & Logging section on the left.

This will display a list of log files on the server. You can select the log file you wish to view, archive, delete, or download the log file to your local computer. Click on the name of the log you wish to view. In this case, select mail.log, and you will be taken to the Log Viewer. You can search for log entries by keywords, applications, date, time, or severity by clicking on Launch Filter.

Working with File Uploads

We looked at the <cffile> tag earlier in Chapter 3 and briefly discussed the upload action. You can use this action to upload files from a client's machine onto the server. Unlike some other server-side languages, ColdFusion makes it very simple to do this. However, there are some minor complications, which we discuss in this section.

Let's start by creating a simple file upload application.

1. Open Dreamweaver, create a new file called uploadForm.cfm, and add the following code to it:

```
<form action="doUpload.cfm" method="post" enctype="multipart/form-data">
  <table>
    <tr>
      <td>File</td>
      <td><input type="file" name="file_to_upload"></td>
      <td><input type="submit" value="Upload file"></td>
    </tr>
  </table>
</form>
```

The first complication arises at the very first tag; notice the addition a new attribute, enctype, to the <form> tag. Whenever uploading files, you must set the enctype to multipart/form-data, or the upload will not work, because the web browser will just pass the filename to the action page instead of uploading the file to the server. Also notice that, for the <input type="file">, you are using a regular HTML <input> tag and not a <cfinput>. This is because the <cfinput> tag supports only a few HTML input types, such as Radio, Checkbox, Text, and Password. Other types, such as File, Hidden, Image, Submit, and Reset, are available only when you use the <input> tag.

2. Next, create another file in Dreamweaver named doUpload.cfm and enter the following code:

```
<cfif IsDefined("Form.file_to_upload") AND➡
  Len(Trim(Form.file_to_upload)) GT 0>
  <cffile action="upload" filefield="file_to_upload"➡
    destination="#ExpandPath( '.' )#" nameconflict="makeunique">
  <cfoutput>
    <a href="#cffile.serverfile#">
      click here to download</a>
      this file.
  </cfoutput>
  <cfdump var="#cffile#">
  <cfelse>
    missing parameter, "Form.file_to_upload".
</cfif>
```

This template first checks whether the necessary form field is defined and is not an empty string. This is where the next complication arises. A bug exists in Internet Explorer 5 for Mac; when a Mac user uploads a file, some spaces are automatically appended onto the end of the filename, and an error message is generated. Because the Mac browser is actually appending spaces, you must use not only the #Len()# function, but also the #Trim()# function to remove these spaces. Using only #Len()# would return the length of the string including appended spaces, which could lead to unexpected results.

Now look at the second line of the code. You must be very careful with the filefield attribute. Do not put any pound signs around this variable, because they will cause problems. Most new developers would be tempted to put # signs around file_to_upload in filefield. This would cause the upload to fail, because ColdFusion is looking for the name of the field, not the value. The value of a variable is passed when pound signs are used, and the name of the field is passed when no pound signs are used.

In this example, you are uploading the file to the same directory as the current file, so the #ExpandPath()# function is used. If you wanted to upload to a different directory, you could either enter #ExpandPath('.\downloads\')# to upload into a subfolder called downloads, or you could hardcode the upload path, such as C:\CFusionMX\wwwroot\images\.

Next, the template outputs a link to the file just uploaded to the server, and the name of the file is saved in a variable called #cffile.serverfile#. We have set the nameconflict attribute in the <cffile> tag to makeunique. This ensures that, if a client were to upload a filename that already exists in the destination directory, ColdFusion would create a unique filename for the newly uploaded file. For example, if a user tried to upload a file named cf_logo.gif that already existed in that directory, ColdFusion would rename that file to cf_logo1.gif. To see the name of the file on the user's computer before upload, you could use the variable #cffile.clientfile#.

If you run the uploadForm.cfm template in a web browser, choose an image to upload, and submit the form, the doUpload.cfm template dumps the contents of the #cffile# structure to the browser window, as shown in Figure 5-9.

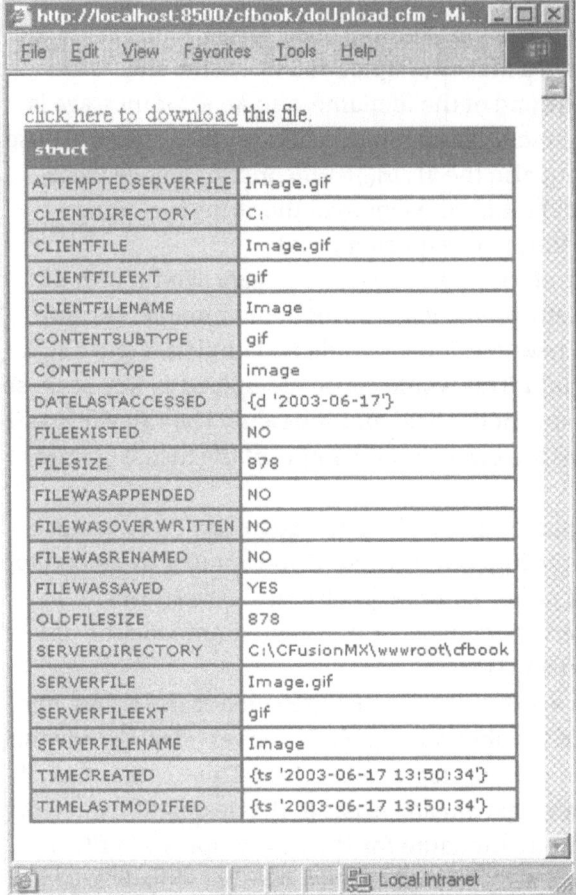

Figure 5-9. The variables available after the upload is complete

This shows all the variables available after the upload is complete. Some of the more useful #cffile# variables are explained further in the following list (for a full list, refer to the documentation):

- clientfile: The name of the file on the client's machine before upload

- clientdirectory: The directory where the user's file was located before upload

- clientfileext: The file extension of the file the user uploaded

- clientfilename: The file name of the file the user uploaded (without extension)

- contenttype: The main content type of the file uploaded

- contentsubtype: The content subtype of the file uploaded

- fileexisted: Whether or not the file name already existed on the server before upload

- filesize: The size of the file in bytes

- filewasoverwritten: Whether or not the file was overwritten (used only if the nameconflict attribute was set to overwrite)

- filewasrenamed: Whether or not the file was renamed after upload

- serverdirectory: The path that the uploaded file was saved to

- serverfile: The name of the file on the server (with file extension)

- serverfileext: The file extension of the file on the server

- serverfilename: The file name of the file on the server (without extension)

So, ColdFusion takes care of most of the hard work involved with file uploading. One limitation of this upload process is that it doesn't upload entire directories to the server. A user would have to manually compress the directory and upload a .zip file, and then the site administrator would have to manually unzip the file (or write a custom tag to do it on the fly using CFML).

Luckily, custom tags that can zip and unzip files are already available at places such as the Macromedia Exchange, which you can find at http://www.macromedia.com/cfusion/exchange/index.cfm?view=sn130.

Uploading Multiple Files with <cffile>

You can upload multiple files by using the same kind of form, but you must be careful, because you must store the values returned by the <cffile> tags. Unless you do this, the values in the #cffile# structure will be overwritten the next time you call <cffile>. Open Dreamweaver, create another new file called uploadForm2.cfm, and add the following code to it:

```
<cfform action="doUpload2.cfm" method="post"
  enctype="multipart/form-data">
  <table>
    <tr>
      <td>Thumbnail image</td>
      <td><input type="file" name="thumbnail_img"></td>
```

```
      </tr>
      <tr>
        <td>Full image</td>
        <td><input type="file" name="full_img"></td>
      </tr>
      <tr align="center">
        <td colspan="2"><input type="submit" value="Upload file"></td>
      </tr>
    </table>
</cfform>
```

Next, add the following to another new file (doUpload2.cfm):

```
<cfif IsDefined("Form.thumbnail_img") AND➥


  Len(Trim(Form.thumbnail_img))>
  <cffile action="upload" filefield="thumbnail_img"➥
    destination="#ExpandPath( '.' )#" nameconflict="makeunique">
    <cfset thumbnail_serverfile = cffile.serverfile>
</cfif>
<cfif IsDefined("Form.full_img") AND Len(Trim(Form.full_img))>
  <cffile action="upload" filefield="full_img"➥
  destination="#ExpandPath( '.' )#" nameconflict="makeunique">
  <cfset full_serverfile = cffile.serverfile>
</cfif>
<cfoutput>
  <cfif IsDefined("thumbnail_serverfile")>
    Thumbnail was uploaded: #thumbnail_serverfile#<br />
  </cfif>
  <cfif IsDefined("full_serverfile")>
    Full was uploaded: #full_serverfile#<br />
  </cfif>
</cfoutput>
```

Most of the code in uploadForm2.cfm is the same as you have seen before. You only added a new <input type="file"> tag and renamed the form fields. You have made some big changes in the doUpload2.cfm file, though. First, you have renamed the fields that you are trying to upload.

> **TIP** *Whenever you change the names of the fields on the form page, you must change the names of the values passed on the action page as well.*

The next change is that you are saving the value of #cffile.serverfile# to a new variable after calling <cffile action = "upload">. If you didn't save the value to a separate variable, the value of #cffile.serverfile# would be overwritten with the new value the next time you called <cffile action = "upload">.

This example is somewhat limited because it only uploads the file to the server. Typically, you would insert this record into a database so that users would be able to search image galleries. You could build a simple gallery by uploading images to the server and saving them into specific directories. You could then use <cfdirectory action = "list"> to list the images within that gallery and display them to a user. However, this would require you to follow a strict naming convention for the images (such as prefixing thumbnails with th_, or saving thumbnails in a directory called thumb and full images in a directory called full) to make it easier for you to code. In the long run, it is much easier to insert the image names into a database.

Forms and Checkboxes

When working with forms on the Web, you often may want to use checkboxes to allow users to select multiple options, or perhaps select a "Remember me" option on a login form. You should know a couple of important things before working with forms and checkboxes. Probably the most important point is that in HTML forms, if you do not check the checkbox, the form field is not passed to the action page.

Before we try to explain this concept, let's look at an example.

1. Open Dreamweaver, create a new file called checkboxes.cfm and enter the following code:

    ```
    <cfform action="doCheckboxes.cfm" method="post">
      Select a color:<br />
      <cfinput type="checkbox" name="color" value="Red">Red<br />
      <cfinput type="checkbox" name="color" value="Green">Green<br />
      <cfinput type="checkbox" name="color" value="Blue">Blue<br />
      <input type="submit" value="giddy up">
    </cfform>
    ```

2. Create another file called doCheckboxes.cfm and type in the following:

    ```
    <cfdump var="#Form#">
    ```

3. View the checkboxes.cfm in your web browser, and you should see a little form similar to the one shown in Figure 5-10.

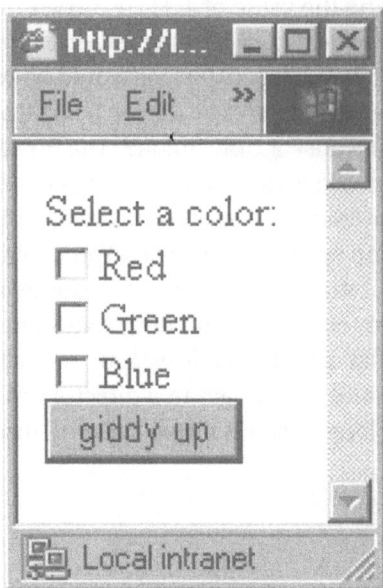

Figure 5-10. A simple form containing checkboxes

4. Make sure that none of the checkboxes is checked, then click on the "giddy up" button. The doCheckboxes.cfm template uses <cfdump> and outputs all the variables in the #Form# scope. Notice that the structure outputted to the screen is actually empty. Because no checkboxes were selected, no values were passed along to the action page. So, if the action page was trying to output the value of #Form.color#, ColdFusion would generate an error because the variable wouldn't exist. You would have to test whether the variable existed by using the #IsDefined()# function, or by using the <cfparam name="Form.color"> tag and setting a default value.

5. Go back to your browser and view the checkboxes.cfm file again. This time, check all checkboxes and click the "giddy up" button. The result should look like Figure 5-11.

   This time, the value of #Form.color# is actually a list of values. When you submit multiple checkboxes (all checkboxes must be given the same name), you get a comma-separated list on the action page. This can cause frustration while programming, because you may be expecting color to equal a single value or a number. If no checkboxes were checked and the form was submitted, no value would be passed to doCheckboxes.cfm, and you would encounter an error if you tried to access the variable. When you use <cfdump> to view the contents of the variable, it generates a list of values you are working with. We could loop through this list of values by using a list loop with the <cfloop> tag, similar to the following snippet:

```
<cfloop list="#Form.color#" index="thisColor">
  <cfoutput>You selected #thisColor#<br /></cfoutput>
</cfloop>
```

The preceding code would output each color checked off in the check-boxes.cfm template on its own separate line. The output would look something like this:

```
You selected Red
You selected Green
You selected Blue
```

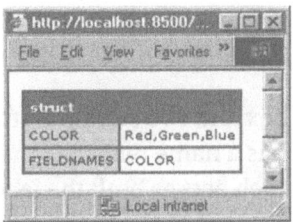

Figure 5-11. Our checkbox form variables

6. Back in the web browser, go to checkboxes.cfm one last time, but this time check only one of the checkboxes and click on the giddy up button. The <cfdump> tag should now output just the value of the one selected checkbox.

The same rules apply to radio buttons. Unless you set an initial value to checked (<input type="radio" name="color" value="Red" checked>), you can still submit the form and have no value defined on the action page (similar to step 4). Likewise, you can select one value and submit the form, and only that one checked value will be passed (similar to step 6).

> **TIP** *The major difference between checkboxes and radio buttons is that with radio buttons, you can select only a maximum of one value from a group; you can select as many (or few) options as you want from a group of checkboxes.*

Multiple Submit Buttons

Another technique developers often use is to have multiple submit buttons for a single form. This allows programmers to reuse certain forms and write a little less code. Let's look at a simple example and discuss one problem that this approach can sometimes introduce.

1. In Dreamweaver, create a new page called multipleSubmit.cfm and enter the following code into it:

```
<table>
  <cfform action="doMultipleSubmit.cfm" method="post">
    <tr>
      <td>Name</td>
      <td><cfinput type="text" name="Name" required="yes"↪
              message="Please enter a name."></td>
      <td><input type="submit" name="submit" value="Search"></td>
      <td><input type="submit" name="submit" value="Create"></td>
    </tr>
  </cfform>
</table>
```

Notice that you have a single text input box and two submit buttons, Search and Create. Each submit button has a name (which is the same for both buttons) and a unique value (which acts as both the label for the submit button and the value that will be passed to the action page). You could also have named your submit buttons different things and used the CFML IsDefined() function to determine which button was pressed.

2. Create a second file called doMultipleSubmit.cfm and enter the following code into it:

```
<cfdump var="#Form#">
  <cfparam name="Form.submit" default="" type="string">
  <cfswitch expression="#Form.submit#">
  <cfcase value="Search">
    You want to search for something or someone.
  </cfcase>
  <cfcase value="Create">
    You want to create something or someone.
  </cfcase>
  <cfdefaultcase>
    I have no idea what to do.
  </cfdefaultcase>
  </cfswitch>
```

The first thing this template does is dump the contents of the #Form# structure. This allows you to see which values are passed from the previous template. Next, you set a default value for #Form.submit# if it isn't currently defined. We'll get back to this bit of code in just a minute. Finally, you use a <cfswitch> block to evaluate the expression and determine which submit button the user clicked (if any).

3. Open the web browser and view the file created in step 1. You will see the screen shown in Figure 5-12.

    Enter a name and click on the Search button. You will be redirected to the doMultipleSubmit.cfm template, and you will see "You want to search for something or someone." and the <cfdump> of the #Form# variables. So far, everything is working as expected.

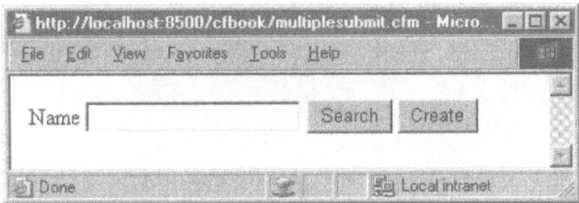

Figure 5-12. The multiple submit button form

4. Click on the Back button in the browser to return to MultipleSubmit.cfm. This time, click the Create button, and you will be redirected to the action page and see the #Form# variables and the text "You want to create something or someone."

5. Return to the previous page one last time. Make sure your cursor is in the text field and press Enter on your keyboard. You will see the dumped form variables as usual, but this time you will also see the text "I have no idea what to do." This is the behavior in Internet Explorer only; browsers such as Safari or Netscape will act as if the Search button was pressed. Because you didn't actually click on one of the submit buttons, no value was passed for #Form.submit#. If you don't have that <cfparam> tag near the beginning of the file, ColdFusion generates an error when it reaches the <cfswitch> tag, because the variable #Form.submit# has not been defined.

> **TIP** *Even though having multiple submit tags can help us write some pretty*
> *interesting code, always remember the following: If users don't click on the*
> *submit button, certain values won't always be passed. You can also run into*
> *the same complications if you use JavaScript to submit the form.*

Using Pre-built Server Behaviors

Dreamweaver offers some very impressive server behaviors that allow developers to create code quickly for common tasks. We are going to look at five server behaviors in this section, most of which can be found in Application ➤ + ➤ Server Behaviors ➤ User Authentication. The behaviors are Log In User, Log Out User, Restrict Access To Page, Check New Username, and Insert Record, as shown in Figure 5-13.

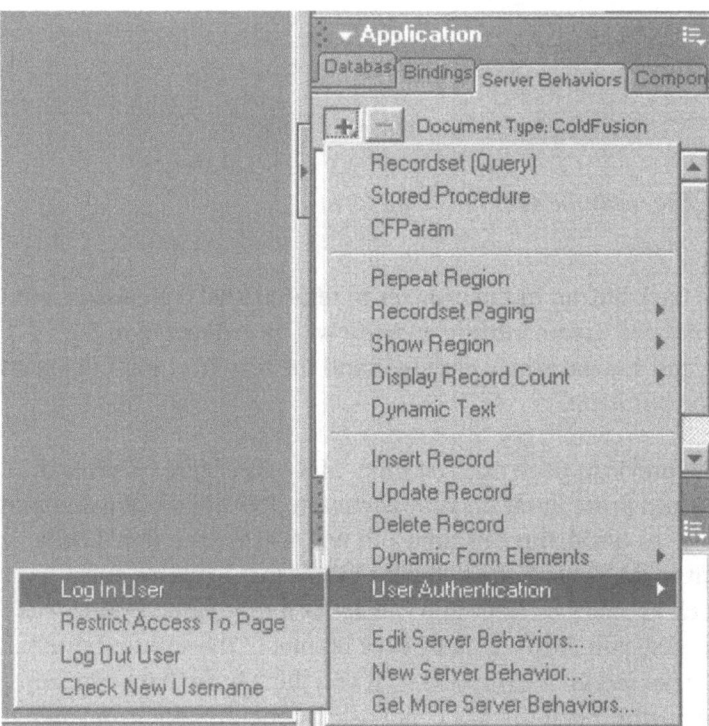

Figure 5-13. The Dreamweaver Application panel showing the User Authentication server behaviors

You are going to create a basic application that allows you to password-protect certain parts of the site so that users must log in before they are able to view those pages. You will also allow users to log out of the application once they've successfully logged in, and you will create a simple page where users can register for the site and enter their names and passwords into a database.

Before getting started, let's set up the folders. In the cfbook site, create a new subfolder called home. Within this directory, create another new subfolder called secured.

Log In User

The first server behavior we examine is the Log In User behavior. Before you can use any server behaviors, make sure that you have completed the five prerequisites (the ones containing links) listed in the server behaviors window, as shown in Figure 5-14.

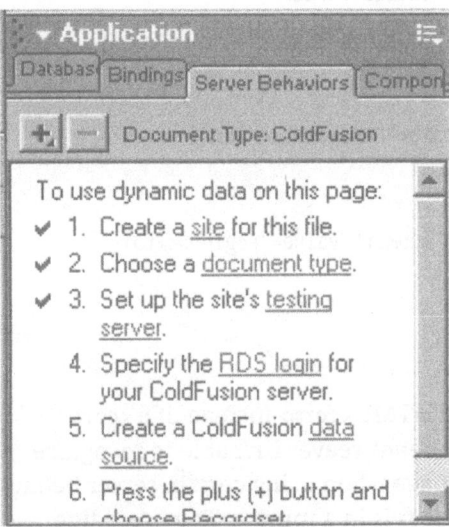

Figure 5-14. The Application panel showing the list of prequisites you must meet before using server behaviors

The RDS login is the one you set for your ColdFusion server when you installed ColdFusion. If you can't remember the password or want to assign a new one, go to the Security section of the ColdFusion Administrator and click on RDS Password, near the bottom. Enter a new password in the New Password text field, and again in the Confirm Password text field.

For the data source, you'll use the same one you set up in Chapter 2. So, before continuing, you should have a data source named CompanyInfo set up for the company.mdb database in the C:\CFusionMX\db\ folder.

When these prerequisites have been met, you can start building your application, as follows:

1. Open Dreamweaver, create a file named index.cfm within the home directory you created, and enter the following code:

```
This is the home page.<br />
<a href="login.cfm">Click here to log in</a>, or <a⟶
href="secured/index.cfm">click here to go to the secure area.</a>
```

2. Create another file named login.cfm in the same folder and enter the following code:

```
<form action="doLogin.cfm" method="post">
  <table>
    <tr>
      <td>User ID</td>
      <td><input type="text" name="UserID"></td>
    </tr>
    <tr>
      <td>Password</td>
      <td><input type="password" name="Password"></td>
    </tr>
    <tr align="center">
      <td colspan="2"><input type="submit" value="Login"></td>
    </tr>
  </table>
</form>
```

Notice that you are using a simple HTML <form> instead of a <cfform> tag. This is because it seems that Dreamweaver isn't able to recognize the <cfform> as a form within the page when using certain server behaviors. We describe how to get around this in a minute. The preceding code simply creates a form with two fields, UserID and Password, and a Submit button. So far, there is no new code at all. You could also add server-side validation and create some hidden variables called UserID_required and Password_required, but keep it simple for now. Also take note of the action attribute in the <form> tag, which is currently going to submit to a page called doLogin.cfm.

3. Within the Server Behaviors panel, select + ➤ User Authentication ➤ Log In User. A Log In User dialog box will open.

4. In the Username text field at the top of this dialog box, make sure that you select UserID, and similarly, select Password for the Password text field. You are telling ColdFusion which form variables you are going to get the username and password from.

5. Next, from the Validate Using Data Source drop-down menu, select the CompanyInfo data source. From the Table drop-down menu, select LoginInfo. This is where you tell ColdFusion which table in the database you want to validate the username and password values against. When you change the table in this drop-down, the values in the Username Column and Password Column change too.

6. From the Username Column drop-down, select UserID, and in the Password Column drop-down, select Password. This is how you tell ColdFusion which columns in the database match the Username Field and Password Field you defined in step 4.

7. In the If Login Succeeds, Go To field, enter **secured/index.cfm** and check the Go To Previous URL (if it exists) checkbox. In the If Login Fails, Go To text field, enter **loginError.cfm**.

8. The Log In User dialog box should now look like Figure 5-15. Click on OK to close this window and return to the document window.

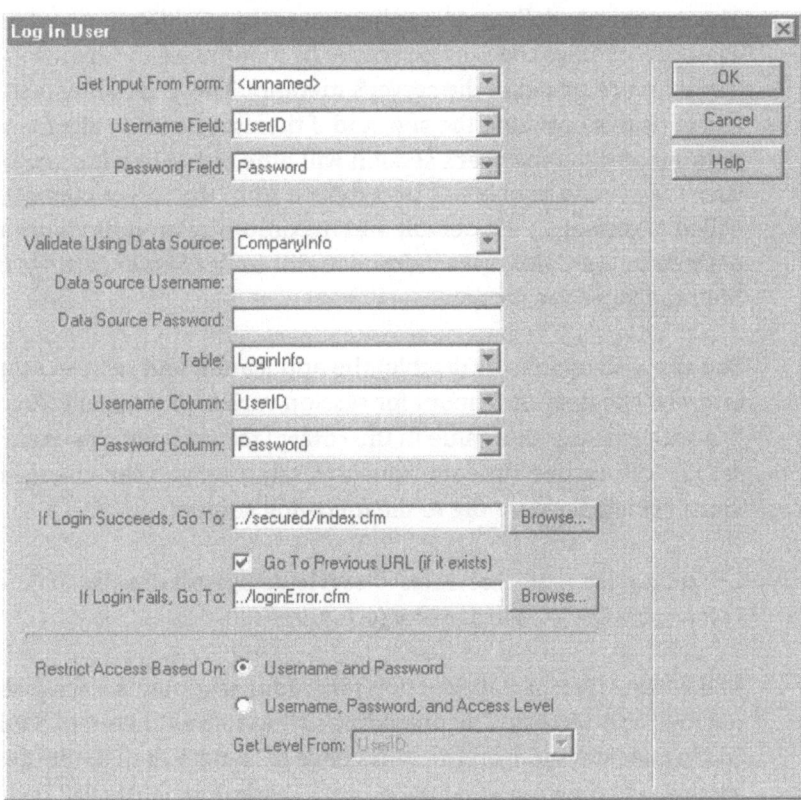

Figure 5-15. The completed Log In User server behavior dialog box

9. Before testing this template in a web browser, you must create the pages defined in step 7. So, within the secured folder, create a file named index.cfm that contains the following code:

```
This is a secured page.<br />
you would put all sorts of secret password protected stuff here.<br />
<a href="logout.cfm">Click here to log out</a>
```

10. Create a template called loginError.cfm in the home folder and enter the following code:

```
Invalid UserID/Password combination. Please try again.<br />
<a href="login.cfm">try again</a>
```

11. Create one last file called Application.cfm within the home folder and enter the following code:

```
<cfapplication name="secureTest" sessionmanagement="yes">
```

This tag simply defines an application within ColdFusion and, in this example, enables the Session scope. As mentioned in Chapter 4, session variables are stored in the server's memory. These variables last as long as the user is browsing the site, and if the user remains idle for a certain amount of time, the user's session will time out. When it times out, the user's session variables will be removed from the server memory. This is called a "timeout"; the default and maximum session timeouts are defined in the ColdFusion Administrator under Server Settings in the Memory Variables section.

You can also enable (or disable) the application and session scopes entirely. The default timeout for session variables is usually 20 minutes, but we can lower this value in the <cfapplication> tag. For example, to set the idle session timeout value to 5 minutes, you can change the previous <cfapplication> tag to the following snippet:

```
<cfapplication name="secureTest" sessionmanagement="yes"➥
sessiontimeout="#CreateTimeSpan(0,0,5,0)#">
```

The #CreateTimeSpan()# function takes four arguments: days, hours, minutes, and seconds. The preceding listing sets a timeout of 5 minutes, so if a user stays idle on the same page for longer than 5 minutes, the session will time out and all the user's session variables will be lost. We'll get back to why you need session variables enabled in a minute.

Now let's examine some of these files more closely. Open the login.cfm template and look at the code that Dreamweaver generated:

```
<cfif IsDefined("FORM.UserID")>
  <cfset MM_redirectLoginSuccess = "secured/index.cfm">
  <cfset MM_redirectLoginFailed = "loginError.cfm">
  <cfquery  name = "MM_rsUser" datasource = "CompanyInfo">
    SELECT UserID,Password
    FROM LoginInfo
    WHERE UserID = '#FORM.UserID#'
    AND Password = '#FORM.Password#'
  </cfquery>
  <cfif MM_rsUser.RecordCount NEQ 0>
    <cftry>
    <cflock scope = "Session" timeout="30" type  ="Exclusive">
      <cfset Session.MM_Username = FORM.UserID>
      <cfset Session.MM_UserAuthorization = "">
    </cflock>
      <cfif IsDefined("URL.accessdenied") AND true>
      <cfset MM_redirectLoginSuccess = URL.accessdenied>
    </cfif>
    <cflocation url = "#MM_redirectLoginSuccess#" addtoken = "no">
    <cfcatch type = "Lock">
      <!--- code for handling timeout of cflock --->
      </cfcatch>
    </cftry>
  </cfif>
  <cflocation url = "#MM_redirectLoginFailed#" addtoken = "no">
<cfelse>
  <cfset MM_LoginAction = CGI.SCRIPT_NAME>
  <cfif CGI.QUERY_STRING NEQ "">
<cfset MM_LoginAction = MM_LoginAction & "?" & CGI.QUERY_STRING>
  </cfif>
</cfif>
```

If you view this page in a browser, the #IsDefined("FORM.UserID")# evaluates to FALSE. ColdFusion evaluates the <cfelse> block and sets a variable called #MM-LoginAction# that contains the value of #CGI.SCRIPT_NAME# (the path and file name of the current template). If any URL variables are in the Querystring (anything after the "?" in the address bar), then you append the Querystring to the #MM_LoginAction# variable. This variable, #MM_LoginAction#, is used here as the "action" URL in the <form> tag.

You were originally going to submit your form information to a page called doLogin.cfm, but if you look at the <form> tag, you see the following:

```
<form action="<cfoutput>#MM_loginAction#</cfoutput>" method="POST">
```

ColdFusion will now submit this page back to itself, and once the form has been submitted, the #IsDefined("FORM.UserID")# will evaluate to TRUE and it will execute the <cfif> block instead of the <cfelse>.

Now, focus on the <cfif> block at the top. ColdFusion creates two new variables, #MM_redirectLoginSuccess# and #MM_redirectLoginFailed#, which hold the two URLs you entered in step 7. Next, ColdFusion executes a query and checks the LoginInfo table for a record with a UserID and Password that match the #Form.UserID# and #Form.Password# variables.

If the query returns no matching records, then you know that a user with the given UserID and Password does not exist. If the query returns more than one record, then you know that a match has been found. Don't worry about understanding all the code generated by Dreamweaver at this point, because we will cover most of these tags in detail later in the book; <cflock> is covered in Chapter 7, and the <cftry> tag is covered in Chapter 8.

Next, two variables are set, #Session.MM_UserName# and #Session. MM_UserAuthorization#. #Session.MM_UserName# holds the value of #Form.UserID#, which was the username that the user logged in with. In the example, #Session. MM_UserAuthorization# is set to an empty string. #Session.MM_UserAuthorization# is used to hold which roles a user belongs to. To use this variable, you must store a list of roles (that this user belongs to) in the database, and you must also set the Restrict Access Based On radio button to Username, Password, and Access Level in the Log In User window (as seen in step 3).

You then check to see if the variable #URL.accessdenied# exists, and if so, you overwrite the value of #MM_redirectLoginSuccess# with this value.

Finally, relocate to the URL defined in the #MM_redirectLoginSuccess# variable. If zero records were returned by the query, the <cfif> block is skipped completely, and you immediately redirect the user to the URL defined in the #MM_redirectLoginFailed# variable.

Testing Your Application So Far

Open the browser and view the index.cfm page. You will see a brief welcome message and two links, as shown in Figure 5-16.

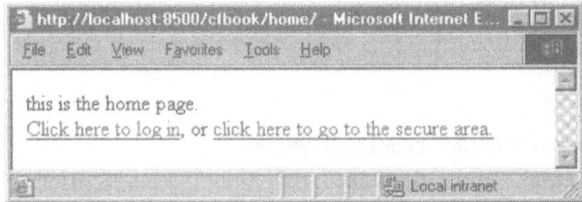

Figure 5-16. The index.cfm page

The first link takes us to a login page where you can enter your username and password, and the second link takes you to the secured area. At this point, you can easily go into the secured area without logging in, but later in this chapter we'll cover securing access to pages by using the Restrict Access To Page server behavior.

Click on the login link to go to login.cfm. Now all you need is a username and password to experiment with; let's get these from the database itself. Back in Dreamweaver, select the Databases tab, navigate to the CompanyInfo data source, and expand the Tables node. Right-click on the LoginInfo table and from the Context menu, select View Data. You will see three records in the database, as shown in Figure 5-17.

View Data			
Record	UserID	Roles	Password
1	BobZ	Employes,Sales	Ads10
2	JaniceF	Contractor,Documentation	Qwer12
3	RandalQ	Employee,Human Resources,Ma...	ImMe

Figure 5-17. The LoginInfo database table showing the accepted username and password combinations

If you enter any of these UserID/Password combinations into the login form, you should be taken to the secured/index.cfm template. If you are taken to the loginError.cfm template, then you have entered an incorrect UserID and/or Password, or you may not have session variables enabled in the <cfapplication> tag in the Application.cfm (as outlined in step 11).

That's all there is to the Log In User server behavior! You learned in step 2 that Dreamweaver doesn't seem to be able to recognize <cfform> as a form on a page, so you have used a simple HTML <form> tag instead.

Note that this is a problem only when you add the server behavior; you can go back and change the <form> into a <cfform> after Dreamweaver has added the code. Open the login.cfm template and change the form to look like the following:

```
<cfform action="#MM_loginAction#" method="POST">
  <table>
    <tr>
      <td>User ID</td>
      <td><cfinput type="text" name="UserID" required="yes"➠
            message="Please enter    your User ID.">
          <input type="hidden" name="UserID_required"➠
            value="Please enter a  User ID."></td>
    </tr>
    <tr>
      <td>Password</td>
      <td><cfinput type="password" name="Password" required="yes"➠
            message="Please enter your Password.">
          <input type="hidden" name="Password_required"➠
            value="Please enter a Password."></td>
    </tr>
    <tr align="center">
      <td colspan="2"><input type="submit" value="Login"></td>
    </tr>
  </table>
</cfform>
```

Notice that you also changed the <input> tags to <cfinput> tags, made them both required, and provided an error message. You also backed up the client-side validation of <cfform> with server-side validation by adding hidden_required fields. The final change you made was to remove the <cfoutput> tags around the #MM_loginAction# in the form's action attribute. The <cfform> tag automatically recognizes the variable as a ColdFusion variable and displays the actual URL. That's it! Again, Dreamweaver did all the hard work, and all you had to do was create a couple of simple pages and fill out some dialog boxes!

It should be mentioned that once you change the <form> tags to <cfform>, Dreamweaver's server behaviors will no longer recognize the code. If you need to edit the behaviors in the future, you will need to temporarily change them back to <form> tags. Let's move on to the Log Out User server behavior.

Logging Out Users

The next step is to allow users to log out once they are finished browsing. We should always give users the ability to log out of an application in case they are using a public computer and don't want other people to view their private information.

1. Open Dreamweaver and create a file named `logout.cfm` within the secured directory.

2. From the Application panel set, select Server Behaviors ➤ + ➤ User Authentication ➤ Log Out User to bring up the Log Out User dialog box.

    If you had a header and footer file, you could add a logout link to one of those that would allow users to log out of the application from any page of the site. However, you will instead include the logout link (pointing to `logout.cfm`) on your `index.cfm` page only. The Log Out User behavior will log out the user automatically when the `logout.cfm` page loads.

    Click on the Page Loads radio button under the Log Out When section. Finally, in the text field beside When Done, Go To, enter **../index.cfm**. This will take you back to the `index.cfm` page in the home directory. You can also create a new page that says "You have been logged out. Thank you!" and give the users a confirmation that they have been logged out of the site.

3. The `logout.cfm` template should now contain the following code:

```
<cftry>
  <cflock scope="Session" type="Exclusive" timeout="30">
    <cfset Session.MM_Username="">
    <cfset Session.MM_UserAuthorization="">
  </cflock>
  <cflocation url="../index.cfm" addtoken="no">
  <cfcatch type="Lock">
    <!--- code for handling timeout of cflock --->
  </cfcatch>
</cftry>
```

This code clears the user's `#Session.MM_Username#` and `#Session.MM_UserAuthorization#` variables. It sets them both to empty strings, then redirects the user to the parent directory's `index.cfm` template.

This is all you need to do to create a logout for an application. In three simple steps, you have managed to create a page that automatically logs a user out of an application. All that remains is to generate some code that will restrict users from viewing a template unless they are logged in. We cover this in the next example, which uses the Restrict Access To Page server behavior.

Restrict Access to a Page

This behavior is used when you are building an administrative section for a web site and want to limit random users from viewing the pages, or you are creating a forum site and want only registered users to be able to post a comment in the forum (hence they have to log in first).

1. In Dreamweaver, open the index.cfm page in the secured folder. Currently, no code restricts users from viewing the page, so any users can view this page if they know the URL. Let's change this. In the Application panel set, select Server Behaviors ➤ + ➤ User Authentication ➤ Restrict Access To Page. A Restrict Access To Page dialog box will open.

2. Leave the Restrict Based On radio button set to Username and Password.

   If you were using roles (otherwise known as Access Levels in Dreamweaver) in this example, you would be able to select the Username, Password, and Access Level radio button and also select which access levels should be able to view this page. (For example, we could build a site where only the sales department is able to view the sales records.)

3. In the If Access Denied, Go To text field, enter the path to the login form. In this case it would be **../login.cfm**. Once you're finished, click the OK button to exit the dialog box.

Dreamweaver has now added 12 lines of code to the secured/index.cfm page, which should look like so:

```
<cflock scope="Session" type="ReadOnly" timeout="30" throwontimeout="no">
  <cfset MM_Username =➡
    Iif(IsDefined("Session.MM_Username"),"Session.MM_Username",DE("")))>
  <cfset MM_UserAuthorization =➡
        Iif(IsDefined("Session.MM_UserAuthorization"),➡
    "Session.MM_UserAuthorization",DE("")))>
</cflock>
<cfif MM_Username EQ "">
  <cfset MM_referer=CGI.SCRIPT_NAME>
  <cfif CGI.QUERY_STRING NEQ "">
    <cfset MM_referer=MM_referer & "?" & CGI.QUERY_STRING>
  </cfif>
  <cfset MM_failureURL="../login.cfm?accessdenied=" &➡
    URLEncodedFormat(MM_referer)>
  <cflocation url="#MM_failureURL#" addtoken="no">
</cfif>
```

First, ColdFusion sets a local variable called #MM_UserName# to either the value of the #Session.MM_UserName# variable or an empty string.

We haven't discussed the #Iif()# function yet. This function allows developers to write <cfif> statements in a shorthand method, but it is generally more confusing and not as efficient as rewriting the code as a <cfif> block. For example:

```
<cfset MM_Username =➡
  Iif(IsDefined("Session.MM_Username"),"Session.MM_Username",DE(""))>
```
is shorthand for:
```
<cfif IsDefined("Session.MM_Username")>
  <cfset MM_Username = Evaluate(Session.MM_Username)>
<cfelse>
  <cfset MM_Username = Evaluate(DE(""))>
</cfif>
```

We can condense five lines of <cfif> code into a single line by using the #Iif()# function, but we'll let you be the judge of which is easier to read and debug. Walking through the code, it is saying "If #Session.MM_Username# is defined, set a local variable, #MM_Username#, to the value of #Session.MM_Username#. If #Session.MM_Username# is *not* defined, set the local variable, #MM_Username#, to an empty string."

The #DE()# function stands for *delay evaluation*; it delays the evaluation of a string until it is passed to the #Evaluate()# function. The #Evaluate()# function is another we haven't covered yet; it is the function responsible for evaluating the value of a variable. Under most circumstances, this function isn't necessary, but if you are trying to evaluate a really complex expression, it is sometimes needed. For example, if you were looping a list of form variables, you could use the #Evaluate()# function to evaluate the value of each variable, as shown in the following snippet:

```
<cfloop list="Username,Password" index="thisField">
  <cfoutput>#thisField# is #Evaluate("Form. "& thisField)#<br /></cfoutput>
</cfloop>
```

This usually isn't as efficient as just treating the #Form# variable as a structure and referring to the variable by using the following syntax:

```
<cfloop list="Username,Password" index="thisField">
  <cfoutput>#thisField# is #Form[ thisField ]#<br /></cfoutput>
</cfloop>
```

This is just a general overview of #Iif()#, #DE()#, and #Evaluate()#. These functions can be substituted for other functions or techniques in most circumstances, but sometimes they are invaluable when handling dynamic data.

Getting back to the code snippet in this step, you are setting local variables for both #MM_Username# and #MM_UserAuthorization#, and then checking to see if the value of #MM_Username# is a blank string, in which case you will execute the <cfif> code block.

The following <cfif> code block sets another local variable named #MM_referer# to the value of #CGI.SCRIPT_NAME#, which is the web path and file name of the current template. If any URL variables are present along with the Querystring, you append those values to the #MM_referer# variable. ColdFusion then sets a new local variable, named #MM_failureURL#, to the value that you supplied in step 2 (In the If Access Denied, Go To text field), appends a URL variable named accessdenied, and finally appends the URL encoded value of MM_referer.

```
<cfif MM_Username EQ "">
  <cfset MM_referer=CGI.SCRIPT_NAME>
  <cfif CGI.QUERY_STRING NEQ "">
    <cfset MM_referer=MM_referer & "?" & CGI.QUERY_STRING>
  </cfif>
  <cfset MM_failureURL="../login.cfm?accessdenied=" &➥
    URLEncodedFormat(MM_referer)>
  <cflocation url="#MM_failureURL#" addtoken="no">
</cfif>
```

Finally, you relocate to the value of the #MM_failureURL# variable, which in this example is the login screen. You also pass a URL variable called #URL.access-denied#, which holds the value of the page the user came from. This allows you to redirect users back to the page that they came from before logging in.

> **NOTE** *It is important to remember that users are redirected only if they are not currently logged in. It is also worth noting that you would have to include this server behavior on each page you wanted to secure. We could also put this server behavior into a separate template and include this template on each page, although this would require that the path to the login page is always the same. Or, you could provide a relative URL to the login form, such as /cfbook/home/login.cfm. The one drawback of including the preceding code is that it will make the server behavior disappear from the server behavior's panel.*

Testing Your Restrict Access Functionality

Fire up the web browser and test this code. Start in the /home/index.cfm page and try viewing the secured content without logging in. You will be redirected to the login screen before you can access the secured content. Once you're logged in, you should also have a login link in the secured area, which you can use to log out.

Even though this is a simple example, you can create multiple pages within the secured area and make sure that each restricts access to the content until the user logs in. The #Url.accessdenied# variable also holds the location the user came from, so if you are trying to access a secured page, you will be redirected to the login form, then sent back to that page once you successfully log in.

That wraps up the Restrict Access To Page server behavior. Now we'll finish off the chapter with a brief walkthrough of two more server behaviors, Insert Record and Check New Username, which will allow you to add new users automatically into the LoginInfo table of the CompanyInfo data source.

Insert Record

In this section, you build a form that will allow users to sign up and add their details to the database. You will do this by using the Insert Record behavior, the nature of which is quite obvious, and the Check New Username behavior, which ensures that two users cannot have the same username in the database. You don't always have to use these two server behaviors together, but they work well for this example.

1. In Dreamweaver, create a new template called register.cfm in the home directory and enter the following code:

```html
<h1>Registration Form</h1>
<form action="" method="post">
  <table>
    <tr>
      <td>User ID</td>
      <td><input type="text" name="UserID"></td>
    </tr>
    <tr>
      <td>Password</td>
      <td><input type="password" name="Password"></td>
    </tr>
    <tr align="center">
      <td colspan="2"><input type="submit" value="Register"></td>
    </tr>
  </table>
</form>
```

This is just a simple two-field form, similar to the login form. For the sake of this example, you're collecting only the UserID and Password. If this were an actual application, you would probably want to collect the user's name, e-mail address, and registration date.

Again, notice that you are using a regular HTML <form> tag instead of <cfform>. Dreamweaver doesn't recognize the <cfform> tag as a form, so you must use a <form> tag while adding the server behavior, then change the code afterward. Also, you have added a text label that says "Registration Form" at the top of the page, because the form looks strikingly similar to the actual login form. An action attribute is not entered in the <form> tag, because Dreamweaver will overwrite the original value anyway.

2. Select Server Behaviors ➤ + ➤ Insert Record. You'll see the Insert Record dialog box.

    Change the Data Source drop-down menu to the CompanyInfo data source. Next, change the table that the data will insert into. Change the value of the Insert Into Table drop-down menu to LoginInfo. The value in the columns text box will change to reflect the change in the database table, as shown in Figure 5-18.
    You need to be concerned about only two columns: UserID and Password. Make sure that the values look as they do in Figure 5-18 and insert a value of login.cfm for the After Inserting, Go To text field. Finally, click the OK button to return to the document window.

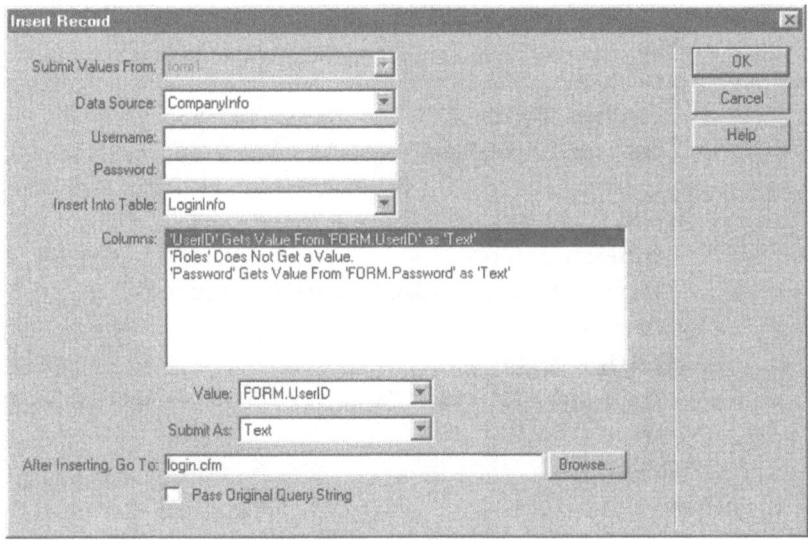

Figure 5-18. The Insert Record dialog box

Dreamweaver has added no fewer than 19 lines of code to our page:

```
<cfset CurrentPage=GetFileFromPath(GetTemplatePath())>
<cfif IsDefined("FORM.MM_InsertRecord") AND➡
  FORM.MM_InsertRecord EQ "form1">
  <cfquery datasource="CompanyInfo">
    INSERT INTO LoginInfo (UserID, Password)
    VALUES (
    <cfif IsDefined("FORM.UserID") AND #FORM.UserID# NEQ "">
      '#FORM.UserID#'
    <cfelse>
      NULL
    </cfif>
      ,
    <cfif IsDefined("FORM.Password") AND #FORM.Password# NEQ "">
      '#FORM.Password#'
    <cfelse>
      NULL
  </cfif>
  )
  </cfquery>
  <cflocation url="login.cfm">
</cfif>
```

First, ColdFusion sets a local variable pointing to the current template, which allows the form to submit itself. Then the code checks to see if a variable named #Form.MM_InsertRecord# has been defined with a value form1, after which it can proceed with inserting the record into the database (this variable was added to the form that you created previously, and it is passed as a hidden variable).

Dreamweaver also changed our <form> tag to the following:

```
<form name="form1" action="<cfoutput>#CurrentPage#</cfoutput>" method="POST">
```

Here you use the #CurrentPage# variable to submit the form back to the original page. The code within the <cfif> block inserts a new record with the supplied #Form.UserID# and #Form.Password#. If either value is blank, ColdFusion inserts a NULL in its place. The NULL has a special meaning in SQL; it means "no value present" rather than a value of zero. This can be a little dangerous when working with registration forms, which hold usernames and passwords; you probably don't want to allow users to have no password or no username. For this reason, it is a good idea to add some client-side and server-side validation to this form so users are not able to register unless they choose a UserID and Password.

After the record is inserted into the database, you redirect the users to the login.cfm template.

This is all you need to insert a record into a database. Next we'll look at the Check New Username server behavior to ensure that users can't have the same login credentials as one another.

Check New Username

The final server behavior we cover in this chapter is Check New Username, which allows you to check whether a username already exists in a database before inserting a new record (it can actually be used to check if any value in a column exists, so it is a very powerful function indeed). Before you can add this server behavior to a template, it is necessary to have already embedded the Insert Record server behavior.

1. Open Dreamweaver and load the register.cfm template created earlier.

2. Select Server Behaviors ➤ + ➤ Select User Authentication ➤ Check New Username. A Check New Username dialog box will open with two form controls. From the drop-down menu, select FORM.UserID and enter **userAlreadyExists.cfm** into the If Already Exists, Go To text field. This defines where ColdFusion will redirect the user if that username already exists in the database. Click OK to return to the document window and see the generated code.

3. Eight lines of code are automatically generated by Dreamweaver and inserted into the document window:

```
<cfif IsDefined("FORM.UserID")>
  <cfquery name="MM_search" datasource="CompanyInfo">
    SELECT UserID
    FROM LoginInfo
    WHERE UserID='#FORM.UserID#'
  </cfquery>
  <cfif MM_search.RecordCount GTE 1>
    <cflocation url="userAlreadyExists.cfm?requsername=#FORM.UserID#"➥
      addtoken="no">
  </cfif>
</cfif>
```

This code appears at the very top of the template and checks whether the variable #Form.UserID# is defined. If the variable hasn't been defined yet, it probably means the form has not been submitted yet. This may happen when you are looking at the form for the first time; in this case, the entire <cfif> block is skipped over. If the variable is defined, execute an SQL query that checks whether any records in the database already have this specific UserID. If the Recordset contains one or more records, then ColdFusion redirects the user to the page that you provided and passes the UserID the user attempted to create as a URL variable called #URL.requsername#.

4. Before you can test this in a browser, you must create a new page called userAlreadyExists.cfm and save it in the same folder as the registration form. Create the file and add the following code:

```
We're sorry, but that UserID,➡
"<cfoutput>#URL.requsername#</cfoutput>", already exists.<br />
Please <a href="register.cfm">try again</a>.
```

5. Once you've saved all of your template, direct a browser window to the register.cfm template in the home directory and create a new user account. Be sure to enter a value for UserID and Password, because there is no client-side or server-side validation (yet). If you submit the form without a UserID, ColdFusion will generate an error. After you've entered a new user or two, try using the same username as an existing user. With a little luck, you should be redirected to your userAlreadyExists.cfm page (where you can always add a little message and link that allows users to try again).

Before closing Dreamweaver, go back to the registration form and add some validation. Change the <form> to a <cfform> and each of the <input> tags to <cfinput> tags. Set both tags to required and supply an error message. Don't forget that when you change the <form> into a <cfform>, you must remove the <cfoutput> tags around the action attribute so that it looks like the following:

```
<cfform name="form1" action="#CurrentPage#" method="POST">
```

As with previous examples, once you change the <form> tags into <cfform>, you will no longer be able to modify the server behavior by double-clicking on its name.

Summary

In this chapter, we looked at many aspects of using forms and ColdFusion. We discussed:

- Client-side and server-side validation

- Sending mail by using the `<cfmail>` tag

- Setting the Mail Settings in the ColdFusion Administrator

- Navigating log files via the ColdFusion directory and the Web

- Navigating the Mail directory to see spooled and undeliverable mail

- Installing SMTP services for those using IIS

You should now have a basic understanding of how to upload files from a user's computer by using the `<cffile action="upload">` tag, and you should also be familiar with how checkboxes and radio buttons perform on the Web. Finally, you saw some of the impressive server behaviors that Dreamweaver provides. These server behaviors allow you to create sites quickly without having to write any CFML code. All you did was create some simple forms and add behavior settings via dialog boxes.

Dreamweaver's server behaviors are very powerful, and they are designed to be generic. Although they allow you to create a working site quickly, they may not always do exactly what you need. Sometimes you will need to modify the generated behavior code to fit your specific needs.

The next chapter focuses on database interaction and storing data collected via forms in a database.

Database Manipulation

IN CHAPTER 2, you learned how to create a data source for an Access database. We also discussed the basic structure of a database, and how to create Recordsets by using the simple and advanced modes in Dreamweaver. Finally, we covered some basic SQL syntax and performed a handful of simple SELECT queries, and provided an overview of INSERT, UPDATE, and DELETE queries.

This chapter goes deeper into the SQL syntax, and you'll create some more complex queries. We also cover how to display query results by using <cfloop> and <cfoutput> and how to page through Recordset results, for example, how to show ten items per page.

Recordsets and Dynamic Tables

As you found out in Chapter 2, creating a Recordset or query to retrieve records from a database is extremely simple, and often you don't need to write any SQL whatsoever. In this chapter, you will build Web interfaces for these Recordsets and use Dreamweaver to generate some code to insert and update some of the records. By letting Dreamweaver do all the hard work, you can have an application up and running in no time.

Let's begin by creating a simple SELECT query to display all the records on the Web.

1. Open Dreamweaver and select the cfbook site. In this, create a new folder named chapter6. Create a new file called viewEmployees.cfm within this folder.

2. In the Application panel, select the Bindings tab, then + ➤ Recordset (Query). The Recordset dialog box will pop up, and you can create the query in either simple or advanced mode. Click on Advanced to give the Recordset a name. You'll be selecting a list of employees, so name the Recordset getEmployees.

3. Select the CompanyInfo data source from the Data Source drop-down menu.

4. Expand the Tables tree at the bottom of the dialog box and highlight the Employee table. Click on the SELECT button on the right to select all columns within this table.

5. Expand the Employee table in the database items section, click on LastName, and click on the ORDER BY button on the right. Then, select FirstName from the database items, and click on the ORDER BY button again.

    Your SQL should now look like this:

    ```
    SELECT *
    FROM Employee
    ORDER BY Employee.LastName, Employee.FirstName
    ```

6. Click on the Test button to view the results of the query. Make sure that the Recordset contains some data. Click on OK twice: once to close the Test SQL Statement dialog box, and again to close the Recordset dialog box.

    Dreamweaver will insert a <cfquery> block in the document window, and SQL statements will be between the <cfquery> and </cfquery>.

7. Go to the Application tab in the Insert bar and click the Dynamic Table button to open the Dynamic Table dialog box. The getEmployees Recordset should be selected automatically. Select the All Records radio button from the Show option and add some padding and spacing, as shown in Figure 6-1.

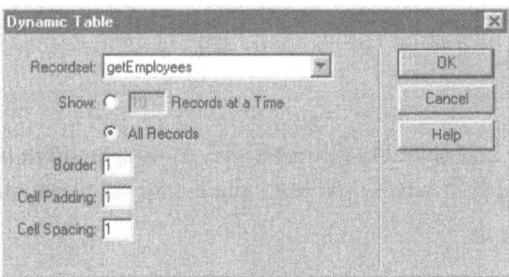

Figure 6-1. The Dynamic Table dialog box

For now, you'll display all records in one long list, but later in this chapter, you'll create a Recordset that pages through results ten records at a time.

Click on OK when you are finished, and Dreamweaver will generate code similar to the following:

```
<table border="1" cellpadding="1" cellspacing="1">
  <tr>
    <td>Emp_ID</td>
    <td>FirstName</td>
    <td>LastName</td>
    <td>Dept_ID</td>
    <td>StartDate</td>
    <td>Salary</td>
    <td>Contract</td>
  </tr>
  <cfoutput query="getEmployees">
  <tr>
    <td>#getEmployees.Emp_ID#</td>
    <td>#getEmployees.FirstName#</td>
    <td>#getEmployees.LastName#</td>
    <td>#getEmployees.Dept_ID#</td>
    <td>#getEmployees.StartDate#</td>
    <td>#getEmployees.Salary#</td>
    <td>#getEmployees.Contract#</td>
  </tr>
  </cfoutput>
</table>
```

Save the file and view the page in your web browser. You will see a table showing all the records sorted by last name.

To format the data between the `<td>` and `</td>`, just highlight the data you want to format and click on the Dynamic Text button in the Application tab of the Insert bar, which brings up the dialog box in Figure 6-2.

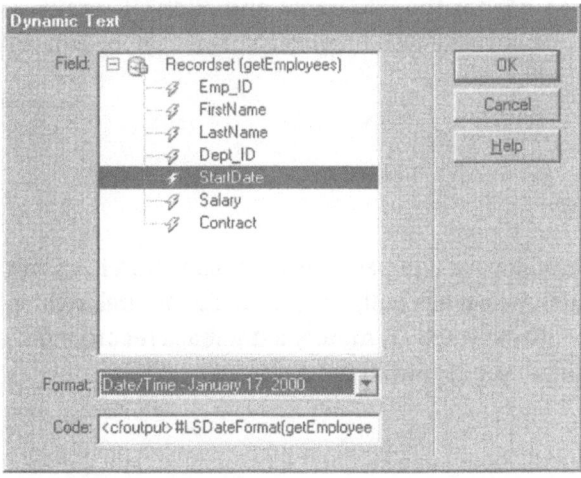

Figure 6-2. The Dynamic Text dialog box

Select the value you want to embed in your code, which in this case is StartDate. In the Format drop-down menu, select any formatting style you want to apply (a date format being appropriate here). The code Dreamweaver generates is shown in the Code text box at the bottom of this dialog box.

You can add custom formatting at any stage.

Adding an Edit Page

Next, you will add another table row and provide a link to an *edit page* (editEmployee.cfm) where users can update the data in the database.

1. After the Contract column at the top of the table, add the following code:

   ```
   <td> </td>
   ```

2. Before the closing </tr> at the bottom of the page, add the following code:

   ```
   <td>
     <a href="editEmployee.cfm?Emp_ID=#getEmployees.Emp_ID#">Edit</a>
   </td>
   ```

This link can also be created through Dreamweaver as follows: add <td>Edit</td> to the page via Design or Code view, then highlight the Edit text. Click the folder icon to the right of the Link text box in the Properties inspector to bring up a file selection dialog box. In this dialog, click the Parameters... button at the bottom right and fill in the name of the URL parameter (Emp_ID) into the Name field. Next, click on the lightning bolt icon that appears and select Emp_ID. Click OK to go back to the file selection dialog box, then enter editEmployee.cfm for the File name and click OK again.

Save the file and view it in your favorite web browser. Notice that an Edit link has been added next to each record.

Building the Edit Page

Now that you have provided a link to your edit page, let's actually build it. In this section, you learn how to use Dreamweaver's built-in Update Record behavior, which automatically builds the form that lets us modify a database record, and creates the SQL necessary to update the record in the database.

1. Begin by creating a new CFML page called editEmployee.cfm in Dreamweaver. Save the file in the same folder as the viewEmployees.cfm page you built in the previous example.

2. Now you need to create a Recordset. Click the Recordset button in the Application tab.

3. Go to the advanced view. Name the Recordset by entering **getEmployee_byEmployeeID** in the Recordset dialog box and choose CompanyInfo as the data source. Enter the following SQL in the SQL text field:

```
SELECT *
FROM Employee
WHERE Employee.Emp_ID = #URL.Emp_ID#
```

The preceding code will return a single record from the database where the employee's ID matches the ID you passed in the URL. Click OK when you're finished to insert the code into the document.

Now you get Dreamweaver to write the entire update form and the SQL to update existing records. Select the Application tab in the Insert bar and click on the Record Update Form Wizard button (located at the extreme right). The Record Update Form dialog box will open, as shown in Figure 6-3.

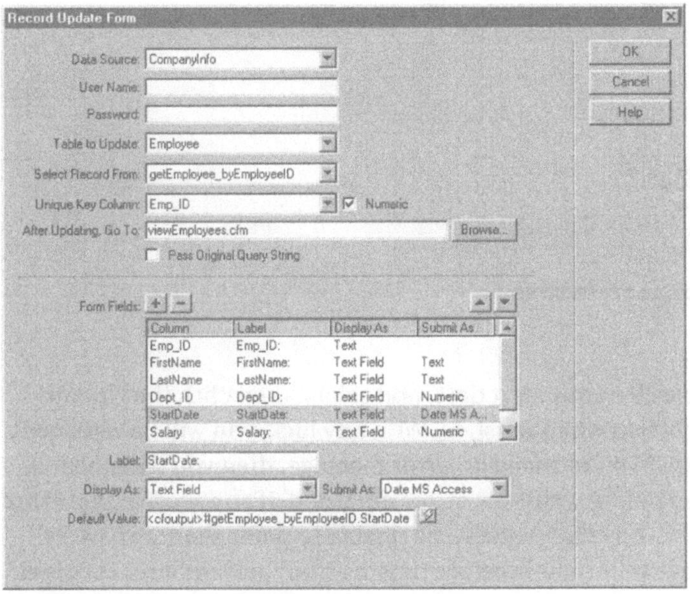

Figure 6-3. The Record Update Form dialog box

From the Data Source drop-down menu, select CompanyInfo, and in the Table to Update drop-down menu, select Employee. From the Select Record From drop-down menu, select getEmployee_byEmployeeID, and in the After Updating, Go To text field, enter **viewEmployees.cfm**.

What does this do? After the record is updated in the database, ColdFusion will redirect you back to the employee list so you can choose a new employee to edit. At the bottom of this dialog box is a list of columns, labels, and data types. These are all used to define how the data appears in the form and how the data is inserted into the database (Text, Numeric, Date, or Checkbox).

Highlight the StartDate column and select Date MS Access from the Submit As drop-down menu. Click OK when you are finished.

Notice that Dreamweaver has generated 82 lines of code. We won't go through it line by line, because it would take too long. The first 43 lines cover updating an existing record in the database after you click the Submit button on the form. The last 39 lines simply display the form that the user will use to modify the record.

Now let's test the page. Open the viewEmployees.cfm file in a web browser and click on the Edit button beside one of the employees. You will be taken to the editEmployee.cfm page, which is similar to Figure 6-4.

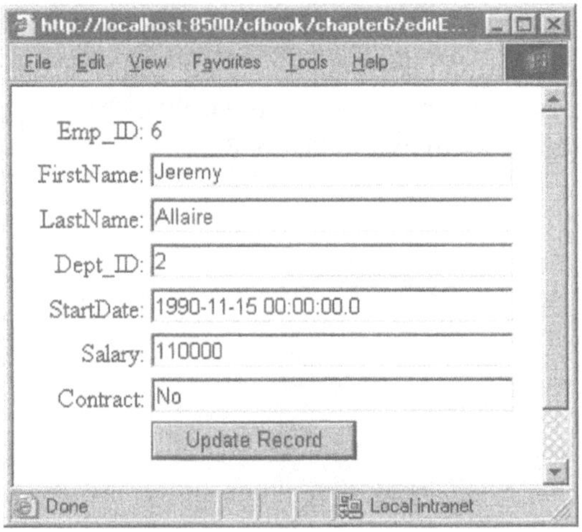

Figure 6-4. The editEmployee.cfm *page*

Change the employee's name, start date, and salary, then click the Update Record button at the bottom when finished. With any luck, you will be returned to the list of employees. If you received an error message, then you will need to roll up your sleeves and debug whatever errors are listed. If you received an error after updating, it's most likely that Access was unable to parse the #StartDate# variable, so you will have to format it before passing it to the database. Let's look at fixing this now.

Switch back to Dreamweaver and look for the following code (which should be around line 23):

```
<cfif IsDefined("FORM.StartDate") AND #FORM.StartDate# NEQ "">
  ###FORM.StartDate###
  <cfelse>
  NULL
</cfif>
```

The error was most probably occurred because Access is struggling to convert the value of ###FORM.StartDate### to a date. You may have to rewrite this in the following way to make the query work properly:

```
<cfif IsDefined("FORM.StartDate") AND #FORM.StartDate# NEQ "">
  #CreateODBCDateTime(FORM.StartDate)#
  <cfelse>
  NULL
</cfif>
```

It isn't always necessary to use the #CreateODBCDateTime()# function when dealing with dates, but it often helps to achieve compatibility with a wider range of date formats.

Save the page and retry editing the employee. If you're still having problems with this page, make sure that the first few lines in the file are as follows:

```
<cfset CurrentPage=GetFileFromPath(GetTemplatePath())>
  cfif IsDefined("FORM.MM_UpdateRecord") AND FORM.MM_UpdateRecord EQ "form1">
  <cfquery datasource="CompanyInfo">
  UPDATE Employee SET FirstName=
```

In some circumstances, Dreamweaver seems to insert the form at the top of the page, which causes errors because ColdFusion is trying to refer to variables that have not been defined yet. The order of the page should be:

```
<cfset CurrentPage= ... >
<cfif IsDefined("...") AND ... >
<cfquery>
UPDATE...
</cfquery>
<cflocation url="...">
</cfif>
<cfquery>
SELECT...
```

```
</cfquery>
<form>
...
</form>
```

Building an Insert Page

Building an insert page is very similar to building the update page—it even includes the same problems. In this example, we are going to extend the employee application and give users the ability to add new employees to the database.

1. Open Dreamweaver and create a new file called addEmployee.cfm in the same folder as the previous two files.

2. One difference between inserting and updating records is that this time you don't need to create a Recordset before beginning, because you are creating a new record. Simply click on the Application tab in the Insert bar, then click on the Record Insertion Form Wizard button. Unsurprisingly, the Record Insertion Form dialog box will open.

3. Most of these settings are similar to the previous example. The Data Source is CompanyInfo, Table is Employee, and in the After Inserting, Go To text field, enter or browse to viewEmployees.cfm, which redirects to the list of employees after you finish inserting a record.

4. In the Form Fields text field, highlight the Emp_ID column and click the minus sign (–) to the right of the Form Fields label to delete it. Because it is an AutoNumber, we don't want to insert a value for Emp_ID, so Access will set a unique value for us. Also, highlight the StartDate column and change the value of Submit As from Text to Date MS Access. Click OK when finished.

To link to this page, open viewEmployees.cfm and include the following code snippet before the </table> tag:

```
<tr>
  <td colspan="8" align="right">
    <a href="addEmployee.cfm">Create new employee</a>
  </td>
</tr>
</table>
```

Notes on Validation

In the past two examples, you haven't performed any sort of data validation to ensure that the data being supplied exists and is the correct data type; these examples were only an overview of using the code that Dreamweaver generates, and how to build applications quickly. Before you put this generated code on a live site, change all the <form> tags to <cfform> tags and set up your client-side JavaScript validation, and include some _required hidden tags for basic server-side validation. You can't always count on users to have JavaScript enabled on their browsers, so you can't rely on only the client-side validation techniques. Also, before using any variables on the page, you should check that the variables exist. Otherwise, the application will throw errors.

In the employee edit form we built previously, check that a #URL.Emp_ID# variable is defined before trying to get its value, and also make sure that it is a numeric value and not a string. This can be done in the following ways. First, you can use the #IsDefined()# function to check that the variable exists. If the variable isn't defined, you should relocate the user back to the viewEmployees.cfm file. You can also check whether a variable is numeric by using the #IsNumeric()# function. This function takes one argument, which is the value you want to check. If the argument is numeric, the function returns TRUE. Otherwise, the function returns FALSE. This code would look similar to the following:

```
<cfif NOT IsDefined("URL.Emp_ID") OR NOT IsNumeric( URL.Emp_ID )>
  <cflocation url="viewEmployees.cfm">
</cfif>
```

Be careful where you place this code. If you put the code at the very beginning of the file, it will be triggered after the user submits the form. Instead of inserting the data into the database, the user will be redirected to the viewEmployees.cfm file. This is because once the form is submitted, the variables will be in the Form scope instead of the URL scope.

To use this snippet, we will need to place it after the initial <cfif> block but before the SELECT query half way down the page. The reason the code will not throw errors in this section of the page is because after you've submitted the form and updated the record in the database, you are already doing a <cflocation> and redirecting to the other page. At this point in the page, you know that if the form is displayed, you haven't already submitted it.

Another method of testing is to use a <cfparam> tag similar to the following:

```
<cfparam name="URL.Emp_ID" type="numeric">
```

This code ensures that a numeric variable is defined, #URL.Emp_ID#. If the variable is not defined or doesn't have a numeric value, an error message will be thrown. Typically, you would want to use this method of testing with a <cftry>/<cfcatch> block, discussed in Chapter 8.

Master Detail Page Set

A master detail page set is a couplet of pages: a list of record summaries or titles containing links for each title (the *master* page) that can be clicked on to bring up full details for each record (the *detail* page). You may also hear master/detail page sets referred to as *Data Drill Down Interfaces*. The two mean the same thing, and offers users an alternative to search forms for navigating your data. For a database table with lots of columns, it isn't sensible to display every row and column on a single page, so this is a much more user-friendly alternative. Let's create one.

1. Open Dreamweaver and create a new page named master.cfm in the same location as the others.

2. Before proceeding, create a Recordset by clicking the Recordset button in the Application tab of the Insert bar. Select Advanced mode, name the Recordset getEmployees, and select CompanyInfo from the Data Source drop-down menu. Enter the following SQL in the SQL box:

```
SELECT *
FROM Employee
ORDER BY Employee.LastName, Employee.FirstName
```

Click on OK when finished to return to the document window.

4. Now, click the Master Detail Page Set button (fifth from the right) in the Application tab of the Insert bar. Clicking this button opens the Master Detail Page Set dialog box shown in Figure 6-5. Here you can define the main master page and the details page.

Let's focus on the master page first. Make sure that the getEmployees Recordset we created in step 2 is selected in the Recordset drop-down menu. You can choose which fields are shown in the master page by using the plus (+) and minus (–) buttons on the right of the Master page fields label. You can also reorder how the fields appear on the master page by using the up and down arrows to the right of the plus and minus buttons. For this example, you are interested only in displaying the FirstName, LastName, and Salary on the master page, so select the other columns (Emp_ID, Dept_ID, StartDate, and Contract) and click the minus button. To remove multiple fields at once, hold down the Shift or Ctrl key while clicking on fields.

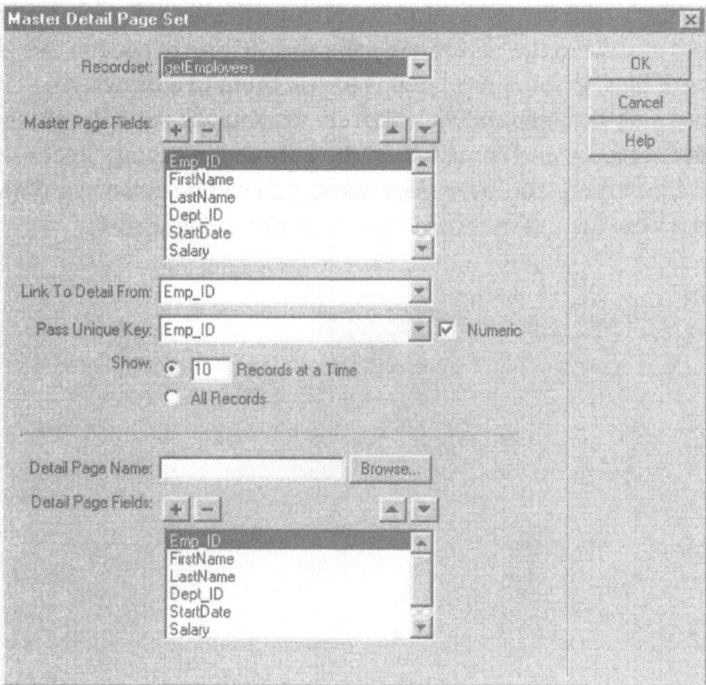

Figure 6-5. The Master Detail Page Set dialog box

5. Next, you must change the order in which the fields appear. Click on the LastName field and click the up arrow button. Change the Link To Detail From drop-down menu to LastName as well. This drop-down menu controls which column in the master page will be hyperlinked to the details page that Dreamweaver will generate after you click on the OK button. Under the Show label are two radio buttons that control how many records are displayed at once on the master page. If you select All Records, ColdFusion will display a list of all the employees in the database (which is similar to the viewEmployees.cfm page that you built earlier). If you select the 10 Records at a Time radio button, ColdFusion will show only ten records on each page and build the "next page/previous page" navigation for you. Select the 10 Records at a Time radio button.

6. Now concentrate on the details page. The bottom half of the Master Detail Page Set dialog box controls the filename of the details page and the text fields that will be displayed. In the Detail Page Name text field, enter **detail.cfm**. Dreamweaver will automatically create this page. Select the fields you want to display and the order in which to display them. You can click the up and down arrows to reorder the fields and the plus and minus buttons to add and remove fields, but leave it as is.

When finished, click the OK button, and Dreamweaver will generate approximately 48 lines of code in the master.cfm page and 36 lines of code in the detail.cfm page. Save both files, and the next step is to test them in a browser.

Open your web browser and view master.cfm. You will see a list of ten employees, Next and Last links, and some text at the bottom left saying "Records 1 to 10 of 19." If you click on an employee's last name, you will be taken to a details page where you can view the entire record. This is shown in Figure 6-6.

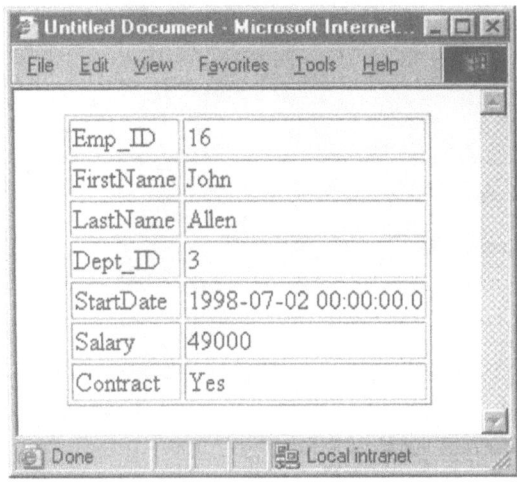

Figure 6-6. The details page

That's it! All you needed to do was create a single Recordset within Dreamweaver and enter some settings into a dialog box. Ideally, you should go back and add some validation to the detail.cfm to make sure the proper URL variables exist prior to being called. You also can format the data in detail.cfm by adding #DateFormat( )# to the StartDate and #DollarFormat( )# to the Salary.

Recordset Paging

You already saw Recordset paging in the previous example, but now we will discuss how to add paging to your existing applications instead of using the prebuilt Master Detail Page Set action. Recordset paging becomes extremely useful when you have a table in a database that contains a large number of records. You certainly wouldn't want to display hundreds of records on a single page and force users to scroll down for miles to find the information they want. Displaying the results in pages makes it easier for users to go through the data quickly, and doesn't force them to download a single large file which could take minutes to render in a browser.

Dreamweaver makes it easy to add Recordset paging by providing a few pre-built server behaviors. The first we look at is Repeat Region. Before you can use Repeat Region (sometimes referred to as Repeated Region), you must set up a Recordset.

1. Create a page called `master2.cfm` in Dreamweaver. This will be similar to the `master.cfm` page you built in the previous example. Create a Recordset named `getEmployees` using the `CompanyInfo` data source. Enter the following SQL into the SQL text field:

    ```
    SELECT Employee.Emp_ID, Employee.FirstName, ➡
    Employee.LastName, Departmt.Dept_Name, Departmt.Location
    FROM Employee, Departmt
    WHERE Departmt.Dept_ID = Employee.Dept_ID
    ORDER BY Employee.LastName, Employee.FirstName
    ```

    This is a simple join between the Employee and Departmt tables.

2. Next, create a region that you want to repeat for each record in the Recordset. Create a simple table with one row and three columns. In the first column, you will display the LastName and FirstName from the Recordset. Position your cursor between the first `<td>` and `</td>` and click on the Dynamic Text button in the Application tab of the Insert bar. The Dynamic Text dialog box will pop up. Simply click on the LastName field within the `getEmployees` Recordset and click on OK.

    Repeat this process again for the FirstName field within the same `<td>`. In the other two columns of the table, enter the Dept_Name and Location columns. Your table code will look like this:

    ```
    <table>
      <tr>
        <td><cfoutput>#getEmployees.LastName#</cfoutput>,
            <cfoutput>#getEmployees.FirstName#</cfoutput></td>
        <td><cfoutput>#getEmployees.Dept_Name#</cfoutput></td>
        <td><cfoutput>#getEmployees.Location#</cfoutput></td>
      </tr>
    </table>
    ```

3. To create a repeated region, highlight the block of code you want to repeat for each record in the Recordset (the code between the `<tr>` tags in this case) and click on the Repeated Region button in the Application tab (fourth button from the left).

From here, you can choose whether to repeat the region for all records within a single page, or page through ten records at a time. Select 10 Records at a Time and click OK. Dreamweaver generates about seven lines of code. If you view the page in a web browser, you will notice that Dreamweaver hasn't yet generated "previous page" and "next page" links.

4. Adding the First, Previous, Next, and Last navigation links is as easy as clicking the Recordset Navigation Bar button in the Application tab (sixth button from the left). The Recordset Navigation Bar dialog box will pop up, and you can choose which Recordset to provide navigation for and whether you want to choose text links or images. If you choose images, Dreamweaver will even create the four images necessary (`First.gif`, `Last.gif`, `Next.gif`, and `Previous.gif`) and copy them to the same directory as your page.

5. Dreamweaver also makes it easy to add navigation status text (for example, Records 1 to 5 of 10) to the page by providing a Recordset Navigation Status behavior. To add this text, click on the Recordset Navigation Status button in the Application tab (sixth from the left) to bring up the Recordset Navigation Status dialog box. Select the Recordset you want to add navigation to, and click on the OK button to embed the code and return to the document window.

Before proceeding to the next section, format the page a little more. In Dreamweaver, you can reorder the HTML tables and use a style sheet to make it look prettier, but what if you want to alternate row colors for the employees? It is actually quite simple. Locate the following snippet of code within the page:

```
<table>
<cfoutput query="getEmployees"➥
  startRow="#StartRow_getEmployees#"➥
  maxRows="#MaxRows_getEmployees#">
  <tr>
    <td>#getEmployees.LastName#, #getEmployees.FirstName#</td>
    <td>#getEmployees.Dept_Name#</td>
    <td>#getEmployees.Location#</td>
  </tr>
</cfoutput>
</table>
```

We will add a `bgcolor` attribute to the opening `<tr>` tag. Change the `<tr>` tag to look like the following:

```
<tr bgcolor="<cfif getEmployees.CurrentRow MOD➥
  2 EQ 0>##EEEEEE<cfelse>##FFFFFF</cfif>">
```

Each time we execute a query, ColdFusion creates three variables for that Recordset: RecordCount, CurrentRow, and ColumnList. You've seen the #RecordCount# variable before; it simply returns the number of records within a resultset. #CurrentRow# tells you which record you are currently looking at within the Recordset. In the preceding code, you are checking the #CurrentRow# while looping over a Recordset, so the value of #CurrentRow# is incremented each time you go through the loop. The final variable, #ColumnList#, returns a comma-separated list of columns within the Recordset object.

To output the value of #getEmployees.ColumnList#, you would have a value of "DEPT_NAME,EMP_ID,FIRSTNAME,LASTNAME,LOCATION" returned. Notice that each column name in the Recordset has been converted to uppercase, and all are sorted alphabetically.

The only other new piece of code in the preceding snippet is the MOD operator, which returns the remainder after dividing two numbers. For example, in this code you are looping over the 19 records in the Employee table. For each record, you check #getEmployees.CurrentRow# (which is an integer from 1 through 19) and return the remainder after dividing that number by 2. This will always return either 0 or 1, so you simply check whether it is 0, and if so, the expression within the <cfif> evaluates to TRUE. In this case, you set the background color to #EEEEEE. Otherwise, the expression evaluates to FALSE, and you use a different color, #FFFFFF.

All the <cfif> tag is saying is "If the #CurrentRow# is even, use color A; otherwise, use color B."

Save your page and view the results in a browser. You will see results similar to Figure 6-7.

Figure 6-7. Our nicely formatted master2.cfm *page, with navigation links and navigation status*

Notice that you have two pound signs (#) before the colors. Because ColdFusion views pound signs as special characters, you must put two together when you want to output a # to the screen. When ColdFusion sees ## within a <cfoutput> tag, it understands that you want to display a pound sign and not a variable. When returning code to the user's browser, ColdFusion automatically will replace the ## with a single #. If there were only a single pound sign before the color, ColdFusion would think that EEEEEE was a variable name and generate an error because there is no closing #, and CF would be unable to find a variable named #EEEEEE#.

Deleting an Employee

Deleting an employee is probably one of the easiest things to code. Dreamweaver has a Delete Record behavior that handles all the work for you.

1. Open Dreamweaver and create a new page called deleteEmployee.cfm in the same location as before.

2. In the Application Panel set, select Server Behaviors ➤ + ➤ Delete Record. This opens the Delete Record dialog box, as shown in Figure 6-8.

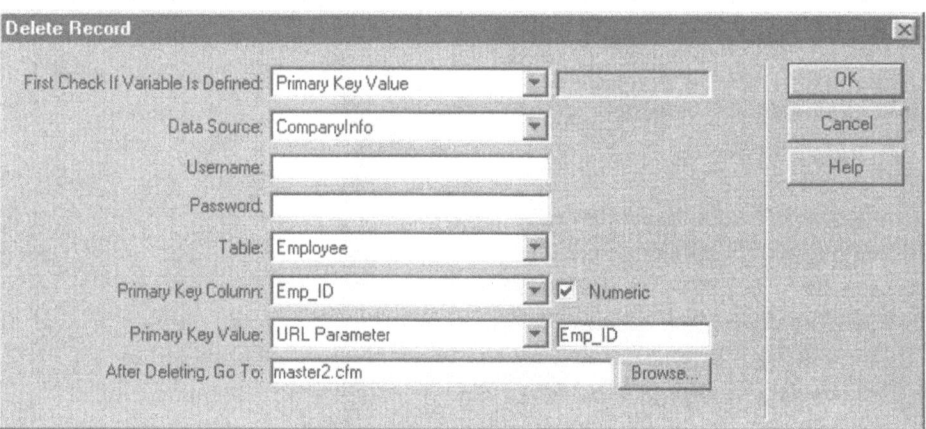

Figure 6-8. The Delete Record dialog box

3. Change the value of the Data Source drop-down menu to CompanyInfo, and for Table select Employee. The only other field you need to modify is the After Deleting, Go To field, which we set to master2.cfm. Click on OK to return to the document window.

The document window will now contain the following code:

```
<cfif IsDefined("URL.Emp_ID") AND #URL.Emp_ID# NEQ "">
  <cfquery datasource="CompanyInfo">
  DELETE FROM Employee WHERE Emp_ID=#URL.Emp_ID#
  </cfquery>
  <cflocation url="master2.cfm">
</cfif>
```

This code checks that a variable named #URL.Emp_ID# exists and isn't an empty string. If this expression evaluates to TRUE, it will delete the employee in the database whose Emp_ID matches the one provided in the URL. Finally, the snippet will redirect the user back to the list of employees.

The only other thing you must do is create a link from the employee list in master2.cfm to the deleteEmployee.cfm page. In master2.cfm, add another column to the table right after <td>#getEmployees.Location#</td>:

```
<td><a href="deleteEmployee.cfm?Emp_ID=#getEmployees.Emp_ID#">Delete</a></td>
```

Save the page and view master2.cfm in a browser. You will see a display similar to Figure 6-9.

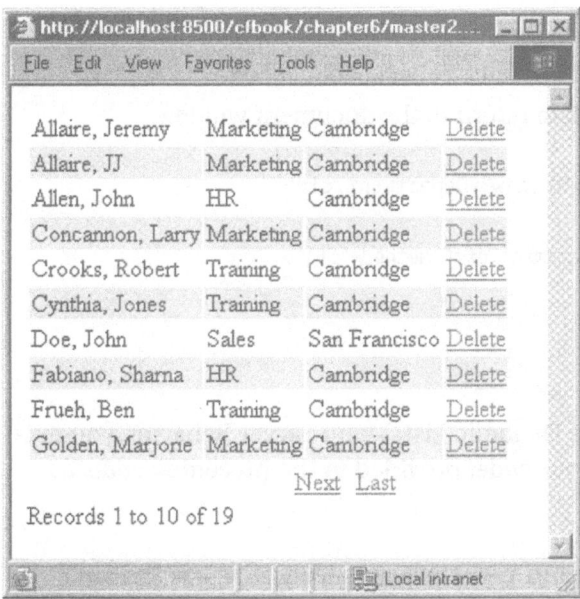

Figure 6-9. The master2.cfm *page with "delete record" links*

If you click on the Delete button to the right of an employee record, you will delete that employee from the database. Be careful, though, because there is no confirmation page or any sort of warning before the record is permanently deleted from the database. This is why it's good idea is to put the Delete button on the detail.cfm page. That way, a user must look at the employee's record before being able to delete the employee from the database. This reduces the chances of an employee being accidentally deleted.

Adding Multiple Server Behaviors in a Single CFM File

In this section, we discuss a few issues that can arise when you have several Recordsets and server behaviors on the same page. We will look at a simple employee list, but this time you will create a dynamic list/menu (like HTML's <select> tag) and allow users to filter only the departments for which they want to see employees.

1. In Dreamweaver, create a new file called viewByDepartment.cfm and add a Recordset to store a list of departments. Like the previous examples, select the CompanyInfo data source, but this time select the Departmt table and name the Recordset getDepartments. Enter the following SQL into the dialog box:

```
SELECT *
FROM Departmt
ORDER BY Departmt.Dept_Name
```

When finished, click OK to return to the document window.

2. Add the following code to viewByDepartment.cfm:

```
<form action="viewByDepartment.cfm" method="GET">
<select name="Dept_ID">
</select>
</form>
```

Before you can add the Dynamic List/Menu Server Behavior, you must have a <select> tag in our code, provided in the preceding code, as you can see.

3. From the contextual menu, Select Server Behaviors ➤ + ➤ Dynamic Form Elements ➤ Dynamic List/Menu. You will see the dialog box shown in Figure 6-10.

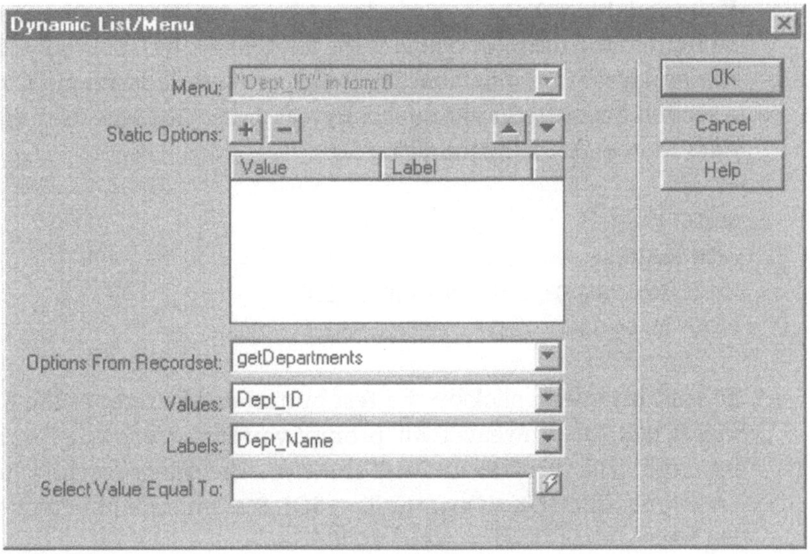

Figure 6-10. The Dynamic List/Menu dialog box

4. In the Options From Recordset drop-down menu, select the name of the Recordset. For Labels, select Dept_Name and for Values select Dept_ID. Click OK to return to the document window. You will now see the following code in your page:

```
<form action="viewByDepartment.cfm" method="get">
<select name="Dept_ID">
  <cfoutput query="getDepartments">
  <option value="#getDepartments.Dept_ID#">#getDepartments.Dept_Name#</option>
  </cfoutput>
</select>
</form>
```

Before the closing </form> tag, add a Submit button (<input type="Submit" value="View">) and view the page in a browser. You will see a drop-down list of departments from the database and a submit button.

5. Back in Dreamweaver, at the bottom of the page add the following code to select employees for a selected department:

```
<cfif IsDefined("URL.Dept_ID")>
<!-- form was submitted -->
</cfif>
```

If the variable #URL.Dept_ID# is defined, you can be sure that the user has submitted the form (or typed in the complete URL). So, you will select all employees in the database belonging to this department. Create a second Recordset named getEmployees_byDeptID using the CompanyInfo data source. Enter the following SQL:

```
SELECT *
FROM Employee
WHERE Employee.Dept_ID = #URL.Dept_ID#
ORDER BY Employee.LastName, Employee.FirstName
```

To test this query, click on the Test button on the right of the Recordset dialog box. Dreamweaver will prompt you for a test value for the #URL.Dept_ID# variable, and will show you the query results when you enter one. Click OK to exit the Test SQL Statement and Recordset dialog boxes.

In the document window, notice that Dreamweaver has embedded the code at the top of the page, which will not work for you in this example. Because you are submitting the form to itself, you can't always be sure that the variable exists yet. The #URL.Dept_ID# variable exists only after the form is submitted, so you will need to copy the getEmployees_byDeptID query within the <cfif> block at the bottom of the page.

6. Next, you will need to create a simple HTML table to display the employee information. Create a simple table near the bottom of our page:

```
<table>
  <tr>
    <td></td>
    <td></td>
    <td></td>
    <td></td>
  </tr>
</table>
```

Using the Dynamic Text button in the Application tab (in the Insert bar), add LastName and FirstName between the first <td></td>. In the second, third, and fourth <td></td> tags respectively, enter **StartDate**, **Salary**, and **Contract**. Separate them by a comma.

Next, highlight the whole of the `<tr>` element and it's contents, and add a Repeat Region server behavior by clicking on the Repeated Region button in the Application panel. Make sure you select getEmployees_byDeptID from the Recordset drop-down. Also, change the number of records from 10 to 5 Records at a Time before clicking on the OK button to finish. Your table will now look like this:

```
<table>
<cfoutput query="getEmployees_byDeptID"➥
  startRow="#StartRow_getEmployees_byDeptID#"➥
  maxRows="#MaxRows_getEmployees_byDeptID#">
<tr>
    <td>#getEmployees_byDeptID.LastName#,
#getEmployees_byDeptID.FirstName#</td>
    <td>#getEmployees_byDeptID.StartDate#</td>
    <td>#getEmployees_byDeptID.Salary#</td>
    <td>#getEmployees_byDeptID.Contract#</td>
  </tr>
</cfoutput>
</table>
```

View the viewByDepartment.cfm page in a browser, and you will see the drop-down menu with department names, as shown in Figure 6-11.

If you select a department and click the View button, you will now see a list of employees belonging to that department. Now you must return to Dreamweaver and add the department page navigation.

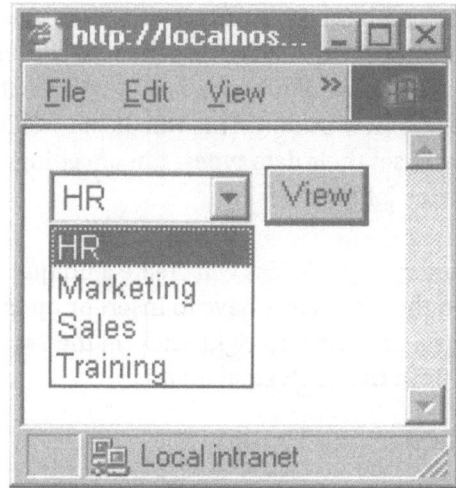

Figure 6-11. Your finished viewByDepartment.cfm *page*

7. Make sure your cursor is within the `<cfif>` code block, either before or after the `<table>` tag. In the Application tab, click the Recordset Navigation Bar button (fifth from left) to add previous and next page navigation. After clicking the Recordset Navigation Bar, make sure that you select the `getEmployees_byDeptID` Recordset from the list. Click OK to return to the document window.

Now when you view a department, there will be a previous and a next link on the page if the department has more than five employees. If you click on that link, ColdFusion will also pass the current Dept_ID you were looking at along the address bar.

Creating a Dynamic Image Gallery in ColdFusion

In Chapter 5, you learned how to upload files from a user's computer to the server by using the `<cffile action="UPLOAD">` tag. In this example, you are going to insert those image filenames into a database so you can easily build an image gallery by using Dreamweaver.

First, you must create a new database to store the image names in. We assume that you have Microsoft Access, but this example will also work in MySQL, SQL Server, Oracle, or any other database product that you may have. The only difference is that the data types and options will be slightly different. Consult your database vendor's documentation for data type information.

Creating the Database

First, open Access and create a blank database. Save this file as `cfbook.mdb` somewhere outside your `Web-root` so that it is not accessible from the web site, and users cannot directly download your database. Put it in the `C:\CFusionMX\db` folder.

Click on the Create table in Design view button. This will display a blank table where you can add columns and set their data types. You are going to create five fields in your table. They are as follows:

- ImageID (`AutoNumber` and primary key): Access will create a unique number for each record for you so that you never have to insert or update this column. To set this column as a primary key, right-click on the `ImageID` field and select Primary Key from the contextual menu.

- ImageThumbSrc (text): This will hold the filename of the thumbnail image uploaded by the user. If you click on this field, you will see at the bottom of the window the Field Properties section, where you can define the field size, etc. Field size controls the maximum number of characters that will be stored in this field. By default, Access sets this number to 50, meaning that a filename (you will store only the name of the image, not the path) can be a maximum of 50 characters. If you need more characters, you can enter a maximum field size of 255 in Access.

- ImageFullSrc (text): This will hold the filename of the full image uploaded by the user. Same as with the thumbnail, if you think you'll have filenames longer than 50 characters, change the file size in the Field Properties section at the bottom.

- ImageAltTag (text): In addition to storing the filenames of the thumbnail and full images, you will also store some alt text so that users can type a brief comment about the image. You can change the maximum field size of a text field to 255 characters, or you can change the data type to Memo to accommodate much longer text.

- ImageOrder (date/time): This field is optional. You will use this field to sort the records so that the newest images appear first in the gallery. You can also set the data type to Number. This helps when you want to customize the order in which images were displayed.

When finished, click on File ➤ Save to save the database. You will be prompted to provide a name for your table; enter **Images** and click the OK button.

Close Access and create a data source using by the ColdFusion Administrator. Log in to the Administrator and click on the Data Sources link under the Data & Services section. For Data Source Name, enter **cfbook**, and for Driver, select Microsoft Access. Click the Add button when finished.

Either type the path (C:\CFusionMX\db\cfbook.mdb) to the database file in the Database File box or click the Browse Server button to the right of the text field. Click on the Submit button when finished.

> **TIP** *If ColdFusion wasn't able to create the data source successfully, refer to the following Macromedia TechNote (23381) entitled "ColdFusion MX: Data source settings needed to connect to Microsoft Access databases," which you can find at* http://www.macromedia.com/v1/handlers/index.cfm?ID=23381&Method=Full.

Uploading Images

Once the data source has been successfully created, open Dreamweaver and create a new folder named gallery in the cfbook site. Within this folder, create a new file called newImage.cfm and enter the following code:

```
<cfif IsDefined("URL.message")>
  <cfoutput>#URL.message#</cfoutput><br/>
<cfelse>
  <br />
</cfif>
<cfform action="uploadImage.cfm" method="post" enctype="multipart/form-data">
<table>
<tr>
  <td>Thumb:</td>
  <td>
    <input type="file" name="ImageThumbSrc">
    <input type="hidden" name="ImageThumbSrc_hidden"➥
      value="Please enter a thumbnail image.">
  </td>
</tr>
<tr>
  <td>Full:</td>
  <td>
    <input type="file" name="ImageFullSrc">
    <input type="hidden" name="ImageFullSrc_hidden"➥
      value="Please enter a full image.">
  </td>
</tr>
<tr>
  <td>Alt:</td>
  <td><textarea cols="20" rows="3" wrap="soft"
name="ImageAltTag"></textarea></td>
</tr>
<tr>
<td colspan="2"><input type="submit" value="Upload Image"></td>
</tr>
</table>
</cfform>
```

You have seen all of this code before in the previous chapter, but some basic server-side validation is added this time to make sure that the user has supplied a thumbnail and full image. The top <cfif> statement passes messages back to this page to say if the required fields were present of not.

> **NOTE** *Remember that when working with file uploads, you must set the* enc-
> type *of the form to* multipart/form-data, *or else the files will not be uploaded.*

Create another new file named uploadImage.cfm in the same folder and enter
the following code into the document window:

```
<cfif NOT IsDefined("Form.ImageThumbSrc")➡
      OR NOT IsDefined("Form.ImageFullSrc")➡
      OR NOT IsDefined("Form.ImageAltTag")>
  <cflocation url="newImage.cfm?message=#UrlEncodedFormat➡
    ('Thumbnail and Full image are required.')#">
</cfif>
<cfif Len(Trim(Form.ImageThumbSrc)) GT 0 AND Len(Trim(Form.ImageFullSrc)) GT 0>
<cffile action="upload" filefield="ImageThumbSrc"➡
  destination="#ExpandPath('images')#" nameconflict="makeunique">
  <cfset ThumbSrc = cffile.serverfile>

  <cffile action="upload" filefield="ImageFullSrc"➡
    destination="#ExpandPath('images')#" nameconflict="makeunique">
  <cfset FullSrc = cffile.serverfile>

  <cfquery name="insertImage" datasource="cfbook">
    INSERT INTO Images (
      ImageThumbSrc, ImageFullSrc, ImageAltTag, ImageOrder
    )
    VALUES (
      '#ThumbSrc#',
      '#FullSrc#',
      '#Trim(Form.ImageAltTag)#',
      #CreateODBCDateTime(Now())#
    )
  </cfquery>
  <cflocation url="newImage.cfm?message=#UrlEncodedFormat➡
    ('Image inserted successfully.')#">
</cfif>
<cflocation url="newImage.cfm">
```

The first <cfif> code block ensures that the required variables have been
passed to this page. If any of the three form fields is missing, the user is redirected back to the newImage.cfm form page and an error message is displayed.
The second <cfif> block checks that the user hasn't entered blank strings for the
thumbnail and full image paths. Next you use <cffile> to upload the two files to

the server. You saw an example of this in Chapter 5. Finally, you insert the images into the database by using an INSERT query. Notice that you are formatting the date before passing it to the database. After you insert the data into the database, you redirect the user back to the insert form.

Before testing this code in your browser, create a subfolder named images under the gallery directory, which is where ColdFusion will save the images.

Test newImage.cfm in your browser and upload a handful of images to the server. Next, you will create a page that allows you to browse the images four at a time. To test the paging, you'll need at least five thumbnails in the database.

Browsing Your Images

Create a page named viewImages.cfm in Dreamweaver and save it to the gallery folder. Create a Recordset named getImages and select the cfbook data source. Using either the simple or advanced Recordset mode, create a query that will select all columns from the images table and order them by ImageOrder. Your SQL query will look like so:

```
SELECT * FROM Images ORDER BY ImageOrder ASC
```

Next, you must create a simple table to structure the display. Create a table with one <tr> and <td> element. Within the <td> element, create an <img> tag either by right-clicking on the <img> tag and selecting Edit Tag <img> from the contextual menu, or by highlighting the tag and pressing Ctrl+F5 to bring up the Tag Editor - Img dialog box, as shown in Figure 6-12.

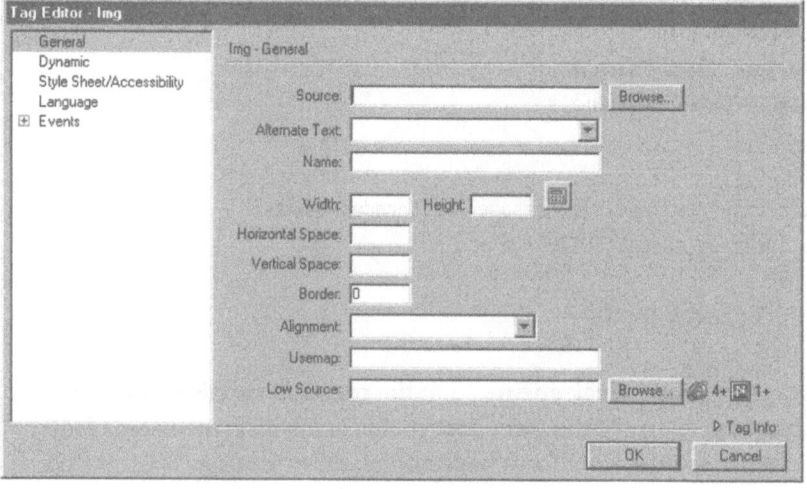

Figure 6-12. The Tag Editor - Img dialog box

In the Source text field, enter images/#getImages.ImageThumbSrc#, and within the Alternate Text field, enter #getImages.ImageAltTag#. Click OK to close this window, and return to the document window. The following code should have been generated:

```
<cfquery name="getImages" datasource="cfbook">
  SELECT *
  FROM Images
 ORDER BY ImageOrder ASC
</cfquery>
<table>
  <tr>
    <td>
      <img src="images/#getImages.ImageThumbSrc#"➥
        alt="#getImages.ImageAltTag#" border="0">
    </td>
  </tr>
</table>
```

Highlight everything between (and including) the opening and closing <td> tags, and then click on the Repeated Region button in the Application tab of the Insert bar. Select how many images you want to show per page (in this example, four) and make sure that the getImages Recordset is selected from the drop-down menu. Click on the OK button when you are finished to return to the document window.

Next, click on the Recordset Navigation Bar button in the Application panel to add navigation to the gallery, and then test the code in your browser.

Viewing Your Full-Size Images

The only task remaining is to create a page to show the full images. In Dreamweaver, create a file called viewFull.cfm in the gallery folder and add the following code:

```
<cfoutput><img src="images/#URL.ImageFullSrc#" border="0"></cfoutput>
```

Naturally, you'd want to add some formatting and make it look a little nicer in the long run, but for now this will do.

Open viewImages.cfm in Dreamweaver. You need to link the thumbnail to the full image, so change the following code snippet from this:

```
<td>
  <img src="images/#getImages.ImageThumbSrc#"➥
    alt="#getImages.ImageAltTag#" border="0">
</td>
```

to this:

```
<td>
  <a href="viewFull.cfm?ImageFullSrc=➥
    #UrlEncodedFormat(getImages.ImageFullSrc)#">➥
    <img src="images/#getImages.ImageThumbSrc#"➥
      alt="#getImages.ImageAltTag#"  border="0">
  </a>
</td>
```

You've added a hyperlink to the viewFull.cfm page, and you are passing the name of the full image as a URL variable named #URL.ImageFullSrc#. You must URL encode the file name in case it contains any special characters (such as &) that may affect the query string.

Test the application in a browser. This is pretty complete—aside from nice formatting, there is not much else left to do, besides perhaps providing a little more error checking to the application by checking if any images are in the database. You could also check if #URL.ImageFullSrc# exists on the viewFull.cfm, and if the image exists before displaying it.

Advanced SQL Topics

To round off this chapter, we will look at some more advanced topics in SQL, such as Stored Procedures and Views.

Stored Procedures

Stored procedures are queries stored within SQL Server (or Oracle, or most other enterprise level database products) and allow the database server to optimize the query that will be executed.

Although they can be a bit more complex and may be more effort to set up than normal queries, stored procedures provide some pretty impressive benefits. With a stored procedure, you can return multiple Recordsets to the calling page, and they are often faster than executing embedded queries. Stored procedures can even offer a greater level of security than embedding queries in your CFML files. In the following sections, we assume that you are using Microsoft SQL Server 2000. The specific menus and syntax will vary slightly from product to product. Refer to your specific database vendor's documentation for exact details on how to set these up for your system. It should be noted that Microsoft Access doesn't currently provide stored procedure functionality.

Here is a simple query you saw earlier in this chapter:

```
SELECT *
FROM Employee
WHERE Employee.Dept_ID = #URL.Dept_ID#
ORDER BY Employee.LastName, Employee.FirstName
```

To change it to a stored procedure, you would change the code as follows:

```
CREATE PROCEDURE [dbo].[sp_getEmployees_byDeptID]
@Dept_ID int
AS
SELECT *
FROM Employee
WHERE Employee.Dept_ID = @Dept_ID
ORDER BY Employee.LastName, Employee.FirstName
```

Notice that the SQL portion of this is very similar to the original query you wrote. The only real difference is that instead of using #URL.Dept_ID#, you are using @Dept_ID. You also had to tell SQL Server that you are creating a procedure and giving it the name sp_getEmployees_byDeptID. Finally, you declare a variable called @Dept_ID that is an integer (int) within the stored procedure.

Calling the stored procedure is different from using a <cfquery> tag, but luckily Dreamweaver has a server behavior that allows you to create new stored procedures easily. Within the Server Behaviors tab, select + ➤ Stored Procedure to bring up the dialog box shown in Figure 6-13.

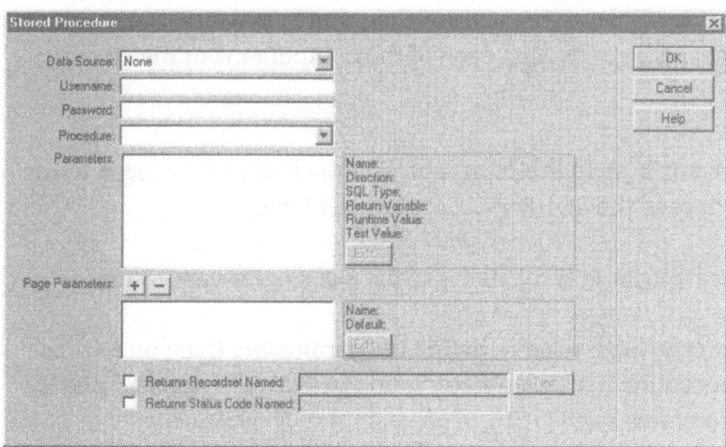

Figure 6-13. The Stored Procedure Server Behavior dialog box

From the Data Source drop-down menu, select your SQL Server data source. If you need to use a username and password to connect to your data source, provide those in the Username and Password fields. From the Procedure drop-down, select the name of your stored procedure; in this case it should be `dbo.sp_getEmployees_byDeptID`. Dreamweaver will list all the parameters needed for this stored procedure. There will be a single entry named `@Dept_ID` in the Parameters box. Click on the `@Dept_ID` parameter and click on the Edit button to bring up the Edit Stored Procedure Variable dialog box.

This is where you specify whether SQL will set variables in your ColdFusion page, or where to get the variables to pass into the stored procedure. Change the Runtime Value from `#Dept_ID#` to `#URL.Dept_ID#`. If the stored procedure is returning a Recordset to the calling page, click on the Returns Recordset Named checkbox in the previous screen and provide a name for the Recordset in the supplied textbox. Because the stored procedure is a `SELECT` query and returns that Recordset to the ColdFusion page, check this box and name it `getEmployees_byDeptID`.

This method allows you to return only a single Recordset using this interface, but once Dreamweaver embeds the code into the page, you can add as many return Recordsets as the stored procedure returns. After you click the OK button, Dreamweaver will create the following code in your page:

```
<cfstoredproc procedure="dbo.sp_getEmployees_byDeptID" datasource="cfbook_sql">
<cfprocparam type="IN" dbvarname="@Dept_ID"➡
  value="#URL.Dept_ID#" cfsqltype="CF_SQL_INTEGER">
<cfprocresult name="getEmployees_byDeptID">
</cfstoredproc>
```

Although the stored procedure may look fairly intimidating at first, it is quite simple once you understand what each component does. A stored procedure can be compared to a function; you are passing it variables, and it passes back a result. Obviously, it is a little more complex than that in practice, but the principle is still the same. Let's go through each of the components of the stored procedure:

- The `procedure` attribute in the `<cfstoredproc>` tag is the name given to the stored procedure in the SQL Server Enterprise Manager.

- The `datasource` attribute is the name of the SQL Server data source.

- The `<cfprocparam>` tag is used to define the parameters that you pass to the stored procedure. Each parameter being passed (or returned) needs its own `<cfprocparam>` tag.

- The type attribute is where you define whether the parameter is being passed into the stored procedure as a parameter, or whether it is being passed out from SQL into the ColdFusion page.

- The dbvarname attribute tells you which SQL Server variable you are defining. You'll notice that the value in the dbvarname is prefixed with an @ symbol, just like when you defined the variable within the stored procedure itself (@Dept_ID int).

- The value attribute is the value of the dbvarname that is passed into the stored procedure. So, if the value of #URL.Dept_ID# is 2, ColdFusion will set the value of @Dept_ID to 2.

- The final attribute, cfsqltype, is the data type of the parameter. This is where you define whether it is an integer, bit, text field, date/time, etc. This also helps you validate that each parameter is of the correct data type before being inserted into the database.

The <cfprocresult> tag lets you name the Recordsets being returned to ColdFusion from the stored procedure. In this example, you have a single result being returned, to which you assign the name getEmployees_byDeptID. This is the same as the name attribute in the <cfquery> tag. We now have a Recordset with the name getEmployees_byDeptID available to use within the CFML page. If the stored procedure returned two Recordsets, you would use code similar to the following to assign each a name:

```
<cfstoredproc procedure="dbo.sp_getEmployees_byDeptID" datasource="cfbook_sql">
  <cfprocparam type="IN" dbvarname="@Dept_ID"➥
    value="#URL.Dept_ID#" cfsqltype="CF_SQL_INTEGER">
  <cfprocresult name="getEmployees" resultset="1">
  <cfprocresult name="getDepartments" resultset="2">
</cfstoredproc>
```

Note that we have added a resultset attribute and assigned each resultset a unique number. For this example to work, the stored procedure in SQL Server must return two Recordsets to the page. Let's look at the revised stored procedure:

```
CREATE PROCEDURE [dbo].[sp_getEmployees_byDeptID]
@Dept_ID int
AS
SELECT *
FROM Employee
WHERE Employee.Dept_ID = @Dept_ID
```

```
ORDER BY Employee.LastName, Employee.FirstName
SELECT *
FROM Departmt
ORDER BY Departmt.Dept_Name
GO
```

Stored procedures also have another interesting benefit. When you insert records by using a stored procedure, it is possible to immediately retrieve the value of the primary key and return it to the ColdFusion page. This makes it easier to build online wizards where you need to insert an item (such as an employee) into a database and then immediately retrieve the Emp_ID of that employee so you can assign the employee to a department or follow another step in a wizard.

Although this is possible using a combination of <cfquery> tags, it isn't always foolproof. For instance, if you have two users trying to add items at the same time, there is a slight possibility of returning the wrong primary key to one of the users. Let's take a look at the SQL code for creating a stored procedure to insert an employee into an SQL Server database (sp_insertEmployee.sql):

```
CREATE PROCEDURE [dbo].[sp_insertEmployee]
@FirstName nvarchar(50),
@LastName nvarchar(50),
@Salary smallmoney,
@StartDate smalldatetime,
@Dept_ID int,
@Contract nvarchar(3)
AS
INSERT INTO
  Employee (
    FirstName,
    LastName,
    Salary,
    StartDate,
    Dept_ID,
    Contract
  )
VALUES
  (
    @FirstName,
    @LastName,
    @Salary,
    @StartDate,
    @Dept_ID,
    @Contract
  )
```

```
SELECT
  Employee.Emp_ID
FROM
  Employee
WHERE
  Employee.Emp_ID = @@Identity
GO
```

This is a little longer than the previous example. This time, you set six incoming variables for the stored procedure. The nvarchar is SQL Server's version of a text field, and the 50 is the length of the column. So, you are saying that the @FirstName and @LastName variables will not exceed 50 characters. You also set @Salary to the smallmoney data type, which you will use to hold the employee's salary. @StartDate is the same as it was in the Access database you saw in Chapter 2. It simply holds the date when the user joined the company. @Dept_ID is an integer, and finally, @Contract is a nvarchar that will hold a maximum of three characters. Typically, if you had a field that was simply holding a Boolean value, you would set it to a bit data type within SQL Server or Access. However, it is left the same as it was in the Access database to make it easier to follow along with the example.

Next, you have the INSERT query. This query inserts a user into the database and is pretty similar to using a <cfquery> tag, except you are inserting SQL variables instead of ColdFusion URLs or form variables. This final bit of code is as follows:

```
SELECT
  Employee.Emp_ID
FROM
  Employee
WHERE
  Employee.Emp_ID = @@Identity
```

This snippet selects from the database an employee whose Emp_ID is the same as the variable @@Identity. @@Identity has a special meaning in SQL Server; it holds the value of the primary key for the record that was just inserted. So, the SQL statement is saying "Select the Emp_ID column for the record that you just inserted in the database." This SQL statement is returned to the <cfprocresult> tag as a Recordset with the name that you provide. Let's look at the ColdFusion stored procedure needed to insert an employee into the SQL Server database:

```
<cfstoredproc procedure="dbo.sp_insertEmployee" datasource="cfbook_sql">
  <cfprocparam type="IN" dbvarname="@FirstName"➥
    value="#Form.FirstName#" cfsqltype="CF_SQL_VARCHAR">
  <cfprocparam type="IN" dbvarname="@LastName"➥
    value="#Form.LastName#" cfsqltype="CF_SQL_VARCHAR">
  <cfprocparam type="IN" dbvarname="@Salary"➥
    value="#Form.Salary#" cfsqltype="CF_SQL_MONEY">
```

```
    <cfprocparam type="IN" dbvarname="@StartDate"➥
      value="#Form.StartDate#" cfsqltype="CF_SQL_TIMESTAMP">
    <cfprocparam type="IN" dbvarname="@Dept_ID"➥
      value="#Form.Dept_ID#" cfsqltype="CF_SQL_INTEGER">
    <cfprocparam type="IN" dbvarname="@Contract"➥
      value="#Form.Contract#" cfsqltype="CF_SQL_VARCHAR">
    <cfprocresult name="getEmpID">
</cfstoredproc>
```

This stored procedure is fairly similar to the ones you created earlier in this section. You are passing six parameters into the stored procedure and receiving a single resultset, getEmpID, containing the primary key for the Employee table.

Creating Views with SQL Server

SQL Server also allows you to create a View, which is sort of like a virtual table. Using views allows you to perform joins on different tables and query the virtual table to simplify our queries. For example, you could create a view named Employee2 between the Employee and Departmt tables. The Employee2 view would contain each of the columns in the two tables, allowing you to query the view instead of having to perform joins every time you wanted to see the data from both tables. Let's look at an example.

The Employee table contains the following columns: Emp_ID, FirstName, LastName, Salary, StartDate, Dept_ID, and Contract. The Departmt table contains the following columns: Dept_ID, Dept_Name, and Location. To return a query containing an employee and the name of the employee's department, you would have to join the Employee and Departmt tables. To see this data on other pages, you would have to perform the join again and again. This can become quite cumbersome!

You can make the task easier by performing the join only once and creating a virtual table (view) containing the employee's name, salary, department name, and location. Then, whenever you need to return an employee's name and department, you only have to perform a simple query on the view rather than having to constantly joining the tables.

Let's look at the syntax for creating a view in SQL server:

```
SELECT
E.Emp_ID, E.FirstName, E.LastName, E.Salary, E.StartDate, E.Contract,
D.Dept_ID, D.Dept_Name, D.Location
FROM
Employee E, Departmt D
WHERE
E.Dept_ID = D.Dept_ID
```

You can create a view in SQL Server Enterprise Manager by expanding the database in which you want to create the view. Right-click on the View node (located below the Tables node in the tree) and select New View... from the contextual menu, and you will see the "New View in '<database name>' on '<server name>'" window.

In the SQL pane, add the preceding SQL statement and click the Save button in the top menu. SQL Server will prompt you for a name to save the view as. Enter **v_Employee** and click the OK button. That's all there is to it; you've created a view!

You can then create a Recordset in Dreamweaver and look at the data in your view, or you can run the SQL Query Analyzer from within SQL Server by selecting Tools ➤ SQL Query Analyzer from the menu at the top of the SQL Server dialog box.

From within the SQL Query Analyzer, navigate to the database where you added your view. You can change databases by using the drop-down menu at the top of the dialog box. Type the following SQL statement into your query analyzer:

```
SELECT * FROM v_Employee
```

Now click on the little "play" button at the top of the screen to execute the query.

Once the query has been executed, a grid of the query results appears at the bottom of the window. If you do not see any results, check that your tables are not empty and that each employee has a valid Dept_ID. If you look at the columns headings displayed in the results, you'll notice that you are seeing all the columns from the Employee table and the Dept_Name and Location from the Departmt table.

When to Use Views

Views are very useful when you want to limit the data that users or developers can see. If you are a database administrator and don't necessarily want the programmers to see all columns within a table, you could create a view that would show all columns within a table except for salaries or perhaps credit card numbers. If you allow developers to query only views and not the tables directly, you can control what data they can see within certain tables. Also, if you force programmers to use only stored procedures, you can control which columns they can write to or which columns are returned to the ColdFusion Server.

Views and stored procedures are advanced SQL concepts; by using a larger enterprise level database solution (such as SQL Server and Oracle), you can set user rights to tables and objects. You would do this so that only certain users could use certain tables or procedures. You also can configure ColdFusion to use certain usernames and passwords when connecting to a data source, and therefore limit the tables that the ColdFusion Server can access.

This last technique is recommended when you are building a complete secure application. Typically, you would never want to allow ColdFusion to have full administrative rights to the data source. This way, even a malicious hacker who obtained access to your server and was able to run custom CFML scripts wouldn't necessarily have full access to all the tables, views, and stored procedures.

Query of Queries

First introduced in ColdFusion 5, this allows you to query the contents of an existing query rather than having to return to the database. This has some definite advantages in certain cases. In some ways, this is similar to an SQL view, although the performance hit is greater, and a more limited subset of SQL is available for use in the query.

Querying an existing query can be a lifesaver when you actually need it, but it often isn't the most efficient method of performing a task. Let's look at an example of where it is useful. Looking back at the previous query to retrieve all employees, you had the following ColdFusion query:

```
<cfquery name="getEmployees" datasource="CompanyInfo">
  SELECT * FROM Employee
</cfquery>
```

This will return a Recordset named getEmployees with every employee in the Employee table. If you want to filter this Recordset to return only employees who have a last name starting with the letter A, you could query the Recordset to filter out the specific records you're interested in, like so:

```
<cfquery name="getEmployees_A" dbtype="query">
  SELECT * FROM getEmployees WHERE LastName LIKE 'A%'
</cfquery>
```

The first query you created would return 19 records—every record in the table. The second query would return only those employees found in the first query that have a last name starting with A, which is only three records.

Look at the last query; instead of providing a data source attribute, you specify dbtype and give it a value of query. This tells ColdFusion that you are not querying a database, but rather an existing query that is in server memory. Notice that instead of specifying a table to retrieve records from, you specify an existing query name after the FROM keyword.

> **TIP** *It is important to note that not all SQL keywords or functions are supported when you're querying a query. For more information on supported query of queries syntax, refer to this ColdFusion documentation:* `http://livedocs.macromedia.com/cfmxdocs/Developing_ColdFusion_MX_Applications_with_CFML/using_Recordsets.jsp`.

Querying an existing query allows a developer to do something never possible before it's introduction to CFML: easily join data from two completely different data sources into one query. If you create two queries from two different data sources, it is possible to join those two queries and create a single Recordset.

Caching Queries

If your data rarely changes and is accessed frequently (for example, your navigation or your department IDs), you can cache the queries in the server's memory for better performance. This way, instead of ColdFusion sending the request to the database server and creating more network and resource overheads, the server simply stores and retrieves the cached query in server memory for fast access. Caching queries is as simple as adding another attribute to the <cfquery> tag:

```
<cfquery name="getDepartments"➡
  datasource="CompanyInfo"➡
  cachedwithin="#CreateTimeSpan(0,0,15,0)#">
  SELECT *
 FROM Departmt
</cfquery>
```

By adding the cachedwithin attribute, you are telling ColdFusion to retrieve the Recordset from server memory if it has been created within the past time span. The #CreateTimeSpan()# function takes four parameters: days, hours, minutes, and seconds. The preceding snippet will return the cached query from server memory only if it is less than 15 minutes old; otherwise, the query will be executed again from the database. Although this will result in increased performance, any changes to your database won't be reflected in your application until the next 15-minute cycle elapses. There is also a cachedafter attribute for the <cfquery> tag that will return the query from server memory only if it is older than a certain time span, although this is very rarely used compared to cachedwithin.

Query Parameters

The final topic we discuss in this chapter is query parameters. ColdFusion offers another excellent method of data validation that uses a tag called <cfqueryparam>. This allows you to validate the data type for data before passing it to the database. Unfortunately, this tag isn't widely used in CFML projects (it should be), even though it helps keep your code secure, and in some cases, increases query performance. The <cfqueryparam> tag does this by:

- allowing you to set maximum lengths for strings

- specifying data types so, for example, errors will be generated if a user tries to pass text into a numeric field

- specifying data types so errors will be generated if users try to pass harmful parameters to a query that could delete records or drop tables from a database

The <cfqueryparam> tag can be used only within a <cfquery> code block:

```
<cfparam name="URL.Dept_ID" default="1">
<cfquery name="getDepartments" datasource="cfbook_sql">
  SELECT *
  FROM Departmt
  WHERE Dept_ID = <cfqueryparam value="#URL.Dept_ID#" cfsqltype="cf_sql_integer">
</cfquery>
```

Notice that you no longer need to use single quotes around the <cfqueryparam> tag, because ColdFusion now knows that it is dealing with strings and can handle the data internally. You also do not need to apply any special formatting to dates or numbers, because the <cfqueryparam> tag handles all this.

What happens if a user tries to modify the URL variable and tamper with existing data within the database? The <cfqueryparam> tag will escape the entire string, making it much more difficult to pass malicious code to delete records from the database. For example, look at the following code, which is similar to the previous listing except that the <cfqueryparam> tag is absent:

```
<cfparam name="URL.Dept_ID" default="1">
<cfquery name="getDepartments" datasource="cfbook_sql">
  SELECT *
  FROM Departmt
  WHERE Dept_ID = <cfqueryparam value="#URL.Dept_ID#" cfsqltype="cf_sql_integer">
</cfquery>
```

If you passed a variable along the query string, such as `?Dept_ID=2;` `DELETE+Employee`, and reloaded the page, this would delete every record from the Employee table. Scared? If not, imagine that it was a table full of shopping cart orders from your e-commerce site, or perhaps all the messages in your extensive message board system, or all of your customers' personal information. You could have avoided this particular disaster by checking that the required variable was numeric by adding a `type` attribute to the `<cfparam>` tag. But what about the next time?

Using `<cfparam>` helps speed up queries slightly, provides some excellent protection from potential malicious code, and helps build a more robust application. It is always a good habit to use the `<cfqueryparam>` tag with all your queries. One slight gotcha with `<cfqueryparam>` is that you cannot cache any queries that use it.

Summary

We covered much in this chapter; if you are still unsure of anything, go back and reread the relevant sections until they sink in, because we'll be using databases in most of the remaining chapters in this book.

Databases are truly the cornerstone for most dynamic sites today. It is possible to add interactivity to a site without using a database, but databases allow data to be retrieved and sorted quickly, and are fast and efficient at the specific task they were designed to do. Finally, we discussed how to create views and stored procedures within SQL Server.

This chapter has just scratched the surface of the SQL language. We recommend picking up a general book on the SQL language (such as *The Programmer's Guide to SQL* by Cristian Darie and Karli Watson; Apress, 2003) and a manual on your specific database product to learn all the ins and outs of your software.

Chapter 7 covers state management and the Web. We will revisit session and client variables and discuss how to store Recordsets and other data structures in a persistent variable scope so that multiple users can share the same data without having to requery the database on each request.

Maintaining State

As we have discussed before, one of the main problems with the Web is that it is "stateless." The web server doesn't have a concept of who a user is and what the user is doing; it simply accepts an incoming request and returns the parsed information. Most variable scopes within ColdFusion are destroyed after the template has finished being processed. The point of persistent variables is to allow you to create a variable once and have that variable persist (not be destroyed) for a specified duration. One benefit of this is the ability to uniquely identify visitors to your web site. Performance is the other benefit; performance improves because variables do not have to be recreated on each request or even for each visitor to the site. In this chapter we focus primarily on the former benefit: the ability to track users on your site and to associate values with a user.

As we briefly mentioned in Chapter 4, a few special scopes are able to persist variables across multiple requests. Without state management, it wouldn't be possible to keep track of users across multiple requests. You wouldn't be able to log in to a site once and look at all the content; instead, you would be required to log in for each page request, or pass a variable along every URL or form submission to tell ColdFusion that you have already logged in.

In this chapter, we are going to look at three main variable scopes: Session, Client, and Cookie. You are probably familiar with cookies already, but you will soon see how Session and Client variable scopes allow you to expand on cookies and store user information on the server instead. We will also take a closer look at another persistent variable scope: Application.

You had a brief introduction to Session-, Cookie-, and Client-scoped variables in Chapter 4, and you also used the Session scope in Chapter 6, where you learned that before you could use the Session scope, you had to enable session management in a <cfapplication> tag.

Using Cookies

You've undoubtedly used cookies on the Web in some form or another—if you've ever logged in to a site or checked a "remember me" check box, for example. Sometimes, just visiting a site sets a cookie. Using cookies has a few advantages, such as being able to access them by using languages like JavaScript, ASP, and PHP. Cookies are stored on the site visitors' machines by their web browser (in a text file). Because the cookie information is stored on the user's machine rather than the server, cookies offer the performance advantage of not taking up any server resources.

> **NOTE**   *It is important to note, especially if you are accessing cookies using a case-sensitive language such as JavaScript, that ColdFusion creates cookies using capital letters.*

Cookies also have some limitations; they can hold only simple values (such as strings, numbers, and Booleans), they can be disabled easily by a user, their size is limited (4KB each), the number of cookies that can be set on a user's machine for a single domain is limited (20), and because they're in a text file on the client, they are not generally very secure.

To further limit the number of cookies you can set, ColdFusion automatically sets some cookies for its own use (CFID and CFTOKEN), reducing the number of available cookies you can set to 18 per host. Both CFID and CFTOKEN are used to track users throughout your site. When a user comes to your site, these two cookies are set and allow ColdFusion to identify that user's session. These two variables are needed for using Session or Client variables. Note that cookies are domain-specific; you cannot read cookies set by other websites, and they cannot access yours either.

There is another cookie, JSESSIONID, that ColdFusion uses in lieu of the CFID/CFTOKEN combination, if J2EE session variables are enabled in the ColdFusion Administrator. The JSESSIONID variable is set when a session is created and can be used to share Session variables between ColdFusion, JSP, and Java servlets. These topics are beyond the scope of this book, but there are some excellent resources at http://www.macromedia.com and http://livedocs. macromedia.com/. It is important to note that when J2EE sessions are enabled in the ColdFusion Administrator, the CFID and CFTOKEN variables are not set, so you are able to set 19 cookies per host instead of 18. One other difference is that J2EE sessions expire as soon as users closes their browser windows, which is not the case with traditional ColdFusion session management.

You can use ColdFusion to set a cookie on a user's machine in one of two ways: either by directly setting a variable in the Cookie scope by using <cfset Cookie.UserID = 14>, or by using the <cfcookie> tag. When using the <cfcookie> tag, you are able to set extra attributes, such as when the cookie expires, whether or not the cookie should be "secure," and the domain and path that the cookie is valid for. Here's an example of the <cfcookie> tag:

```
<cfcookie name="UserID" value="14">
```

The preceding snippet will create a cookie named UserID with a value of 14. Because you haven't defined when this cookie will expire, it will reside in the user's memory until the browser is closed. At this point the cookie will be deleted. This is often referred to as a session cookie because it lasts for only a single user session. If you define when the cookie expires, it will be written to a text file (cookies.txt if you are using Netscape, or individual files if you are using Internet Explorer) on the user's computer and will remain there for the specified time. CFML allows you to define when the cookie expires in the following ways:

- An exact date: `<cfcookie name="xyz" expires="12/3/2004">`

- A fixed number of days: `<cfcookie name="xyz" expires="100">`

- NOW: `<cfcookie name="xyz" expires="NOW">`

- NEVER: `<cfcookie name="xyz" expires="NEVER">`

If you specify an expiration date of NOW, the cookie is deleted from the user's cookies.txt file or individual file on the user's local computer as soon as the `<cfcookie>` tag executes. Specifying an expiration date of NEVER will set the cookie to expire in 30 years.

Because cookies can be set to persist on a client machine for any duration, they are an excellent way to build "remember me" functionality into an application so users don't have to log in to a site each time they visit. Also, because cookies are stored on the client's machine, you don't have to worry about taking up large amounts of server memory or filling a database.

In the following simple example, you will see how you can set cookies that persist only as long as the user's browser remains open, and how to create cookies that last for a certain number of days.

1. Use Dreamweaver to create a file called getName.cfm within a new subfolder called Ch7 in your cfbook site, then enter the following code:

```
<cfform action="showName.cfm" method="post">
  <cfinput type="Text" name="Name" value="" required="yes"➡
  message="Please enter your name.">
  <input type="Submit" value="Submit">
</cfform>
```

There is nothing interesting about the preceding code. You are simply creating a form to allow users to type in their names.

2. Create another file called showName.cfm within the same folder containing the following code:

```
<cfparam name="Form.Name" type="string">
<cfcookie name="Name" value="#Form.Name#">
<cfoutput>Your name is: #Cookie.Name#<br /></cfoutput>
<a href="anotherPage.cfm">Another page</a>
```

In this step, you are setting a cookie called Name to the value of the form field that the user filled out. You then display the value of the cookie along with a link to anotherPage.cfm.

3. Create a third file, anotherPage.cfm, and enter the following line into it:

```
<cfoutput>#Cookie.Name#</cfoutput>
```

Now test your files. Navigate to the getName.cfm file, enter your name in the text box, and click the Submit button. You name will be stored in a cookie, and you will see the cookie's value output to the window in showName.cfm.

If you then click on the hyperlink at the bottom of showName.cfm, you will go to anotherPage.cfm, which also displays the value of the cookie; you didn't have to explicitly pass the variable to anotherPage.cfm because it was able to retrieve it from the Name.cookie. You can even leave this page, navigate to another site, then return to anotherPage.cfm, and you will still see the name you entered in getName.cfm.

Because you didn't specify an expiration time for this cookie, it will remain in your memory until you close your browser. Therefore, if you close your web browser, open a new one, then navigate back to anotherPage.cfm, you will receive an "Element NAME is undefined in COOKIE" error; the cookie is no longer on your system.

This happens because the cookie expires as soon as the browser is closed—it was never even written to the disk. If you change the code in showName.cfm to the following snippet (showName2.cfm), the cookie will be saved on the user's hard drive and would still be defined after the browser was closed and reopened:

```
<cfparam name="Form.Name" type="string">
<cfcookie name="Name" value="#Form.Name#" expires="7">
<cfoutput>Your name is: #Cookie.Name#<br /></cfoutput>
<a href="anotherPage.cfm">Another page</a>
```

By adding the expires attribute to the <cfcookie> tag as shown, you are telling ColdFusion to save this cookie on the user's system for seven days, after which time it will expire. You could also set an actual date for the cookie to expire on.

Cookies can be useful if you want to track users around a site. You might want to create a snippet of code that creates a record of which users were viewing which pages and inserts into a database. You could then paste that snippet at the bottom of each web page and build your own simple stats package. You would be able to query the database and see how many times a certain page was browsed on a particular day, or track to see which pages were viewed by a particular user, and in which order.

Session **Variables**

There are a few important differences between Session variables and cookies. Cookies are stored on the user's computer, whereas Session variables are stored in the server's memory. Cookies are limited to simple values and lists, but Session variables can hold Recordsets, arrays, objects, or XML documents. Session variables use slightly more resources than cookies, but have fewer limitations.

One very important consideration when using Session variables is that you must be careful to "lock" the variable every time you read or change its value in versions of ColdFusion prior to MX. ColdFusion is able to tell which user the Session variables belong to by using the CFID and CFTOKEN (or JSESSIONID) cookies, so for sessions to work, a user's cookies must be enabled.

In ColdFusion MX and MX 6.1, you do not have to lock access to session variables for memory threading issues, but you do have to lock them anytime there is a possibility of a *race condition*. (A race condition is anytime one piece of code could change the value of a variable at the same time another piece of code tries to access it, which could result in invalid data being read.) Race conditions can be prevented if locks are used appropriately. This problem holds true with any of the variable scopes that are persisted in server memory: Session, Application, and Server. The main differences among these three scopes are as follows:

- Session variables are tied to a specific user.

- Application variables are available to all users of a certain application.

- Server variables are available to all users in all applications on the server.

Because Session variables are stored within the server's memory, they have a much shorter lifespan than Client variables or Cookies. Session variables by default are stored in the server's memory for only 20 minutes. If a client is idle on your site (no page requests) for more than 20 minutes, the session variables will be deleted from the server's memory and will no longer exist.

As you saw in Chapter 1, Session variable timeouts (along with Application variables) can be set in the ColdFusion Administrator on the Memory Variables page in the Server Settings section. This is where you can disable or enable these two scopes entirely, or else set their default timeout and maximum timeout values. You can also define timeout values by using the <cfapplication> tag in your site, if you want to customize timeout values on a site-by-site basis.

It is also important to note that, if the timeout value within your <cfapplication> tag exceeds the maximum timeout value in the ColdFusion Administrator, the value from the ColdFusion Administrator will be used instead (the shortest of the two values is always the one used).

Using the <cflock> Tag

Let's look at a simple example showing how you use the <cflock> tag when reading or modifying the contents of a Session variable. This example locks access to the entire session scope by using the <cflock> tag's scope attribute. If few variables need to be locked, a better practice is to use the <cflock> tag's name attribute (all locks with the same name "obey" each other).

1. In Dreamweaver, open the showName.cfm file you made earlier in this chapter. Remove any existing code and add the following (see showName3.cfm in the code download):

```
<cfparam name="Form.Name" type="string">
<cflock timeout="15" type="exclusive" scope="session">
  <cfset Session.Name = Form.Name >
</cflock>
<cflock timeout="10" type="readonly" scope="session">
  <cfoutput>#Session.Name#</cfoutput>
</cflock>
```

You are using <cflock> tags to eliminate the chances of users seeing a different user's session variables. When you set a Session variable, you must set the lock type to "exclusive" so that no other threads are able to read or write to this variable while the current thread is accessing it.

2. Now view the getName.cfm template again, fill out the form, and submit it. You will either see the name displayed on the screen, as in the previous example, or you will get an error similar to the one shown in Figure 7-1. If you receive this error, you need to create an Application.cfm template in the same folder (or parent folder) and enable the session scope by adding the following code to it:

```
<cfapplication name="cfbook" sessionmanagement="yes">
```

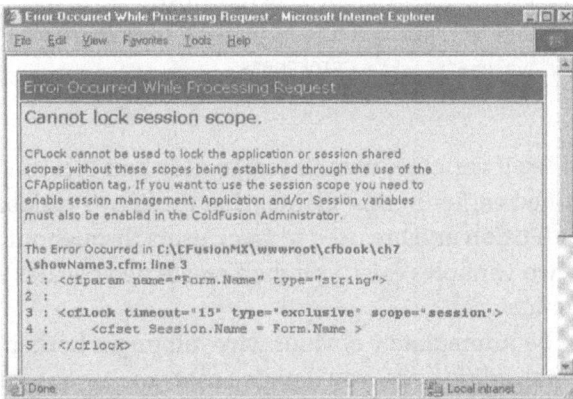

Figure 7-1. An error caused because you haven't enabled the session scope yet

3. Retest getName.cfm, and this time you should see your name being output to the browser. If you still receive an error message, check the ColdFusion Administrator and make sure that the Session scope hasn't been disabled.

Session variables, like Cookies, last a certain amount of time. You saw earlier in this chapter that it's possible to close the browser and navigate back to the anotherPage.cfm template and still view the value of the Cookie. The same holds true with Session variables, assuming they haven't expired. You can get it to persist for a prescribed length of time like so:

Open anotherPage.cfm again and change the code to the following (see anotherpage2.cfm in the code download):

```
<cflock scope="session" timeout="10" type="readonly">
  <cfoutput>#Session.Name#</cfoutput>
</cflock>
```

Now close your browser, reopen it, and navigate back to the anotherPage.cfm template. You will still see your name displayed on the screen (unless the variables have timed out already). Even if the user closes the browser, the user's Session variables still remain in the server's memory until they time out.

But what if you wanted to have users' sessions end once they close their browsers? You need to set the Cookie.CFID and Cookie.CFTOKEN cookies to expire when a user's browser is closed. To achieve this, add the following code into your Application.cfm file below the current line (see Application2.cfm in the code download):

```
<cfif IsDefined("Cookie.CFID") AND IsDefined("Cookie.CFTOKEN")>
  <cfcookie name="CFID" value="#Cookie.CFID#">
  <cfcookie name="CFTOKEN" value="#Cookie.CFTOKEN#">
</cfif>
```

This code checks to see if variables named Cookie.CFID and Cookie.CFTOKEN already exist. We mentioned earlier in this chapter that these two variables are set automatically by ColdFusion and are used to track users throughout their visit to the site. If these two variables exist, you then create two cookies with the exact same names and values.

Although it may not be immediately obvious why you might bother doing this, if you examine the preceding code, you'll notice that you haven't defined an expiration date for these cookies. As we mentioned earlier in this chapter, if you do not define an expiration date, the cookies will not be saved to the users' disks and will expire when the users close their browsers.

So effectively, the users' CFID and CFTOKEN values will now expire when their values are closed. Note that this doesn't actually destroy the users' Session variables; it simply "disconnects" them from the current session. All of their session variables will still remain in server memory (though inaccessible unless the same CFID/CFTOKEN combination are passed) until they time out and are destroyed.

This technique can be very useful for logging out users from an application when their browsers close. If you weren't using the preceding code listing and a user exited the browser without hitting a logout button, the user would still be logged in if the Session variables weren't timed out. If that user (or a different user entirely) were to reopen the browser and navigate back to your site, the new visitor could still use the logged in functionality of the site.

Session variables aren't limited to simple strings. For an e-commerce site, you could create a user's shopping cart and store it in a Session variable instead of storing carts in a database. This has the benefit that, if a user abandons the cart and leaves your site, the Session variable will be deleted when the session times out. If you stored all the items in the user's cart within a database, you would need to run a cleanup routine to delete carts not modified in the past day or two.

Saving Recordsets with Session Scope

Next we will look at a couple of techniques for saving Recordsets within the Session scope. Most developers would put a <cflock> around the entire query, although this could negatively affect server performance if the query took a long time to execute. You can see an example of this here (recordsetSession.cfm):

```
<cflock type="exclusive" scope="session" timeout="10">
  <cfquery name="Session.getDepartments" datasource="CompanyInfo">
    SELECT * FROM Departmt
  </cfquery>
</cflock>
```

```
<cflock type="readonly" scope="session" timeout="10">
  <cfoutput query="Session.getDepartments">
    #Dept_Name#<br />
  </cfoutput>
</cflock>
```

Again we are illustrating code that, for whatever reason, we want to protect against a race condition. So, whenever writing to a session-scoped variable, you set the lock type to exclusive, and whenever you are simply reading from the Session scope, you set the type to readonly. Instead of creating locks each time you access this session variable, you can copy it into a scope that doesn't require locking, such as the Request or Variables scope, as shown here (altScope.cfm):

```
<cfif NOT IsDefined("Session.getDepartments")>
  <cfquery name="getDepartments" datasource="CompanyInfo">
    SELECT * FROM Departmt
  </cfquery>
  <cflock type="exclusive" scope="session" timeout="10">
    <cfset Session.getDepartments = getDepartments >
  </cflock>
</cfif>
<cflock type="readonly" scope="server" timeout="10">
  <cfset getDepartments = Session.getDepartments >
</cflock>
<cfoutput query="getDepartments">
  #Dept_Name#<br />
</cfoutput>
```

Now, instead of locking the entire query and display, you lock only the code that copies the Session variables into a different scope. In the preceding listing, you are using the Variables scope. However, you could use the Request scope instead, and the Recordset would then be available to every template, custom tag, and component within this request. As mentioned earlier, you need to use locking only when the possibility of a race condition exists, so copying the session variables to the request scope doesn't offer many benefits. It's an important concept to understand nonetheless, because this was a very common practice before ColdFusion MX, and it is still useful in some scenarios.

If you run this snippet within a web browser, the first time it runs, it will execute the query and copy the Recordset into the Session scope. The second time you run this code, the variable will already be defined, and ColdFusion will skip over the <cfif> block.

Next, you copy the Session variable back into the Variables scope and display the results of the query. The code is slightly longer, but you always want to lock as little code as possible. When you have an exclusive lock for a scope, no other request can access that scope until the lock has finished executing.

Exclusive locks let only a single process use that scope at a time, whereas a read-only lock lets multiple users access the variable simultaneously.

Locking variables can sometimes be tricky, because poorly nested <cflock> tags can create what is called a *deadlock*. A deadlock occurs when you nest a <cflock> in such a way that it is blocking itself and the lock can never be attained. For example, consider the following code (deadLock.cfm):

```
<cflock type="readonly" scope="session" timeout="10">
  <cfif NOT IsDefined("Session.uhOH")>
    <cflock type="exclusive" scope="session" timeout="10">
      <cfquery name="Session.getDepartments" datasource="CompanyInfo">
        SELECT *
        FROM Departmt
      </cfquery>
    </cflock>
  </cfif>
</cflock>
```

This code will throw errors because the entire code block is enclosed within a read-only lock of the Session scope. If a variable isn't defined, you will create a nested exclusive lock and execute the query. This fails for one important reason: the exclusive lock can never be attained because you already have a readonly lock open. If you attempt to run this template in your web browser, the page will freeze for about 20 seconds until providing an error message similar to the one shown in Figure 7-2.

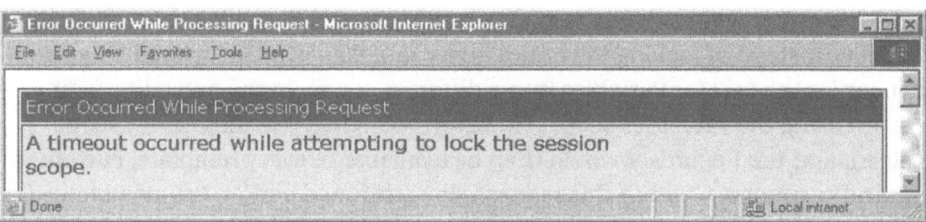

Figure 7-2. An error caused by a deadlock in your code

Named Locks vs. Scoped Locks

ColdFusion has two methods for locking code. Each of the examples you've seen in this chapter so far have involved locking an entire scope so that only one thread is able to access the Session scope at a particular time. This might be much too restrictive for your application if you are storing many variables within a shared memory variable scope and you have many threads stuck in a queue waiting for the previous thread to release an exclusive lock. This doesn't happen too often when accessing the Session scope (because they're accessed by a single user), but is common when accessing the application scope. It can happen with the Session scope when users reload a page before it's done loading, or when using framesets, for example.

In this situation, the alternative mentioned earlier might be better: named locks. Named locks allow you to assign a name to a lock, which can then be invoked individually, instead of locking the entire scope. Now, instead of having only one thread access an entire scope at any particular time, you can be more specific by naming your locks and increase the performance of your application. You can see the differences between scoped locks and named locks in the following block of code (differentLocks.cfm):

```
<!--- Scoped Locks --->
<cflock scope="session" timeout="10" type="exclusive">
  <cfparam name="Session.Name" default="Barney" type="string">
</cflock>
<cflock scope="session" timeout="10" type="readonly">
  <cfoutput>#Session.Name#</cfoutput>
</cflock>
<!--- Named Locks --->
<cflock name="getName" timeout="10" type="exclusive">
  <cfparam name="Session.Name" default="Barney" type="string">
</cflock>
<cflock name="getName" timeout="10" type="readonly">
  <cfoutput>#Session.Name#</cfoutput>
</cflock>
```

Deadlocking is still possible if you use nested locks in your code, and one other problem can arise when using named locks; if you fail to name your locks properly, you end up not locking your code at all. For the previous named locks, for example, if you used two different lock names when reading and writing the #Session.Name# variable, ColdFusion would not lock #Session.Name#, and other users could modify it while you were using it.

Locking and ColdFusion Structures

You've already seen how to lock your Session variables effectively, but you should be aware of one important point when using structures (and Java objects, COM objects, and Recordsets). When you copy a structure from or into another variable, you are copying only a "reference" but not the structure itself.

Create a new file in Dreamweaver called structDuplicate.cfm and enter the following code:

```
<cfset myStruct = StructNew()>
<cfset myStruct["a"] = "one">
<cfset myStruct["b"] = "two">
<cfset otherStruct = myStruct>
<table>
  <tr bgcolor="EEEEEE">
    <td colspan="2">PRE</td>
  </tr>
  <tr>
    <td><cfdump var="#myStruct#" label="myStruct"></td>
    <td><cfdump var="#otherStruct#" label="otherStruct"></td>
  </tr>
  <cfset otherStruct["a"] = "seven">
  <tr bgcolor="EEEEEE">
    <td colspan="2">POST</td>
  </tr>
  <tr>
    <td><cfdump var="#myStruct#" label="myStruct"></td>
    <td><cfdump var="#otherStruct#" label="otherStruct"></td>
  </tr>
</table>
```

This code produces the output shown in Figure 7-3.

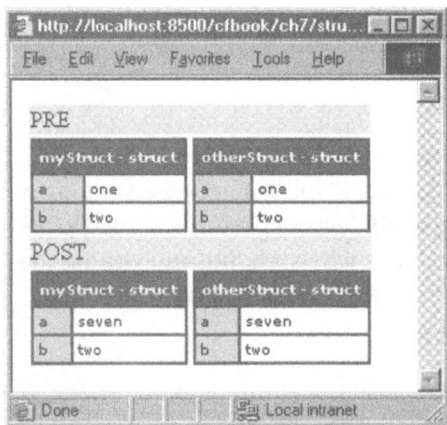

Figure 7-3. Copying variable structures creates only a reference, not an exact structural copy.

You can see that even though you changed a value in the #otherStruct# structure, the value was also changed in the original #myStruct# structure. This is because instead of copying the structure completely, ColdFusion simply creates a "pointer" or "reference" to the original structure. If you want to copy the structure completely, use the #Duplicate()# function, as shown here (trueDuplicate.cfm):

```
<cfset myStruct = StructNew()>
<cfset myStruct["a"] = "one">
<cfset myStruct["b"] = "two">
<cfset otherStruct = Duplicate(myStruct)>
<table>
  <tr bgcolor="EEEEEE">
    <td colspan="2">PRE</td>
  </tr>
  <tr>
    <td><cfdump var="#myStruct#" label="myStruct"></td>
    <td><cfdump var="#otherStruct#" label="otherStruct"></td>
  </tr>
  <cfset otherStruct["a"] = "seven">
  <tr bgcolor="EEEEEE">
    <td colspan="2">POST</td>
  </tr>
  <tr>
    <td><cfdump var="#myStruct#" label="myStruct"></td>
    <td><cfdump var="#otherStruct#" label="otherStruct"></td>
  </tr>
</table>
```

This code produces the output shown in Figure 7-4.

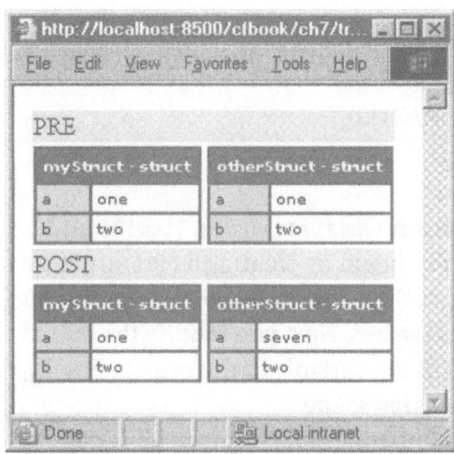

Figure 7-4. To copy structures exactly, you must use the #Duplicate()# function.

You can see here that the original structure remains the same and only the copy is being modified. This is important when you have a structure being stored in a Session, Application, or Server scope. If you simply copy the reference to the structure rather than duplicating it, you are still modifying the original structure. This probably isn't what you intend to do. Note that if there are nothing but simple values (no nested structures, queries, or XML) in a structure, the #structCopy()# function will make a complete duplicate as well. If you use #structCopy()# and there are nested complex variables, pointers to those variables are created. For this reason, it's easier to always use the #Duplicate()# function when you want to be sure that a new variable is created without pointers.

Now let's look at some general code to illustrate a shopping cart stored in a structure in the Session scope (cart.cfm).

```
<cfparam name="Form.ItemID" type="numeric">
<cfparam name="Form.Quantity" type="numeric">
<cflock name="myCart" type="exclusive" timeout="10">
  <!--- if Session cart does not already exist, create it. --->
  <cfif NOT IsDefined("Session.myCart")>
    <cfset Session.myCart = StructNew()>
    <!-- Cart Created. -->
  </cfif>
</cflock>
<cflock name="myCart" type="readonly" timeout="10">
  <!--- copy user's cart into the Request scope. --->
  <cfset Request.myCart = Duplicate(Session.myCart)>
</cflock>
<!--- code to insert the product into cart here or update➥
  quantity if it already exists. --->
<cfset Request.myCart[Form.ItemID] = Form.Quantity>
<cfdump var="#Request.myCart#">
<cflock name="myCart" type="exclusive" timeout="10">
  <!--- copy user's cart back into the Session scope. --->
  <cfset Session.myCart = Duplicate(Request.myCart)>
</cflock>
```

The preceding example requires two form variables, #Form.ItemID# and #Form.Quantity#, to be passed to the page. You begin by creating a cart structure in the Session scope if it doesn't already exist, then you copy the Session cart into the Request scope to avoid locking reads and writes. Next you modify the cart in the Request scope and display the contents of the variable to the screen. Finally, you duplicate the structure back into the Session scope.

This is a very simplistic example, but it illustrates locking and the necessity for duplicating the cart structure to and from the Request scope. Also, take note that you have named your locks the same. This way, no ColdFusion processes can create a lock and write to the #Session.myCart# using an exclusive lock as long as you have a read-only lock open.

Deleting Session Variables

If you need to delete a variable from the Session scope, you can use a function called #StructDelete()#. Because the Session scope is treated as a structure, you can use each of the structure functions on this scope (and most other scopes).

If you were storing an administrator's #AdminName# and #AdminID# in the Session scope once this administrator logged into the admin site, you could log out this administrator by simply deleting these two variables, like so:

```
<cfset StructDelete( Session, "AdminName" ) >
<cfset StructDelete( Session, "AdminID" ) >
```

Application **Variables**

The Application scope is ideal when you want to cache queries that don't change often, or variables that never change throughout an application. This way, you don't have to keep setting variables for each user on each page refresh.

Here's a useful trick: Instead of continually querying the database for menu and submenu items for each user request, you can query the database once and store the Recordsets in the Application scope. Assuming that each user sees the same menu and that the menu changes very infrequently, this will save you countless resources on wasted queries and the like.

You will put this to use in this section's example; you will cache the query within the Application scope instead of grabbing the results from the database every time.

You need to understand how Application variables differ from Session variables. Session variables are specific to a particular user, whereas Application variables are the same for all users within an application.

Using Dreamweaver, create a new a new file called cacheQuery.cfm and enter the following code into the document window:

```
<cflock type="readonly" name="companyInfo_departmt" timeout="15">
    <cfset dptQryDefined = IsDefined("Application.getDepartments")>
</cflock>
<cfif NOT dptQryDefined>
  <cfquery name="getDepartments" datasource="CompanyInfo">
    SELECT *
    FROM Departmt
```

```
        ORDER BY Dept_Name ASC
    </cfquery>
    <cflock type="exclusive" name="companyInfo_departmt" timeout="15">
        <cfset Application.getDepartments = getDepartments>
    </cflock>
</cfif>
<cflock type="readonly" name="companyInfo_departmt" timeout="15">
    <cfset Request.getDepartments = Application.getDepartments>
</cflock>
<cfform action="index.cfm" method="post">
<cfselect name="Dept_ID" query="Request.getDepartments"➡
    value="Dept_ID" display="Dept_Name"></cfselect>
<input type="submit" value="View Employees">
</cfform>
```

Test this file in a web browser. The first time you run the code, the variable #Application.getDepartments# will be undefined and the first block of code will execute. For each subsequent call to this template, the Application variable will exist, and this code block will be skipped.

You will not need to requery the database unless you restart the server or the variable expires. You must put this code either on every page where you need this query or, even better, in the Application.cfm template so that you won't need to check for the Application variable's existence on several different templates.

Creating a Content Management System

Next we will look at creating a simple content management system in ColdFusion. By storing your content in a database, you can easily allow administrators to change text on a page without having to use FTP or RDS to make simple text changes. Also, it allows you to limit what people are allowed to change. For example, on your home page you might want to allow people to change only the welcome message. If the content is stored in a database, people could update the text as often as they like without having access to the rest of the site. If you assign users to particular "roles," you can limit which users can update which content.

The following example retrieves the site's content from a database and stores it in an Application variable, then copies that Application variable into the Request scope so you don't have to worry about locking throughout the application. By retrieving the content from the database only once and caching it in the Application scope, you dramatically reduce the number of calls necessary to the data source.

Retrieving Content from a Database

In the `cfbook` folder create a new subfolder named `ContentManager` and create an `Application.cfm` file inside it. Enter the following code:

```
<cfapplication name="ContentManagementSystem">
<cflock type="readonly" name="cfbook_content" timeout="10">
  <cfset content_init = IsDefined("Application.ContentManager")>
</cflock>
<cfif NOT content_init>
  <cfquery name="getContentManagerPages" datasource="cfbook_sql">
    SELECT PageName, PageContents
    FROM ContentManager
  </cfquery>
  <cfset Request.ContentManager = StructNew()>
  <cfloop query="getContentManagerPages">
    <cfset Request.ContentManager[ PageName ] = PageContents >
  </cfloop>
  <cflock type="exclusive" name="cfbook_content" timeout="10">
    <cfset Application.ContentManager = Duplicate(Request.ContentManager)>
  </cflock>
<cfelse>
  <cflock type="readonly" name="cfbook_content" timeout="10">
    <cfset Request.ContentManager = Duplicate(Application.ContentManager)>
  </cflock>
</cfif>
```

Naming your application by using the `<cfapplication>` tag allows ColdFusion to know which `Application` variables belong to which site. Next you check to see if a variable named `#Application.ContentManager#` already exists. If this variable has already been defined, then the application has already been initialized and you won't need to retrieve the latest content from the database. If the variable has not been defined, you must query the database and grab all records from the `ContentManager` table within the database (available in the code download as `ch7_cms.mdb`). Also remember to set up a data source and connection for the database, as we described in Chapter 2. Call the data source `cfbook_sql`.

This is a simple table with only two columns, `PageName` and `PageContents`. `PageName` is a text column and allows you to assign a name to the content. The table has only a single row with some content named `home_intro`, which will hold the site's welcome message. The next column, `PageContents`, is the actual text that you want to display. Because it may need to hold a large amount of text, set the data type to Memo (assuming you are using Access; if using SQL Server, set it to an nvarchar data type with a maximum length of about 4,000 characters). Just be careful that you don't set the maximum length of the fields too small, or you will receive data truncation errors if your users try to enter too much text in the field.

After querying the database, you create a new structure named ContentManager within the Request scope. For each record in the Recordset, create a new entry in the structure. This will allow you to retrieve the PageContents from the structure by passing the PageName as a key, for example, #Request.ContentManager['home_intro']#, as you will see in the following admin template.

Finally, copy the Request structure into the Application scope so the next time you need to display text from the content manager, you can use the cached values in the Application scope instead of having to query the database again. If the #Application.ContentManager# variable is already defined, then the <cfelse> code block will execute and you will simply have to duplicate the structure from the Application scope into the Request scope to avoid future locks. Because this code is all stored in the Application.cfm file, it will execute before each page request, and you can be sure that the #Request.ContentManager# structure exists within your templates.

Displaying Content

Next, create a file called index.cfm within the same directory as the Application.cfm file and enter the following code into it:

```
<table>
  <tr>
    <td><cfoutput>#Request.ContentManager['home_intro']#</cfoutput></td>
  </tr>
</table>
```

This code doesn't need too much explanation. It just has some basic formatting and outputs the value of #Request.ContentManager['home_intro']# to the window. You can create as many pages for the content management system as you want. For example, you could create a generic header and footer to include on each page, or create some content for a Contact or an About page, and include contact details throughout the site. By storing the site's text in a database, you can allow users to modify the text as often as they want without giving them access to your files, thereby avoiding the risk of damage to your site code). The other added bonus is that, because you've cached all the content in the Application scope, you don't have to query the database several times per user request to get the latest content.

Adding and Editing Content

Create another file called admin.cfm, which you will use to edit the content and add new pages, and add the following code to it:

```
<cfform action="admin.cfm" method="post">
  <select name="PageName">
    <cfloop list="#StructKeyList(Request.ContentManager)#" index="thisPage">
    <cfoutput><option value="#thisPage#">#thisPage#</option></cfoutput>
    </cfloop>
  </select>
  <input type="Submit" value="Edit Page">
</cfform>
<cfform action="createNewPage.cfm" method="post">
  <cfinput type="text" name="PageName" value=""➥
    required="yes" message="Please enter a page name.">
  <input type="Submit" value="Add Page">
  <input type="Hidden" name="PageName_required" value="Please enter a page name.">
</cfform>
<cfif IsDefined("URL.ErrorMessage")>
  <cfoutput>#URL.ErrorMessage#</cfoutput>
</cfif>
<cfif IsDefined("Form.PageName")>
  <cfoutput>
    <h1>#UCase(Form.PageName)#</h1>
    <cfform action="updatePageContent.cfm" method="post">
      <textarea cols="80" rows="25" wrap="soft" name="PageContents">
        #Request.ContentManager[Form.PageName]#
      </textarea>
      <br />
      <input type="Submit" value="Update Content">
      <input type="hidden" name="PageName" value="#Form.PageName#">
    </cfform>
  </cfoutput>
</cfif>
```

This page is broken into four sections. The first section is a form that displays the list of pages in a drop-down menu along with a Submit button. You are using a new function here called #StructKeyList()#, which returns all the keys within the structure. In the #Application.ContentManager# structure, you are using the page names for keys. So, each option in the drop-down menu is the name of a page. When you have finished your application, selecting a page and clicking the Edit Page button will result in the contents of that page being displayed at the bottom of the web page for edit.

The second section is a form containing a text input field and a Submit button. This is where you create new pages for the content manager by simply typing in a new name for a page and clicking the Add Page button. You'll look at the exact code later in this section.

The third section is where ColdFusion displays an error message if it is unable to successfully create or update a page. If there is a variable called #URL.ErrorMessage#, then ColdFusion displays it to the screen.

The final section is shown only if the user selects a page from the drop-down menu at the top of the template and clicks the Edit Page button. If the #Form.PageName# variable exists, the page name is shown along with a large text area in which you can change the existing page's content.

Create another page called createNewPage.cfm, again in the same directory, and enter the following code into it:

```
<cfparam name="Form.PageName" type="string">
<cfquery name="checkPageNameExists" datasource="cfbook_sql">
  SELECT PageName
  FROM ContentManager
  WHERE PageName = <cfqueryparam value=➡
    "#Form.PageName#" cfsqltype="cf_sql_varchar">
</cfquery>
<cfif checkPageNameExists.RecordCount EQ 0>
  <cfquery datasource="cfbook_sql">
    INSERT INTO
      ContentManager (
        PageName,
        PageContents
      )
    VALUES
      (
        <cfqueryparam value="#Form.PageName#" cfsqltype="cf_sql_varchar">,
        <cfqueryparam value="" cfsqltype="cf_sql_varchar">
      )
  </cfquery>
  <cflock type="exclusive" name="cfbook_content" timeout="10">
    <cfset Application.ContentManager[ Form.PageName ] = "" >
  </cflock>
  <cflocation url="admin.cfm">
<cfelse>
  <cflocation url="admin.cfm?ErrorMessage=#URLEncodedFormat("This PageName
already exists in the database. Unable to create page.")#">
</cfif>
```

You've already seen most of the CFML in this file in previous examples. First you are checking that you have passed a variable called #Form.PageName# by using the <cfparam> tag. Of course, this code is fairly simplistic, and you'll want to add some better error handling and trapping (we look at this in greater detail in Chapter 8).

This template begins by checking to see if a record by this name already exists in the database, and if not, it inserts one. You must be very careful here: Remember that you also have to replicate the changes in the database and in the #Application.ContentManager# structure. If you apply the changes to only the database, they will not be reflected on the front end of the site until after you reboot the server and ColdFusion recreates the #Application.ContentManager# variable.

Conversely, if you update only the #Application.ContentManager# variable and not the database, when your server reboots (or if the application variables expire) and the latest content from the database is grabbed, all of the changes will be lost. If a record with this page name already exists, ColdFusion executes the <cfelse> block, redirects the user back to the admin.cfm template, and passes an error message along the query string.

Create a final template called updatePageContent.cfm in the same directory as the two preceding files and enter the following code into it:

```
<cfparam name="Form.PageName" type="string">
<cfparam name="Form.PageContents" type="string">
<cfquery datasource="cfbook_sql">
  UPDATE
    ContentManager
  SET


  PageContents =
  <cfqueryparam value="#Form.PageContents#"➡
    cfsqltype="cf_sql_varchar" maxlength="4000">
  WHERE
    PageName = <cfqueryparam value="#Form.PageName#"
              cfsqltype="cf_sql_varchar">
</cfquery>
<cflock type="exclusive" name="cfbook_content" timeout="10">
  <cfset Application.ContentManager[ Form.PageName ] = Form.PageContents >
</cflock>
<cflocation url="admin.cfm">
```

This template is very similar to createNewPage.cfm, except that this time you are making sure that both the #Form.PageName# and #Form.PageContents# variables exist before updating the database. As before, you update the

#Application.ContentManager# structure as well so the content is current in both the database and the structure. Finally, ColdFusion redirects users to the admin.cfm page, where they can create a new page or modify an existing one.

You have now built a basic content management system that enables users to modify their own content. Now you can modify your site's content from any computer with an Internet connection.

The same general concept of caching your content can be applied to several other applications as well. By using code similar to your content management systems, you are able to add content easily to your site from a remote news feed. You could create a file that grabs a remote XML feed from Macromedia or one of the millions of "blogs" on the Internet, parse the XML, and save the results to an Application-scoped variable (you will learn more about XML in Chapter 11). This way, you wouldn't need to parse the XML each time a user visits the page, but instead will be synchronizing the content on an hourly basis or setting up a scheduled task in the ColdFusion Administrator that runs regularly. This would download the latest version of the XML document and update the Application variable. This method of content caching allows you to keep content relatively current without the huge overhead of parsing a remote data feed every time the user wants to view the page.

Counting Online Users

Although there are no supported built-in methods of counting the number of currently active sessions within ColdFusion, it isn't that difficult to write some code that creates this kind of functionality. By using a combination of the Session, Application, and Variables scopes, you can create a structure to hold each user's unique token and the date and time the user last connected.

Create another new folder named SessionTracker within your cfbook site. Within this folder create a new Application.cfm file and enter the following code:

```
<cfapplication name="countOnineUsers"➡
  sessionmanagement="Yes"➡
  sessiontimeout="#CreateTimeSpan(0,0,15,0)#">
<cflock type="EXCLUSIVE" name="user_init" timeout="10">
  <cfparam name="Session.UniqueID" default="#CreateUUID()#">
  <cfset Variables.thisUniqueID = Session.UniqueID >
</cflock>
<cflock name="app_init" type="READONLY" timeout="10">
  <cfset app_init = IsDefined("Application.onlineUsers") >
</cflock>
<cfif NOT app_init>
  <cfset Variables.onlineUsers = StructNew() >
```

```
<cfelse>
  <cflock name="app_init" type="READONLY" timeout="10">
    <cfset Variables.onlineUsers = Application.onlineUsers >
  </cflock>
</cfif>
<cfset StructInsert( Variables.onlineUsers, Variables.thisUniqueID, Now( ), TRUE
) >
<cfloop collection="#Variables.onlineUsers#" item="thisUUID">
  <cfif DateDiff( "n", Variables.onlineUsers[ thisUUID ], Now() ) GT 16>
    <cfset StructDelete( Variables.onlineUsers, thisUUID ) >
  </cfif>
</cfloop>
<cfset Request.numOnlineUsers = StructCount(Variables.onlineUsers) >
<cflock type="EXCLUSIVE" name="app_init" timeout="15">
  <cfset Application.onlineUsers = Duplicate( Variables.onlineUsers ) >
</cflock>
```

First add the <cfapplication> tag, enable session management, and set the sessions to expire after 15 minutes of the user being idle. Next you create a #Session.UniqueID# variable (if it hasn't already been defined) using the <cfparam> tag, then copy the Session variable into the Variables scope to avoid future locks.

The next block of code creates a read-only lock, where you set a variable that checks if the Application variable (#Application.onlineUsers#) has been defined yet. If the variable has not been defined, a new structure named #Variables.onlineUsers# is created in the Variables scope; this will hold the current user's unique ID and the date the user last accessed the site. If the variable has been defined, the <cfelse> block executes, and you create a read-only lock to copy the Application structure into the Variables scope.

The #StructInsert()# function then inserts the current user's unique ID and timestamp into the #Variables.onlineUsers# structure. To make sure the latest timestamp is used, #StructInsert()# overwrites the value if it already exists.

Next, ColdFusion loops through each user in the #Variables.onlineUsers# structure and uses the #DateDiff()# function to see when the user last accessed the system. The #DateDiff()# function compares the date/time the user last viewed a page with the current date/time, and a user who hasn't viewed a page in the past 16 minutes is deleted from the structure. If the user has viewed a page within the past 16 minutes, that user is still active within the site and remains in the structure.

Next you set a variable called #Request.numOnlineUsers#, which holds the number of keys still in the #Variables.onlineUsers# structure.

Finally, you create an exclusive lock where you copy the #Variables.onlineUsers# structure back into the Application scope.

To test this code, create a new file called index.cfm within the SessionTracker folder and enter the following line of code:

```
<cfoutput>
  There are currently #Request.numOnlineUsers# active user(s) online.
</cfoutput>
```

View the index.cfm template in a web browser, and you will see an output similar the display in Figure 7-5.

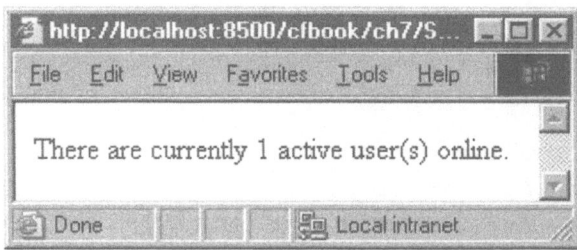

Figure 7-5. Your session tracker showing one user currently online

The application should have only one active user at the moment (you). If you have a second computer, you can view index.cfm from there, too, and see two users now online.

Client **Variables**

Client scope variables are specific to a particular user and, like Session scope variables, rely on the #Cookie.CFID# and #Cookie.CFTOKEN# variables. Unlike Session variables, they never need to be locked and are stored in one of three places: a database, the server's registry, or within cookies. Client scope variables also require a bit more setup than Session scope variables do, and they have one important limitation: Client variables can use only simple values such as strings, numbers, lists, Booleans, and so on. However, there is one slight workaround that allows you to store queries, arrays, and structures in the Client scope by using the <cfwddx> tag.

Enabling Client Variables

First let's take a look at how to enable Client scope variables on your site. Open a browser, load the ColdFusion Administrator (http://localhost:8500/CFIDE/administrator/), and click on the Client Variables link on the left-hand menu. This should open the window shown in Figure 7-6.

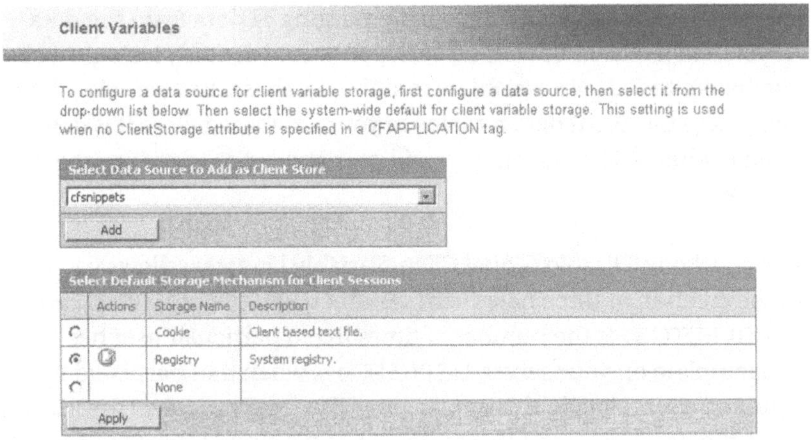

Client Variables

To configure a data source for client variable storage, first configure a data source, then select it from the drop-down list below. Then select the system-wide default for client variable storage. This setting is used when no ClientStorage attribute is specified in a CFAPPLICATION tag.

Select Data Source to Add as Client Store

| cfsnippets | ▼ |

| Add |

Select Default Storage Mechanism for Client Sessions

	Actions	Storage Name	Description
○		Cookie	Client based text file.
◉	🗑	Registry	System registry.
○		None	

| Apply |

Figure 7-6. The ColdFusion Administrator Client Variables screen

This is where you can select which data sources are used for Client variable storage.

You have three options for storing Client variables: a data source, the registry, or client cookies. You can specify the default storage method (if one isn't provided) within the <cfapplication> tag. The best place to store client variables is within a database. The system registry wasn't designed to have multiple users storing large amounts of data, and we've already discussed the limitations imposed on setting cookies on the user's system. In the very least, you should create a default database to store Client variables instead of storing them in the system registry.

Because you will be using a database to store Client variables, you first must create a data source before enabling Client variables. Because you created a data source for the cfbook database in Chapter 6, you will use that same data source to hold the Client variables too.

To enable Client variable storage for the data source, select cfbook from the drop-down menu at the top of the screen and click the Add button.

The next screen that appears is where you configure client storage settings for this particular data source:

- The text area at the top of the page allows you to enter some text or notes if desired.

- The first checkbox allows you to tell ColdFusion whether to create the database tables automatically. These tables will be used to hold the client data and should be checked only if this is the first time you are setting up the Client variable store. If these tables already exist in your database, ColdFusion will throw an error.

- The second checkbox lets you disable the purging of data from the database. If you had a cluster of web servers, you would set only a single web server to delete the Client variables from the database. You can also define how many days the client data remains in your database before it is deleted. The default value is 90 days, but you will probably want to reduce this to a week or less.

- The final checkbox, Disable Global Client Variable Updates, allows you to disable the creation of three new client variables: HITCOUNT, LASTVISIT, and TIMECREATED. HITCOUNT is the number of times that a particular user has viewed a template on your server. LASTVISIT logs when that particular user last requested a template in this application. The final variable, TIMECREATED, logs when the user's session was created. In some circumstances you may find these Client variables useful, but if you are not going to use them within your application, check the checkbox to stop them from being updated; disabling this option will slightly improve your application's performance.

After you have finished making changes, click the Submit Changes button to apply them and return to the previous window.

If you want to set the default data storage location for Client variables, you can now click on the radio button beside the cfbook data source and click the Apply button. From now on, when you enable client management within your <cfapplication> tag and don't specify a data source to use for variable storage, it will default to this database.

Now, to use Client variables within your application, all you must do is update the <cfapplication> tag within your Application.cfm, like so:

```
<cfapplication name="cfbook" clientmanagement="yes">
```

If you didn't set the default Client variable storage location to the cfbook data source within the ColdFusion Administrator, or if you wanted to use a different data source, you would need to change the preceding snippet to:

```
<cfapplication name="cfbook" clientmanagement="yes" clientstorage="cfbook">
```

where clientstorage is the desired data source in which you want to store your Client variable data.

Setting Client variables is as simple as creating Form, URL, Variables, or Request scoped variables. Because Client variables are not stored within the server's memory, there is no need to lock access to this scope. If you want to create a variable called #Client.Name#, all you have to do is use the <cfset> tag as shown here:

```
<cfparam name="Form.Name" type="string">
<cfset Client.Name = Form.Name >
```

Similarly, you do not need to perform any locking when writing out to this variable scope; to display this variable, just output #Client.Name#.

Deleting Client *Variables*

Deleting Client variables is somewhat trickier. If you want to actually delete a variable from client storage, you must use a special function: #DeleteClientVariable()#. Here's the syntax for this function:

```
<cfset success = DeleteClientVariable("Name") >
```

Because the DeleteClientVariable() function returns true or false, you can test to see if the deletion was successful. If you don't care whether the Client variable was deleted successfully, you could shorten the preceding snippet to:

```
<cfset DeleteClientVariable("Name") >
```

Be careful about a couple of things here. Note that you need to enclose within double quotes the name of the Client variable you want to delete. Note also that you didn't prepend the variable name with the Client scope.

If you want to get a list of the variables within the Client scope, a function called #GetClientVariablesList()#returns a list (comma-delimited by default) of each current Client variable (excluding CFID, CFTOKEN, etc). The syntax looks like this (clientVariables.cfm):

```
<cfset Client.VarA = "One" >
<cfset Client.VarB = "Two" >
<cfset Client.VarC = CreateDate(2003,2,28) >
<cfloop list="#GetClientVariablesList()#" index="i">
  <cfoutput>#i#: #Client[ i ]#<br /></cfoutput>
</cfloop>
```

This code loops over each of the Client variables and displays their names and values, as shown in Figure 7-7.

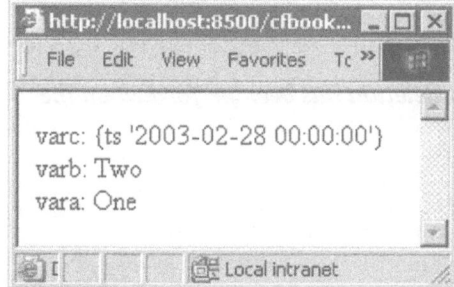

Figure 7-7. Outputting Client variables

You are also able to loop through each Client variable by treating the Client scope as a structure with the following code:

```
<cfloop collection="#Client#" item="i">
  <cfoutput>#i#: #Client[ I ]#<br /></cfoutput>
</cfloop>
```

If you want to delete each of the variables within the Client scope (you would want to do this when a user logs out of your site, for example), you can use code similar to the following:

```
<cfloop list="#GetClientVariablesList()#" index="i">
  <cfset DeleteClientVariable(i) >
</cfloop>
```

If you were to use <cfdump> to look at the contents of the Client scope after deleting all the variables, you could build a template using something as simple as this (see deleteClient.cfm for full code):

```
<cfdump var="#Client#">
```

This would create the output shown in Figure 7-8.

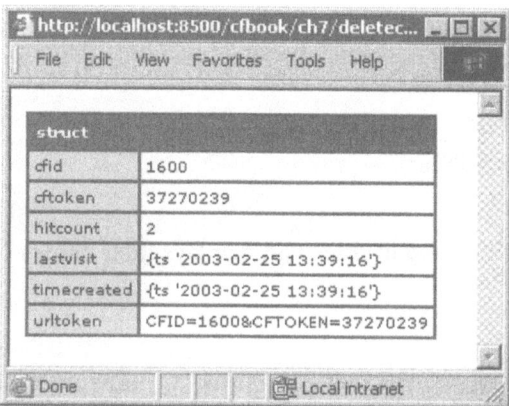

Figure 7-8. The variables still defined after a deletion has been performed on the Client *scope*

As you can see in Figure 7-8, not all variables have been deleted from the Client scope. There should be three to six client variables still defined:

- CFID

- CFTOKEN

- HITCOUNT

- LASTVISIT

- TIMECREATED

- URLTOKEN

If you disabled the global client variable updates in the ColdFusion Administrator, you would see only the first three variables instead of all six. We've already covered CFID and CFTOKEN, but look at the URLTOKEN value in Figure 7-8 and notice that it is simply the CFID and CFTOKEN variables concatenated together. This makes it easier for developers to pass these variables along the Querystring if they need to. You will need to do this in a few particular circumstances; for example, when cookies are disabled or when the same application is split between two domain names. If you've used the <cflocation> tag before, you may have noticed that it automatically appended the CFID and CFTOKEN variables along with the address for you.

Using WDDX

We also mentioned earlier that it is possible to display complex values within the Client scope. To do this, you first must look at another tag, <cfwddx>. WDDX stands for Web Distributed Data Exchange, and is a free, XML-based technology developed by Allaire for ColdFusion 4.0. One of WDDX's major benefits is that it is supported by most programming languages, including JavaScript, PHP, Perl, ASP, and Java. WDDX allows any CFML data type, including structures, queries, and the like, to be converted (serialized) into XML (which can be transmitted as text) and then converted back (deserialized) on the destination system. WDDX is no longer controlled by any one company and is now an open standard. You can learn more at http://www.openwddx.org.

You've already seen how easy it is to create Client variables with CFML; now we're going to show you how simple it is to convert arrays and structures into WDDX packets.

1. In Dreamweaver, create a new file called serializeWddx.cfm in the ch7 folder and enter the following code:

```
<cfset myString = "Hello World">
<cfwddx action="cfml2wddx" input="#myString#" output="myWddxPacket">
<cfoutput>#HTMLEditFormat( myWddxPacket )#</cfoutput>
```

The #HTMLEditFormat()# function escapes any special HTML characters (such as ", >, <, or &) with " > < and &. This allows you to output a string safely to the screen and not have it render as HTML. The preceding snippet will output the following:

```
<wddxPacket version='1.0'>
<header/><data><string>Hello World</string></data>
</wddxPacket>
```

ColdFusion has converted the string into a WDDX packet, akin to an XML document. Although you wouldn't really need to convert a simple string into a WDDX packet, you will see shortly that it is just as easy to convert an array or Recordset to WDDX.

2. Create another file in Dreamweaver called serializewddx2.cfm and enter the following code into it:

```
<cfset myArray = ArrayNew(1) >
<cfset myArray[1] = "One" >
<cfset myArray[2] = "Two" >
<cfset myArray[3] = "Three" >
<cfwddx action="cfml2wddx" input="#myArray#" output="Client.myWddxPacket">
<cfoutput>#HTMLEditFormat( Client.myWddxPacket )#</cfoutput>
```

If you have not enabled Client variable support, you will get an error like this:

```
Exception during WDDX
operation.coldfusion.runtime.NoOperScope$ScopeDisabledException:
The requested scope client has not been enabled.
```

To solve this, create file called Application.cfm and enter the following code:

```
<cfapplication name="Ch7" clientmanagement="yes">
```

This code snippet generates a packet:

```
<wddxPacket version='1.0'><header/>
<data>
  <array length='3'>
    <string>One</string>
    <string>Two</string>
    <string>Three</string>
  </array>
</data>
</wddxPacket>
```

The CFML that converts a variable into a WDDX packet is exactly the same. You set the WDDX action to cfml2wddx, which tells ColdFusion that you want to create a WDDX packet from a ColdFusion variable. Finally, you specify the variable to convert (enclosed in a pair of pound signs). In the input and output attributes, you are telling ColdFusion which name to assign to the resulting WDDX packet. The WDDX packet itself can be treated like a string and then saved to a client variable, as you did previously.

3. Now let's look at how you convert this WDDX packet back into an array. Create another page named deserializeWddx2.cfm and enter the following code into it:

```
<cfparam name="Client.myWddxPacket" type="string">
<cfwddx action="wddx2cfml" input="#Client.myWddxPacket#"
output="myArray">
<cfdump var="#myArray#">
```

This time, the <cfwddx> tag is converting a WDDX packet back into CFML, as shown in <cfwddx>'s action attribute. The input attribute holds the #Client.myWddxPacket# variable, which is the actual WDDX packet. The result is saved into a new variable called myArray.

If you run serializewddx2.cfm and then deserializewddx2.cfm, you will see the output shown in Figure 7-9.

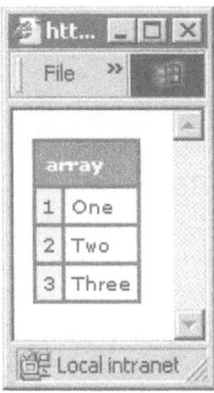

Figure 7-9. The result of transforming an array into a WDDX packet and back again, then outputting the array to a browser

The <cfwddx> tag is able to serialize any sort of CFML object. If you need to store more than simple variables in Client variables, you must use <cfwddx> and serialize and deserialize packets whenever you need to use them, because Client variables are able to store strings but not complex data types. The benefit is that you don't have to worry about locking variables before accessing them, and you can store complex values in a format such as a cookie, database, HTTP Request, or text file. However, the drawback is that you always must be actively converting back and forth between WDDX and CFML, which has some performance cost.

In the long run it may be easier for you to use Session variables and lock all the reads and writes, but it is always nice to know that you can use Client variables if you need to. In addition, using <cfwddx> makes it very easy to syndicate data to other sites, even though proprietary XML formats are much more widely used, and, since the release of ColdFusion MX, the CFML language has had full support for XML. (XML is covered in Chapter 11.)

Understanding Cookieless Sessions

As explained earlier in this chapter, Client and Session variables rely on two cookies: #Cookie.CFID# and #Cookie.CFTOKEN# (or JSESSIONID). But what happens if users do not have cookies enabled? Luckily, you can still use state management, but it isn't quite as easy. If users have disabled cookies on their systems, you must explicitly pass the CFID and CFTOKEN variables to each page. This means that for each form, you must include the CFID and CFTOKEN as hidden variables for each link on your site, and you need to append CFID and CFTOKEN to the address.

This isn't as bad as it sounds initially, but verifying that each form and link are passing the correct values can be time consuming. ColdFusion makes this slightly easier by supplying a variable called #Client.URLTOKEN# or #Session.URLTOKEN#, which is a combination of #CFID# and #CFTOKEN# and can be used easily in URLs. Instead of having to type the following code:

```
<a href="index.cfm?CFID=#Client.CFID#&CFTOKEN=#Client.CFTOKEN#">link</a>
```

you can use this:

```
<a href="index.cfm?#Client.URLTOKEN#">link</a>
```

The #Client.URLTOKEN# and #Session.URLTOKEN# variables make it easier to append the CFID and CFTOKEN variables onto a URL.

If your users do have cookies enabled, you don't need to pass these variables along the address bar for each link and form. ColdFusion MX introduced a new function called #URLSessionFormat()# that appends the CFID and CFTOKEN variables into the URL if the user has cookies disabled. If the user has cookies enabled, the CFID and CFTOKEN variables are not appended. This function leads to much tidier URLs and makes development a little easier because you do not need to explicitly pass variables for each link. Also, you don't need to test whether a user has cookies enabled if you are using session management. Another reason that using this function is a good practice is that it is aware of whether J2EE Sessions are being used, and will construct the session token appropriately. We present an example of the #URLSessionFormat()# function in this section.

Open Dreamweaver, create a new file named sessionFormat.cfm in the Ch7 folder, and enter the following code into the document window:

```
<cfoutput>
  <a href="index.cfm?CFID=#Client.CFID#&CFTOKEN=#Client.CFTOKEN#">
    link A
  </a><br />
  <a href="index.cfm?#Client.URLTOKEN#">link B</a><br />
  <hr />
  <a href="#URLSessionFormat('index.cfm')#">link C</a><br />
  <a href="#URLSessionFormat('index.cfm?error=true')#">link D</a><br />
</cfoutput>
```

Test the results in a web browser, and you will see four links on the page. If you hover your mouse over each link, you can see that the first two links explicitly pass the CFID and CFTOKEN variables to the target page, and the final two links will pass the CFID and CFTOKEN variables only if users have cookies disabled on their machines. You can test this by disabling your cookies, restarting your browser, and viewing the sessionFormat.cfm template in the browser again.

Determining Whether a User's Cookies Are Enabled

Testing whether or not a user has cookies enabled can be slightly tricky. You cannot set a cookie on a CFML template and check for its existence on the same page. Even if cookies are disabled, ColdFusion will think that the cookie was successfully created. To test if cookies have been enabled, set the cookies on one page and redirect the user to a new page to see if the cookie was actually set. Let's look at an example:

Create a new folder named checkCookies within the cfbook site. Within this, create a new file called index.cfm and enter the following code:

```
<cfcookie name="cookies_enabled" value="1">
<cflocation url="checkCookie.cfm">
```

This is a fairly basic file that sets a session-based cookie and redirects the user to a new page. It is important to note that the preceding code will not work in versions of ColdFusion prior to MX. Previous versions of ColdFusion would redirect the browser before setting the cookie on the client's machine, so you would need to revise the preceding listing to use either a meta refresh or a JavaScript redirect to the following target page.

Next create another new template called checkCookie.cfm and enter the following code:

```
<cfoutput>Cookies are enabled: #IsDefined( "Cookie.cookies_enabled" )#</cfoutput>
```

If you view the index.cfm template in a web browser, you will be redirected to checkCookie.cfm and see output similar that shown in Figure 7-10.

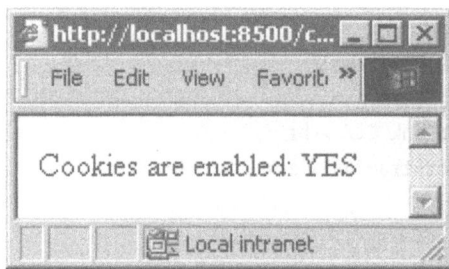

Figure 7-10. Your cookie settings tester in action

If you then disable cookies on your browser, close all open browser windows, and recheck the file, you will see that it tells you cookies are not enabled.

Summary

In this chapter you learned how to create and destroy cookies, as well as the difference between session cookies and persistent cookies. You also learned about Session and Application variables and why it is sometimes important to lock access to variables stored in the server's memory. You should now also understand how to copy a structure effectively by using the #Duplicate()# function to avoid problems in your code, and you've learned the key differences among the Application, Session, and Client scopes.

Finally, you should now have a very general concept of what WDDX is and how to use it. WDDX is not used very often now that XML is supported by ColdFusion MX and ColdFusion MX 6.1, but WDDX can be very useful when you need to pass data easily between different sites and want to take advantage of the <cfwddx> tag's ability to automatically create a packet for you.

You can find some great articles on session management on the Macromedia site at http://www.macromedia.com/support/coldfusion/session.html and http://www.macromedia.com/support/coldfusion/ts/documents/tn18235.htm. You can find more information on WDDX at http://www.openwddx.org.

Exception Handling
with CFML

A KEY FEATURE OF an application built with any programming language is its ability to gracefully handle business logic or runtime exceptions. CFML provides many constructs that allow you to build structured exception handling into your applications to catch errors and conditions raised by your applications.

Every application has the potential to raise exceptions (throw errors) under certain conditions, and ColdFusion is no exception to this rule. Errors fall into two categories: those generated by business process or coding errors, and those generated by business logic exceptions. You can handle errors at one of three levels: server (one page that handles all errors on a server), application (one page that handles all exceptions of a specific type at the application level), or code (errors are handled in-place at runtime at the level of the code that generated the exception).

In this chapter we cover:

- Configuring the ColdFusion Administrator to handle errors at the server level

- Using `<cferror>` to handle errors at the application level

- Using `<cfcatch>`, `<cftry>`, `<cfthrow>`, and `<cfrethrow>` to build more robust exception handling

- When and how to define and handle custom exceptions

- Best practices and more on structured exception handling

- Using the ColdFusion Administrator Debug settings

- Using `<cfdump>` to debug applications

- Using `<cftrace>` to debug an application

- Using `<cftransaction>` to protect data integrity

Configuring the ColdFusion Administrator to Handle Errors at the Server Level

The broadest error-handling mechanisms available in ColdFusion are the Site-wide Error Handler and the Missing Template Handler. You can find both in the ColdFusion Administrator under the Settings link in the Server Settings section of the menu, as shown in Figure 8-1.

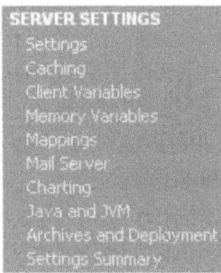

Figure 8-1. The ColdFusion Administrator Server Settings menu section. Note the Settings link at the top.

Ordinarily, when an error occurs, the ColdFusion Server aborts processing of the page, logs the error in a log file (application.log and/or exception.log in the logs subdirectory of your ColdFusion install directory), and returns that all-too familiar blue-and-gray error screen to the end-user.

The Site-wide Error Handler allows you to specify the relative path (from the Web-root) to a page that the server will execute, rather than returning the default error page, in the event that any exception is thrown. This page can contain any valid CFML code. With a Site-wide Error Handler in place, the server will now abort processing the current page when an error occurs and invoke the page specified in the Administrator.

The Missing Template Handler specifies the relative path (from the Web-root) to a page that executes in the event that an HTTP request is sent for a ColdFusion file that is not found (typically referred to as a "404 error"). This assumes that the web server in use is configured *not* to check if a file exists prior to executing. Otherwise, the web server will handle the 404 exception itself. Again, any valid CFML code may be placed in this page.

When you click on the Settings link discussed previously, you will reach the Server Settings screen, which contains two text fields for entering the paths to your Site-wide Error Handler and Missing Template Handler, as you can see in Figure 8-2.

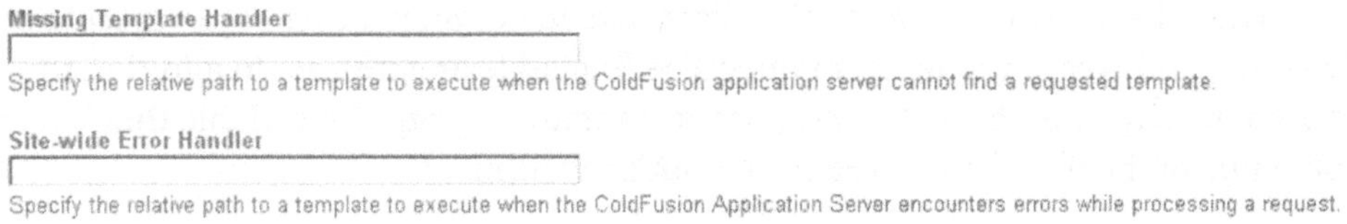

Missing Template Handler

Specify the relative path to a template to execute when the ColdFusion application server cannot find a requested template.

Site-wide Error Handler

Specify the relative path to a template to execute when the ColdFusion Application Server encounters errors while processing a request.

Figure 8-2. The error page handlers in the ColdFusion Administrator Server Settings screen

When either the Site-wide Error Handler or the Missing Template Handler is executed, in addition to the scopes that regularly exist (such as CGI, Cookie, URL, etc.), an Error scope is created and populated with information specific to the error that occurred. This error information can be logged to a file or database, displayed to the user, e-mailed to the web master, etc. The Error scope variables are as follows:

- Browser: The client browser type and version that made the errant request

- DateTime: The current server timestamp

- Diagnostics: Diagnostics information (detail message)

- GeneratedContent: The HTML generated by the errant request

- HTTPReferer: The HTTP page that referred the client to the erroneous requested page

- Mailto: The web master's e-mail address (generally populated by <cferror>)

- Message: The short error message

- QueryString: The URL Querystring of the errant request

- RemoteAddress: The client IP address

- RootCause: Runtime execution diagnostics structure for the tag that generated the error

- TagContext: Array of structures of execution diagnostics for executed custom tags

- Template: Relative path to the erroneous page that was requested

- Type: ColdFusion error type

When the Missing Template Handler is executed, only the Message, TagContext, Template, and Type variables from the preceding table are present. In addition to those four error variables, the Error scope contains a _template variable that holds the name of the file that was requested but not found.

Using <cferror> to Handle Errors at the Application Level

Although the Site-wide Error Handler is a good alternative to the ugly error messages we developers are used to seeing when testing code, it does have limitations. For one, the default look and feel of the site the users are browsing will be lost when they are redirected to the Site-wide Error Handler unless the server is a dedicated server for that site and the error handling page is tailored to fit in. It is usually very generic-looking and must be shared by all applications and web sites on the server.

The Site-wide Error Handler is also limited because it is called for all errors that occur, which means the error-handling code is generally very generic and often limited to presenting a simple error message and logging the error. When the Site-wide Error Handler executes, the original caller page is aborted, and users will be on their way to a new file.

The <cferror> tag provides developers with the same functionality as the Site-wide Error Handler, but each <cferror> tag is specific to a single application and can be configured to listen for and handle only one specific type of error.

Any time the ColdFusion Server encounters a <cferror> tag, it creates a listener that will request the file specified by its template attribute whenever an error of the type specified by the <cferror> type attribute is thrown.

The listener waits to see if an error of that type occurs during the current request. If not, it does nothing. If that error type does occur, the <cferror> tag catches the exception and redirects users to the file specified in the template attribute. ColdFusion aborts processing the file containing the error as soon as the exception is raised. First let's look at the <cferror> tag's attributes and their possible values:

- type: This attribute refers to the type of error this tag raises and passes to the error handler. Valid values are request, validation, and exception. Note that prior to ColdFusion MX there used to be a fourth valid value, monitor, which is now deprecated.

- template: This contains the path to the ColdFusion file that executes for this error type, which is relative to the current page (the page containing the <cferror> tag).

- mailto: This contains an e-mail address that will populate error.mailto in the page that handles the error.

- exception: If the type attribute is set to exception, this is the type of exception that occurred. Possible values include any, application, database, missinginclude, expression, lock, security, template, object, and user-defined error types

When ColdFusion encounters an exception, and a <cferror> tag catches that exception, the file that controls that error is executed. The Error scope and all of its attributes (as discussed in the previous section) is created and populated, and is available to the code in that page. The type of error caught determines what is allowable code in the page:

- request: HTML and error variables allowed, but no other CFML code

- validation: HTML and error variables allowed, but no other CFML code

- exception: HTML and/or CFML code allowed

You will note from the preceding points that CFML code is not valid in a page that processes a request or validation error, but the error variables are allowed. These pages can contain any HTML needed to display text and markup to the user. If you want to display the values of error variables in the page, you embed the error variables (prefixed with error) surrounded by pound signs in the page in the same way that variables are ordinarily displayed to users. The difference is that no <cfoutput> tags are required—or even allowed—to render the variables. This is not really an issue, because <cferror> is generally used as a last-resort error handler—try/catch error handling is generally considered a more preferable method of handling exceptions. We will discuss try/catch error handling later in this chapter.

For an error to be caught by <cferror>, ColdFusion must process a <cferror> tag in the same request as the request for the errant page. Because of this, and because generally you will want to reuse one error page on many requests, the <cferror> tag(s) are placed in an Application.cfm file as a best practice. If you have error-handling pages for various types of error, you should code one <cferror> tag in the Application.cfm file for each error type. Remember that ColdFusion processes a page from the top down, so put the more specific error type handlers above more general ones. The top of an Application.cfm file might look like the following:

```
<cferror template="noRecs.cfm" type="exception" exception="noRecsFound">
<cferror template="validate_error.cfm" type="validation"➧
  mailto="shorwith@figleaf.com">
<cferror template="generic_err.cfm" type="request">
```

Note that the more specific error types are at the top of the stack; they become more generic as the CFML parser moves toward the bottom.

An exception error is thrown whenever an exception of any possible type occurs and a <cferror> tag is able to name the specific exception type with its exception attribute. We discuss exception type errors in greater detail in the next section.

A validation error is thrown whenever a user submits a form that contains ColdFusion server-side validation, and the validation conditions are not met. To implement ColdFusion server-side validation, an HTML form must contain a hidden form field for each regular form field that you wish to validate. The hidden form field should have the same name as the form field that it validates, concatenated with one of several allowable suffixes that determine the type of validation to perform. The allowable suffixes are:

- _date: Field must be a date in a common format (mm/dd/yy or mm/dd/yyyy). If you omit the year, it will default to the current year.

- _time: Field must be a time in any of the commonly accepted time formats.

- _eurodate: Field must be a date in European format (dd/mm/yy or dd/mm/yyyy). If you omit the year, it will default to the current year.

- _integer: Field must be a whole number (no decimal value allowed).

- _float: Field must be a number (decimal values are allowed).

- _range: Field must be a number in a specific range. To specify the range, add MIN= and/or MAX= along with the desired limitation to the form control value attribute.

- _required: Field must have a value. An empty space does count as a value.

If you assign the hidden form field a value, this value will display within the bulleted list of error messages if it fails validation. Server-side validation is useful for data validation redundancy in the event that any other client-side validation fails. Here is a simple example in which the age field value must be from 0 to 100 (age_validation.cfm).

```
<form action="create_err_validation.cfm" method="post">
  What is your age?
<input type="text" name="age"><br />
<input type="hidden" name="age_range" value="Age MIN=0 and MAX=100">
<input type="submit" value="Generate Error!!">
</form>
```

When a validation error occurs, there are three variables in the Error scope that do not exist with other error types: #error.ValidationHeader#, #error.InvalidFields#, and `#error.ValidationFooter#`. You can output these in a simple error page, for example (`create_err_validation.cfm`):

```
<cfoutput>#error.ValidationHeader#</cfoutput><br />
<cfoutput>#error.InvalidFields#</cfoutput><br />
<cfoutput>#error.ValidationFooter#</cfoutput>
```

Try saving both the preceding files in a directory on your ColdFusion server and testing them. When you try to submit an age outside the value range 0 to 100, you'll be presented with an error like the one shown in Figure 8-3.

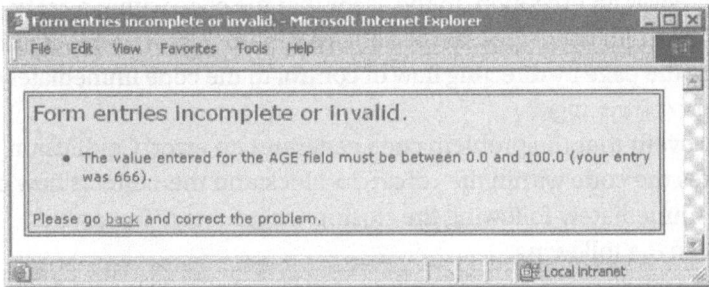

Figure 8-3. A simple custom error screen created by outputting variables contained within the Error *scope*

Note that the preceding code validates *only* that the form field value is in a specific range. A second hidden form field called `age_required` would need to be added to the form to make it a required field.

Most if not all errors fall into the category of request, so the request type `<cferror>` tag is generally used for error-catching redundancy in case no other `<cferror>` tag catches an exception. Therefore, the request `<cferror>` tag is always the last `<cferror>` tag in a page (from top to bottom). It acts as the last-ditch attempt to catch the error.

Using `<cfcatch>`, `<cftry>`, `<cfthrow>`, and `<cfrethrow>` to Build More Robust Exception Handling

Although preventing ugly error messages by implementing `<cferror>` tags is good, the `<cferror>` tag alone does not provide the tools you need to build truly robust exception handling. More localized and functional exception handling can be implemented by use of the `<cftry>` tag. To implement structured exception handling in an application, you must first identify any CFML code that is error prone.

No steadfast rules exist for doing this, but a good rule of thumb is to look for any code that is dependent on a resource or resources other than the ColdFusion server itself. Some tags to look for are <cfquery> (which relies on a database), <cffile> and <cfdirectory> (which rely on the local file system), <cfobject> and <cfinvoke> (which rely on external objects), <cfhttp> and <cfftp> (which rely on external servers), etc.

The <cftry> tag does not have any attributes; you simply surround the potential "problem" code with opening and closing <cftry> tags. By itself, <cftry> does nothing to prevent or handle errors, but it does enable the use of other error handling tags within its opening and closing tags, specifically the <cfcatch>, <cfthrow>, and <cfrethrow> tags.

The <cfcatch> tag allows developers to write code and have that code execute only when the prior block of code (the problem code immediately following the opening <cftry> tag) raises an exception. In the event that the code within a <cftry> executes without error, ColdFusion ignores the code within the <cfcatch> block and continues processing the page by directing flow of control to the code immediately following the closing </cftry> tag.

However, in the event that the problem code generates an error, ColdFusion immediately executes the code within the <cfcatch> block and then directs flow of control to the code immediately following the closing </cftry> tag. The pseudo code for this looks like the following:

```
<cftry>
  problem code here
  <cfcatch>
    error handling code here
  </cfcatch>
</cftry>
control of flow continues here
```

When a <cfcatch> block is executed, a scope known as the cfcatch scope is created and populated with all the error variables for the error that just occurred. The cfcatch scope is available only to the code inside the <cfcatch> tag block and does not exist outside of the <cfcatch> tags. Inside the <cfcatch> structure, the following values may exist (cfcatch keys vary by error type):

- Detail: Detailed error message

- ErrNumber: ColdFusion internal error number

- Message: The general error message

- MissingFileName: Name of file that could not be included

- TagContext: An array of structures representing the tag stack execution block

- Type: The error message "type"

- `RootCause`: Structure of error variables specific to the code being executed that threw the exception

- `SQLState`: A database driver error code

- `LockOperation`: Lock operation that failed ("timeout," "unknown," or "create mutex")

- `ExtendedInfo`: A custom error message that does not usually display in default error messages

- `ErrorCode`: Custom error code

- `LockName`: Name of the lock that failed ("anonymous" if the lock has no name)

- `NativeErrorCode`: A database driver error code

- `Name`: The name of the variable that could not be resolved

Several `<cfcatch>` blocks may be nested within a single `<cftry>` block—but not directly within each other. To nest a `<cfcatch>` within another `<cfcatch>`, you have to actually nest the `<cfcatch>` within a `<cftry>` within the `<cfcatch>`.

As was mentioned in the prior discussion about `<cferror>`, ColdFusion processes code from the top down. When an exception is thrown within a `<cftry>` block, ColdFusion begins searching down the page by starting with the line of code immediately following the code that threw the exception. Flow of control enters the first `<cfcatch>` block encountered, which is listening for the same type of error that was thrown, and then jumps to the code immediately following the closing `</cftry>`.

However, if no `<cfcatch>` block that matches the error type is found, ColdFusion aborts the current page and searches for a `<cferror>` tag within `Application.cfm` that handles this error type. Flow of control then moves to the page specified by the first `<cferror>` template that meets this criteria, and no other `<cferror>` tag is executed.

If no qualifying `<cferror>` is found within `Application.cfm`, ColdFusion raises an exception that will be handled by a Site-wide Error Handler if one is specified in the Administrator. Finally, if there is no Site-wide Error Handler either, the default ColdFusion error page is returned.

The `<cfcatch>` tag has a single attribute, `type`. Its allowed values are `any`, `application`, `database`, `security`, `template`, `expression`, `lock`, `searchengine`, `missinginclude`, `object`, or a user-defined error type (more on this in the next section).

As mentioned previously, in addition to being able to embed multiple `<cfcatch>` blocks within a single `<cftry>` block, you can also embed a `<cftry>/<cfcatch>` block within a `<cfcatch>` block. A situation in which this may be desirable is to handle failed database operations. Suppose an e-commerce application inserts customer order information in a SQL Server database, but that database undergoes a two-hour maintenance outage once per week. Ideally, the application will have 100-percent uptime. To handle an error thrown in the event that the SQL Server is offline, the query that inserts a new order is placed inside a <cftry> block, and another query is run inside the <cfcatch>. This query attempts to record the order in an Access database that has been designed to serve as a backup for the SQL Server. In the event that this query fails, an e-mail could be sent to the web master and a message displayed. The code might look something like this:

```
<cftry>
  <cfquery name="qAddOrder" datasource="mySQLServerDSN">
    query to INSERT order into the sql server
  </cfquery>
  <cfcatch type="Database">
  <!--- catch sql server insert attempt --->
    <cftry>
      <cfquery name="qAddOrder2" datasource="myAccessDSN">
        query to INSERT order into the access database
      </cfquery>
      <cfcatch type="Database">
      <!--- catch access insert attempt --->
        <cfmail from="#myAppEmailAddress#"➥
          to="#webmasteremail#"➥
          subject="#cfcatch.type# Error">
          An error occurred at #Now()#
          Error message: #cfcatch.message#
          Details: #cfcach.details#
        </cfmail>
        An error occured trying to record your order. Never fear,
        the webmaster has been notified.
      </cfcatch>
    </cftry>
  </cfcatch>
</cftry>
```

Note that it is very important not to place any unnecessary code within a <cftry> block, because all code within a <cftry> must be run within a special "protected" scope. The more code contained within a <cftry>, the greater the impact on performance, and the greater the possibility that an error will go uncaught.

When calling custom tags, UDFs, and ColdFusion CFCs, it makes more sense to return any errors to the page that called the tag, UDF, or CFC (the "caller" page) and handle the errors locally on that page. This allows the pages that make calls to external code to maintain their flow of control over the application and its display. To accomplish this, you can use the <cfrethrow> tag, which has no attributes and must be placed within a <cfcatch> block.

When an error is caught by a <cfcatch> and the <cfcatch> is either ill-equipped to handle that type of error or must have the original file that called the current page so it can handle the error, the <cfrethrow> tag is used within a <cfcatch> to raise the error to the next outermost <cftry>, or to the caller page if the current <cftry><cfcatch><cfrethrow> block is not nested within a local <cftry> block.

The pseudo code for throwing an error from a custom tag to the caller page looks like so:

```
<!--- mytag.cfm - a custom tag --->
<cftry>
  <cfquery name="qFoo" datasource="myDSN">
    some errant SQL code here
  </cfquery>
  <cfcatch type="Database">
    <cfrethrow>
  </cfcatch>
</cftry>

<!--- caller page --->

<cftry>
  <cf_mytag>
  <cfcatch type="Database">
    handle error raised by custom tag query here!!
  </cfcatch>
</cftry>
```

When throwing exceptions from a ColdFusion CFC, the exception type is maintained. When an exception occurs while attempting to invoke a component or component method, an application type exception is always thrown. Nothing more than <cftry><cfcatch> must be placed around component instantiation code in this case, but method calls may be placed inside <cftry> with various <cfcatch> blocks.

When and How to Define and Handle Custom Exceptions

Not only must the code in an application obey the syntactical rules that govern CFML, but it must also obey the business rules of the processes that define their purpose. When a condition exists that violates business rules but has not generated a ColdFusion error, the <cfthrow> tag can be used to raise a user-defined exception. Unlike <cfrethrow>, which must be coded within a <cfcatch> block, <cfthrow> may be coded anywhere within a <cftry> block.

The <cfrethrow> tag simply throws an exact duplicate of whatever <cfcatch> error variable had been passed to that <cfcatch> block (up to a <cfcatch> block less local to the original exception), but <cfthrow> allows an application to define or redefine the <cfcatch> variable. The <cfthrow> tag is capable of throwing only errors of type application or a user-defined type.

User-defined error messages are useful for treating business logic exceptions as if they were actual ColdFusion errors. This is particularly useful in building an API for other developers to implement your application framework. Your framework, when called from other tags and pages, will return structured errors with error messages, details, names, and even different error codes. When you are implementing an API, this makes it easy to know exactly why errors are occurring based on the error information generated and to gracefully handle such errors.

Custom exception handling is also very useful for raising more simple (less structured) errors when business logic criteria aren't met. When ColdFusion encounters a <cfthrow> tag, it immediately generates an exception. If there is no <cfcatch> or <cferror> to handle a thrown exception, the user receives the default ColdFusion error page. Because errors aren't supposed to be thrown consistently for no reason, <cfthrow> tags are usually contained within a <cfif> block that tests a business condition. The <cfthrow> tag has the following attributes:

- detail: The detailed message for the error (ColdFusion appends the error description to this value)

- message: The general error description

- type: The type of error thrown (application—the default—or user-defined)

- extendedinfo: Custom error information

- errorcode: Custom error code

- object: Allows you to throw a Java exception from a CFML page

As you saw previously, application is the default <cfthrow> error type. An application error is one of two default error types and will be caught by a <cfcatch> with no attributes. However, if a <cfthrow> tag has a user-defined type attribute specified, there must be a <cfcatch> tag with that same error type value (or any) specified. To catch a user-defined exception with <cfcatch>, simply use that user-defined name as the value of the type attribute of the <cfcatch> tag.

An example of this is as follows. Say you want to throw an error whenever a user attempts to withdraw more money from a savings account than the user's current account balance allows:

```
<cftry>
  <cfset savingsAccount = savingsAccount - withdrawAmount>
  <cfif savingsAccount lt 0>
    <cfthrow type="accountBalance"
            message="Your savings account balance is below zero"➡
            detail="Please do not attempt to withdraw more than you have"➡
            errorcode="19">
  </cfif>

  <cfcatch type="accountBalance">
    <cfoutput>
      #cfcatch.message#
    </cfoutput>
  </cfcatch>
</cftry>
```

In addition to being able to catch user-defined errors by using the <cfcatch> tag, it is also possible to catch them with a <cferror> tag. To use <cferror> with user-defined exceptions, you set the type attribute of the <cferror> tag to exception and the exception attribute equal to the user-defined error name. This allows you to set up one page to handle a particular condition whenever it occurs.

For example, suppose a site wanted all users who run a database query yielding no search results to be shown a "no search results found" message. The <cfthrow> and <cferror> tags make this easy: First, the message template is created. Next, you add the following to the Application.cfm file:

```
<cferror template="../errortemplates/noRecs.cfm" type="exception"➡
    exception="noRecsFound">
```

Last, each query that searches the database and returns zero records is surrounded by <cftry> tags, a <cfif>/<cfthrow> pair, and a <cfcatch>/<cfrethrow> pair, like so:

```
<cftry>
  <cfquery name="qMyQuery" datasource="myDSN">
    SELECT someCols
    FROM someTables
    WHERE someExpression = someValue
  </cfquery>
```

```
<cfif not qMyQuery.RecordCount>
    <cfthrow type="noRecsFound" detail="Your query returned no results"➡
        message="No records were found"➡
        extendedinfo="Please use your back button and try re-submitting➡
        your search with more general search terms">
</cfif>
<cfcatch>
    <cfrethrow>
</cfcatch>
</cftry>
```

Best Practices and More on Structured Exception Handling

So why use structured exception handling? Well, for one, exception handling keeps the user's experience pleasant by preventing ugly error messages intended for developers from being returned to the user. This gives site visitors more confidence in the site.

Also, developer error messages are a security risk because they can show sensitive information like database schemas, server file system paths, and the like to users who are not privy to this information.

Exception handling also allows code to be made self-repairing. An example of this would be an attempt to insert a record into a SQL Server database that, on error, attempts to insert the same data into an Access or other database, thus preventing the data from being lost and allowing users to continue using the web application without even being made aware that an error had occurred.

When building a ColdFusion application, you must make some considerations regarding the formulation of an error-handling strategy. Although it may be tempting to catch errors and implement user-defined errors to handle every possible business logic exception that may occur, it is generally not a good idea to use exception handling too much.

With regard to performance, <cftry> does come with some overhead; a block of code will never execute as fast within a <cftry> as it will without the <cftry> wrapper. For this reason, it is an absolute best practice not to enclose more code than necessary within <cftry>. Along the same line of thought, do not place a <cftry> block around code that clearly isn't error prone. In addition to it being a best practice to keep <cftry> blocks as localized to the code as possible, one of the rules of the CFML programming language is that every <cftry> must be closed in the same page; you cannot <cfinclude> a file that contains an opening <cftry> and then <cfinclude> another file containing the closing </cftry>. Attempting to do so will result in error.

One more reason to keep the number of <cftry> blocks to a minimum is that exception handling itself must be troubleshot. Generally, it is not considered ideal to spend as much (or even more) time debugging an application's error-handling code as the application itself! That said, this is sometimes the case when developers get carried away with their exception handling. It is important to find a balance between overdeveloping error handlers and not providing enough error handling for common conditions.

Another best practice is to implement exception handling only after an application is built. Though you may never want the default error messages returned by ColdFusion to be displayed to site visitors, the error messages do come in very handy while a site is under development. If a developer cannot see the error messages being returned by the server, it is much more difficult to troubleshoot the code producing the error. It is for this reason that developers should troubleshoot and debug their ColdFusion applications before implementing any type of error-handling mechanism. Another benefit of adding exception handling after the application is developed is that the application can be load tested for performance analysis before any error-handling logic is in place, then tested again afterward to easily analyze the performance hit being made by the error-trapping code.

With this in mind, we will now examine tools and best practices for debugging an application without the use of CFML exception-handling tags.

Debugging Using the ColdFusion Administrator Debug Settings

The ColdFusion Administrator can be configured to show debug information to aid in application development troubleshooting. Debug output contains information about variables and their values, execution times, etc. This information is useful for tracking down business logic exceptions and for determining why a page is not displaying information as expected.

You can view the debug settings for your ColdFusion Server by browsing to the ColdFusion Administrator and clicking on the Debugging Settings link under the Debugging and Logging section of the menu, as shown in Figure 8-4.

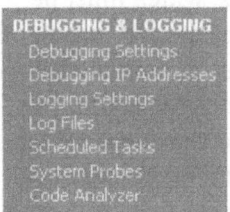

Figure 8-4. The ColdFusion Administrator Debugging and Logging menu section. Note the Debugging Settings link at the top.

In the debugging settings window, you have the ability to specify which, if any, debug information and/or variable type values you wish to see in the debug output, as shown in Figure 8-5.

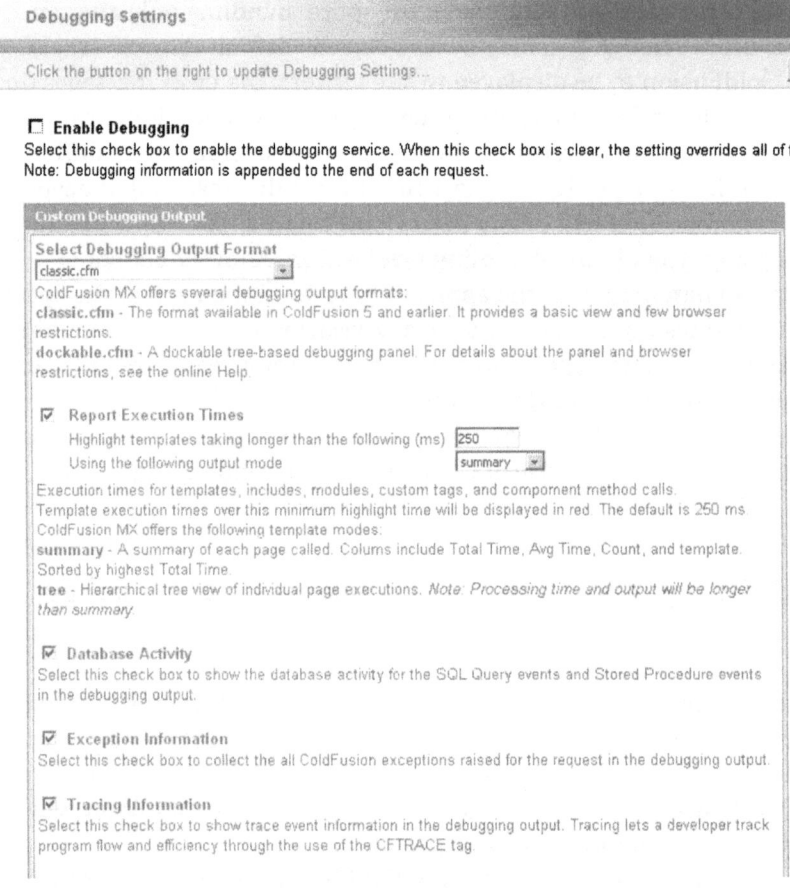

Figure 8-5. The Debugging Settings window

Of particular interest on this screen is the first checkbox, which must be checked to allow any debug information to be returned from the server. Generally, there is no harm in enabling everything (checking all checkboxes). However, one exception to this rule is the Enable Performance Monitoring checkbox. Unless you absolutely need to view the CPU cycle use of the server in real-time, do not select this. Performance monitoring comes with a lot of overhead, because the ColdFusion service will have to communicate back and forth with the operating system performance monitor at all times, which is usually unnecessary.

In addition to turning on debugging, it is important to add the IP address of any and all development machines to the Debugging IP Addresses window. This window is opened by clicking on the Debugging IP Addresses link in the menu you saw previously. When debugging is enabled on a ColdFusion Server, all page requests will have the debug information appended to the end of each HTTP response. As soon as one or more IP addresses are entered in the Debugging IP Addresses interface, only machines matching those IP addresses will receive debug information. For this reason it is good practice to enter **127.0.0.1** as a debugging IP address immediately after enabling debugging. This means that only server requests originating from the server will have debug information appended to the response.

Once debugging is enabled and the IP address for your development machine has been added to the server, you can find the debug information at the bottom of any page requested with a web browser. If the page is browsed using the Dreamweaver Server Debug browsing mode, the debug information will not display with the page output but rather will be used to populate a "debug" tree control found in the Dreamweaver Results panel, as shown in Figure 8-6. (You can view this panel by choosing Window ➤ Results ➤ Server Debug.)

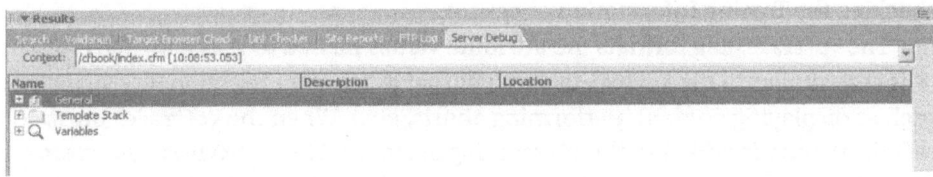

Figure 8-6. The Dreamweaver MX Results panel

Whenever a page containing a query does not show the expected results, the first thing most developers do is look at the debug information to determine what SQL string the query ran, how long the query took to run, how many records were returned, etc. Debug output could also be used to view the execution times for all pages that were executed. This helps you find out why a page containing custom tag calls and/or <cfinclude>s is taking so long to execute. The Session and Application scope variables and their values (as well as those of the Form, URL, Request, and other memory scopes) are displayed in debug output, which also helps in identifying why conditional logic isn't behaving as expected. The list of uses for the debug information goes on and on; it is definitely an invaluable weapon in every developer's arsenal.

Using <cftrace> to Debug an Application

The <cftrace> tag was introduced in ColdFusion MX to aid with debugging applications. A very common practice among ColdFusion developers when debugging an application is to put a <cfoutput> or <cfdump> tag in the page, followed immediately by a <cfabort>, to view the value of a variable at a specific point in the execution of a page and then halt execution of the rest of the page. This has always been the easiest and fastest way to figure out why a variable has been assigned the value (or lack thereof) that it contains at the end of page execution. By viewing variable values at various points in the execution of a page, you are able to deduct where in the code the value becomes corrupt.

> **NOTE** *Execution times may be significantly increased when the <cfdump> tag is executed on a page, so they should not be used while evaluating page load time issues.*

The <cftrace> tag was introduced in ColdFusion MX to give developers added functionality when viewing variable values at points throughout a page. To use the <cftrace> tag, debugging must be enabled in the ColdFusion Administrator by checking the Tracing Information checkbox.

The <cftrace> tag formats the attribute values passed to it as a log file entry (it is very similar to the <cflog> tag, except that it has extra functionality available, such as displaying content, performing aborts, etc.). When the <cftrace> tag is called, an entry is added to the cftrace.log file in the CfusionMX\logs\ directory. A number of options are available here. You can have the tag display the log file entry on the screen, or just log it in the log file. You can abort processing after execution, or allow the code to continue running. You can associate a variable with the trace, and you can also associate meta data such as log entry type, category, and a text message with the log entry. The attributes of the <cftrace> tag are all optional and are as follows:

- category: A user-defined string that identifies the trace. Multiple calls to <cftrace> with the same category value are associated with each other as part of one group.

- text: This user-defined text is used as the log entry message.

- inline: A Boolean value specifying whether to display the log file entry in the page and in the debug output (the trace summary area at the bottom of the request), or just in the debug output. The default is No.

- abort: A Boolean value indicating whether to abort the page processing immediately after the <cftrace> or to let the page continue loading. The default is No.

- var: The name of a variable to dump (display). The variable can be a simple or complex variable.

- type: The level of severity to associate with the log entry—Information, Warning, Error, or Fatal Information. The default is Information.

Let's have a look at an example. The following code contains one inline trace that monitors the value of a variable i that is incremented by a loop (cftrace.cfm):

```
<cfloop from="1" to="3" index="i">
  <cftrace var="i" abort="No" category="loopvar" inline="No"➡
    text="The value of 'i' within the loop is #i#" type="Information">
</cfloop>
<cftrace var="i" abort="No" category="loopvar" inline="Yes"➡
  text="The value of 'i' after the loop is #i#" type="Information">
```

Open this code in Dreamweaver and press F12 to test it. With server debugging enabled, its output will look like Figure 8-7.

●[CFTRACE 16:42:39.039] [3906 ms]
[C:\CFusionMX\wwwroot\cfbook\ch8\TMPdv6wraz7q9.cfm @
line: 6] - [loopvar] *The value of 'i' after the loop is 4*
i 4

Figure 8-7. `<cftrace>` *inline output*

The debug output for the trace will look like Figure 8-8.

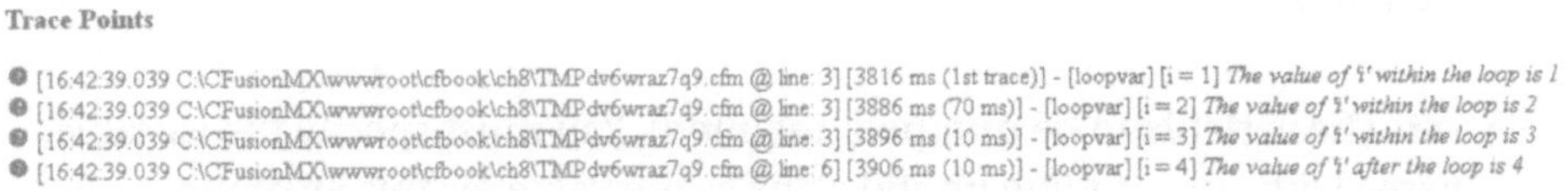

Trace Points

● [16:42:39.039 C:\CFusionMX\wwwroot\cfbook\ch8\TMPdv6wraz7q9.cfm @ line: 3] [3816 ms (1st trace)] - [loopvar] [i = 1] *The value of 'i' within the loop is 1*
● [16:42:39.039 C:\CFusionMX\wwwroot\cfbook\ch8\TMPdv6wraz7q9.cfm @ line: 3] [3886 ms (70 ms)] - [loopvar] [i = 2] *The value of 'i' within the loop is 2*
● [16:42:39.039 C:\CFusionMX\wwwroot\cfbook\ch8\TMPdv6wraz7q9.cfm @ line: 3] [3896 ms (10 ms)] - [loopvar] [i = 3] *The value of 'i' within the loop is 3*
● [16:42:39.039 C:\CFusionMX\wwwroot\cfbook\ch8\TMPdv6wraz7q9.cfm @ line: 6] [3906 ms (10 ms)] - [loopvar] [i = 4] *The value of 'i' after the loop is 4*

Figure 8-8. The debug output of `<cftrace>` *trace points*

Finally, the log file entries will look like the following:

```
"Severity","ThreadID","Date","Time","Application","Message"
"Information","jrpp-29","02/09/03","00:57:21",,"[20 ms (1st trace)]➡
[F:\Inetpub\mycfmxroot\DWCF_Book\errorHandling\wwwroot\trace_test.cfm @ line: 3] -➡
[loopvar] [i = 1] The value of 'i' within the loop is 1 "
"Information","jrpp-29","02/09/03","00:57:21",,"[30 ms (10)]➡
[F:\Inetpub\mycfmxroot\DWCF_Book\errorHandling\wwwroot\trace_test.cfm @ line: 3] -➡
[loopvar] [i = 2] The value of 'i' within the loop is 2 "
```

```
"Information","jrpp-29","02/09/03","00:57:21",,"[40 ms (10)]➥
[F:\Inetpub\mycfmxroot\DWCF_Book\errorHandling\wwwroot\trace_test.cfm @ line: 3] -➥
[loopvar] [i = 3] The value of 'i' within the loop is 3 "
"Information","jrpp-29","02/09/03","00:57:21",,"[50 ms (10)]➥
[F:\Inetpub\mycfmxroot\DWCF_Book\errorHandling\wwwroot\trace_test.cfm @ line: 7] -➥
[loopvar] [i = 4] The value of 'i' after the loop is 4 "
```

The <cftrace> tag is most useful because it makes the process of tracking the value of a variable throughout its existence in a page or application relatively easy to do. Diagnosis of business logic errors is made much simpler with the <cftrace> tag. <cftrace> is also particularly helpful when debugging ColdFusion CFCs and methods, which are notorious for being difficult to debug. One noteworthy behavior is that, if you set inline to true, you can generate <cftrace> outputs even within CFC methods that have their output attribute set to false!

Using `<cfdump>` to Debug Applications

The <cfdump> tag was introduced in ColdFusion 5 to provide a way to dump very quickly and easily the contents of any variable—complex or simple—to the screen. If the variable being "dumped" is anything other than a simple variable, the variables contained within the variable and their values are displayed in a DHTML table that allows users to click on a variable name in the left-hand column and expand and collapse the right-hand column containing the variable value(s). Not only does <cfdump> display variables and their values in a collapsible tree, but it color-codes variables of different types. The ability to collapse rows and view variable types by color-code makes it very easy to sort through the data stored in complex variables. The <cfdump> tag has three attributes, only the first of which (var) is required:

- var: The variable to be dumped (required). You must specify the variable name with surrounding pound signs as the value for this attribute.

- label: A label to put in the dump table header. Useful when doing several dumps in a single request.

- expand: A Boolean specifying whether to expand the table entries when the table loads (the default is yes).

The colors used by <cfdump> to display ColdFusion variables are as follows:

- Simple variables: no color

- Structure: blue

- Query: purple

- Array: green

- Function or component method: orange

- Component or Java object instance: red

- WDDX packet: black

- XML DOM: gray

Variables serialized as WDDX (complex data represented as a WDDX XML string—see Chapter 7 for more information) and then passed to <cfdump> show up as their native data type color surrounded by a black border. For example, a WDDX packet serialization of a structure will display as a blue table contained within a black table. In ColdFusion, virtually every scope that has a name exists as a structure (an associative array). This means that you can pass the name of a scope (with pound signs) to the <cfdump> tag to view all the data in a specific scope.

Let's see <cfdump> in action. The following code (cfdump.cfm) creates several local variables on a page. It then dumps the Variables scope, so you can view all of the local variables in your browser window:

```
<cfscript>
  firstName = "Simon";
  lastName = "Horwith";
  email = "simon@horwith.com";
  hobbies = arrayNew(1);
  hobbies[1] = "Chess";
  hobbies[2] = "Billiards";
  hobbies[3] = "Scuba Diving";
</cfscript>

<cfdump var="#variables#" label="My Local Variables">
```

Test the code in a browser, and you should see the display shown in Figure 8-9.

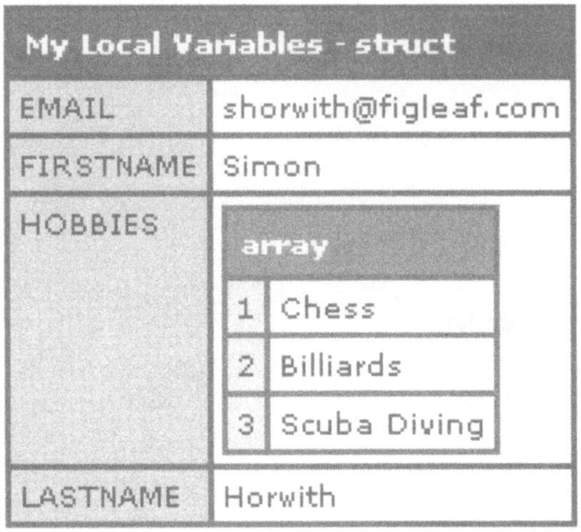

Figure 8-9. `<cfdump>` *of the local variables scope*

Using `<cftransaction>` to Protect Data Integrity

In addition to providing developers with the ability to execute code in a kind of safe mode with the `<cftry>` and `<cfcatch>` tags, the ColdFusion Application Server also provides functionality for performing database operations in a "safe mode" with the `<cftransaction>` tag.

The database server treats all `<cfquery>` tags contained within a `<cftransaction>` block as one logical unit. The use of `<cftransaction>` is governed by the database management system (DBMS) in use. The `<cftransaction>` tag accomplishes this by leveraging the native database transactional mechanisms for whatever database type(s) its enclosed `<cfquery>` tags connect with.

The `<cftransaction>` tag has two attributes (both optional): action and isolation. The action attribute specifies the action to perform on the database transaction. Its valid values are:

- begin: Identifies the beginning of a transaction (the default).

- commit: Commits all query operations that make up the pending transaction to the database. Once a transaction is committed, no "undo" command is available.

- rollback: Rolls back a database transaction. None of the query operations that make up the pending transaction is committed, and the data stored in the database retains the same value(s) as before the transaction.

A very common use of the <cftransaction> tag is to insert a new record and then retrieve the unique ID column value for the row that was just added. It is important to perform these two database operations in a single transaction to assure that the ID retrieved from the database matches the same row that was just added. (Too many concurrent users requesting the same page can result in the wrong ID being returned to the wrong user if transactional processing is not being leveraged.) To ensure that an INSERT and SELECT are treated as a transaction, place the two <cfquery> tags within opening and closing <cftransaction> tags. No tag attributes are required.

Explicitly performing a rollback or commit requires the action attribute to be supplied to an empty <cftransaction> tag, which sits within the opening and closing <cftransaction> tags that the queries are embedded within. Usually, the <cftransaction> that performs the commit or rollback is nested within conditional logic of some sort. As an example of rolling back a transaction, consider a user attempting to withdraw more money than allowed by a current savings account balance; the rollback might look like this:

```
<cftransaction>
  <cfquery name="qUpdSavings" datasource="myDSN">
    UPDATE Savings
    SET actBalance = actBalance - #withdraw_amt#
    WHERE actID = #act_id#
  </cfquery>
  <cfquery name="qGetBalance" datasource="myDSN">
    SELECT actBalance
    FROM Savings
    WHERE actID = #act_id#
  </cfquery>
  <cfif qGetBalance.actBalance lt 0>
    <cftransaction action="ROLLBACK" />
    <h1>Invalid Transaction!!</h1>
    <h3>
      You have attempted to withdraw too much money from your account.
      Your transaction was cancelled.
    </h3>
  <cfelse>
    <cftransaction action="COMMIT" />
    <h1>Transaction Complete!!</h1>
    <h3>Your transaction was successfully completed.</h3>
  </cfif>
</cftransaction>
```

In addition to being able to specify what action the <cftransaction> will perform by using the action attribute, you can also control the level of locking to use when executing a transaction by using the isolation attribute. The values allowed for the isolation attribute behave exactly like their equivalent database isolation level locking values:

- read_uncommitted: Sometimes called a "dirty read," read_uncommitted transactions read in database data with no regard for current exclusive locks that other transactions may have, and do not place any shared lock on the data being accessed. During an uncommitted read, read-in data may be changed by other transactions, resulting in inaccurate data being returned in the Recordset.

- read_committed: Transactions given this value use shared locks to ensure that only currently committed data is read (other transactions are obeyed) and that no other transaction modifies data rows currently being used. This type of transaction does not prevent other transactions from modifying the current data set after those data rows have been read in but before the transaction is completed. The read_committed value is the default transaction type used by most relational database management systems (RDBMSs).

- repeatable_read: These isolation level locks behave the same as read_committed, except the rows used in the Recordset are exclusively locked until the transaction is finished. Additional data rows may still be added to the table(s) being used by the repeatable_read transaction. Because of the high level of locking used by repeatable_read transactions, its use is discouraged.

- serializable: Transactions of this isolation level are the most data-consistent transactions but also have the most overhead. A serializable transaction places an exclusive lock on every data table in use for the duration of the transaction. Essentially, access to database tables is single-threaded when serializable transactions are used. Because the locking level is so high, serializable transaction use is strongly discouraged.

Some developers believe that <cflock>, the tag that allows programmatic threading of code execution, is a better alternative to <cftransaction>. This is only partially true. It has been found that <cflock> is more reliable and performs slightly better than <cftransaction> under heavy load. However, if <cflock> is used to thread execution of queries, the database is unaware of the lock. This means that any other application that accesses the database resource(s) being "locked" will execute as if there were no other current transaction. As a best practice, named <cflock>s should be used, but they should be used in conjuncture with <cftransaction> tags.

Summary

One of the most important aspects of web applications is the user experience. One of the sure signs that an application has been well developed is its ability to handle exceptions gracefully and to prevent the end-user from even knowing that an error has occurred. The structured exception handling mechanisms discussed in this chapter should help you to build such applications. Specifically, we discussed:

- Configuring the ColdFusion Administrator to handle errors at the server level

- Using <cferror> to handle errors at the application level

- Using <cfcatch>, <cftry>, <cfthrow>, and <cfrethrow> to build more-robust exception handling

- When and how to define and handle custom exceptions

- Using <cftrace> and <cfdump> to debug applications

- Using <cftransaction> to protect data integrity

- Best practices

The tools discussed in this chapter are a developer's best friends; get to know them well. You will find that the time it takes to develop applications will decrease as you become more proficient at debugging your applications.

CHAPTER 9

Dreamweaver MX 2004 Extensions

ONE OF THE MAIN reasons Dreamweaver MX 2004 has been so successful is undoubtedly its extensibility: its potential to be customized as required. Thanks to the efforts of some early Dreamweaver adopters—who have spent a lot of time digging into it's program folders to find out ways to improve the application—the number of extensions available for Dreamweaver has reached a startling amount. Macromedia has always kept a close eye on this phenomenon and welcomed it with open arms, offering more and more tools and features to facilitate the development, distribution, and consumption of these extensions, as well as publishing numerous extensions in the form of Dev Net Resource Kits.

What distinguishes Dreamweaver extensibility from that of other web development tools is that most of the core program itself is built using the same API provided to developers for building extensions. Therefore, you don't need to go far to find the functionality necessary for you to start developing extensions, and to gain insight into building your own functionality, you just need to have a look at how Dreamweaver's core functionality has been created. What you will discover is that much of this great Dreamweaver functionality is built using familiar technologies such as HTML, XML, or JavaScript.

In this chapter we will:

- Look at the Macromedia Extension Manager and how it is used it to install, disable, and remove extensions, and package new extensions we have written ready for distribution

- Showcase a couple of the most popular extensions—the Yaromat Check Form extension, and the Massimocorner CF Upload extension

- Learn how to use the Dreamweaver Server Behavior Builder to build a CFML form mailer

Exploring Extensions

An extension is something that permits us to add functionality to an application beyond its core out-of-the-box functionality. Extensions are employed to further increase productivity and reduce time spent solving problems during development by automating repetitive tasks or adding functionality to the base program. In Dreamweaver, extensions are nothing more than additional objects, behaviors, commands and the like added to the existing product.

To facilitate their distribution and installation, Macromedia Extensions are usually made available as Macromedia Extension Package (MXP) files (similar to zip archives) that contain all the files necessary to install an extension. These files contain Macromedia Extension Installation (MXI) files, which we show you how to create at the end of this chapter.

Managing Extensions with the Macromedia Extension Manager

Dreamweaver is not the only product that Macromedia made easily extensible. Flash and Fireworks can take advantage of custom extensions as well. For this reason, instead of enabling each one of these applications to handle the installation and packaging of extensions individually, Macromedia developed a program called Macromedia Extension Manager, which serves extensions to all of them, and presents other useful features.

> **NOTE** *Although Dreamweaver, Flash, and Fireworks are not the only Macromedia products that can be extended, they are the MX Studio products that take advantage of the Extension Manager. Programs such as Director and Freehand can be extended using extensions called Xtras. For more information on these, see* http://www.macromedia.com/software/xtras/.

The Extension Manager has reached version 1.6 and is able to manage extensions for Dreamweaver 4, Dreamweaver MX, Dreamweaver MX 2004, UltraDev 4, Fireworks MX, Flash 5, Flash MX, and Flash MX 2004. Extension Manager is usually installed by default with Dreamweaver or any other of the previously mentioned software packages, but it can also be downloaded for free from the Macromedia web site at http://www.macromedia.com/exchange/em_download/.

> **TIP** *Though Dreamweaver does install the Extension Manager by default, it is always worth visiting the Macromedia Exchange to check if a new version of the Extension Manager is available. If you create extensions using version 1.5 or above, developers who want to install the extension will also have to download the new version of the Extension Manager if it is not already installed on their machine.*

When launched, the Extension Manager presents us with a list of installed extensions, as shown in Figure 9-1. Please be aware that if you are working on an operating system that allows multiple user configurations (such as Windows 2000, Windows XP and Mac OS X), you will be able to view only the extensions installed in the current user's account and those installed by the system administrator.

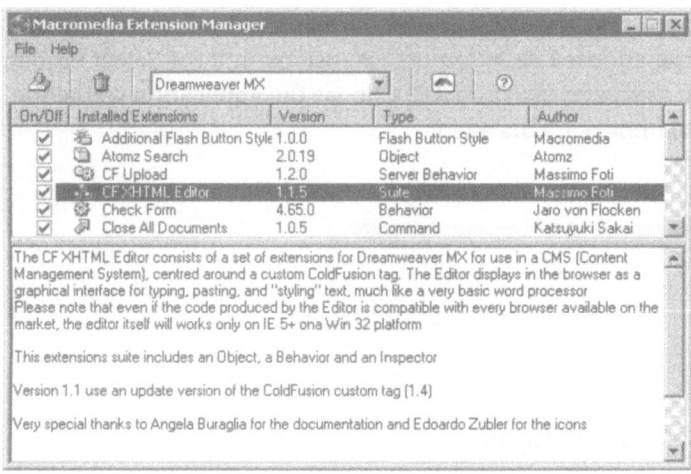

Figure 9-1. The Macromedia Extension Manager

Extensions can be installed by choosing File ➤ Install Extension, clicking on the Install New Extension button (the icon in the top left of Figure 9-1), or simply by double-clicking the MXP file.

Although the Extension Manager permits it, you are strongly discouraged from installing an extension into a version of the application other than what it was intended for (for example, installing a Dreamweaver 4 extension into Dreamweaver) unless you test the extension thoroughly before using it. You may have compatibility problems if you don't heed this advice.

Once an extension has been installed, it will be displayed along with the others in the Extension Manager. Extensions that are no longer needed can be disabled or removed. When you have a large number of extensions installed, this can affect Dreamweaver's performance, so it is a good idea to disable extensions that you are not currently using. To disable an extension, just uncheck its checkbox in the On/Off column, or select the extension and press the spacebar. To enable it, simply reverse the process.

If you would like to permanently remove an extension, you first must select it, then either select File ➤ Remove Extension, or click the Remove Extension button (the trash can icon).

In addition to installing new extensions, the Extension Manager enables us to import them from other instances of Dreamweaver present on a local network or disk. This feature is very useful, for example, if you are working in a team and each member needs to use certain extensions to increase productivity. Another possible scenario is when upgrading to a newer version of Dreamweaver and you want to import all your previously installed extensions in a single operation (although, as stated before, when moving extensions between different product versions, it is be better to install and test each extension singularly to avoid possible compatibility issues).

To import extensions, first select the product from the drop-down menu on the main interface. Next, choose File ➤ Import Extensions, and the Select Product dialog box will appear, as shown in Figure 9-2. Choose the application where the extensions you want to import are installed.

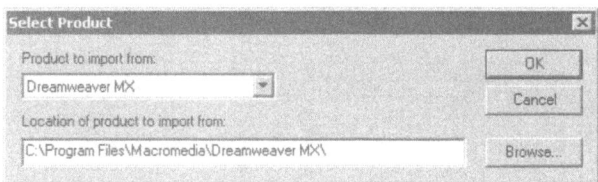

Figure 9-2. The Select Product dialog box

Click OK, and the Import Extensions dialog box should appear, as shown in Figure 9-3. From here choose the extensions you want to import, enabling them in the Import column. Once you have chosen, click the Import button to import the extensions.

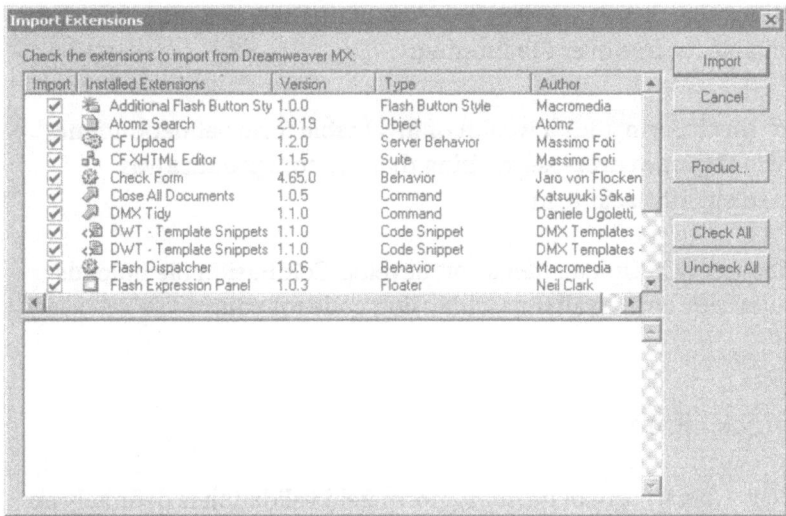

Figure 9-3. The Import Extensions dialog box

The Extension Manager also contains functionality to allow us to package the extensions we write and submit them to the Macromedia Exchange (for more on packaging extensions, see the "Distributing Server Behavior" section later on). The Macromedia Exchange is a great online resource where you can download extensions and upload your own.

To go to the exchange, either click on the Go To Macromedia Exchange button (or choose File ➤ Go To Macromedia Exchange) in the Extension Manager, or type the following URL into a browser: http://www.macromedia.com/exchange/.

Extensions Online Resources

Without doubt, the Macromedia Exchange is the biggest extensions resource available on the Web; however, it isn't the only one. Each day, more and more extensions for Dreamweaver and other Macromedia products are created or updated by a number of third-party developers. It may happen, for example, that more recent or exclusive versions of extensions published on the Macromedia Exchange have been made available by their developers only on their personal web sites.

Many of these developers are well known and respected "extensionologists"—developers who have been creating and distributing extensions since the early days of Dreamweaver. To list all their web sites would take up more space than we have available, but you will find a useful list of the better extension sites to visit at http://www.dwfaq.com/Resources/Extensions/default.asp.

In the sections that follow, we showcase two of the best and most popular extensions available for free over the Internet:

- Yaromat Check Form adds a wealth of invaluable form validation functionality to Dreamweaver—something that the core product was considered slightly lacking in.

- Massimocorner CF Upload helps you develop ColdFusion file uploads really quickly by writing all the ColdFusion code for you.

Yaromat Check Form

Jaro von Flocken's Check Form behavior for form field validation is definitely an extension that should be part of your developer toolbox. The latest version of Check Form (version 4.66.0) has been selected by Macromedia as one of the top three extensions currently available for Dreamweaver: `http://www.macromedia.com/software/dreamweaver/special/extensions/`.

You can download Check Form for free from the previous link, and Jaro's web site at `http://www.yaromat.com` (it is easy to navigate to).

As we learned in previous chapters, client-side form validation using JavaScript is very useful to check for data consistency before submitting it to the server.

> **TIP** *As stated in Chapter 5, be aware that users can disable JavaScript in their browsers. Therefore, it is always good practice to combine client-side and server-side validation.*

Dreamweaver ships with a behavior called Validate Form, which offers basic form field validation. And, as we described earlier in the book, ColdFusion has some useful built-in form validation facilities in its `<cfform>` (and associated) tags.

Nevertheless, neither of these client-side validation options offers the same flexibility and amount of features as Check Form provides. The Validate Form behavior, for example, doesn't present any kind of control for date and time format validation, doesn't validate anything but text fields, and doesn't allow the customization of the error message. Forms created with `<cfform>` also have some problems: even if correctly rendered in Design View, they won't be recognized by Dreamweaver as valid form instances, with the result that you won't be able to apply behaviors or server behaviors to them.

After you install it, the Check Form extension is available from the Behaviors panel (+ ➤ Yaromat ➤ Check Form), ready to be applied to the form you want to validate. The Check Form extension has many options for validating form elements, which vary according to the field type. The following is a list of controls Check Form lets you implement:

- Required: Checking this option denotes the field as required.

- Anything: The field can accept any value.

- A number from . . . to . . . : The field can accept any number within the specified range.

- E-Mail Address: This control checks if the value entered into the field constitutes a valid e-mail address.

- Date: Use this to choose from many date format validation options (including MySQL date format) to ensure valid database entries. It not only checks that the value is in a proper date format, but also if the date in fact exists (for example, the 30th of February 2003 is not a valid date).

- VTime: Use this to choose from many different time format validation options.

- This must be checked too: You select this to create dependency between radio buttons or checkboxes and other form fields. For example, you can make it so that a check box has to be checked before content in a text field is accepted.

- This must be the same: Extremely useful for password validation—this option allows you to specify that the contents of two different fields must be the same.

- Menu: This control lets you force the user to make a selection from a pop-up menu.

- Textarea: Here you can specify the minimum number of characters that the user must enter in a text area field.

- Checkbox: This control tests to see if a check box is checked, and lets you define a dependency between a checkbox and other form fields.

- Radiobutton: This control offers the same function as Checkbox, but for radio buttons.

- Error message: Us this to define a custom error message for every field that does not succeed the validation control.

To appreciate some of these features, let's build a simple survey form:

1. In Dreamweaver, create a new folder called Ch9 inside the cfbook folder. Create a new file called checkform.cfm within this folder.

2. Open checkform.cfm in Design View and insert a new form into it (click the Form button in the Forms tab of the Insert bar). Name the newly created form surveyForm (enter the name into the Properties panel, as shown in Figure 9-4).

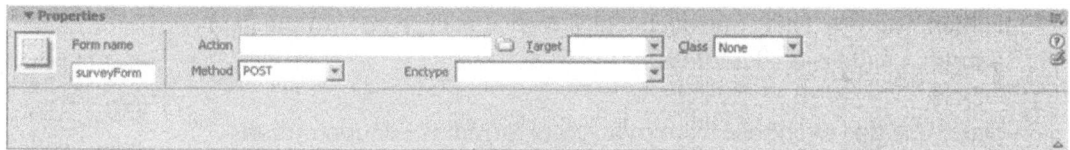

Figure 9-4. The Dreamweaver Properties panel, showing the details of the new form

3. Enter the text **What is your preferred ColdFusion Book?** into the form.

4. Now click on the Radio Group button in the Forms tab of the Insert bar to open the Radio Group dialog box. Fill it in as shown in Figure 9-5, and click OK.

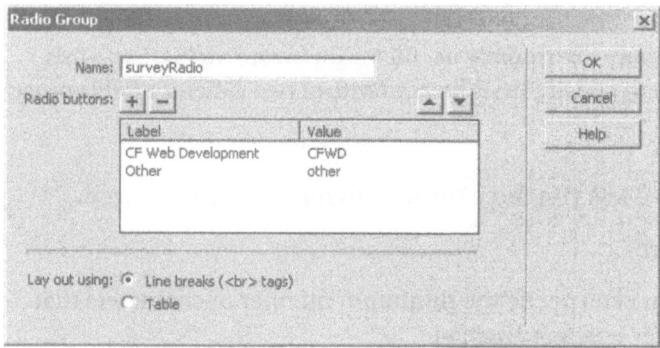

Figure 9-5. The Dreamweaver Radio Group dialog box

A radio button group should now be inserted on the page for you.

5. Below it, type the text **If 'Other', please specify:**. Below this, insert a blank text field into the form by clicking on the Text Field button in the Forms tab of the Insert panel. Name it otherField.

6. Lastly, insert a Submit button by clicking on the Button icon in the Forms tab of the Insert panel and save your file. Your survey form is ready, and should look like the one shown in Figure 9-6.

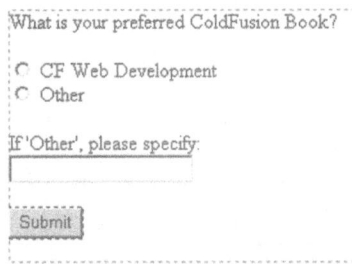

Figure 9-6. Our finished survey form

Now it's time to add JavaScript validation to the form by using Jaro's Check Form behavior. Select the <form> tag (displayed as <form#surveyForm>) from the tag selector on the bottom bar of the document window (as shown in Figure 9-7) to select the entire form.

Figure 9-7. The tag selector for the current page

From the Behaviors panel, click on the + sign and choose Yaromat ➤ Check Form. The Check Form dialog box will open, as shown in Figure 9-8.

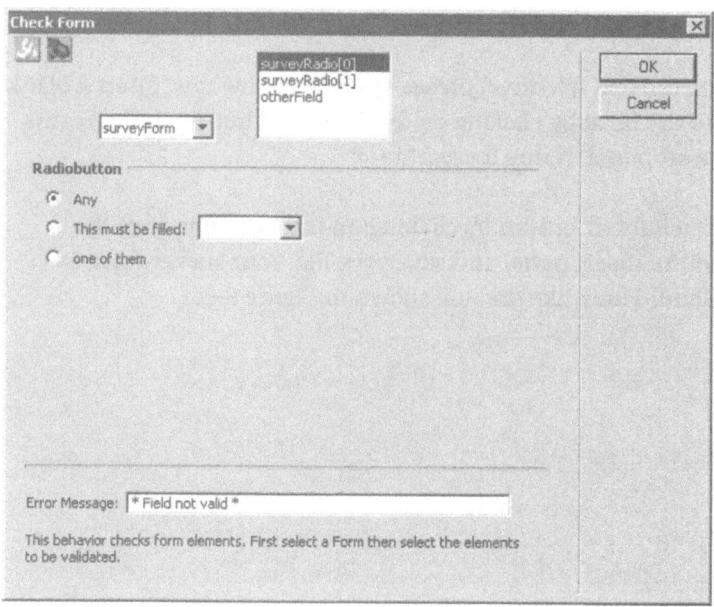

Figure 9-8. The Yaromat Check Form dialog box, showing the choices available for our first radio button

Now, with surveyRadio[0] selected, click the radio button labeled "one of them" and enter **Please choose a book** in the Error Message field.

Next, select surveyRadio[1], click the radio button labeled "This must be filled," and choose otherField from the pop-up menu (which should be the only field available in the pop-up menu anyway). Enter **Please specify a title** in the Error Message field and click OK.

Looking at the Behaviors panel, you will notice that the Check Form behavior has been applied to the onSubmit event of your form, which is usually the best place to apply client-side form validation. If you now look in Code View, you will see that JavaScript code has been added to your page to validate form entries.

Test the form in a browser. Now if you try to submit the form without making any choice, the "Please choose a book" error message will be displayed, and if you choose the Others radio button without specifying a title for it on the text field, the "Please specify a title" error message will pop up. Fairly impressive, isn't it?

Massimocorner CF Upload

Massimo Foti is surely one of the most prolific and recognized extension developers today. He won the title of "Best Extension Developer" during the Macromedia Best Extension Developer Awards in 2000. CF Upload is only one of the many

Dreamweaver extensions committed to speeding up ColdFusion development in Dreamweaver (it was originally designed for Dreamweaver 4). You can download it for free from his personal web site at http://www.massimocorner.com. (On the main page, click on the Ultradev menu option, then the ColdFusion submenu option, and you should find it there.)

We have already seen how, when the action attribute of <cfform> is set to upload, it can be used to provide a mechanism for uploading files to the server. Massimo's CF Upload server behavior further simplifies the process of creating a file upload form by completing the CFML code for you, and implementing a rock-solid validation routine that checks for bad file types.

After you install it, CF Upload is available from the Server Behaviors panel when working with a ColdFusion site in Dreamweaver. To use the CF Upload server behavior, we first require a simple HTML postback form. A *postback* form (also known as a self-posting form) is nothing more than a form that submits information entered into it to itself. In other words, the same page is responsible for processing the data input and displaying the results.

The form must contain an input field with the type attribute set to file. If CF Upload doesn't find this, it will promptly warn you to insert it. In addition, if you forget to include or set the enctype attribute of the form tag to multipart/form-data, or the method attribute to post, a warning dialog will appear and ask if you want CF Upload to fix these for you before inserting the CFML code into the page, as shown in Figure 9-9.

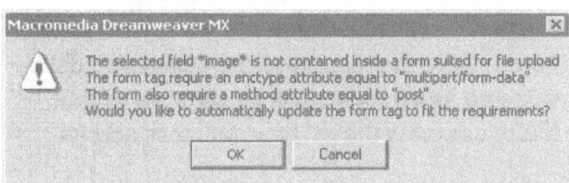

Figure 9-9. CF Upload warns you if everything is not in place prior to its use and offers to fix any problems it detects.

CF Upload has many options available that mainly replicate the properties of <cffile> when its action attribute is set to upload. In addition to these, you can specify redirection to another page once the uploading process has successfully completed, which comes in handy to give positive feedback to users. The following is a list of settings available in CF Upload:

- Max Size Allowed (KB): Use this to specify the maximum allowed size (in kilobytes) of the file that has been uploaded. The validation process for this feature of CF Upload is the result of a pretty effective combination of CGI variables and HTTP header controls.

- Form Field: You select the form and the file field to apply CF Upload to.

- Destination Directory: Here you specify the pathname of the directory where the uploaded files will be stored on the server.

- Handle Name Conflicts: Taking advantage of the nameConflict attribute of the <cffile> tag, this option lets you decide which action ColdFusion should take when the name of a newly uploaded file conflicts with the name of a file already stored on the server. Allowed options are: Make Unique Name, Report an Error, and Overwrite.

- After Uploading, Go To: Use this to redirect users to another page after a successful file upload.

- Allowed Type: This series of checkboxes lets you choose which file MIME types are allowed for upload to the server.

If something goes wrong during the upload process, CF Upload will display an error message to the users. This message varies depending on the main cause of the problem.

In Chapter 6 we described how to use Dreamweaver to create a CFML-driven dynamic image gallery. In the following example, we show how you can efficiently apply CF Upload to that example to create an upload form more quickly.

The following example assumes you have gone through "Creating a Dynamic Image Gallery in ColdFusion" section in Chapter 6, or at least have downloaded the code for it. We assume here that you have the cfbook.mdb database and that it is successfully registered as a data source. In addition to that, make sure your cfbook site root folder contains the gallery directory and its images subfolder.

1. In the Ch9 folder, create a new file and call it success.cfm. Enter **Image has been successfully uploaded to the server.**, then save the file and close it.

2. Now create another file in the same location and call it cfupload.cfm. Insert a blank form into the page in Design View, as in the last example.

3. Next, insert a file field into the form by choosing Form Objects ➤ File Field from the Insert menu.

4. Finally, insert a Submit button into the form, as before. Your upload form is ready, and should look like Figure 9-10.

Figure 9-10. Your form, ready to have CF Upload applied to it

We will now proceed to apply the CF Upload server behavior to the form. From the Server Behaviors panel, choose + ➤ Massimocorner ➤ File ➤ File Upload. You should be presented with the dialog box in Figure 9-11.

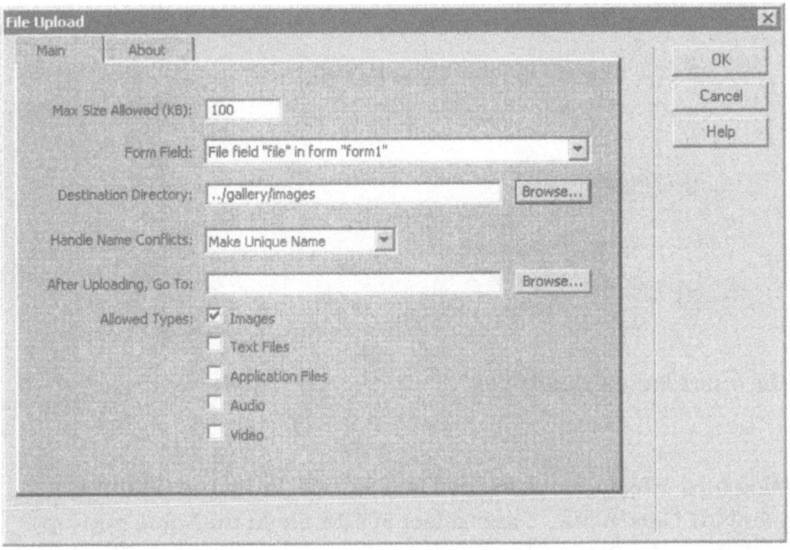

Figure 9-11. The CF Upload File Upload dialog box

In the dialog box, increase the Max Size Allowed (KB) value from 30 to 100, leave the Form Field drop-down menu as it is, and set the Destination Directory as gallery/images. Leave Make Unique Name as the rule for the Handle Name Conflicts option, and make sure the only allowed type for upload is Images.

The allowed values for the Handle Name Conflicts option originate from the nameConflict attribute of the ColdFusion <cffile> tag. For a complete description of the available actions, please consult the ColdFusion CFML Reference documentation or refer to Chapters 3 and 5 of this book.

Because CF Upload works smoothly in combination with standard server behaviors, we won't redirect users to another page now, but will first use the Insert Record server behavior to add the value returned from CF Upload as an entry to our database. Providing a URL in the After Uploading, Go To field at this point will result in no data being entered into the database, so leave it empty and click OK to exit this dialog box and apply the behavior.

Now let's finish off our page. Choose Server Behaviors ➤ + ➤ Insert Record. The Insert Record dialog box will pop up, as shown in Figure 9-12.

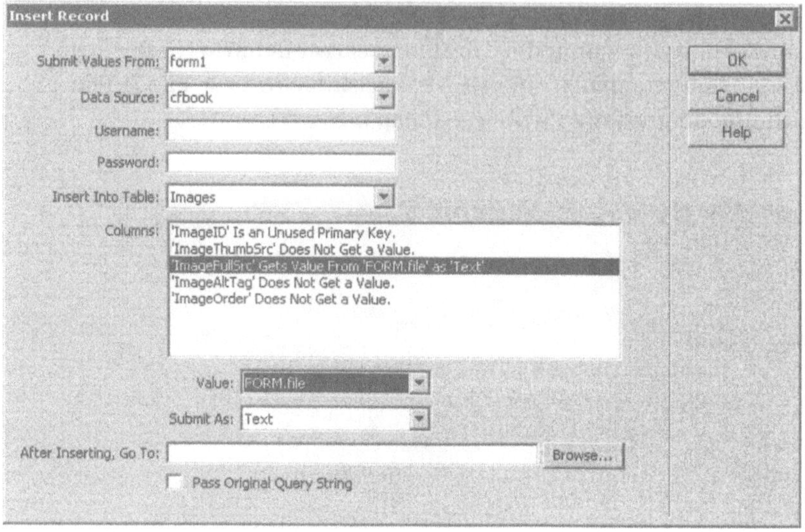

Figure 9-12. The Insert Record dialog box

In this dialog box, select cfbook as the Data Source. From the Columns box, select "'ImageFullSrc' Gets Value...", and select FORM.file in the Value pop-up menu. Finally, click on the Browse button, browse to the success.cfm file, then click the OK button to close the dialog box and apply the behavior.

Now test the page in a browser, and try to upload images. If the image upload process and database insertion is successful, you will be redirected to the success.cfm page; otherwise, an error message will be displayed.

If the upload process is successful, CF Upload will automatically set the value of the FORM variable passed by the file field to the value of the FILE.ServerFile variable, facilitating its use with other server behaviors.

Dreamweaver's Server Behavior Builder

After so much talk about extensions and how you can benefit from using ready-made ones, we now take a look at one of the main ways in which you can create your own: the Server Behavior Builder.

Over the course of this book we have seen how useful Dreamweaver server behaviors are, and how much time they can save you during web development. Well, now you can create your own: introduced in Dreamweaver UltraDev 4, The

Server Behavior Builder enables you to turn code snippets into powerful server behaviors. The Server Behavior Builder automates the creation of all the necessary files that make up the server behaviors. They consist of an HTML file and two or more Extension Data Markup Language (EDML) files.

The HTML file contains all the needed scripts and all the elements of the interface that will allow the user to use the server behavior, whereas the EDML files (which are basically XML files) are mainly used by Dreamweaver to identify and interpret the various code blocks that comprise the server behavior.

To better understand the content of the EDML files, a short digression on how a server behavior works is required. As you should have noticed in previous chapters, server behaviors differ from regular behaviors in the way they can be applied to your HTML code. In fact, because server behaviors mainly comprise server-side code, they can be placed on any part of your source code, even around selected areas. Each single code block of a server behavior is called a *participant* and is made up of an EDML file, while the list of all the participants needed by a server behavior to work is called a *participants group*, and is represented by another EDML file.

When inserting a server behavior into a document, Dreamweaver needs to know where to insert each code block, what each code block looks like, and what data must be entered by the user or replaced at runtime. Each single participant EDML file stores its own information, and the participants group EDML file lists all the participants that make up the server behavior.

Creating a Generic CFML Form Mailer Server Behavior

Using the Dreamweaver Server Behavior Builder, you are now going to create a generic ColdFusion-driven Form Mailer. A Form Mailer is used to process and send all the fields of an HTML form to a specified address as an e-mail.

Before considering turning code into a server behavior, make sure it is bug free and fully tested. Inserting a buggy server behavior into your pages will cause all kinds of problems that will be difficult to debug. In addition to this, make sure that the code you want to be available as a server behavior is really suitable; if it doesn't accept parameters or cannot be easily reused, it is not the right candidate for a server behavior. Code blocks that need no or few parameters to be entered should instead be turned into snippets, as we will see in the next chapter.

Building the Server Behavior Code

The following listing is the ColdFusion code we are going to turn into a server behavior (`CFmailer.cfm`):

```
<cfif isdefined("form.fieldnames")>
  <cfset mail_body = "">
  <cfset cr = Chr(13) & Chr(10)>
  <cfloop index="form_element" list="#form.fieldnames#">
    <!--- Append each form element to message body --->
    <cfset mail_body = ➡
      mail_body & form_element & ": " & Evaluate(form_element) & cr>
  </cfloop>
  <cfmail to="info@mysite.com" from="myform@mysite.com" subject="Contact Form">
    #mail_body#
  </cfmail>
  <cfset mail_redirect="success.cfm">
  <cfif mail_redirect NEQ "">
    <cflocation url="#mail_redirect#">
  </cfif>
</cfif>
```

The code starts by checking that the Form.Fieldnames variable exists. If so, it loops over each form field, adding their names and values to the message body (the mail_body variable), which will be sent as an e-mail by using the <cfmail> tag. After the message has been sent, the <cflocation> tag will stop the code execution and open a new page, as long as the mail_redirect variable is not empty.

For the sake of the example, when turning the preceding ColdFusion code into a server behavior, you will convert only the to and from attributes of the <cfmail> tag and the value of the mail_redirect variable into custom parameters, although it is possible to change other parts of the code, such as the subject attribute.

1. Start by choosing + ➤ New Server Behavior from the Server Behavior panel. The New Server Behavior dialog window should appear, as shown in Figure 9-13.

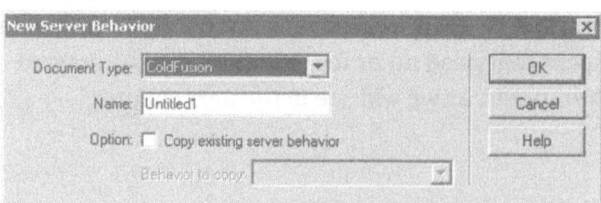

Figure 9-13. Specifying the Document Type and Name of your server behavior

Make sure ColdFusion is selected in the Document Type drop-down menu and enter **CF Form Mailer** in the Name field.

Checking the "Copy existing server behavior" option will enable the "Behavior to copy" drop-down menu, which shows a list of all the available server behaviors we can copy from. You don't want to copy a server behavior in this case, so leave it unchecked.

2. Now click OK, and the main dialog window of the Server Behavior Builder will appear, which should look like Figure 9-14.

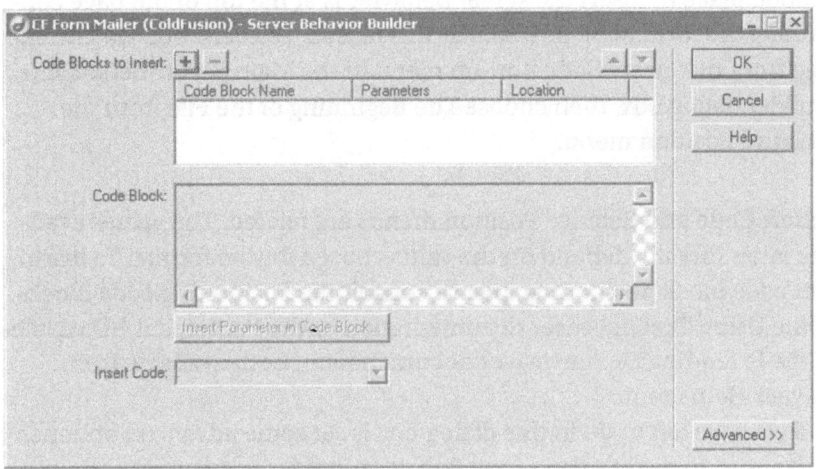

Figure 9-14. The main Server Behavior Builder dialog box

3. Click on the + sign to add a new code block. Dreamweaver will name it CF Form Mailer_block1. Click OK to accept this name.

4. Insert the CFML Form Mailer code (CFmailer.cfm) into the Code Block field.

5. Now it's time to convert part of the code into some custom parameters. You want to be able to define the values of the <cfmail> tag's first two attributes and to choose which URL to redirect users to after they submit the form. Highlight the <cfmail> tag's first attribute value (info@mysite.com) and click on the Insert Parameter in Code Block button. The dialog box in Figure 9-15 appears.

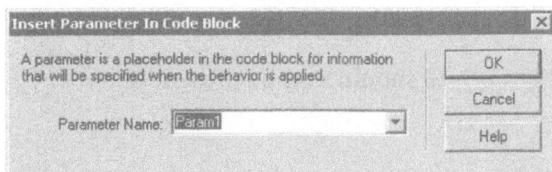

Figure 9-15. Inserting a parameter in the code block

Enter **Send Form To** in the Parameter Name field and click OK. The chosen parameter name will be inserted into the code block surrounded by @@ blocks, replacing the info@mysite.com address.

6. Repeat step 5, this time replacing myform@mysite.com with From, and replacing success.cfm (which is the value of the mail_redirect attribute of the <cfset> tag) with **Go To Page**.

7. A good place to insert the server behavior is at the top of the page containing the form to be posted. For this reason, select Above the <html> Tag from the Insert Code pop-up menu in the Main Server Behavior Builder dialog box, then choose The Beginning of the File from the Relative Position menu.

The Insert Code and Relative Position menus are related. The values available for the latter directly depend on the value chosen for the former. To learn more about code block positioning, please consult the Positioning code blocks section of the Using Dreamweaver documentation or the Participant EDML files section of the Extending Dreamweaver documenation, both available from Dreamweaver's Help menu.

Now all we have left to do in this dialog box is set some advanced options. Click on Advanced to display the Server Behavior Builder's advanced options.

Make sure the Identifier checkbox is selected so that the server behavior will be recognized by Dreamweaver and displayed on the Server Behaviors panel. The Server Behavior Title field is where you define the name your server behavior will appear under in the Server Behaviors panel, and the Code Block pop-up menu defines which code block will be highlighted when the server behavior is selected. Lastly, change the default [No Selection] value with CF Form Mailer_block1 and click on Next.

Building the Server Behavior Interface

We have covered the first step of making your server behavior. Next you must specify an HTML interface that you will use to enter custom parameter values into the server behavior. You don't have to actually build a GUI yourself; you just specify what you want to appear in it, then Dreamweaver does most of the hard work.

1. The dialog box shown in Figure 9-16 should now be present in Dreamweaver.

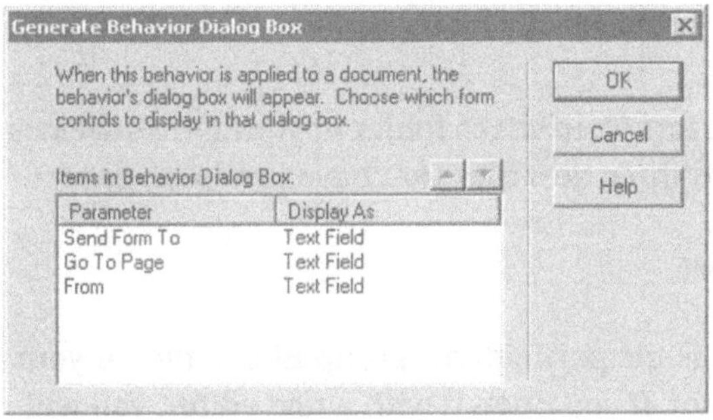

Figure 9-16. The dialog box that allows you to specify how the GUI (dialog box) for your server behavior will look

Select the Go To Page parameter. A small down arrow will appear at the right of its value in the Display As column. Click on the arrow to display all the available interface controls for user input.

2. Because the Go To Page parameter defines which URL users are sent to after the form is posted, choose URL Text Field.

3. The up and down arrows to the top-right corner of the main dialog change the order in which the parameters appear on the final HTML interface. Leave the Go To Page parameter selected and click on the down arrow to move it to the bottom of the list. Click OK.

The CF Form Mailer server behavior should have been added the Server Behaviors panel, and is ready to be applied to any page you choose. The main dialog of your newly created server behavior should look like Figure 9-17. Try it out on a form of your own!

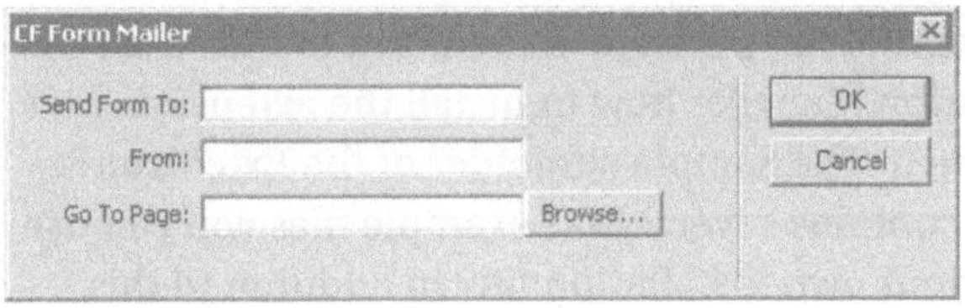

Figure 9-17. Your new server behavior's dialog box

What Files Compose the Server Behavior?

If you now look into the ServerBehaviors/ColdFusion folder in your Dreamweaver Configuration directory, you will find three new files that have just been generated by the Server Behavior Builder.

The three new files are as follows:

- CF Form Mailer.edml: This file is the participants group EDML file for your CF Form Mailer server behavior. If you open it with a text editor, you will see that it contains information about which version of Dreamweaver created it, and the text that will appear in the Server Behaviors panel after you apply the server behavior to a page. It also contains a list of all the participant EDML files.

- CF Form Mailer_block1.edml: This file is a participant EDML file and contains all the information needed by Dreamweaver to distinguish it as a code block and to correctly apply it to files when the server behavior is applied.

- CF Form Mailer.htm: This is the interface of the CF Form Mailer main dialog that appears when the server behavior is called within Dreamweaver. Because it is simple HTML, you can edit it to create a more satisfactory user interface if wished.

Distributing Server Behavior

To distribute your new server behavior, you can use the Extension Manager, which allows you to create an MXP and submit it to the Macromedia Exchange (http://www.macromedia.com/exchange).

For the Extension Manager to be able to package your server behavior, you must prepare a Macromedia Extension Installation (MXI) file. These files are basically XML files used to document the name of the extension, its version number and type, and the content of the package. In addition to this, the MXI file tells the Macromedia Extension Manager how to install the extension, and tells users how to access and use it. The Sample subfolder of the Extension Manager application directory contains several MXI example files you can use as starting templates to create your own installation file. In addition to this, a complete reference about MXI files is available on the Macromedia web site at http://www.macromedia.com/go/em_file_format/.

We will now guide you through the creation of a simple MXI file you can use to package your CF Form Mailer server behavior for distribution:

1. Start by creating a folder on your desktop (or wherever you prefer on your local machine) and name it CFBook Form Mailer. This is where you will copy all the files that will form the extension package.

2. Copy the three files created by the Server Behavior Builder for your CF Form Mailer extension into this folder: `CF Form Mailer.htm`, `CF Form Mailer.edml`, and `CF Form Mailer_block1.edml`. They should be in the `Configuration\ServerBehaviors\ColdFusion` subdirectory of your Dreamweaver install directory.

3. Open your text editor of choice. Now you start to build the MXI file. First add the following tag to the file, which provides data about the extension to the Extension Manager, including name, version, and type, and whether a restart of Dreamweaver is required after installation:

```
<macromedia-extension name="CF Form Mailer"
   version="1.0"
   type="serverBehavior"
   requires-restart="false">
</macromedia-extension>
```

4. Next you specify the products the extension has been built for, which in your case is Dreamweaver only. Add the following lines inside the `<macromedia-extension>` tag (note that Dreamweaver corresponds to version 7 of the application):

```
<products>
   <product name="Dreamweaver" version="6" required="true"  />
</products>
```

5. Other required information is as follows: the name of the extension's author (contained in the `<author>` tag `name` attribute), a short explanation of its use (in the `<description>` tag), and instructions on how to access it from inside the application (in the `<UI-access>` tag).

    The last two tags must contain a `CDATA` section and use a `VARCHAR` data type with a limit of 2,000 characters. In addition to this, you can use the `<br />` HTML tag and nonbreaking spaces (specified by the   escape code) to format the text inside those tags. Add the following lines directly below the `</products>` tag:

```
<author name="CFBook"></author>

<description>
  <![CDATA[
    Generic ColdFusion Form Mailer
  ]]>
</description>
```

```
<UI-Access>
 <![CDATA[
   You can run this Server Behavior by choosing:<br />
   Server Behaviors > CF Form Mailer
 ]]>
</UI-Access>
```

6. Now it's time to provide the list of files that must be installed in the application as part of the extension. This is done using the `<files>` tag, which contains `<file>` child tags—one for each file installed.

   The `<file>` tag has two attributes: source and destination. The first attribute contains the name of the file to be installed, and the second contains the path to the destination folder. Add the following lines to your code, just below the `<UI-Access>` tag:

```
<files>
  <file source="CF Form Mailer.htm"
    destination="$Dreamweaver/Configuration/ServerBehaviors/ColdFusion/">
  </file>
  <file source="CF Form Mailer.edml"
    destination="$Dreamweaver/Configuration/ServerBehaviors/ColdFusion/ ">
  </file>
  <file source="CF Form Mailer_block1.edml"
    destination="$Dreamweaver/Configuration/ServerBehaviors/ColdFusion/ ">
  </file>
</files>
```

Our MXI file should now be ready for packaging—save it as `cf_form_mailer.mxi` in the same location as your `.htm` and `.edml` files (check that it is correct by comparing it to the `cf_form_mailer.mxi` file in the code download for this chapter, available at `http://www.apress.com`).

Now double-click your `cf_form_mailer.mxi` file. The Macromedia Extension Manager will now launch and present you with the dialog box shown in Figure 9-18.

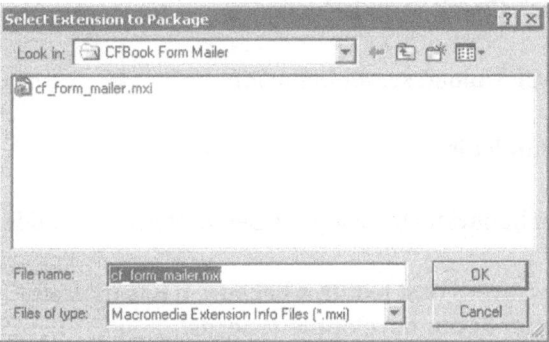

Figure 9-18. The Extension Manager prompts you to choose an extension to package when you click on an MXI file.

Click the OK button, and the Extension Manager will propose a name for the MXP file. Accept the default offered by clicking OK again, and the extension package will be created.

Our CF Form Mailer extension can now be installed in Dreamweaver. Always remember to test carefully each new extension you package before distributing it. Macromedia Exchange provides a set of useful extension testing guidelines at http://www.macromedia.com/exchange/.

Summary

In this chapter you have learned about several aspects of Dreamweaver extensibility. You now know:

- What a Macromedia Extension is

- What the Macromedia Extension Manager is and where to get it

- How to install, remove, and manage extensions by using the Macromedia Extension Manager

- Where to download additional extensions to add to Dreamweaver

- How to use Jaro von Flocken's Check Form behavior

- How to use Massimo Foti's CF Upload server behavior

- What the Server Behavior Builder is

- How to create custom server behaviors by using the Server Behavior Builder

Extensibility is one of Dreamweaver's best features because it lets us easily customize our environment to better fit our development needs.

CHAPTER 10

Code and Component Reuse

IF YOU EVER FIND yourself writing the same code over and over again on different pages or on similar projects, you should consider adopting a more efficient way to code that permits you to save precious development time. Sure, it requires a little more effort in the planning stage of your application development, but code reuse has a number of benefits. Not only does the practice of reusing code save you a considerable amount of development time, but splitting your code into small chunks will result in tidier code that is easier to read, debug, and maintain.

Both ColdFusion MX 6.1 and Dreamweaver MX 2004 offer developers several ways to implement reusable elements and code blocks. Some, for example Dreamweaver MX snippets, simply save you from having to retype the same lines of code over and over, whereas others, such as ColdFusion Components (CFCs), provide a more flexible architecture to the whole application, making code more readable and enabling the clear separation of the business logic from the presentation layer.

This chapter presents you with an overview of the most important and common reusable elements that you'll want to use in your work, specifically:

- The <cfinclude> tag

- CFML UDFs

- CFML custom tags

- CFCs

- Dreamweaver snippets

- Dreamweaver library

- Dreamweaver templates

- Dreamweaver tag libraries

The ColdFusion <cfinclude> tag

As we showed in Chapter 3, you use the <cfinclude> tag to add the content of another ColdFusion file into the current page. When executing a .cfm file, if ColdFusion encounters a <cfinclude> tag, it reads the content of the page specified in the template attribute as if it were part of the page that contains the <cfinclude> tag, making the code and variables specified in the include file available to the page containing the include.

Because the <cfinclude> tag doesn't allow you to pass parameters to the included file, but makes available to it all the variables available to the calling page, it is usually used to incorporate common blocks of code into multiple pages, such as headers and footers, allowing extra control over layout consistency on a web site. This also saves time: if you wish to change some content in these common blocks, you have to make the changes only once rather than updating every single page on your site. The <cfinclude> file also comes in handy when you want to divide large documents into smaller chunks.

For practical examples using the <cfinclude> tag, refer back to the "Understanding Common ColdFusion Tags" section of Chapter 3.

ColdFusion UDFs

ColdFusion offers a vast number of built-in functions that allow developers to perform a variety of tasks, from handling arrays to formatting dates and everything in between. Functions are a good example of code reuse, because they allow us to execute their encapsulated logic and operations to perform tasks as many times as you want just by calling them and passing them the information to be processed.

UDFs work exactly the same way as built-in CFML functions, but are created by developers (they are not part of the CFML language). You can write functions to solve specific problems and needs to meet an application's business requirements.

Introduced in ColdFusion 5, UDFs had to be written using CFScript, a scripting language similar in syntax to JavaScript. CFScript is considered by many developers to be more readable than its ColdFusion tag-based code counterpart, but is limited in that it cannot contain other tags.

However, three new tags were introduced in ColdFusion MX that allowed user-defined functions to be written with tag based syntax: <cffunction>, <cfarguments>, and <cfreturn>. With these now available, there's no longer any need to write UDFs using CFScript, even though you still can. One on the main reasons is that, using this tag-based alternative, you can incorporate all the available ColdFusion MX 6.1 tags into your functions, which was not possible by only using CFScript.

The following is a very simple example showing how to define and call a CFScript-based UDF (the pre-ColdFusion MX way of doing things). The function accepts a single parameter (a string) and returns a welcome message (scriptUDF.cfm):

```
<cfscript>
function SayHello(FirstName){
  var HelloMessage = "Hello, " & FirstName;
  return HelloMessage;
}
</cfscript>

<cfoutput>#SayHello("Edo")#</cfoutput>
```

As you can see, you must wrap CFScript code within a <cfscript> element, within which you declare the function and define the accepted parameters, just as if you were writing a common JavaScript function. The main difference is that CFScript-based functions are executed server-side rather than client-side, so that you can reference ColdFusion variables, functions, and expressions from within them. You call the UDF in exactly the same way you would call a predefined CFML function.

Now let's see how you would write exactly the same UDF, this time using the three new tags introduced in ColdFusion MX (tagUDF.cfm):

```
<cffunction name="SayHello">
  <cfargument name="FirstName" type="string" required="Yes">
  <cfset HelloMessage = "Hello, " & Arguments.FirstName>
  <cfreturn HelloMessage>
</cffunction>

<cfoutput>#SayHello("Edo")#</cfoutput>
```

> **TIP** *If you want to learn more about UDFs, a good starting point (other than the Macromedia Documentation) is the Common Functions Library Projects found at* http://www.cflib.org. *This site is the biggest ColdFusion UDF repository available on the Internet, and also features a number of useful tools and resources to get you started with UDF development.*

ColdFusion Custom Tags

ColdFusion custom tags are another powerful way to define your own business logic. While UDFs allow you to write functions that behave and are called using the same syntax as CFML functions, custom tags are executed in much the same way as CFML tags.

There are two kinds of custom tags: the first type, formally know as CFML custom tags, are created using CFML code and are made available as .cfm files. The other type is referred to as CFX tags. These are written in programming languages such as Java or C++, and are mostly offered as Java classes or COM objects (which you register in the ColdFusion MX Administrator to make them available to your pages).

> **TIP** *We haven't chosen to discuss CFX tags in this chapter, because they are an advanced topic beyond the scope of this book. If you want to know more about them, please refer to the Building Custom CFXAPI Tags chapter of the Developing ColdFusion Applications with CFML documentation (http://livedocs.macromedia.com/coldfusion/6.1/htmldocs/cfxtags.htm).*

CFML custom tags are similar to pages included using the `<cfinclude>` tag because the code is contained in a separate file, but are different because you can pass attributes to them containing information to be processed. In addition, the content of the custom tag file is not directly included on the calling page, but instead is executed as a single unit, so that internal variables aren't exposed to the calling file. This is referred to as a *protected scope*.

During the previous chapter, we showed how to turn a Form Mailer written in CFML into a server behavior. The original code was as follows:

```
<cfif isdefined("form.fieldnames")>
  <cfset mail_body = "">
  <cfset cr = Chr(13) & Chr(10)>
  <cfloop index="form_element" list="#form.fieldnames#">
    <!--- Append each form element to message body --->
    <cfset mail_body = mail_body & form_element & ": " & form[form_element] & cr>
  </cfloop>
  <cfmail to="info@mysite.com" from="myform@mysite.com"
    subject="Contact Form">
    #mail_body#
  </cfmail>
  <cfset mail_redirect="success.cfm">
  <cfif mail_redirect NEQ "">
    <cflocation url="#mail_redirect#">
  </cfif>
</cfif>
```

With little effort, you can turn it into a CFML custom tag, like this:

```
<cfsilent>
<!---
/**
* ColdFusion MX 6.1 custom tag: "form_mailer"
*
* The tag assemble a very simple email out of all the form field submitted to the
current file
*
* @author              Massimo Foti (massimo@massimocorner.com)
* @version             1.0, 02/25/2003
* @param to            Destination address (required)
* @param from          From  address (required)
* @param subject        Email's subject (optional)
*                       Default is "Contact Form"
* @param redirect       Url for redirection (optional)
 */
 --->

<!--- Required attributes --->
<cfparam name="Attributes.to" type="string">
<cfparam name="Attributes.from" type="string">

<!--- Default attributes --->
<cfparam name="Attributes.subject" type="string" default="Contact Form">
<cfparam name="Attributes.redirect" type="string" default="">

<cfif isdefined("form.fieldnames")>
  <cfset mail_body = "">
  <cfset cr = Chr(13) & Chr(10)>
  <cfloop index="form_element" list="#form.fieldnames#">
    <!--- Append each form element to message body --->
    <cfset mail_body = mail_body & form_element & ": " & form[form_element] & cr>
  </cfloop>
  <cfmail to="#Attributes.to#" from="#Attributes.from#"
     subject="#Attributes.subject#">
    #mail_body#
  </cfmail>
  <!--- Redirect if required --->
  <cfif Attributes.redirect NEQ "">
    <cflocation url="#Attributes.redirect#">
  </cfif>
</cfif>
</cfsilent>
```

The <cfsilent> tag simply suppresses the ColdFusion output (including unnecessary white space created as a result) and is not related exclusively to custom tags. The comments just explain the use and function of the tag attributes. The really important part in the preceding code—which is what makes it into a good reusable custom tag—is the use of Attributes scoped variables. The Attributes scope is populated with all the attributes passed to the custom tag from the page containing it.

Once your custom tag is ready, you can call it from any of your pages as you would a common CFML tag. The name of the CFML custom tag will be composed of the cf_ prefix followed by the name of the file containing the code, without the .cfm file extension. For example, if the previous example was saved as form_mailer.cfm, you could then call it as a custom tag by inserting <cf_form_mailer> into your page, and the attributes you pass to it would then be available internally in the Attributes scope.

Custom tags can be stored in any of the following places if you want them to be directly available to be called from your web pages:

- The folder containing the calling page

- The CFusionMX/CustomTags folder of your ColdFusion server

- A subfolder within the CFusionMX/CustomTags folder

- Any other directory specified in the ColdFusion Administrator

The last three possibilities are not always allowed when deploying your ColdFusion pages on a shared hosting environment. If you don't have the permission to store them in the CFusionMX/CustomTags folder, or you don't have access to the ColdFusion Administrator, the best solution is to place your custom tags on the same directory as the calling pages.

Besides these methods, there are other ways to call custom tags from a page. Other possibilities are the use of the <cfmodule> tag, which permits you to specify the location the custom tag is stored in, and the <cfimport> tag, which imports the custom tag as part of a tag library (which may also contain JSP custom tags!). When you have two tags with the same name, ColdFusion may not know which to use. Therefore, it will first search the folder where the calling page resides and then any additional specified folders. Using <cfmodule> helps you prevent this ambiguity.

For more information, please consult the Creating and Using Custom CFML Tags chapter of the Developing ColdFusion MX Applications with CFML documentation (http://livedocs.macromedia.com/coldfusion/6/Developing_ColdFusion_MX_Applications_with_CFML/contents.htm).

ColdFusion Components

The CFC framework was introduced in ColdFusion MX and offers a more innovative and object-oriented way to facilitate ColdFusion code reuse. A strong point of CFCs is that the application logic encapsulated in a CFC can not only be accessed from ColdFusion pages, but also provides a standard interface allowing client access by a number of other applications/mechanisms, such as the Flash Player (Flash Remoting) or as a web service via SOAP (Simple Object Access Protocol).

For more information on how to access a CFC from a Flash-based application using Flash Remoting, please consult Chapter 12.

Dreamweaver MX 2004 offers various tools to easily create and access ColdFusion components. In the following example, you create a CFC that reads a text file and returns its content to the calling client, which in this case will be a .cfm page:

1. In the cfbook site, create a folder named Ch10, and inside that, a sub-folder named CFC. Create a simple .txt file in the Ch10 folder containing the sentence "Hello, how are you today?". Name this greetings.txt.

2. In Dreamweaver select New from the File menu. From the General tab's Dynamic Page category, choose ColdFusion Component and then click on the Create button.

3. Select Code View, and replace the default code between the opening and closing <cfcomponent> tags with the following:

```
<cffunction access="public" name="readFile" output="false"➡
  returntype="string" hint="Read a text file and return a string">
  <cfargument name="fileUrl" type="string" required="true"
    hint="Relative path to the file">
  <cfargument name="fileCharset" type="string" required="false"
    default="ISO-8859-1" hint="Charset used for the file">
  <cfset fileContent="">
  <!--- Turn relative url to an absolute path --->
  <cfset fileToRead="#ExpandPath(arguments.fileUrl)#">
  <!--- Be sure the file exist --->
  <cfif FileExists(fileToRead)>
    <cftry>
      <!--- Lock file on read --->
      <cflock timeout="10" throwontimeout="yes" type="readonly"➡
        name="#fileToRead#">
```

```
                    <cffile action="read" file="#fileToRead#" variable="fileContent"➥
                        charset="#arguments.fileCharset#">
                </cflock>
                <cfcatch type="any">
                    <!--- Throw an error if something went wrong (read permissions➥
                        or the like) --->
                    <cfthrow message="Error reading file: #fileToRead#"➥
                        type="read_file">
                </cfcatch>
            </cftry>
            <cfelse>
            <!--- Throw an error if the file doesn't exist --->
            <cfthrow message="Argument fileURL point to a non existing file➥
                " type="read_file">
        </cfif>
        <cfreturn fileContent>
    </cffunction>
```

4. Save the component file inside the CFC folder as read_file.cfc, and you're done.

Now click the Components panel tab of the Application panel group and select CF Components from the drop-down menu. You will now find your new component listed with the other components available on your server.

> **TIP** *Depending on the situation, Dreamweaver may fail to refresh the Components panel. If so, you can manually refresh it by clicking on the Refresh button in the top-right corner of the panel.*

Now let's look at how you can utilize this component in a web page:

1. Create a page within the Ch10 folder and name it cfcexample.cfm.

2. From the Components panel, select your CFC's main function, which is represented by the icon seen previously that looks like the end of a wrench with a little arrow circling it. Drag and drop it inside the <body> tag of the cfcexample.cfm page.

3. All of the tags needed to invoke the CFC have been inserted for you by Dreamweaver. You just have to change the value attribute of the <cfin-vokeargument> tag to the path you want the text file to be placed when it is created by the CFC.

4. Lastly, add a `<cfdump>` tag to display the result of the component call, which is given by the `returnvariable` value of the `<cfinvoke>` tag.

The code within the page's `<body>` tag should now look like this:

```
<cfinvoke component="cfc.read_file" method="readFile"➥
  returnvariable="readFileRet">
  <cfinvokeargument name="fileUrl" value="greetings.txt"/>
</cfinvoke>
<cfdump var="#readFileRet#">
```

Test the `cfcexample.cfm` page, and the content of the text file should be displayed.

> **NOTE** *CFCs are a very advanced topic when their more object-oriented features and functionality are used. For more on CFCs, see the Developing ColdFusion Applications with CFML documentation* (http://livedocs. macromedia.com/coldfusion/6/Developing_ColdFusion_MX_Applications_ with_CFML/buildingComponents.htm).

Dreamweaver Snippets

Code snippets are nothing more than blocks of code ready for quick reuse; they wrap around a selection or exist as a single portion of code. You insert them into pages by using the Dreamweaver MX Snippets panel available in the Code panel group, or by choosing Window ➤ Snippets from the main menu, as shown in Figure 10-1.

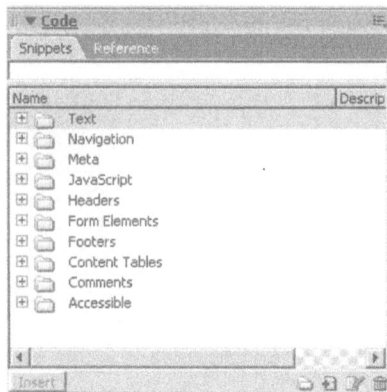

Figure 10-1. The Dreamweaver MX Snippets panel

When considering ColdFusion code for turning into a snippet, make sure it is bug-free and fully tested, exactly as you would when creating a server behavior, for the same reasons we discussed in Chapter 9. If you are not sure whether a code block would be better as a simple snippet instead of a more complex server behavior, here's a general rule.

If you need your code to accept several parameters through an interface, convert it into a server behavior. If, on the other hand, the code you want to reuse doesn't need any parameters to be passed to it (or very few), there's no reason to bother turning it into a server behavior, so turn it into a snippet instead.

In addition, be aware that using lots of server behaviors at the same time can affect Dreamweaver performance—you won't run into this problem using snippets.

The Snippets panel was introduced with the release of Dreamweaver MX. However, the concept of code snippets will be familiar to experienced users of HomeSite or ColdFusion Studio.

Unfortunately, Dreamweaver snippets are not compatible with HomeSite or ColdFusion Studio snippets because a different storing file format has been adopted. Snippets created with Dreamweaver are saved as XML files with a .csn file extension (code snippet), but HomeSite snippets are saved and restored as a combination of two text files with file extensions of .hss (HomeSite Snippet Start) and .hse (HomeSite Snippet End). This means that you can't directly import and use snippets created with HomeSite, ColdFusion Studio, or JRun Studio into Dreamweaver.

Even though Dreamweaver doesn't offer a way to translate snippets from other sources by default, there is a nifty Dreamweaver extension created by Massimo Foti that will allow you to convert and import them into Dreamweaver snippets. The extension is called Snippets Converter and is available as a free download from http://www.dwfaq.com/Snippets/converter.asp.

Now let's look at an example of how to create a code snippet and insert it into a page using the Snippets panel. The ColdFusion code you are going to turn into a snippet prevents browsers caching web pages that it is included on, and looks like so:

```
<cfset gmt=GetTimeZoneInfo()>
<cfset gmt=gmt.utcHourOffset>
  <cfif gmt EQ 0>
    <cfset gmt="">
  <cfelseif gmt GT 0>
    <cfset gmt="+"&gmt>
</cfif>
```

```
<cfheader name="Expires" value="#DateFormat(now(), 'ddd, dd mmm yyyy')#➡
  #TimeFormat(now(), 'HH:mm:ss')# GMT#gmt#">
<cfheader name="Pragma" value="no-cache">
<cfheader name="Cache-Control" value="no-cache, no-store, proxy-revalidate,➡
  must-revalidate">
```

This code an ideal candidate for turning into a code snippet for two good reasons. First, it a useful general function that can be applied to many different situations. Second, it doesn't require any parameters to be passed to it. This is a perfect "write once, use often" code block—ideal for use as a snippet. Now let's look at how you go about creating a snippet from it:

1. From the Snippets panel, click on the New Snippet Folder icon (the little folder icon in the bottom-right corner of the following screenshot) and name the newly created folder ColdFusion, as shown in Figure 10-2.

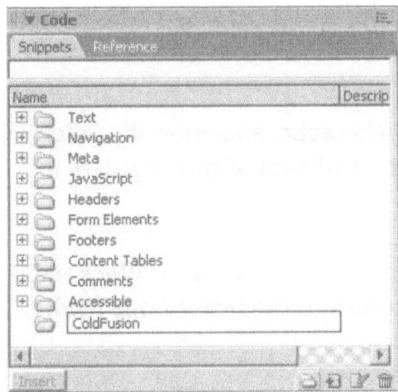

Figure 10-2. The Dreamweaver Snippets panel, showing your new ColdFusion *folder*

2. Select the newly created ColdFusion folder and click on the New Snippet icon (the icon in the bottom-right corner that looks like a document with a plus sign preceding it.) The Snippets dialog box should appear, as shown in Figure 10-3.

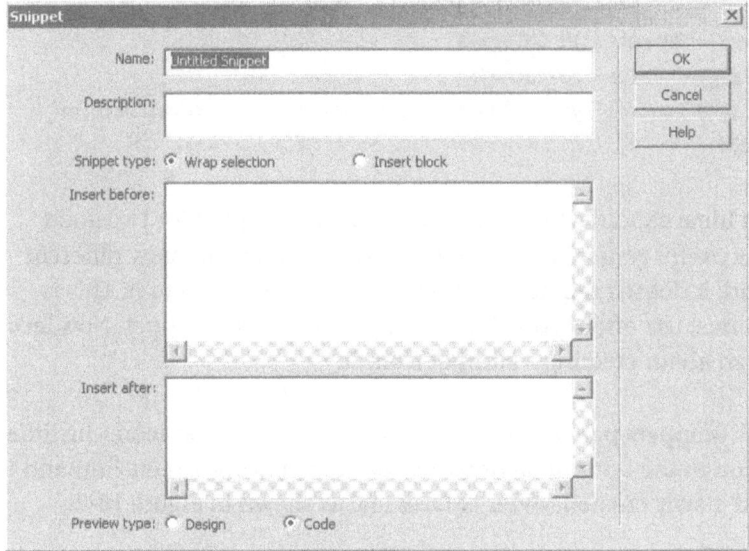

Figure 10-3. The Snippet dialog box, where new snippets are created

Using the dialog box, name the snippet No cache, and enter the following description on the Description field: **Send a set of http headers to
the browser to prevent caching**.

3. We will use this snippet as a single block, so select the Insert Block radio
    button and type the following lines of code into the Insert Code field:

```
<cfset gmt= GetTimeZoneInfo()>
<cfset gmt=gmt.utcHourOffset>
  <cfif gmt EQ 0>
    <cfset gmt="">
  <cfelseif gmt GT 0>
    <cfset gmt="+"&gmt>
</cfif>
<cfheader name="Expires" value="#DateFormat(now(), 'ddd, dd mmm yyyy')#➥
  #TimeFormat(now(), 'HH:mm:ss')# GMT#gmt#">
<cfheader name="Pragma" value="no-cache">
<cfheader name="Cache-Control" value="no-cache, no-store,➥
  proxy-revalidate, must-revalidate">
```

4. Make sure Code is selected from the Preview Type radio buttons. Preview Type defines the way you will see your snippet's code on the Snippets panel preview pane. If you select Design, Dreamweaver will try to render the code in the pane, but if you select Code, Dreamweaver just shows the code, which comes in handy when the code doesn't actually visibly display anything on the page, like in our example.

5. Click OK, and your No Cache snippet will be added to the Snippets panel within the ColdFusion folder.

Many more useful snippets are available for free download from Dreamweaver FAQ's Snippets Exchange at http://www.dwfaq.com/Snippets/default.asp.

Inserting a snippet into a page is even easier. The perfect place for your new No Cache snippet is on top of the page or, even better, in an Application.cfm file. To insert it, you will simply have to place the cursor at the position you want it to be inserted, then double-click the snippet in the Snippets panel. If the snippet you have created is designed to wrap around a selection, with opening and closing tags, highlight the code it is to be placed around. It is also important to note that by clicking Edit ➤ Preferences ➤ Keyboard Shortcuts, you can assign a keyboard shortcut to any snippet you create!

Dreamweaver Library

Dreamweaver's library is accessed from the Assets panel, which is part of the Files panel group. The Assets panel is kind of a central repository for common assets used throughout the development of a web site. These common assets can be images, Flash movies, links, etc.

A library item is somewhat similar in purpose to a snippet, but differs from snippets because of its "linked" status: basically, that means that all instances of the same library item, which can be inserted on different pages, are related. Library items that have been inserted on a page are updated when changes are made to them in the Assets panel, whereas snippets are not.

You can access Dreamweaver's library by clicking the Library icon (the little open-book icon at lower-left in Figure 10-4) on the Assets panel that resides in the File panel group. Alternatively, you can choose Window ➤ Assets from the main menu, then click on the Library icon.

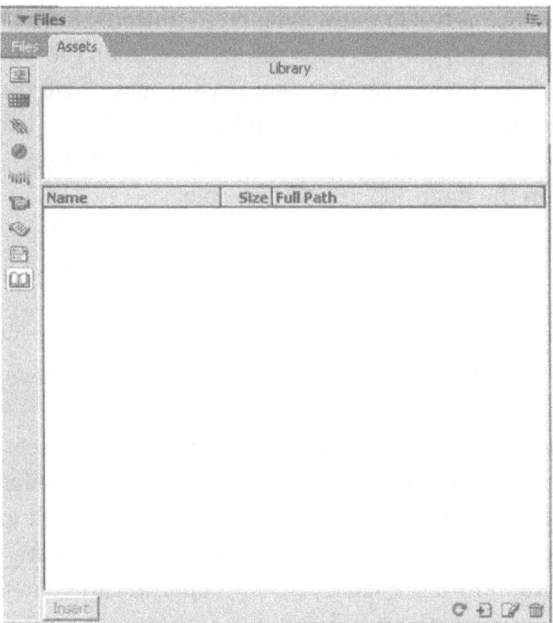

Figure 10-4. The Dreamweaver library

The library items are stored in a folder called Library, which is created in the root of your site by Dreamweaver as soon as you make your first library item. Library items are stored with the file extension .lbi, and contain the code for the item.

To better understand how the library works and how you can speed up your development time by using it, you will build a copyright notice for a fictional company, then store and modify it as a library item:

1. Create a new file inside the Ch10 folder you created earlier within this folder and call it dmxlibrary.cfm. In Design View, add the following text to this file: **This is my fictional company's copyright notice**.

2. Highlight the text you just entered and select Library ➤ Add Object To Library from the Modify menu, or simply drag and drop the selected content into the library. A new untitled item will be added to the library as shown in Figure 10-5.

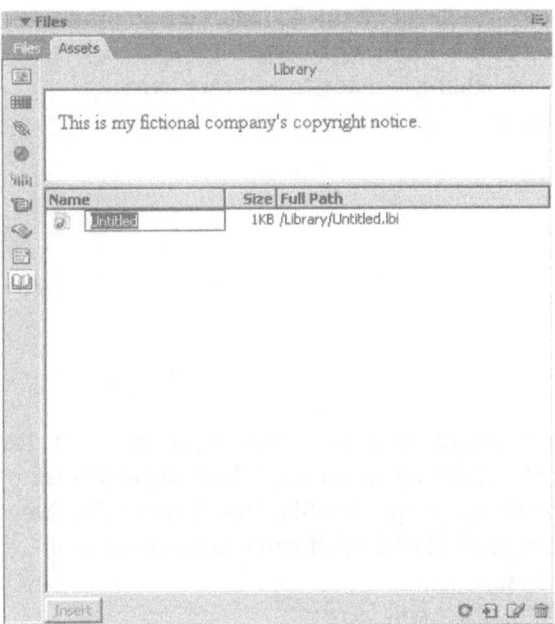

Figure 10-5. Your as yet unnamed library item.

3.   Name your new library item "copyright." Now save the dmxlibrary.cfm
     file. Now look at the code of your page—notice that the following com-
     ments have been added around the sentence you have just turned into
     a library item:

```
<!-- #BeginLibraryItem "/Library/copyright.lbi" -->This is my fictional
company's copyright notice<!-- #EndLibraryItem -->
```

These comments are used by Dreamweaver to identify the wrapped
code as a library item included on the page. It is important that these
comments remain in place; otherwise, Dreamweaver will not be able to
update the item. In addition to this, Dreamweaver will highlight the
item with a bright yellow background color in both Design View and
Code View, so it can be easily identified.

> **CAUTION**   *As you can see, the comment lines added by Dreamweaver contain
> a sort of mapping for the files contained in the* Library *folder created by
> Dreamweaver in the root of your site. Because of this mapping, it is important
> to not rename that folder, or you'll have to update all the references to it and
> to the files within it.*

You have just learned how to create a library item. To insert it into other pages, simply drag it from the panel to the document, or select it and click the Insert button. Now we will look at how changes made to a library item are applied to all the pages that contain it.

First, double-click the copyright item in the library to open the copyright.lbi file. Change the text in the copyright.lbi file by entering **(c) 2003 My Fictional Company. All rights reserved**. Save the copyright.lbi file. The Update Files dialog box will pop up, as shown in Figure 10-6, and ask if you want to update all the files containing the copyright item.

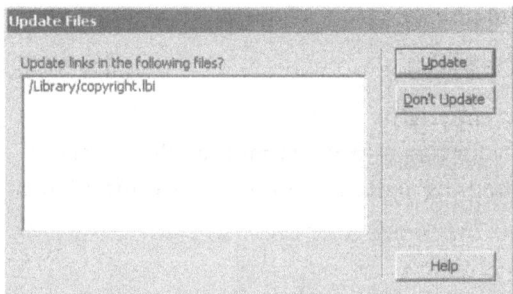

Figure 10-6. The library's Update Files dialog box

Click on the Update button. The Update Pages dialog box appears displaying the report for all modified files. Click on the Close button. Now open the dmxlibrary.cfm file. As you can see, the page has been updated to reflect the changes made to the copyright.lbi file. If the item was contained in other pages, it would have been updated there as well.

Remember that after updating a library item and all the related files that contain it, you must still upload all changes the to the deployment server before they will be reflected on your live site.

Dreamweaver Templates

Dreamweaver templates are far more than simple assets or chunks of code. As implied by their name, they are a special kind of parent page from which you can create multiple child pages. For this reason, templates are primarily used to define and maintain the main layout design of an entire web site, allowing it to be kept consistent easily.

Templates consist of two different kinds of region: non-editable and editable. Non-editable regions are parts of the template that can't be modified on the child pages created from the parent template. Any changes you wish to make to non-editable regions must be made in the parent template's non-editable regions, after which they will be automatically updated in all the child pages made from the parent page, in a fashion similar to how library items are updated. Editable regions, on the other hand, are parts of the template that can be edited on every child page.

For example, if you made a parent template for your company web site, you might have common elements on each page, such as a header including a company logo, a footer, a copyright notice, and maybe even a navigation menu. These would be non-editable regions. You could then define the main content area of the page as an editable region, and then create child pages from this parent template; most of the work for each page would then already be done, leaving you with only the content to fill in on each page.

Dreamweaver templates are stored in a special folder named Templates, which will be created by Dreamweaver in the root of your site when you create a template. Don't rename this folder; otherwise, Dreamweaver will not be able to preserve mapping and ensure automatic updates of all the pages generated from the templates.

Dreamweaver template files are saved into the Templates folder as .dwt files. Macromedia introduced a brand new nomenclature for templates in Dreamweaver MX used to generate dynamic server-side web pages. For example, if you want to create a parent template for generating child ColdFusion pages, you must save it with a file extension of .dwt.cfm.

This new naming convention has been implemented to solve a security issue that used to occur with Dreamweaver UltraDev 4 when common Dreamweaver template files containing server-side code were stored on the deployment server. Because server-side templates used to end with the .dwt file extension, it used to pass these template files directly to the browser without processing the server-side code, which would be exposed to the user. Adding an additional server-side file extension to the .dwt extension ensures that the requested files are processed before being served to the requesting client.

Now let's build a Dreamweaver CFML template from scratch:

1. Make sure your cfbook site is selected from the Site panel (so that the template is associated with the correct site) and choose New from the File menu. The New Document dialog box will pop up, as shown in Figure 10-7.

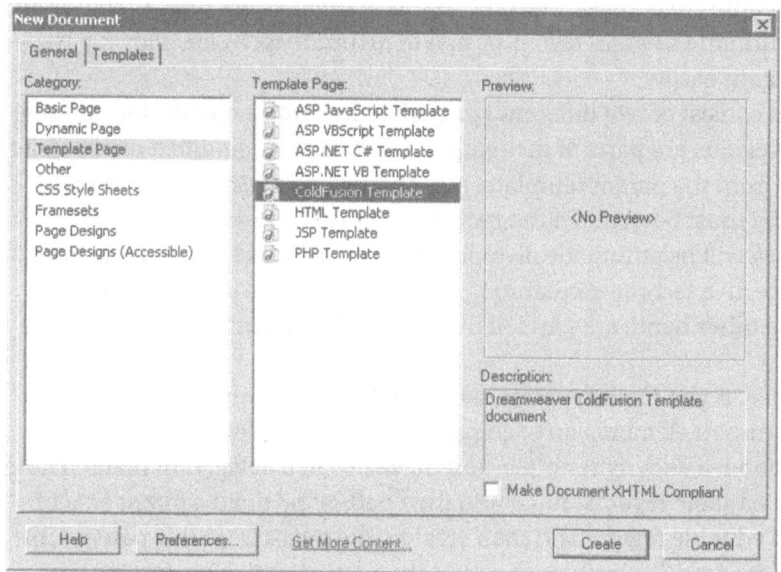

Figure 10-7. Creating a CFML template from the New Document dialog box

2. From the General tab, select Template Page as the Category and ColdFusion Template from the Template Page list, as shown in Figure 10-7. Click on the Create button, and the new template will open in Dreamweaver.

3. Save the template. A warning dialog will pop up informing you that no editable regions have been created. You are going to add them in a moment, so click the OK button to close the dialog box. The Save As Template dialog will now appear. Enter **main** as the template name, then click Save. The newly created template will now be available on the Site panel, within the Templates folder, and on the Assets panel (when you click on the templates button, as shown in Figure 10-8).

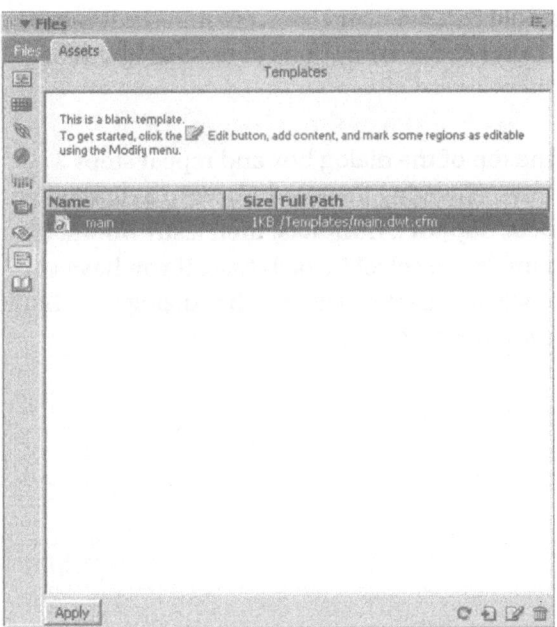

Figure 10-8. The Dreamweaver Assets panel, showing your template available for use

Now let's give your template some content. You will create a navigation bar for your site containing links to all sections of a fictional company web site—Home, Products, Support, Contacts, and About. Note that all the images used for creating the navigation bar are available for download from http://www.apress.com—make sure you have downloaded them and put them in a safe place before you start going through this exercise:

1. Make sure the main.dwt.cfm file is open in Dreamweaver Design View. If it is not, select it from the Template section of the Assets panel and click on the Edit button, or double-click it from the Site panel.

2. Click on the Navigation Bar button, and the Insert Navigation Bar dialog box should pop up. Fill it in as detailed in the next few steps.

3. Type **Home** into the Element name field, click on the Browse button of the Up image field, and select the home_up.gif image.

4. Choose home_over.gif as the Over image and home_down.gif as the Down image.

5. Type **Home** into the Alternate text field, and `home.cfm` into the When clicked, Go to URL field. Leave the other options of the dialog box as they are.

6. Click on the + button at the top of the dialog box and repeat steps 3 through 5 another four times, changing the word *Home* to a different word in each case: **Products**, **Support**, **Contacts**, then lastly **About**. It should be obvious which images to select in each case. If you have correctly completed each step, your Insert Navigation Bar dialog box should now look like the one shown in Figure 10-9.

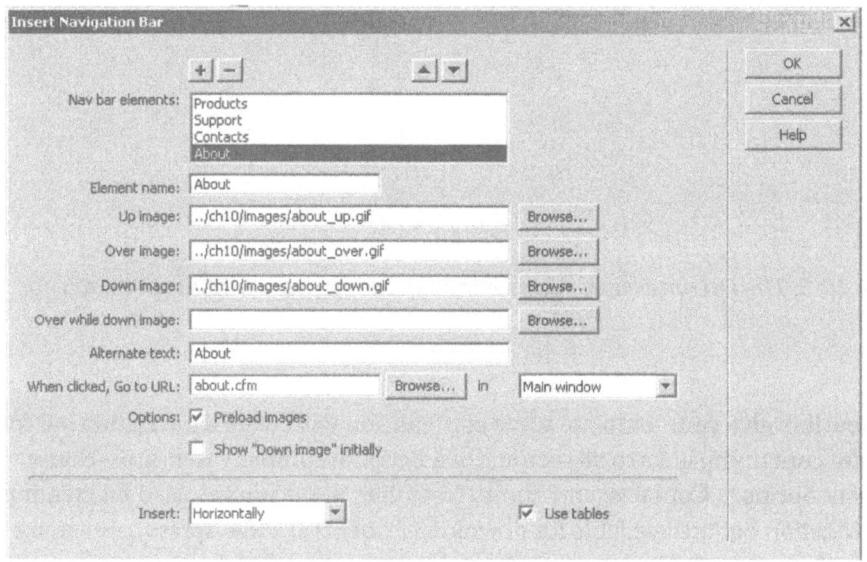

Figure 10-9. The completed Insert Navigation Bar dialog box

Lastly, click OK to close the dialog box and insert the navigation bar on the template page.

You have just created a non-editable region, which consists of the main navigation for your web site. You are now going to insert an editable region that will contain the page content. Once done, you will create a number of child pages:

1. Put your cursor to the right of your new navigation bar and press Shift-Enter to insert a line break below it.

2. Click the Insert Table button from the Common tab of the Insert panel and create a simple 550-pixel-wide table with one column and one row. Click inside this table and select the `<tr>` tag from the tag selector on the bottom bar of the document window. The entire row will be selected.

3. Make sure your cursor is inside the table, then click the Repeating Region button from the Templates tab of the Insert panel and type **ContentCell** into the Name field of the New Repeating Region dialog that appears. Click OK to exit this dialog box.

4. Now position your cursor inside the table again, click on the Editable Region button from the Templates tab of the Insert panel, and type **ContentText** into the Name field of the New Editable Region dialog box that appears. Click OK to exit this dialog box.

Dreamweaver will now display the repeating region and the editable region you have just created on the document window, as shown in Figure 10-10.

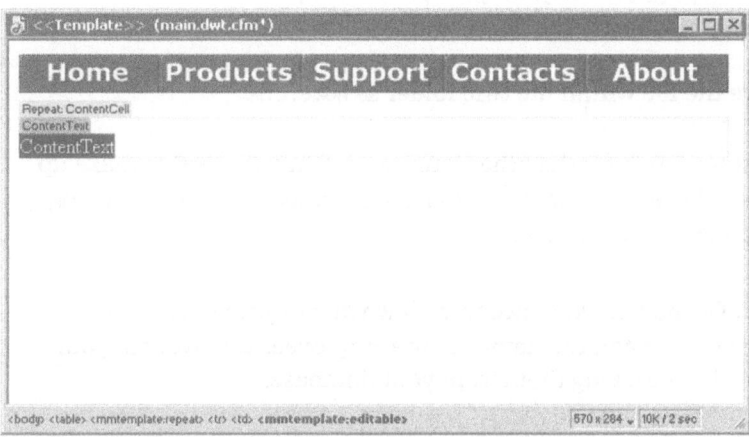

Figure 10-10. Your template, with repeating region and editable region shown. The editable region is contained within the repeating region.

Save and close the main.dwt.cfm template file. You are now ready to generate all the pages for your company web site from the parent template:

1. Select New from the File menu. Click on the Templates tab and select Site cfbook. Dreamweaver will display a list of all available templates (which, in your case, consists only of the main template) and preview the selected template on the Preview pane.

2. Select your main template and click on Create. Dreamweaver will create a new page in the Document window with the navigation bar in place. The page will be surrounded by a bright yellow border, and you won't be able to select any of the navigation bar elements, because this is a non-editable region, as shown in Figure 10-11.

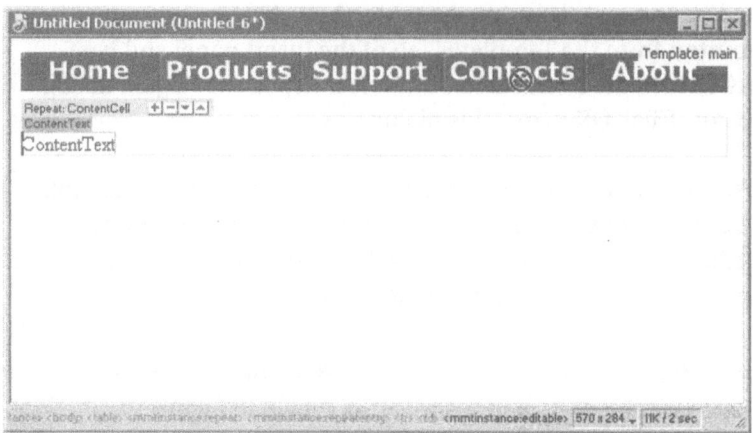

Figure 10-11. A child page created from your parent template

3. Now save the file within the Ch10 folder as home.cfm.

4. Repeat steps 1 to 3 for the other four pages that you need to make up your site—these pages should be saved as products.cfm, support.cfm, contacts.cfm, and about.cfm.

Leave about.cfm open in Dreamweaver. Now you are going to add some content to this page; you will add the names of the employees that work in your fictional company by retrieving them from your database.

1. Create a new Recordset named qry_About by using CompanyInfo as the data source and retrieving the FirstName and LastName columns from the Employee table. Note that creating a Recordset by using Dreamweaver was explained in Chapter 2. Refer back to that chapter for more information.

2. Return to the about.cfm page. Click on the + sign in the Repeat:ContentCell label of the Repeating Region to add an additional row, as shown in Figure 10-12.

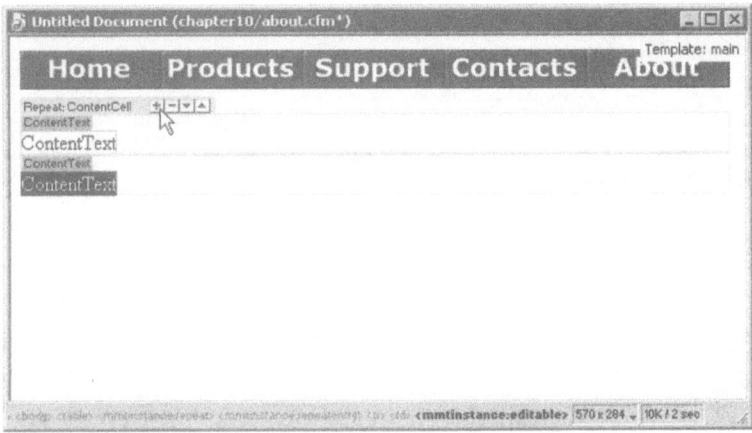

Figure 10-12. Adding another row to the Repeating Region of your about.cfm *page*

Replace the highlighted text in the newly created editable region with the text **Who we are**, then click on the up arrow in the Repeat:ContentCell label of the Repeating Region to bring the new editable region up to the top.

3. Delete the text contained in the other editable region and insert a dynamic table in its place by clicking on the Dynamic Table button on the Application tab of the Insert panel. The Dynamic Table dialog box will now pop up.

4. From the Dynamic Table dialog, select "about_qry" as the Recordset and check the All Records radio button of the Show option. Click OK to close the dialog box and add a dynamic table to your page.

Now save your about.cfm page and test it in a browser. It should look like Figure 10-13.

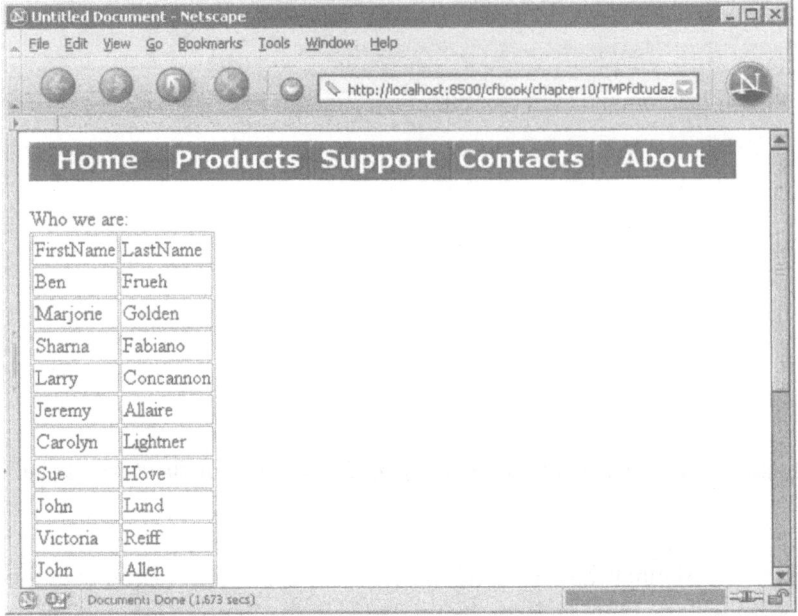

Figure 10-13. Your about.cfm *page, viewed in Netscape 7*

Now try browsing the web site by using its navigation bar. As you can see, you have created a fully functional web site structure in no time by taking advantage of Dreamweaver templates.

And if all this wasn't enough, we will now look at another strong point of templates: in a fashion similar to pages containing library items, if you want to make a site-wide change, you can update every child page by modifying just the parent template. Let's say you don't want the Contacts page anymore, so you need to delete the Contacts button from the navigation menu on every page. You can do it quickly and easily, like this:

1. Open the main.dwt.cfm template, either by selecting it from the Template pane of the Assets panel and clicking on the Edit button, or by double-clicking it in the Site panel.

2. Select the Contacts image of the page navigation. Then, using the tag selector on the bottom bar of the document window, select the column containing it by clicking on the <td> tag.

3. Press the Delete key and save the template. The Update Template Files dialog box will now appear, asking if you want to update all the pages generated by this template, as shown in Figure 10-14. Click the Update button, and the Update Pages dialog will appear displaying the report for all the modified files. Click Close to exit the report.

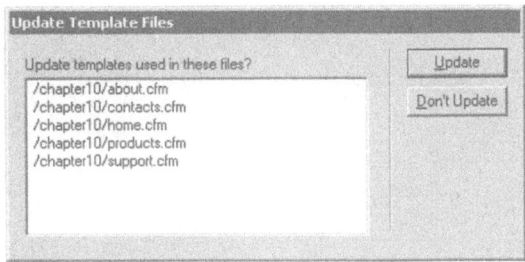

Figure 10-14. The Update Template Files dialog, showing the files that will be updated if you click Update.

All your pages have been updated to reflect the changes to the navigation bar.

Dreamweaver Tag Libraries

The last feature of Dreamweaver MX we will look at in this chapter is technically not a way to reuse code, but is still an important feature that speeds up development when coding in Dreamweaver Code View. We are talking about Dreamweaver Tag Libraries.

If you are familiar with HomeSite, ColdFusion Studio, or JRun Studio, you already know what great timesavers such features as the Tag Chooser and Code Hinting are. The Tag Chooser lets you insert any tags contained in Dreamweaver Tag Libraries into your pages. While coding in Dreamweaver Code View, simply position the cursor where you want to insert a specific tag and right-click and select Insert Tag from the Context menu to display the Tag Chooser, as shown in Figure 10-15.

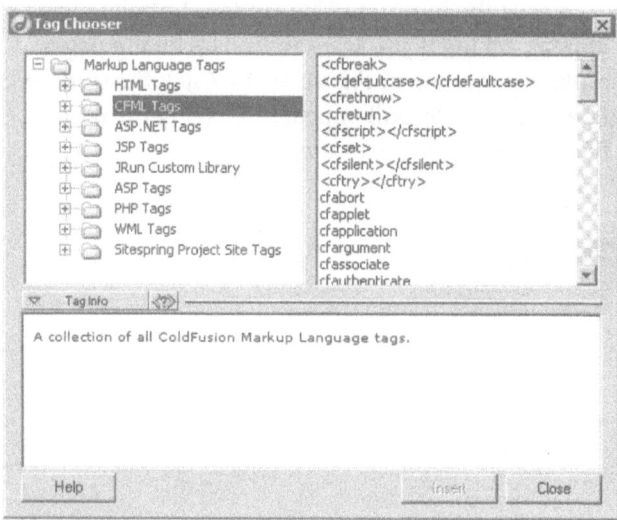

Figure 10-15. The Dreamweaver Tag Chooser

From the Tag Chooser you can select any tag from the libraries tree, receiving information about its syntax and usage. Once you have found the tag you want, simply click the Insert button to enter it into the page you were working on.

> **TIP** *Tags that require attributes to be set before you can insert them are displayed without angle brackets around their names in the Tag Chooser. When you select these tags, the Tag Editor dialog box appears, allowing you to enter the required additional information.*

The Dreamweaver Code Hints feature enables you to complete and edit tags quickly as you type them in Code View. When you start typing code, a context menu appears, as shown in Figure 10-16, displaying all the possible items you could enter to complete your entry, such as available tags, attributes, or any other values that can be filled in.

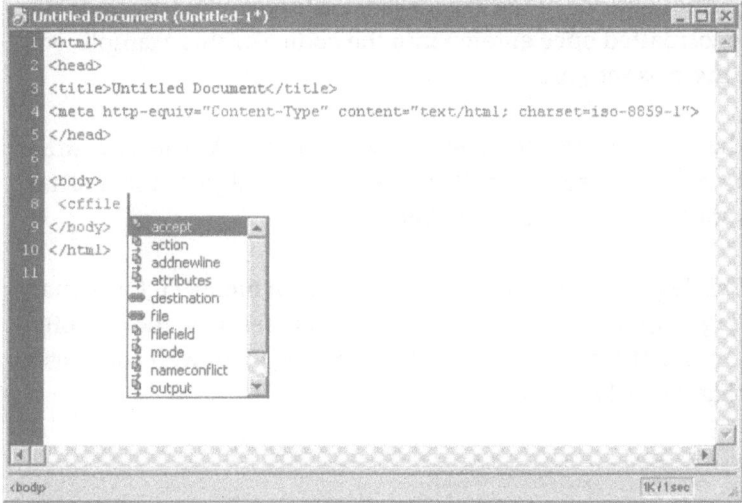

Figure 10-16. An example of code hinting in action in Dreamweaver

All the available code hints come from the Tag Libraries available to Dreamweaver. These Tag Libraries are stored as .vtm files (which can come from HomeSite, ColdFusion Studio, or JRun Studio) in the TagLibraries sub-folder of the Configuration directory of Dreamweaver.

Dreamweaver's implementation of .vtm files differs from that of HomeSite and the other Studio applications, because the interfaces for the various tags contained in the libraries are now stored as a separate HTML file to follow the rules of Dreamweaver extensibility model. Refer back to Chapter 9 for more about the Dreamweaver extensibility model.

Dreamweaver allows you to import additional tag libraries thanks to the Tag Library Editor, which is accessed by choosing Tag Libraries from the Edit menu. External Tag Libraries can be imported into Dreamweaver in various formats such as TLD, JAR, ZIP, XML DTD, etc. In addition, the Tag Library Editor lets you create your own Tag Libraries, as you will see in the following example.

You are now going to create a Tag Library entry for the <cf_form_mailer> custom tag you created earlier in this chapter. This will allow you the benefits of Dreamweaver color coding, code hints, and code validation for this custom tag.

1. Select Tag Libraries from the Edit menu. The Tag Library Editor will now appear. Click on the + sign at the top of the dialog box and choose New Tags. The New Tags dialog box will appear.

2. Make sure CFML Tags is selected from the Tag Library drop-down menu, and enter **cf_form_mailer** in the Tag Names field. Your cf_form_mailer doesn't need a closing tag, so uncheck the Have Matching End Tags option and click the OK button.

3. The Tag Format options of the Tag Library Editor let you define how the tag will be formatted once entered into the code. For this example, you can leave them as they are.

4. Click on the + sign again and choose New Attributes. As you saw earlier, the cf_form_mailer accepts four attributes (to, from, subject, and redirect) that we want to make available as Code Hints.

5. Select CFML Tags from the Tag Library drop-down menu, cf_form_mailer from the Tag drop-down menu, and enter the names of all the accepted attributes in the Attribute Names field, separating them with commas, as shown in Figure 10-17.

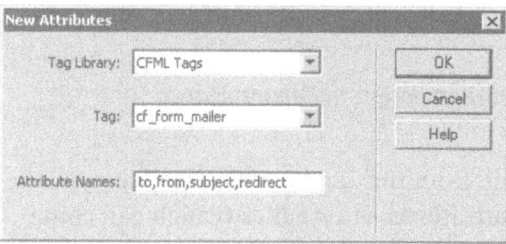

Figure 10-17. Setting the attributes of your <cf_form_mailer> *tag in the Tag Library Editor*

6. Click OK to close the dialog. Now select the redirect attribute and choose File Path from the Attribute Type menu, as shown in Figure 10-18.

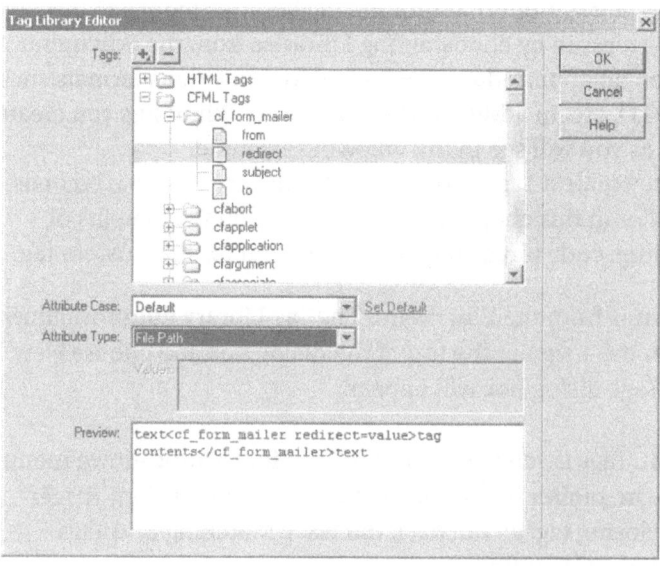

Figure 10-18. The Tag Library Editor dialog box

Click the OK button to close the dialog box. Your new Tag Library is created and you can now take advantage of all the code editing features offered by Dreamweaver when using your own tags, as shown in Figure 10-19.

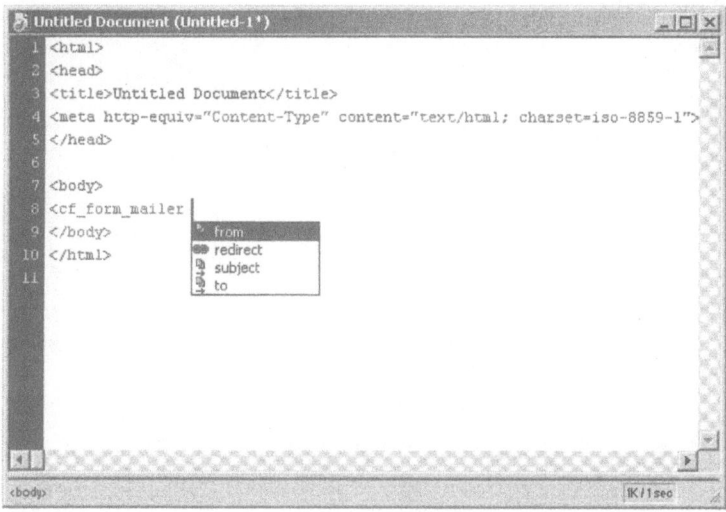

Figure 10-19. You can now utilize code hinting for your own custom tags.

Summary

In this chapter, you have learned about the basics and benefits of code reuse, and how to put it to use in ColdFusion and Dreamweaver. Specifically, we have discussed:

- The benefits of reusing code

- The <cfinclude> tag

- CFML UDFs

- CFML custom tags

- CFCs

- Dreamweaver snippets

- Dreamweaver library

- Dreamweaver templates

- Dreamweaver tag libraries

As you develop web sites and web applications, you will more than likely find that you use the same assets and chunks of code over and over again. Mastering how to reuse them with the various opportunities offered by Dreamweaver and ColdFusion will allow you to speed up development and write code that is easier to read, debug, and maintain.

Working with XML in ColdFusion MX 6.1

COLDFUSION MX 6.1 is the most significant version release to date. Among the many reasons for this significance is the addition of support for two key technologies to the CFML programming language: web services and XML. We delve into PHP/Flash web services in Chapter 12. In this chapter, we examine the new support for XML in CFML; specifically, we cover the following:

- Take a general look at XML, including the ways in which XML is represented in CFML

- Discuss the ways in which XML can be dynamically created in CFML

- Discuss the ways in which XML can be parsed from and written to external source(s)

- Examine the ways in which XML data can be accessed and manipulated

- Learn how to search XML data in CFML by using XPath

- Learn how to transform XML from one "flavor" to another

XML: What Is It? Why Use It?

XML is a web initiative that began in the mid 1990s. The language is based on the idea that text marked up with tag syntax (similar to CFML and HTML) can be used to represent data, and that this data can be passed between and manipulated within any application running on any environment, so long as that environment has the ability to parse the XML text and represent it in a native data format. Document type definition (DTD) files are XML schematic definitions used to enforce the rules of an XML "flavor." This flavor is an XML language that two or more systems agree to use to interact or "talk." There are hundreds of XML languages—you can even create our own! This ability to create your own tag-based metadata language is what makes XML *extensible*.

XML is very strict. Even though you can use it to define our own mark-up language, all XML languages must obey rules. First, all XML is based on tags, and every tag in XML must have a closing tag. If a tag does not contain any content (does not need a closing tag), it can close itself with this syntax:

```
<mytag />
```

Notice that we place the forward slash (usually found at the beginning of a closing tag) at the end of the opening tag, preceded by a space; this is called an *empty tag*. In XML, tag attributes must be enclosed in quotes. Furthermore, if an opening XML tag is in uppercase, its closing tag must also be in uppercase (and vice versa). XML attributes are case-sensitive. XML is also very strict about tag nesting. All nested tags must be properly nested within each other. The following example is invalid in XML, because the tags are not properly nested.

```
<strong><em>Hello World!</strong></em>
```

> **TIP** *Special characters are not allowed to be embedded in XML. To convert these invalid characters to their XML equivalent, use the CFML* xmlFormat() *function. This function replaces all characters (in a string) that are not allowed in XML with a character representation that is. Commonly replaced special characters are single and double quotation marks, ampersands, greater than and less than, etc. One other character to watch out for is a leading blank space or carriage return. Some characters and their* xmlFormat() *representations are given below:*
>
> < is represented as <
>
> > is represented as >
>
> & is represented as &
>
> ' is represented as '
>
> " is represented as "

> **CAUTION** *XML Parsers are notorious for refusing to parse XML strings because of a hidden carriage return at the beginning of the XML packet.*

XML also requires that all XML documents have one base tag surrounding the entire packet. For example, consider the following snippet:

```
<employee fname="Simon" lname="Horwith" />
<employee fname="Dave" lname="Watts" />
<employee fname="Steve" lname="Drucker" />
```

The preceding is not a valid XML packet, but the following is:

```
<figs>
<employee fname="Simon" lname="Horwith" />
<employee fname="Dave" lname="Watts" />
<employee fname="Steve" lname="Drucker" />
</figs>
```

We represent XML in two ways. In its raw state, XML is a string, as you've seen in the examples so far. The fact that XML is a string makes it lightweight, easy to pass between servers via HTTP, and easy to persist to disk or database. Though XML is a string, it is easier to represent the data as a complex data object when working with XML data in development environments. Every environment that has XML support uses software known as an XML parser to take an XML string and represent it as a complex data object. ColdFusion uses a Java Simple API for XML (SAX) parser internally.

> **TIP** *If a DTD exists, the parser validates that all the rules for that language have been obeyed before it parses the XML. The data resultant of XML parsing is known as an XML DOM (document object model). In this chapter, we use this term interchangeably with ColdFusion XML Object. The DOM for an XML document is a tree-like data representation of the XML packet. When we look at an XML string, we talk about tags. When we are working with an XML DOM object, we refer to these tags as nodes or elements of the DOM. For example, every properly formed HTML page has a <body> tag nested within the <html> element. If the HTML string were treated as XML and parsed, we would say that the <html> element (also referred to as the XMLRoot, because it surrounds all the other html code) has a <body> child node. In ColdFusion MX, the XML DOM was introduced as a new data type. There are many methods for working with XML, and there is also a new tag for creating XML.*

XML is good at describing data. Because you can define our own data language by using XML, it is the ideal choice for describing data. XML allows this "described data" to be:

- Easily persisted in an RDBMS or text file

- Easily syndicated and shared with other servers and development environments over HTTP

- Searched for data-subsets by using XPath

- Easily transformed into another language or text format

In other words, XML is an extremely flexible, lightweight, portable solution for meeting data representation needs.

> **NOTE** *WDDX (Web Distributed Data Exchange), which we discuss in Chapter 7, was the first form of XML support in the CFML programming language (WDDX is an XML flavor). WDDX was created for, and is good at, describing raw data, but it is also very verbose—often resulting in huge XML packets. Furthermore, WDDX only describes raw data; the data has no context. In other words, just by looking at a WDDX packet representation of an array, you have no way of knowing whether you are looking at a shopping cart, employee listing, or a user's personal preference settings. XML lets you be much more descriptive and more concise in describing data. For more information about WDDX, read the ColdFusion documentation for the* <cfwddx> *tag, or visit* http://www.openwddx.org.

Dynamically Creating XML

You may be asking "Where does this XML come from?" Well, XML comes from one of two places: it is either created dynamically with code, or it comes from an external source. Right now, let's look at dynamically creating XML with code; we'll look at external sources in the next section. We could create an XML string programmatically by using ColdFusion's string manipulation functions, but we won't waste any time talking about that in this chapter. We're interested in the new, more efficient functionality that comes with the server.

The <cfxml> tag was introduced in ColdFusion MX. This tag gives developers a convenient way to create a ColdFusion XML object. The tag has two attributes, only one of which is required:

- Variable: This is the name of the ColdFusion variable that is created to hold the XML DOM. It is the required attribute.

- CaseSensitive: The default value is No. Specify Yes if you want to maintain the case of DOM elements and attributes.

To create a ColdFusion XML object with the <cfxml> tag, an XML file (all of the tags and attributes for an XML string) is placed between the opening and closing <cfxml> tags. In addition to XML tags, CFML tags can be placed within the <cfxml> block in order to dynamically create XML tags. By way of the variable attribute, we specify the name of a variable (that will be created) whose value is the XML object. Note that only CFML tags will be evaluated, and not CFML functions.

To use a CFML function such an XMLFormat() within a <cfxml> block, be sure to call it within <cfoutput> tags.

The following code snippet (cfxml_dom.cfm) will create an XML DOM (stored in the local xmlEmps variable) from a query recordset of employee information.

```
<cfxml variable="xmlEmps">
  <employees>
    <cfoutput query="qEmployee">
    <employee id="#qEmployee.empID#" fname="#xmlFormat(qEmployee.empFName)#"➥
      lname="#xmlFormat(qEmployee.empLName)#" />
    </cfoutput>
  </employees>
</cfxml>
```

This snippet creates an XML packet with an <employees> root tag and a nested <employee> tag for each row that is returned from the query. If you use the <cfdump> tag to look at the value of the xmlEmps variable created by this code, the output looks somewhat like Figure 11-1.

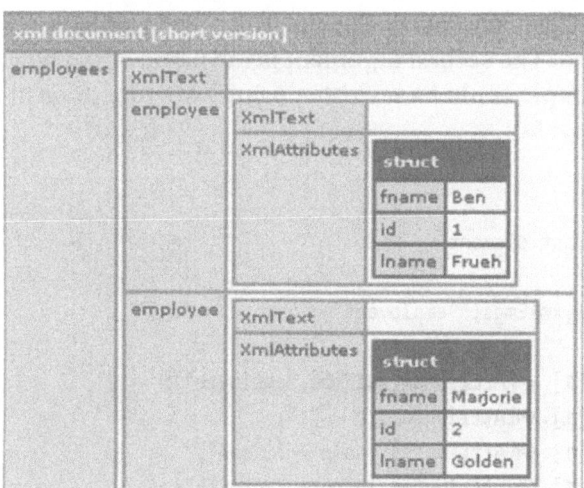

Figure 11-1. <cfdump> *of a ColdFusion XML Object*

Notice that many data values were not represented in the code used to create the DOM, but the values are still present in the DOM. An XML DOM is a variable of the XML DOM type. An XML DOM can be detected with the new isXMLDoc() function, which returns a Boolean yes/no depending on whether the variable passed is an XML DOM. Every valid XML DOM is essentially represented as a structure of structures. Of particular interest is that each node in a DOM is:

- a structure with an XMLText key that is the text between its opening and closing tags

- an XMLAttributes key that is a structure of the attributes (name/value pairs) for this node

- an XMLChildren key that is an array of XML Nodes (the children of this node)

The root node, which surrounds all other nodes, can be referred to by name or as XMLRoot. XML tag attribute names cannot begin with "xml," because ColdFusion uses this internally to identify values.

In addition to the <cfxml> tag, there is another slightly more complex method of creating an XML DOM. We already discussed the fact that XML nodes are structures, and that nodes contained within other nodes exist within their parent's XMLChildren array. This, coupled with two new functions, is all you need to create XML manually!

The first function required to create an XML DOM manually is XMLNew(). It has only one attribute: caseSensitive (Boolean). This is optional and defaults to No. The other method (new to ColdFusion) that allows XML to be created is the XMLElemNew() function. This takes two arguments. The first is the DOM variable in which this node is being created. The second argument is the name of the new element. The prior <cfxml> example could be rewritten using XML functions in <cfscript> like so (cfscript_dom.cfm):

```
<cfscript>
//create object and initialize root element
    xmlEmps = XMLNew();
    xmlEmps.xmlRoot = XMLElemNew(xmlEmps, "employees");
//add first child element
    xmlEmps.xmlRoot.xmlChildren[1] = XMLElemNew(xmlEmps,"employee");
    xmlEmps.xmlRoot.xmlChildren[1].XMLAttributes.id = "1";
    xmlEmps.xmlRoot.xmlChildren[1].XMLAttributes.fname = "Simon";
    xmlEmps.xmlRoot.xmlChildren[1].XMLAttributes.lname = "Horwith";
//add second child element
    xmlEmps.xmlRoot.xmlChildren[2] = XMLElemNew(xmlEmps,"employee");
    xmlEmps.xmlRoot.xmlChildren[2].XMLAttributes.id = "2";
    xmlEmps.xmlRoot.xmlChildren[2].XMLAttributes.fname = "Dave";
    xmlEmps.xmlRoot.xmlChildren[2].XMLAttributes.lname = "Watts";
//add third child element using slightly different syntax to reference the root
    xmlEmps.xmlRoot.xmlChildren[3] = XMLElemNew(xmlEmps,"employee");
    xmlEmps.employees.xmlChildren[3].XMLAttributes.id = "3";
    xmlEmps.employees.xmlChildren[3].XMLAttributes.fname = "Steve";
    xmlEmps.employees.xmlChildren[3].XMLAttributes.lname = "Drucker";
</cfscript>
    <!---:: output xml object ::--->
    <cfdump var="#variables.xmlEmps#">
```

Although the `<cfscript>` syntax may seem much more verbose and less simple to implement, this approach has a few advantages, which we will discuss in the "Manipulating and Accessing XML Data" section of this chapter.

Using XML with External Sources

More than just a format to store persistent data in memory, XML's strength is as a portable data representation. By "portable," we mean that it is easy to share between applications, syndicate to other servers, and persist on disk in files and/or databases. In the previous section, you learned how to create an XML DOM with ColdFusion code. In this section, we will discuss how to create an XML DOM from a preexisting XML source, and how to save an XML DOM for later use.

When XML data is used in an application, the application generally works with the data in the DOM format. To save that XML DOM for later use, it must first be converted to an XML string. This is achieved by using a single line of code with the CFML toString() function. This function will accept an XML DOM object as its first argument and will return the string representation of the XML DOM. toString() also has an optional second argument that specifies the character encoding to use for the string (the default is the encoding of the current page).

> **TIP** *To persist the XML DOM, write that string to file with the `<cffile>` tag or to a database with a `<cfquery>` tag after converting it to a string with* toString().

To create an XML object from an external source, you must first retrieve the XML string. Because an XML string is no different from any other string in ColdFusion, many methods are available for transferring this XML data:

- You could use the `<cffile>` tag to retrieve the contents of an XML file from a file on the server's local file system.

- The `<cfinvoke>` tag, `<cfobject>` tag, or createObject() functions can be used to connect with a remote web service or local ColdFusion component that may have methods that return XML.

- The `<cfhttp>` tag can be used to make an HTTP request for any web-accessible file.

- A `<cfquery>` tag may be used to retrieve the XML from an RDBMS.

It is possible to use other methods to retrieve XML from an external source, but these are by far the most common.

Once an external source has responded to a page's request, a variable (whose contents are an XML string) exists on that page. If you attempt to view this string by outputting the variable in a <cfoutput> block, many browsers will show the data but not the actual tags. To view an XML string in a web page, use the HTMLEditFormat() function. This replaces any necessary characters with their HTML display equivalent. For example, < becomes <. Use the XMLParse() function to take an XML string and convert it to a ColdFusion XML DOM Object. XMLParse() has one required attribute, which is the XML string itself. A second optional argument specifies whether the XML Document and its attributes are case-sensitive. Let's examine some examples.

Save the resulting XML string from the earlier examples as employees.xml in a C:\myXMLDocs directory. An example of retrieving the XML from file and parsing it into an XML DOM is shown in the following code snippet:

```
<!---:: create xml DOM from text file ::--->
<cffile action="READ" file="C:\myXMLDocs\employees.xml" variable="myXMLString">
<cfset myXMLDOM = XMLParse (myXMLString)>
```

The following code creates an XML DOM by requesting a URL that returns an XML string:

```
<cfhttp url="http://www.mysite.com/xmlfiles/foo.xml" method="GET" resolveurl="No">
</cfhttp>
<cfset myXMLDOM = XMLParse(cfhttp.fileContent)>
```

The following code snippet retrieves XML from a web service:
```
<cfinvoke webservice="http://www.mydomain.com/data/xmlFactory" method="getXML"➥
  returnvariable="myXMLString">
<cfset myXMLDOM = XMLParse(myXMLString)>
```

The following code snippet retrieves XML from a database:

```
<cfquery name="qGetXML" datasource="myDSN">
  SELECT myXMLCol FROM someTable
</cfquery>
<cfset myXMLDOM = XMLParse(qGetXML)>
```

When retrieving XML from another environment, you must take great care to ensure success. Earlier, we mentioned that XML parsers have difficulty parsing text whose first character is a space or carriage return (linefeed). So, it is crucial to strip away any leading spaces or carriage returns before the XMLParse() function is called.

Because these methods of retrieving an XML sting require using external resources—and because accessing external resources is probably the most error-prone of all of the things we can do in a ColdFusion template—it is important to implement some sort of error-handling strategy when attempting to retrieve the XML string. Often there is very little guarantee that the string returned will be in proper XML notation—remember, XML is a strict language. Attempting to use XMLParse() on a string that does not meet the format requirements of XML, such as having a base tag, will result in error. For this reason, implement error-handling when parsing a string into an XML DOM object, unless you are sure of your source (see Chapter 8 for more information on structured exception handling).

Putting all this information together, this example retrieves an XML packet from a text file, verifies that it doesn't have any carriage returns in the beginning, parses it into an XML DOM, and dumps the DOM, writing it back to the text file as a string (retrieve-writeXML.cfm).

```
<cfscript>
  thisDir = expandPath('.');
  targetXMLFile = variables.thisDir & "\mydata.xml";
</cfscript>
<cfif not fileExists(variables.targetXMLFile)>
  <h3>Can't find target xml file</h3>
  <cfabort>
</cfif>
<cftry>
  <cffile action="read" file="#variables.targetXMLFile#" variable="originalXMLString">
  <cfcatch>
    <h3>error opening XML file!</h3>
    <cfabort>
  </cfcatch>
</cftry>
<cfset originalXMLString = replace(variables.originalXMLString,chr(13),"","All")>
<cftry>
  <cfset myXMLDOM = XMLParse(variables.originalXMLString)>
  <cfcatch>
    <h3>Error parsing XML!</h3>
    <cfabort>
  </cfcatch>
</cftry>

<cfdump var="#myXMLDOM#" label="My XML Packet From File">

<cfset newXMLString = toString(variables.myXMLDOM)>
  <cftry>
    <cffile action="write" file="#variables.targetXMLFile#"➥
      output="#variables.newXMLString#">
```

```
    <cfcatch>
      <h3>Error Writing to text file!</h3>
      <cfabort>
    </cfcatch>
  </cftry>
```

Accessing and Manipulating XML Data

We have already discussed why XML is an ideal format in which to store data, but how do you actually use this XML in a web application? As with data stored in other complex variables such as arrays or structures, an application may need to output values contained in the XML DOM. Sometimes, data in an XML DOM needs to be added to, deleted, or modified. As mentioned before, XML DOM nodes are represented as structures, and their attributes are stored in the node XMLAttributes key. The text contained in the opening and closing tag is stored in the node XMLText key. If this node has children (nested tags), they are contained within its XMLChildren array as structures. Not only can nodes be referenced as parentNode.XMLChildren[indexPosition], where indexPosition is the nested tag depth from the parent tag, but also as parentNode.xmlElementName[indexPosition], where indexPosition is the nested tag depth from the parent tag among all nodes with the same name. This means that array, structure syntax, and the built-in CFML functions for manipulating these two types of data can be used to add/edit/delete XML data. The best way to understand this is to look at the following examples.

Our first example shows how to add a new attribute to DOM node(s). We start with the XML DOM we looked at earlier:

```
<figs>
  <employee fname="Simon" lname="Horwith" />
  <employee fname="Dave" lname="Watts" />
  <employee fname="Steve" lname="Drucker" />
</figs>
```

Suppose that you want to add an active attribute to each employee tag in this simple XML packet. The code would look like this:

```
<cfscript>
  // add an 'active' attribute to all XML Children off the DOM root➡
  for (i = 1; i LTE arrayLen(variables.myXMLDOM.XMLRoot.XMLChildren); i = i + 1)
  {structInsert(variables.myXMLDOM.XMLRoot.XMLChildren[i].XMLAttributes,➡
  "inactive",1,1);}
</cfscript>
```

This code loops over the array containing all children of the XMLRoot (XMLChildren) and inserts an active key into each child's XMLAttributes structure.

If you wanted to add a new <employee> node to the DOM, the code would look something like the following:

```
<cfscript>
  // get array position of next XML child to add
  newNodePos = arrayLen(variables.myXMLDOM.XMLRoot.XMLChildren)➡
  + 1;
  // add new node then set its attributes
  variables.myXMLDOM.XMLRoot.XMLChildren[variables.newNodePos] =
XMLElemNew(myXMLDOM,"employee");

  structInsert(variables.myXMLDOM.XMLRoot.XMLChildren➡
  [variables.newNodePos].XMLAttributes,"fname","Ashu",1);
structInsert(variables.myXMLDOM.XMLRoot.XMLChildren➡
  [variables.newNodePos].XMLAttributes,"lname","Courchesne",1);
  structInsert(variables.myXMLDOM.XMLRoot.XMLChildren➡
  [variables.newNodePos].XMLAttributes,"active",1,1);
</cfscript>
```

The preceding code snippet determines the array index position in the XMLRoot's XMLChildren array for the new node to add. It then sets that array position equal to a new XML node with the XMLElemNew() function and adds attributes to its XMLAttributes structure.

To modify existing data in an XML DOM, use the same array/structure syntax to access the node or attribute you wish to modify, and assign a new value. The following example changes the lname attribute of the first node from Horwith to Badhwar.

```
<cfscript>
  //set the first employee's last name to 'Badhwar'
  variables.myXMLDOM.XMLRoot.XMLChildren➡
  [1].XMLAttributes.lname = "Badhwar";
</cfscript>
```

Array and structure functions can be used to add data as well as remove data. Suppose you need to remove the second employee node from the XML DOM. The following code would remove the node:

```
<cfscript>
  //remove the second employee
  arrayDeleteAt(variables.myXMLDOM.XMLRoot.XMLChildren, 2);
</cfscript>
```

The following example removes the active attribute from all employee nodes:

```
<cfscript>
  // remove 'active' attribute from all XML Children off of the DOM root
  for (i = 1; i LTE arrayLen(variables.myXMLDOM.XMLRoot.XMLChildren)➡
  ; i = i + 1){
  structDelete(variables.myXMLDOM.XMLRoot.XMLChildren[i]➡
  .XMLAttributes,"active",0);
  }
</cfscript>
```

Alternatively, you can combine structure dot syntax with array notation to access the nodes nested within a DOM. The following is an example of using alternative syntax to set the active attribute of the second employee node to 0:

```
<cfscript>
  // use structure syntax to set the "active" attribute of the second node to "0"
  variables.myXMLDOM.figs.employee[2].XMLAttributes.active = 0;
</cfscript>
```

> **NOTE** *If you don't specify the node array position to be manipulated, the first node will be accessed.*

Here we see an example of using this shorthand syntax to set the lname attribute of the first employee node to Badhwar:

```
<cfscript>
  // use structure syntax to set the "lname" attribute of the first node to "Badhwar"
  variables.myXMLDOM.figs.employee.XMLAttributes.lname = "Badhwar";
</cfscript>
```

In addition to the properties of an XML DOM and its nodes that we've discussed, much more information can be accessed from within an XML DOM. The XML DOM has two sets of data members, the XML Root Keys and the XML Element Keys.

These are the XML Root Keys:

- XMLComment: all comments within this element level

- XMLRoot: the root element

These are the XML Element Keys:

- XMLName: element name

- XMLNSPrefix: prefix of the namespace

- XMLNSURI: URL of the namespace

- XMLText: all text in the element (not in children)

- XMLComment: all comments in this element level

- XMLAttributes: structure of element attributes

- XMLChildren: an array of all the element's children elements

- XMLParent: parent DOM node for this element

- XMLNodes: array of all the XML DOM nodes in this element

Of the data members mentioned previously, all except XMLParent and XMLNodes will be displayed by passing an XML DOM to the <cfdump> tag. When a DOM is "dumped," <cfdump> gives you the option of viewing the DOM in long mode or short mode. The current mode is displayed at the top of the <cfdump> table. Click on this label to switch between modes.

> **TIP** *Some data members display only in "long version," so get into the habit of viewing XML DOMs in "long version" mode if you plan to work with all XML DOM data members.*

XML is capable of very complex operations and data representations. You may want to pick up a book dedicated to XML, or try visiting http://w3c.org/xml to learn more about what some of these data members represent and how they can and should be used. The more complex capabilities of XML are beyond the scope of this chapter.

In addition to the functions already discussed, ColdFusion also has functions for determining whether a node is the root node or another XML node, extracting a specific element based on name and order in the XML children of that name, and many more tasks. These functions are:

- isXMLDoc(): accepts an object name and returns a Boolean to indicate whether it is a properly formed XML DOM

- isXMLElem(): accepts an element name and returns a Boolean to indicate whether it is a DOM element

- `isXMLRoot()`: accepts an element name and returns a Boolean to indicate whether it is the DOM root element

- `toString()`: converts an XML DOM to a string, allowing the XML to be output or written to disk

- `XMLParse()`: converts a string to a DOM and accepts two arguments: an XML string to create the DOM from (required), and `caseSensitive` (an optional Boolean) to indicate case sensitivity (default is false)

- `XMLChildPos()`: Retrieves the nth element of a specific name and accepts three arguments: the element to retrieve the child node from, the name of the element to retrieve, and the element child position to return

Most functions are fairly straight forward, except for `XMLChildPos()`. This function is useful for determining where in the array of all `XMLChildren` a node sits, based on the node's name and its occurrence in the sequence of nodes of that name. When all nodes have the same name (as in our example), this isn't very useful. What if all the elements within a DOM do not have the same name? For example, the `figs` XML packet may contain `employee` and `contractor` nodes to represent employees and contractors. The XML packet would then look like this:

```
<figs>
  <employee fname="Simon" lname="Horwith" />
  <employee fname="Dave" lname="Watts" />
  <contractor fname="Charles" lname="Arehart" />
  <contractor fname="Branden" lname="Hall" />
  <employee fname="Steve" lname="Drucker" />
</figs>
```

To determine the position of the third employee in the `XMLChildren` array, you must determine how many `employee` nodes exist (we don't want to find the `XMLChildren` position for the third `employee` if there are only two), and then use the `XMLChildPos()` function to determine its position. The code to do this is:

```
<cfscript>
  // find out how many employee elements there are
  numContractors = arrayLen(variables.myXMLDOM.figs.employee);
  // if there are at least 3 employees, find out where the third employee is in
the child➡
  elements array
  thirdEmployeePos = XMLChildPos(variables.myXMLDOM.figs,"employee",3);
  thirdEmployeeNode =➡
  variables.myXMLDOM.XMLroot.XMLChildren[variables.thirdEmployeePos];
</cfscript>
```

Though array and structure functions coupled with the XMLChildPos() function do help in finding and extracting the desired data, sometimes these solutions don't perform efficiently enough to meet the needs of an application. XPath addresses many of these limitations.

Searching for and Extracting XML Data with XPath

In the real world, a simple XML schema with one DOM level of tags, all having the same name, often is not capable of meeting an application's needs. This is particularly true of applications storing data that has complex relationships with other data. Sometimes, it is necessary to nest tags within tags, and sometimes the XML schema definition is already made for you. XPath can help you quickly retrieve data nested at various levels in a DOM hierarchy. Another common issue when working with large XML packets is the performance limitation of looping over every node in an XML DOM and performing conditional logic to validate whether each node is one that we are looking for. XPath helps tremendously with this type of functionality.

XPath is the language of representing XML DOM hierarchies with expressions. You may already be familiar with using regular expressions for text pattern matching in CFML, JavaScript, or some other programming language. Think of XPath as regular expressions for XML data hierarchies. If you're not familiar with regular expressions (Regex), they are a language used for specifying text patterns in many programming languages (including CFML). They are useful for parsing and manipulating text when simple find, replace, and list functionality isn't flexible enough to suit your needs. XPath may syntactically look more like Regex to many folks, but it's actually more similar to SQL in terms of functionality. Like SQL, the sole purpose of XPath is to search through a large amount of data and return whatever data it finds to meet our criteria.

> **NOTE** *Unlike SQL, XPath is used for only searching and not for inserting and updating data. However, XPath can be used with other XML tools to update or transform data. In essence, it is a tool for searching XML.*

Just like HTML, CSS, and XML, XPath is an official specification of the World Wide Web Consortium (http://www.w3.org/TR/xpath). As already mentioned, XPath is a tool for searching XML by using expressions. More than that, XPath is a tool for mapping XML nodes. We can use XPath to map the nodes of one XML packet to another when performing transformations, which we cover in the next section of this chapter. XPath is not only good at defining elements (branches in the hierarchy), but also is great at mapping node text values and attribute values.

XPath is implemented in ColdFusion pages with the XMLSearch() function. XMLSearch() accepts two arguments: the first is the DOM object to search, and the second is the XPath expression that we wish to apply to the XML DOM. To use XMLSearch(), you must be somewhat familiar with XPath. These rules will help you create XPath expressions:

- Single forward slashes separate nested elements in a DOM, just like slashes in a URL represent nested folders.

- Double forward slashes are a wildcard. They represent any parent element—any number of nested levels.

- Always enclose XPath comparison statements inside square brackets.

- All nonnumeric attributes or XMLText values to match are enclosed in single quotes.

- All attribute names are preceded with by an @ symbol.

- XPath searches are case-sensitive.

If you follow these rules and experiment a bit, you can master using XPath in no time! To provide some practice with XPath, we've made the XML Schema a little bit more complex. The schema now contains both <employee> and <contractor> tags just beneath the root level. Nested below that level are <active> elements, which contain the text 1 or 0 between the two tags (XMLText). The sample XML looks like this:

```
<figs>
<employee id="1" fname="Simon" lname="Horwith">
  <active>1</active>
</employee>
<employee id="2" fname="Dave" lname="Watts">
  <active>1</active>
</employee>
<contractor id="1" fname="Charles" lname="Arehart">
  <active>1</active>
</contractor>
<contractor id="2" fname="Branden" lname="Hall">
  <active>1</active>
</contractor>
<employee id="3" fname="Steve" lname="Drucker">
  <active>1</active>
</employee>
</figs>
```

Using the preceding XML packet, if we wanted to retrieve all the <contractor> tags directly off of the figs root, it would look like this:

```
<cfscript>
  //get all contractors off the 'figs' root element.
  aAllContractors = XMLSearch(myXMLDOM,"figs/contractor");
</cfscript>
```

If, on the other hand, we wanted all <contractor> tags regardless of where they are in the hierarchy (no matter how many levels deep they are), the code would look like this:

```
<cfscript>
  //get all contractors in the DOM, regardless of parent node.
  aAllContractors = XMLSearch(myXMLDOM,"//contractor");
</cfscript>
```

The following code retrieves all employee nodes found immediately off the <figs> root element, that have a nested <active> node with the value 0 between their opening and closing <active> tags:

```
<cfscript>
  //get all employees off the 'figs' root element that have a nested "<active>"➥
  node with the value 0 between the opening and closing "<active>".
  aActiveEmployees = XMLSearch(myXMLDOM,"/figs/employee[active=0]");
</cfscript>
```

The following code retrieves all employees whose last name is Horwith:

```
<cfscript>
  //get all employees that have an lname of "Horwith"
  aHorwiths = XMLSearch(myXMLDOM,"//employee[@lname='Horwith']");
</cfscript>
```

This snippet finds all nodes that have a first name of Dave and a nested <active> tag set to 1:

```
<cfscript>
  //find all nodes that have an "fname" of "Dave" AND that have their nested➥
  "<active>" tag set to 1
  aActiveDave = XMLSearch(myXMLDOM,"//employee[@fname='Dave' and active=1]");
</cfscript>
```

This last snippet shows how to find all nodes that have a first name of Simon or have their nested <active> tag set to 0:

```
<cfscript>
  //get all employees that have an fname of "Simon" OR that have a nested➥
  "<active>0</active>" child
  aSimonOrInactive = XMLSearch(myXMLDOM,"//employee[@fname='Simon' or active=0]");
</cfscript>
```

Although the preceding example XML packet is not really complex, the sample syntax and rules laid out in this chapter can be applied to XML packets of any size. It is important to note that XPath generally executes very fast, much faster than Query of Queries in tests. This makes it an excellent alternative to Query of Queries in cases where you can easily represent the desired data as XPath expressions. When you need to cross-reference multiple data sources (XML files or queries) with each other (similar to a table join in SQL), XPath is not recommended. XPath is also unsuitable when you require wildcard functionality; for example, if the SQL LIKE keyword needs to be implemented.

> **TIP** *XPath is often the best answer for retrieving data from a single XML source, based on the values of tags and their attributes.*

One last thing to discuss about XPath is its return value. You may have noticed that all the XPath samples set the results to a variable that began with a lowercase "a." This is not required, but was done for naming convention reasons—XPath returns the data it finds as an array of elements. What this means is that we must put that result set into proper XML DOM format to perform operations like XMLSearch(), toString(), etc. Unfortunately, we will have to loop over the array result elements and manually copy their data members into another DOM node. Attempting to insert the actual XPath results array into a second DOM will not work. ColdFusion does not allow elements from one DOM to exist in another, which makes sense when you account for the XMLParent pointer that every element contains. Unfortunately, the XMLParent cannot be deleted from an element, either.

Transforming XML with XSLT

We have shown how to create, access, and manipulate data in an XML DOM. We have also examined the syntax used to search an XML DOM for nodes that match search parameters by using XPath expressions. One last thing we need to examine is how to transform XML from one XML version to another, or from XML to HTML (more useful) for display. This is accomplished by using Extensible Stylesheet Language Transformations (XSLT).

XSLT is the process of combining XML with a style sheet to transform that data into some other format. The result of this combination is that the XML transforms into some other text. The style sheet used to perform the transformation is generally stored in a file and given a `.xsl` extension. You must open this file programmatically by using `<cffile>`. If the XSL file is web accessible, it can be retrieved by using `<cfhttp>`, and its contents can also come from a database or from any variable whose value meets the requirements for extensible style sheet content.

Extensible style sheets use a lightweight scripted programming language to define conditional logic, loops, variable declaration and output, data sorting, and other simple common tasks required to take XML content and redefine its structure. Implementing XSLT in ColdFusion is a trivial task; it's writing the style sheet that most developers find challenging.

To implement XSLT in ColdFusion pages, you use the `XMLTransform()` function. `XMLTransform()` accepts two arguments, both of which are required. The first argument is an XML DOM variable, and the second is an XSL style sheet—not a URL, but the actual style sheet contents.

Before you can implement a style sheet, let's examine the details of writing extensible style sheets. The first line of a style sheet looks the same as the first line of most XML packets: `<?xml version="1.0"?>`. This identifies the remaining text in the page as an XML packet. This first line, as with other XML files, requires no closing tag. The second tag in an XSL document is:

```
<xsl:stylesheet xmlns:xsl="http://www.w3.org/1999/XSL/Transform" version="1.0"➥
   xmlns="http://www.w3.org/TR/REC-html40"➥
   xmlns:xlink="http://www.w3.org/1999/xlink">"
```

This identifies the XML contents as an XSL style sheet and also identifies the URLs for linking, transformation, and namespace specifications. This tag, and all proceeding tags, will have end tags.

The next tag in an XSL style sheet is `<xsl:template match="/">`. This tag uses the `match` attribute to tell the browser at what point in the XML packet it should start an XPath mapping. A value of / specifies that all XPath mappings in this document begin at the document root. Everything between `<xsl:stylesheet><xsl:template>` and `</ xsl:stylesheet></ xsl:template>` comprises the actual text that makes up the transformation output, including other `<xsl:...>` tags that represent style sheet instructions. All extensible style sheet commands are tags with the `xsl:` namespace. Commonly used XSL tags are provided in Table 11-1.

Table 11-1. Common XLS Tags

Tag Name	Attributes	Description
xsl:apply-templates	Select (XPath expression)	Calls one template from another. The attribute determines which node to act upon.
xsl:choose	None	Chooses one of many possible options—equivalent to a switch statement.
xsl:for-each	Select (XPath expression)	Loops through the set of elements specified by the attribute.
xsl:if	Test (Boolean expression)	Performs "if" logic.
xsl:otherwise	None	Executed when no xsl:when statement is executed. Similar to the default in a switch-case statement.
xsl:sort	Order (ascending or descending)	Specifies the sort order for xsl:apply-templates and xsl:for-each statements.
xsl:stylesheet	Version (1.0—optional)	Root element for the style sheet.
xsl:template	Match (XPath expression)	Specifies a set of XSLT tags to execute as a single unit. Applies to node(s) specified by the attribute.
xsl:value-of	Select (XPath expression)	Generates a text string with the value of the attribute. Similar to <cfoutput>.
xsl:variable	Name (value)	Defines a variable and its value. Note: Once a variable is set in XSLT, you cannot change its value.
xsl:when	Test (Boolean expression)	Represents on option in an xsl:choose block. Similar to a case statement.

One thing worth noting is that, unlike traditional programming languages, the value of XSL variables created with the <xsl:variable> command cannot be changed. Let's put all this new information together in a simple example in which you transform the previous XML packet into an HTML table of active employees.

First, let's look at the code that creates the XML DOM, retrieves the XSL style sheet, and performs the actual transformation:

```
<!---:: create XML DOM ::--->
<cfxml variable="myXMLDOM">
<figs>
<employee id="1" fname="Simon" lname="Horwith">
  <active>1</active>
</employee>
<employee id="2" fname="Dave" lname="Watts">
  <active>1</active>
</employee>
<contractor id="1" fname="Charles" lname="Arehart">
  <active>1</active>
</contractor>
<contractor id="2" fname="Branden" lname="Hall">
  <active>1</active>
</contractor>
<employee id="3" fname="Steve" lname="Drucker">
  <active>1</active>
</employee>
<employee id="4" fname="Dave" lname="Gallerizzo">
  <active>0</active>
</employee>
</figs>
</cfxml>

<cffile action="read" variable="myXSL" file="#expandPath('.')#\figsXSL.xsl">

<cfset transformedXML = XMLTransform(variables.myXMLDOM, variables.myXSL)>
<cfoutput>#variables.transformedXML#</cfoutput>
```

Notice that this code creates an XML DOM with two nested active employees, then two active contractors, then another active employee and an inactive employee. We want to return an HTML table with only active employees in it.

The contents of the figsXSL.xsl style sheet are:

```
<?xml version="1.0"?>
  <xsl:stylesheet xmlns:xsl="http://www.w3.org/1999/XSL/Transform" version="1.0"
    xmlns="http://www.w3.org/TR/REC-html40"
    xmlns:xlink="http://www.w3.org/1999/xlink">
  <xsl:template match="/">
<html>
```

```
<head>
  <title>Active Employees</title>
</head>

<body>
<table border="1" width="350">
  <tr>
    <th>First Name</th>
    <th>Last Name</th>
  </tr>
  <xsl:for-each select="/figs/employee">
  <xsl:if test="active=1">
  <tr>
    <td align="center"><xsl:value-of select="@fname"/></td>
    <td align="center"><xsl:value-of select="@lname"/></td>
  </tr>
  </xsl:if>
  </xsl:for-each>
</table>

</body>
</html>


</xsl:template>
</xsl:stylesheet>
```

The resulting output of the ColdFusion page containing the XML DOM declaration, the `<cffile>` tag that opens the XSL document, and the code that performs the transformation and outputs the results is shown in Figure 11-2.

First Name	Last Name
Simon	Horwith
Dave	Watts
Steve	Drucker

Figure 11-2. Results of transforming the figs XML

Style sheets are a very powerful tool for transforming XML from one flavor into another. You can use them to transform XML into HTML, XHTML, another XML flavor, CSV, or any other text format imaginable. Style sheets allow for looping, conditional logic, variable declarations, and lots more. To implement more complex style sheets, you need to study and practice.

As with XPath and XML, entire books are devoted to XSLT. If you need to use XSLT heavily in your applications, we recommend picking up *XSLT Programmer's Reference, 2nd Edition* (Michael Kay, Wrox Press), or visiting the W3C at http://www.w3.org/Style/XSL/.

Summary

The <cfxml> tag makes it very easy to create an XML object without really having to understand the intricacies of XML. The new XML functions, although they do require a little more knowledge of XML, allow developers to manipulate existing XML objects and also create them by using an alternative syntax. The XMLSearch() function adds full support for the retrieval of data by using XPath, and the XMLTransform() function makes it very easy to apply styles programmatically to transform one version of XML to another.

The new XML functionality in ColdFusion MX 6.1 allows for the easy creation, manipulation, transformation, and filtering of XML data. Developers are limited only by their lack of knowledge about XPath, XSL, and XML, so play around with it and have fun! Once you begin to figure out and become comfortable with the basics, pick up an intermediate level book—one that explains not only XML, but also XPath and XSL. One such book is *Beginning XML, 2nd Edition* (Jonathan Pinnock et al., Wrox Press). Once you start using XML to represent application data, you may very well never want to store data in any other format again!

Flash MX 2004, Web Services, and ColdFusion MX 6.1

IN THIS CHAPTER we show you how to use Flash MX 2004, web services, and ColdFusion MX 6.1 together to build Rich Internet Applications (RIA). The web services features in Flash MX 2004 are brand new to this release and come with some great components and classes that allow developers to code minimally, but also have a lot of power and flexibility. In short, a web service is a way of exposing data between technologies in a platform-independent format that is lightweight and seamless. The details of how it is done are hidden to the developer. Web services are platform-independent because at its most basic level, a web service is XML. XML is stored in a text file so, as long as a technology can read a file and have a XML parser, the data is independent of any proprietary platform. Other technologies, such as ASP.NET, Java, PHP, and many others, all have the capability to generate web services that both ColdFusion and Flash can use in applications. This is accomplished by another standard, Simple Object Access Protocol (SOAP). SOAP is a wrapper that uses XML to describe data that is to be shared between technologies. Because SOAP is a standard, many technologies include parsers, much like the XML parser, to read in the data and produce native objects out of that data. These native objects would be a generic object, array, string, number, date, Recordset, user-defined object, and so on. The following example illustrates the process:

1. Flash makes a web service call to a ColdFusion CFC for a list of users.

2. The CFC generates a SOAP document that describes an array of user structs.

3. Flash receives the SOAP document, parses it, and creates an array of user objects that Flash can use.

All this happens with very little effort on your part as the developer. Also, you don't even need to know about XML or SOAP to work with the technology; all this is being done for you by Flash and ColdFusion, so you don't need to spend hours reading up on these technologies (though it doesn't hurt). Also, if you have gone through this book, you should feel very comfortable with this method of data exchange because you have been doing something very similar to this already. Think about working with databases. Data is stored in a database that is very different from the way that ColdFusion uses that data. You use a technology, such as a JDBC database driver, to pass data between the two technologies and transform it into something they both can work with, but you did not need to know how the database driver actually worked—you just used it. SOAP web services are the same; just use them. The hard work is already done.

Web services are not the only communication technology used to pass data between Flash and ColdFusion. Here is a list of some other technologies:

Flash Remoting

Flash Remoting acts just like a SOAP-based web services does, except that it is a proprietary technology built by Macromedia. The advantage of using Flash Remoting is that because it is compiled to a binary format when being sent, it is smaller in file size and has less overhead than SOAP. This makes Flash Remoting much faster and more efficient than SOAP. The disadvantage of Flash Remoting is that this technology is proprietary and cannot be shared with other technologies that are not Flash Remoting–enabled (Flash Remoting can be used with JRun, ColdFusion, .NET, and Java). This takes away many of the benefits of having an open standard for data exchange. Lastly, at the time of this writing, Flash Remoting was originally released for Flash MX, and although it is included in Flash MX 2004, it was not updated to the new ActionScript 2.0 language that came with Flash MX 2004 (we discuss ActionScript 2.0 later in the chapter). At this time, Flash Remoting is still written in ActionScript 1.0 and cannot be used within ActionScript 2.0 classes as you would expect it. In short, to use Flash Remoting within ActionScript 2.0, you must take a step backward from the new way of developing applications in Flash MX 2004.

Flash and ColdFusion Both Understand XML

XML can be read and produced in both Flash and ColdFusion. You can produce and interpret XML manually without using a SOAP web service, but be careful not to re-invent the wheel. As you will see in this chapter, it requires very little effort to create a SOAP web service, so make sure that what you need doesn't already exist. That said, you can come up with reasons for using XML pretty easily. For instance, maybe you do not want to use a ColdFusion back-end and just want access to static data in a file; this would be a good case for storing the data in plain XML and parsing it yourself from Flash. I find this to be really handy for storing configuration data, or client-specific data that would not go into a database or would be used by every user of the application.

loadVariables

Flash uses the loadVariables function to load a text file containing name value pairs for data structure. This is a quick and easy way to expose data, but would not be the preferred way of working with data within Flash. XML is usually more descriptive and supports a hierarchical way of dealing with data—and once again, the preferred way would be to use SOAP web services. It's analogous to parsing data from a comma-delimited file rather than a database.

Using Flash

Traditionally, animators and web designers have made movies using Flash animation to add basic interactivity and animation to web sites. Flash is a multimedia application; its broad scope covers audio, video, animation, graphics, and coding. We can import all sorts of media into Flash, including FLV, MP3, WAV, MOV, AVI, WMV, DV, JPG, and PNG formats, and even specialized formats such as FreeHand, Fireworks, ToonBoom, and Swift3D files. However, in recent years Flash has been increasingly used for creating front-ends for dynamic server-side applications and web sites. Macromedia coined the term *Rich Internet Applications* to describe these apps. With the addition of powerful tools such as Flash Remoting, Flash offers much more for developers, and is capable of much more than mere web animations.

There is no need to feel apprehensive about using Flash even—possibly especially—if you are not a designer. Flash has built-in user interface components and a developer-friendly script-editing tool to make things easier for those not inclined to animate (which includes the majority of developers using Flash for business application development). Flash MX 2004 Professional comes with a forms-based development environment much like the .NET for Visual Basic and JBuilder environments. This form-based approach has clearly made the statement that Flash MX 2004 Professional is here for developers as well. In the following examples, we use the features from Flash Professional. If you do not yet have the Flash software, you can download it from http://www.macromedia.com/downloads/.

As a developer, invest in Flash Professional, because Flash by itself does not contain the advanced features you will want for building Rich Internet Applications.

Once you have the application installed and loaded, you will first notice the start page (examples are shown on Mac OS X: on Windows, everything is identical with the exception of panel docking), shown in Figure 12-1:

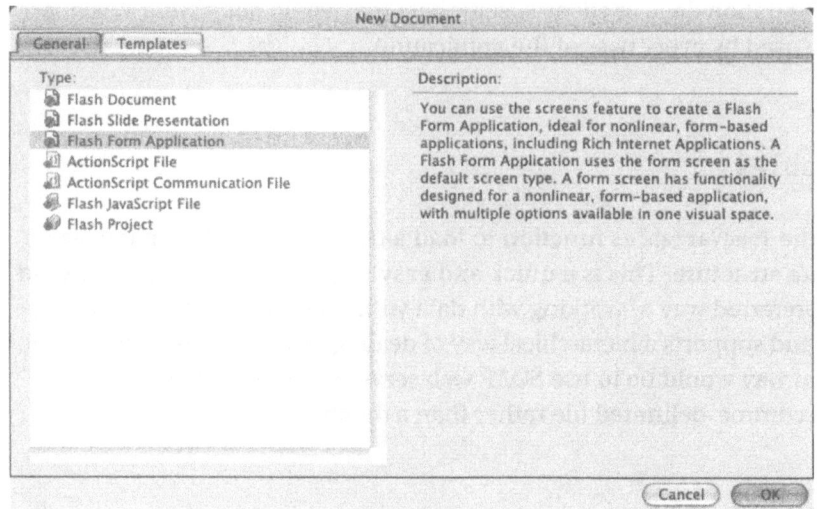

Figure 12-1: The New Document panel provides a list of the available document types.

As you can see, you can choose from many selections. If you click through each option, the description of that option will appear on the right. For this example we are mainly interested in the Flash Form Application. Select this option from the menu and click the OK button.

Once the IDE has opened the blank Flash Form Application, you'll see five areas that we discuss next.

Stage

The Stage is where you visually draw or place objects to create the user interface, as Figure 12-2 shows.

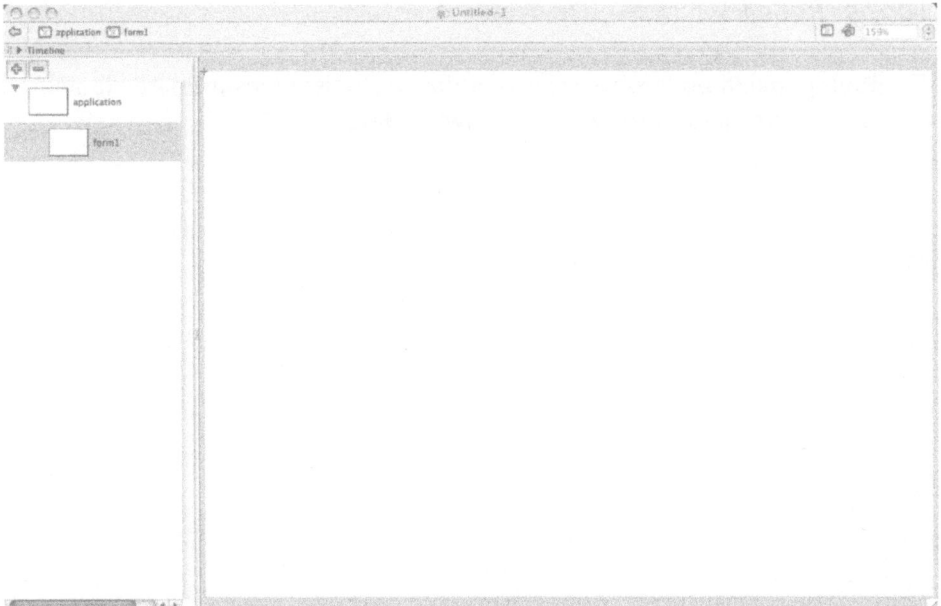

Figure 12-2: The Stage is where you visually place and work with components, text, shapes, and objects.

On the Stage, you will drop objects from the Components panel or use the tools from the Tools panel (both described further on) to construct the user interface elements.

To the left of the Stage is the form tree. This is where you organize your forms. Forms, also known as screens, act as containers for your user interface. You can think of them as structural building blocks organized in a hierarchical system.

Above the Stage and the forms tree is the Timeline. This can be confusing to new developers coming to Flash Professional. The reason for this is that Flash has always been dependent on the timeline to do anything. The timeline was originally intended for doing animations, not application development; because Flash started as an animation tool, the Timeline was an integral part of the interface until Flash Professional was released. As you will see in this chapter, there is no need to use the Timeline when creating business applications. In fact, you can do most of your animations by using ActionScript rather than the Timeline. Therefore, we don't discuss the usage of the Timeline here, but we suggest you experiment with it and see if you can use it in the future (when justified).

Tools Panel

The Tools panel (if not visible, select Window ➤ Tools) holds primarily drawing tools for creating a user interface, as shown in Figure 12-3.

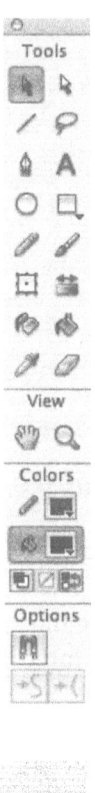

Figure 12-3: The Tools panel is used when drawing or positioning components.

Don't be fooled into thinking that this panel is for designers only. As a developer, you will use basic shapes to break up your interface and add some basic design to your application. Most importantly, the arrow icon (highlighted in the top left of the panel) is your selection tool; you will use it constantly for giving focus to and for positioning items in the user interface.

Components Panel

The Components panel (if not visible, select Window ➤ Development Panels ➤ Tools) is where you access your visual components, as shown in Figure 12-4.

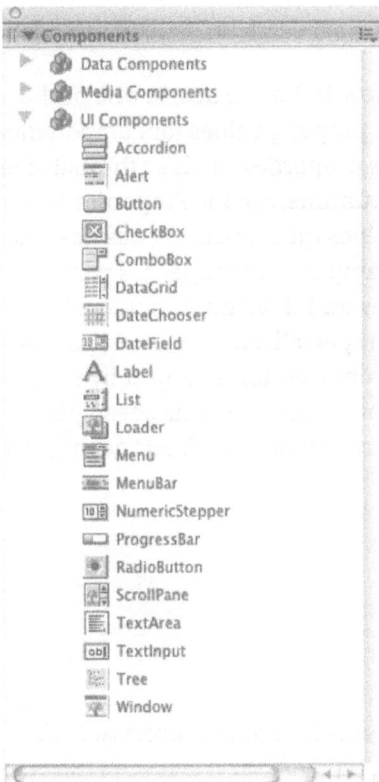

Figure 12-4: The Components panel contains all of the available components that Flash can use.

As you can see, there are quite a few. You drag and drop these components to the Stage for use. The components' properties are accessed via ActionScript, the Properties panel (discussed next), and the Component Inspector (which we discuss later). All of these components are very powerful and a huge time saver when developing applications. These components all follow a standard look and feel (Macromedia has defined this look and feel as *Halo*, but the Halo technology does encompass more) but have a flexible API for customization (skins and isolated property definitions). As you become more comfortable with these components, you can look at the ActionScript 2.0 source that was used to create them here: {flash install directory}/First Run/classes. Before looking into these classes, you may want to create a backup of this directory to avoid any accidental modification of the files.

We will be focusing on the data components and user interface components in this chapter.

Properties Panel

The Properties panel (if not visible, select Window ➤ Properties) is one of the design-time ways in Flash that developers can set property values for components and forms. There are many ways to set values for properties, such as through the Component Inspector or through ActionScript at runtime, but the Properties panel is a very convenient way to assign some basic values quickly during design-time development. As you will see in the following examples, the Properties panel is used primarily for setting some basic properties and does not include all the properties for most components. For those more specialized properties, you will need to use ActionScript to set value(s). To set properties for an object by using the Property panel, shown in Figure 12-5, select the object after it has been placed on the Stage. Once this has happened, the Properties panel will load that object's properties.

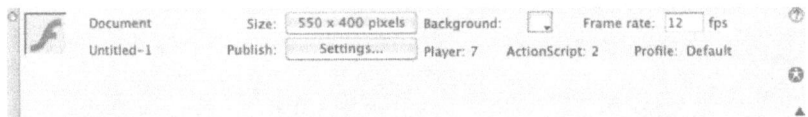

Figure 12-5: The Properties panel is a convienient way of setting properties while dealing with objects on the Stage.

ActionScript Editor

To view the ActionScript Editor, select File ➤ New. Once the New Document dialog opens, select the ActionScript File option and click OK. You will now see a blank ActionScript file in the ActionScript Editor, as shown in Figure 12-6. Some developers and designers place ActionScript on the Timeline as well, but because this chapter deals with ColdFusion application development and not animation, the following examples will be only placing code in external ActionScript files. This method of keeping files in external, self-contained files promotes code reuse, and the ability to use code versioning software and other developer tools that deal with text.

Figure 12-6: The ActionScript Editor is where you edit code.

The ActionScript Editor is a basic text-editing feature that allows you to stay inside Flash while doing your nonvisual work (pure code writing). This editor has code hint ability for objects that it knows (objects on the Stage with an assigned instance name) and will display these hints as you type. This is a common feature included in other development environments such as Visual Studio or JBuilder. Figure 12-7 shows the hints at work.

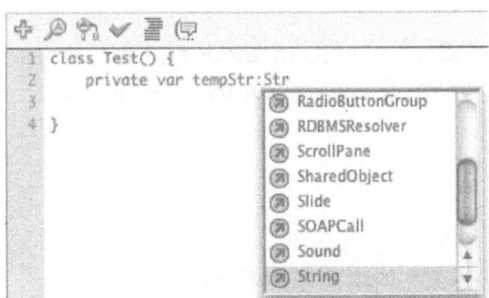

Figure 12-7: Code hinting speeds up code writing and helps prevent typos.

Code hints and color-coded syntax are great features to have in an editor. These two features can save you time while writing code by eliminating the need to look up properties and methods from documentation and help files, and they can help you spot keywords when looking over code.

ActionScript 2.0

A thorough examination of ActionScript 2.0 is beyond the scope of this book, so we will look at the basics here. ActionScript 2.0 is an Object Oriented Programming language that closely resembles JavaScript and is very similar to Java (ActionScript is ECMA-Script compliant). If you are familiar with these or any other ECMA Script language, then you will be able to adapt to ActionScript 2.0 very quickly. Following is a quick ramp-up list of ActionScript 2.0 language features to show you its syntax and functionality.

Declaring Variables

ActionScript 2.0 supports strong data typing, which means that if you misuse a data type, the compiler will catch it and throw an error. To use a variable in Flash, you must declare it explicitly. The format for declaring a variable is as follows:

```
[var] variableName[:type]
```

You start with the keyword *var*, then put the variable name followed by a ":" and a data type, which is any native data type (like String, Number, Array, Date or Object types) or a class or interface you have defined.

Defining Classes and Methods

A class is the definition of an object that defines all of its methods and properties. You will use instances of these classes to create the object for use at runtime.

```
class MyClass {
  // constructor
  function MyClass() {
    // this method will be called everytime the object is instaniated
  }
  // methods are defined within the class
  function myMethod() {
  }
}
```

There are many good books on Object Oriented Programming that go into deeper discussion on classes, and we suggest picking up one to gain a deeper understanding.

Variable Scope

There are four variable scopes in ActionScript 2.0 that you will most commonly use: public, private, static, and _global. You will use these scopes while defining variables and methods to contain a greater control over the access of these variables.

```
[scope] [var] variableName[:type]
```

- public: This scope allows access to the variable to any class that calls it.

- private: This scope allows access only to the class that declares or defines it, or to subclasses of that class.

- static: Very different from public and private, static variables are declared once and used in every instantiated class from that point forward. In short, all classes will share that variable and its value; none will have its own copy.

- global: This scope is similar to the application scope in ColdFusion. If you declare a variable by using global, that variable can be accessed anywhere within the application.

Inheritance

ActionScript 2.0 supports object inheritance. What this means is that by using the *extends* keyword in a class definition, you can inherit all of the properties and methods of another class as a way of reusing code and functionality. This is an extremely powerful language feature that you should consider using as you design the application. As you will see in future exercises, we will be inheriting from the Form class. By doing this, we can take the functionality of the Form that has already been written and add to that within our own class definition. For example, a class definition for a user administration screen may look like this:

```
import mx.screens.Form;
class UserAdminForm extends Form {
}
```

In almost every case, you must import a class to extend it, but some objects, like the MovieClip, are not required to have an import statement to extend. MovieClip is a core object, which means that Flash accounts for it whether or not the developer has. This is true for other objects like the TextField object and many others. That said, almost every time you will be required to import classes and every time you will need to import the user-defined classes you have created.

In later examples you will see that extending a class gives you all the functionality of that parent class. This will promote code reuse and save time during future application maintenance.

Again, this is a very quick overview of ActionScript 2.0 that merely shows a few basic language features so that the examples in this chapter are clear. ActionScript 2.0 has really proven itself to be a full-featured language and deserves a full investigation.

Using Flash Components

In this chapter, we use the user interface components, which are pre-made components installed with Flash MX 2004. Essentially, components are self-contained movie clips designed to perform certain tasks in a Flash movie. Components are particularly useful when you want to create an interface or mock-up quickly by using pre-made items. You may also want to create your own components if you need to reuse elements across multiple Flash movies or distribute it to other Flash developers. Components are very easy to use; you can drag and drop components onto the Stage from the Components panel.

To find the user interface components set, open the Components panel, then use the drop-down menu in this panel to select user interface components.

The user interface component set includes commonly used graphical interface elements, including buttons, panes, and list and combo boxes. In this chapter we use both the ComboBox and Button components. The Button is similar to an HTML button created using Input type=button or Input type=submit. The List is similar in functionality to an HTML select box (Select and Option). Figure 12-8 shows both the ComboBox and Button components.

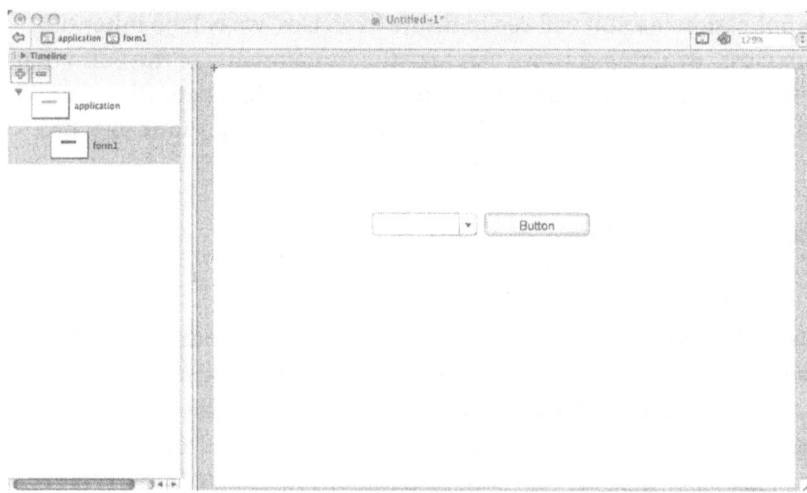

Figure 12-8. A Button and ComboBox on the Stage

You can set values and properties for these by using the Property Inspector. Simply drag a component from the user interface components set onto the Stage, select it, and open the Property Inspector. These values can be used along with the ActionScript you write. Using the parameters and properties, you can control components or change how they look. To respond to a components event, like when the user clicks the button, you will need to write a listener for that component. As you will see in later examples, this code will be written in an external ActionScript file, though many times you will see other developers place code like this in the Timeline. Here's what the listener code looks like:

```
// create the listener object
var myButtonListener = new Object();
// create the event that it will listen for
myButtonListener.click = function(evnt) {
    trace("my_button clicked");
}

// add the listener to the button component
my_button.addEventListener("click", myButtonListener);
```

Publishing a Movie

When working in the authoring environment, we work with .fla documents. When we put Flash on the Web, we need to embed a .swf file into the HTML web page. This is then "played" using the Flash Player browser plug-in. In order to create a .swf file from the Flash document, we need to publish the file.

Typically, as you work with Flash applications, you will need to test the movie often and publish the movie only when you are doing a build to post on the site. The difference is that when you *test* a Flash application, a .swf is created, which is the Flash executable; when you *publish* a Flash application, that same .swf is created, but also any other supporting files, like HTML, QuickTime, or projector files that have been set in the publishing preferences will be created too.

You can test a Flash movie without publishing it by pressing Ctrl+Enter from the authoring environment. This opens a built-in Flash player that you can test movies in. Trace statements, problems with code, and so on will become apparent in the Output window.

You can then publish a movie for the Web by going to File ➤ Publish. The default settings will publish .swf and HTML files in the same directory as the FLA file. Alternatively, you can take the <object> and <embed> code from this file and embed it in an existing web page, or let Dreamweaver generate the code for you by embedding a .swf file into a page. To change the publish settings in the Flash authoring environment, select File ➤ Publish Settings, and the Publish Settings dialog box will open. In this chapter, we stick to the default settings. Some sample code generated by these settings is as follows, for a Flash movie called cfbook:

```
<HTML>
<HEAD>
<meta http-equiv=Content-Type content="text/html; charset=ISO-8859-1">
<TITLE>cfbook</TITLE>
</HEAD>
<BODY bgcolor="#FFFFFF">
<!-- URL's used in the movie-->
<!-- text used in the movie-->
<OBJECT classid="clsid:D27CDB6E-AE6D-11cf-96B8-444553540000"➥
  codebase="http://download.macromedia.com/pub/shockwave/cabs/flash/➥
  swflash.cab#version=6,0,0,0"
  WIDTH="550" HEIGHT="400" id="cfbook" ALIGN="">
<PARAM NAME=movie VALUE="cfbook.swf"> <PARAM NAME=quality VALUE=high>
<PARAM NAME=bgcolor VALUE=#FFFFFF> <EMBED src="cfbook.swf" quality=high➥
  bgcolor=#FFFFFF  WIDTH="550" HEIGHT="400" NAME="cfbook" ALIGN=""
  TYPE="application/x-shockwave-flash"
PLUGINSPAGE="http://www.macromedia.com/➥
  go/getflashplayer"></EMBED>
</OBJECT>
</BODY>
</HTML>
```

Because we are using ActionScript 2.0, which only works with Flash Player 6 and 7, we will publish our movie as a Flash 7 document so it can be viewed in a browser. Also bear in mind that Flash web service support was introduced for, and is specific to, Flash Professional, and requires Flash Player 7. When developing for Flash Player 6, be sure to check that the components you have selected and the language features of ActionScript 2.0 do in fact work for Flash Player 6. There are many new features in Flash MX 2004 that will work in only Flash Player 7.

This is merely a quick introduction to the aspects of the Flash user interface that will be used most in this particular chapter. Many books and online resources are available on this subject to help you learn more about the details of the Flash authoring environment.

We describe what is happening in the ActionScript in each of the following sections, and also provide some pointers on web services in the following examples. We assume a basic working knowledge of JavaScript, which will make it fairly easy to follow along with the ActionScript examples, because the two languages are quite similar. However, ActionScript 2.0 is its own language (which is much too large to delve into here), and you would benefit greatly from reading up on it more deeply.

The (ColdFusion) Server Side of the Service

So far, this chapter has discussed Flash, but our Flash code will need to talk to the server; ColdFusion will be used for the server-side functionality. There are a couple of rules that need to be followed when writing a CFC as a web service.

<cffunction>

Within a CFC, all of your methods will be written within the <cffunction> tag. Normally, the attribute name is the only required attribute, but when developing web services, you will always need to set the access attribute to remote; otherwise, ColdFusion MX Server will not make it accessible to Flash or any other technology as a web service. Also, you must set the returntype attribute, even if the method returns nothing, then it must be set to void.

<cfargument>

The <cfargument> tag is used within the <cffunction> tag to define the arguments taken by the method. When defining an argument for a web service, you must define the name and type arguments as well as set the required attribute to true.

For more information on publishing CFCs as web services, go to http://livedocs.macromedia.com/coldfusion/6/Developing_ColdFusion_MX_Applicat ions_with_CFML/webservices5.htm.

Sending the Current Time to Flash

Now that we have some Flash MX 2004 basics and know the new rules to create a CFC in ColdFusion, let's create a quick CFC and see how Flash works with that web service.

Creating a CFC to Read the Server Time

The first step is to create the CFC that we want to access from Flash. Open Dreamweaver and create a new folder in the cfbook site named ch12. Go to File ➤ New ➤ Dynamic Page ➤ ColdFusion Component and create a page called servertime.cfc. Enter the following code into this page:

```
<cfcomponent>
  <cffunction name="getServerTime" access="remote" returntype="date"➡
    output="false">
```

```
      <cfreturn Now()>
   </cffunction>
</cfcomponent>
```

This is a simple CFC that doesn't take any parameters and simply returns the current time of the server.

Remember that we have to set the access to remote for any functions that we want to use as a web service.

Next create a ColdFusion file named test_servertime.cfm in this folder, which you'll use to test your component. When building web service applications, it is often easiest to work in stages so you can verify that your component fully works before integrating it with Flash. Then you will not have to debug both ColdFusion and Flash files at the same time.

Now add the following code into the test_servertime.cfm file:

```
<cfinvoke component="cfbook.ch12.servertime" method="getServerTime"➥
   returnvariable="currentServerTime" />
<cfdump var="#currentServerTime#">
```

Save the file and view the results in a browser by pressing F12. You will see the server's current date and time displayed to the browser window. Once you've verified that the CFC works, delete this test file and close Dreamweaver. The output will be something like Figure 12-9.

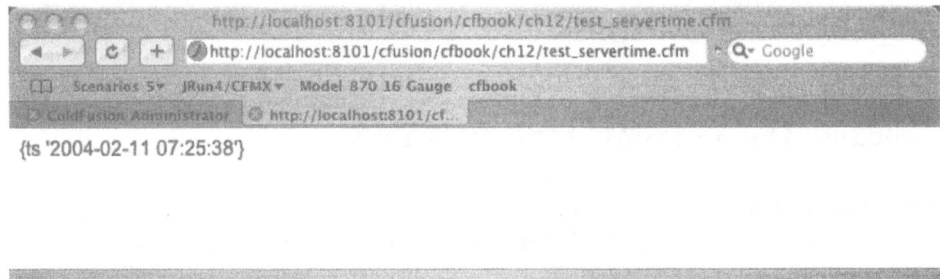

Figure 12-9. Test output for the current date and time on server

Examining the Web Service in Flash MX 2004 Professional

When working with web services, it is often necessary to check the methods and their parameters as you develop your Flash application. Flash MX 2004 Professional has supplied a great tool just for that. Let's start this application by creating a Flash Form Application, Then we will examine the web service we are trying to contact and then put it all together.

First, create a new Flash Form Application from the New Document dialog, then save it as servertime.fla. Now that you have the application saved, let's look at the data that will go into it.

Go to Window ➤ Development Panels ➤ Web Services to open the Web Services panel, shown in Figure 12-10.

Figure 12-10: The Web Services panel allows you to define web services and graphically explore the methods and properties of those services.

This panel allows the developer to define web services and use it as a reference to explore those web services. Click on the world icon to define a web service, then click the plus icon to add a web service. Here you will enter the address to your CFC and add ?WSDL to the end of the address (WSDL stands for Web Service Definition Language). WSDL is an XML format for describing web services. It defines what methods (or operations) are available, what parameters the method will take, and what the method returns. This definition enables tools like the Web Services panel to show the method descriptions. Your URL to your web service should be something like http://localhost:8101/cfusion/cfbook/ ch12/test_servertime.cfm?WSDL, which you can see in Figure 12-11.

> **NOTE** *Edit the URL to match your server setup.*

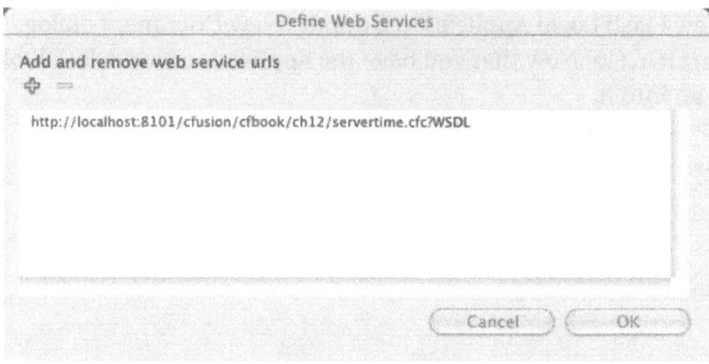

*Figure 12-11: When defining a web service on your development machine, make
sure that the URL is set appropriately to your server configuration.*

Click OK. The Web Services panel now holds a node for the servertime web
service. Drill down the tree to expose the methods and arguments for the servertime web service, as shown in Figure 12-12.

Figure 12-12: The Web Services panel exposing the servertime service.

As you can see, the method getServerTime and its result dateTime are shown.
This tool will become a valuable reference as you develop more web service
applications, especially if you did not create the web service.

Displaying the Time from the Server

Now that the servertime web service exists, you have a way to view the contents
of the web service. You need to set up a way to call the web service and display

the results. In Flash Professional, you can call a web service by using components out of the Data components set, or you can use the WebServices classes. The data components can enable an application to communicate with web services with little to no code by merely setting properties and binding user interface components to those data components via the Component Inspector. When using the WebServices classes, you should create the connection and binding through ActionScript 2.0. In this example, we use the data components and bind them to the user interface components through the Component Inspector panel.

Start by dragging then the Web Service Connector component to the Stage, as Figure 12-13 shows.

Figure 12-13: The Web Service Connector component on the Stage

To set up the Web Service Connector component, follow the following steps:

1. In the Properties panel, name the component serverTime_wsc.

2. Set the WSDL parameter to the URL pointing to your servertime web service (the same way that was done in the Web Services panel).

3. Set the operation parameter to getServerTime.

At this point the Web Service Connector component knows where to look for the web service and what method to call. Figure 12-14 shows the component's properties.

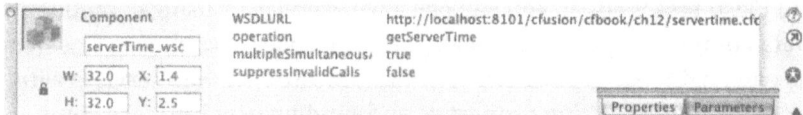

Figure 12-14: Properties panel for the Web Service component

> **TIP** *Now that you know how to add the component and set the parameters manually, there is a shortcut in the Web Services panel. If you select Add Method Call from the menu at the upper-right corner of the Web Services panel, a web service component with all of the appropriate parameters filled out will be placed on the Stage for you.*

Binding Components to Display Data

The Web Services Connector component has the ability to bind parameter and return values to user interface components and other data components. For example, using this technology, you can bind a TextInput component to a parameter, such as search text, then bind a DataGrid component to the result value of the method call to display results, without creating any code. You can complete this step visually through the Component Inspector panel.

For this example, we are going to bind the server time result to a Label component. To do this, follow these steps:

1. Drag a Label component from the user interface components to the Stage and name it result_label. Set the width to 300.

2. Open the Component Inspector panel by going to Window ➤ Development Panels ➤ Component Inspector.

3. Select the serverTime_wsc component, then select the Bindings tab.

4. Click the plus icon to add a binding. When the Add Binding dialog opens, select the results:Date node and click OK.

5. Back in the Component Inspector panel on the Bindings tab, you will see results in the binding list. With results selected, click the bound to property. This will open the Bound To dialog, shown in Figure 12-15.

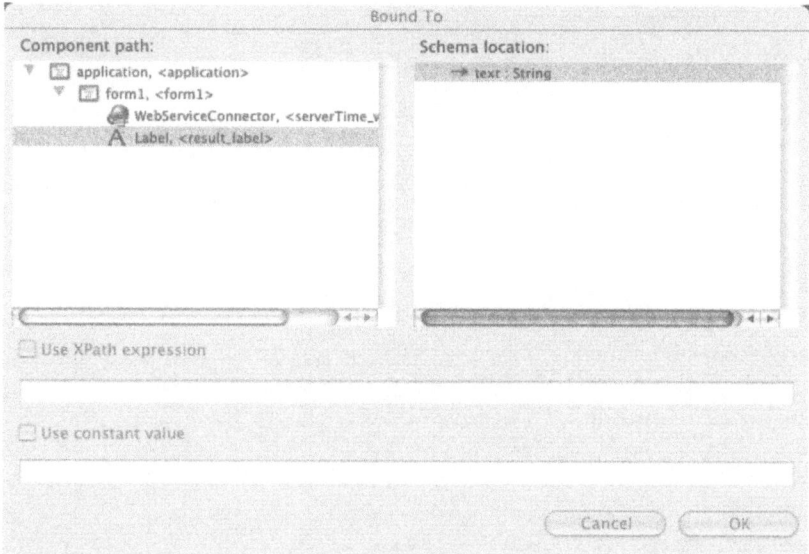

Figure 12-15: The Bound To dialog is where you will bind data to components on the Stage.

6. In the Bound To dialog, select the `results_label` and click OK.

Now that the Web Service Connector is set up and the resulting value is bound to the component, you need to write some code to tell `serverTime_wsc` to make the call; otherwise, the service is never executed. To do this, you will associate an ActionScript 2.0 class with the form that the components are on. Follow these steps:

1. First rename the form to `serverTime_form` so that it is something meaningful. To do this, simply open the Properties panel and change it from `form 1` to `serverTime_form`. You can also double-click the name of the form in the form browser and rename it there.

2. Create a class by creating a new ActionScript file from the New Document dialog.

3. Save the document as `ServerTimeForm.as` in the same directory as the `servertime.fla`.

4. Enter the code from Figure 12-16.

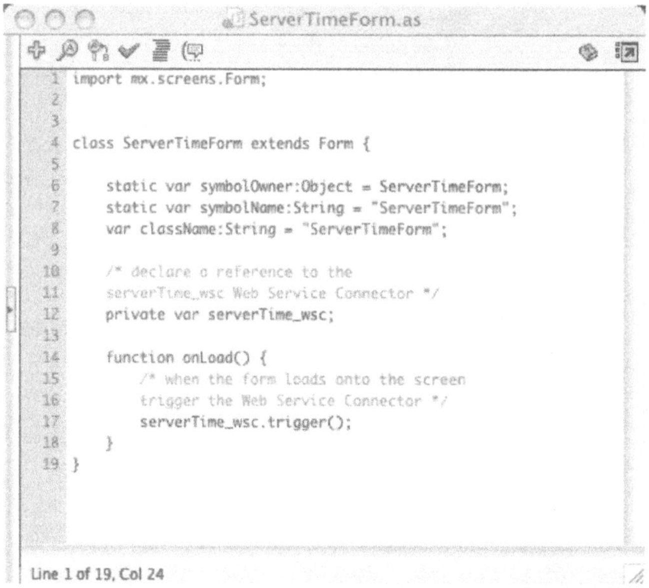

```
ServerTimeForm.as
1  import mx.screens.Form;
2
3
4  class ServerTimeForm extends Form {
5
6      static var symbolOwner:Object = ServerTimeForm;
7      static var symbolName:String = "ServerTimeForm";
8      var className:String = "ServerTimeForm";
9
10     /* declare a reference to the
11     serverTime_wsc Web Service Connector */
12     private var serverTime_wsc;
13
14     function onLoad() {
15         /* when the form loads onto the screen
16         trigger the Web Service Connector */
17         serverTime_wsc.trigger();
18     }
19 }
```

Line 1 of 19, Col 24

Figure 12-16: Code for the serverTime_form *class* ServerTimeForm.as

5. Go back to the Stage and select serverTime_form in the tree on the left and change the Class Name property from mx.screen.Form to ServerTimeForm.

6. Now run the application, and you should see results similar to Figure 12-17.

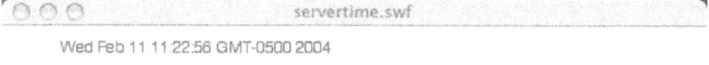

servertime.swf

Wed Feb 11 11:22:56 GMT-0500 2004

Figure 12-17: Test results from running the serverTime Flash application

What happened here? You did a lot; in a nutshell, you created a Flash Form Application with one Form called serverTime_form. This form is associated to an ActionScript 2.0 class called ServerTimeForm. By associating a class to a Form tells Flash to create an instance of that class when the Form is created in memory, and for that class to be the Forms class. We will look at the ActionScript more closely after some more explanation. On the serverTime_form you placed a Web Service Connector component name serverTime_wsc and set the appropriate properties for that component to make a web service call to your web service servertime.cfc. Then you bound the results of the web service call to the result_label component so that the server time could be displayed to the user. With all of that reexamined, lets look at the ActionScript class that we built.

On the first line, you imported the Form class so that we could inherit all of the methods and properties of the Form class. This is required for a Class to be associated with a Form.

```
import mx.screens.Form;
```

Next you defined the Class ServerTimeForm.

```
class ServerTimeForm extends Form {
}
```

After that there are three lines that Flash requires to make the connection between the Class you defined and the one created in the IDE.

```
static var symbolOwner:Object = ServerTimeForm;
static var symbolName:String = "ServerTimeForm";
var className:String = "ServerTimeForm";
```

Flash uses these variable to complete the association. For a more in-depth explanation of these variables, check the help files.

Then we declared a variable to point to the serverTime_wsc. After declaring a variable with the same name as the component on Stage, you will then have a reference to that component in your class. Failure to properly declare a variable will result in a compilation error if you attempt to reference the undefined variable.

```
/* declare a reference to the
serverTime_wsc Web Service Connector */
private var serverTime_wsc;
```

The next bit of code you wrote is a function that is fired when the Form is fully loaded. This is the best point to start interacting with your components that have been dropped onto the Stage; trying to interact with components before this method is fired may result in behavior you did not expect. This is primarily because the component may not be fully loaded yet, so calls to that component may just be ignored.

```
function onLoad() {
}
```

Finally, when the onLoad method is automatically called, the trigger() method is called on the serverTime_wsc component, which then makes the call to the web service.

```
/* when the form loads onto the screen
trigger the Web Service Connector */
serverTime_wsc.trigger();
```

Upon the return result of that call, the value is loaded into result_label.

That is it! The application is complete. Although this application is simple, the technology at work is doing a lot. The implementation has been done so well, however, that you just need to take advantage of it and not spend hours developing it.

Consuming a Web Service with Flash

Although the first example was very basic, creating increasingly advanced applications doesn't necessarily have to be much more difficult. In this example, we will look at one way of using Flash and ColdFusion to consume a third-party web service that provides weather forecasts for specified areas of the United States.

ColdFusion will handle calling the remote web service and returning the results to Flash; the results will then be displayed in a simple Flash interface. Although it is possible to directly consume web services using only Flash and the data components, you will sometimes want to first perform processing on the data returned from a web service before sending it along to Flash (here using ColdFusion).

Looking at the Service

Before coding the ColdFusion Consumer component, look at the service to see what you will be dealing with. To keep consistent with the previous example, view the web service through the Flash development environment. Because we are opening up Flash to view aspects of the project, go ahead and create a new Flash Form Application .fla file that you will be working with called weather.fla, then define a new web service in the Web Services panel by using this URL, http://www.ejse.com/WeatherService/Service.asmx?WSDL, as Figure 12-18 shows.

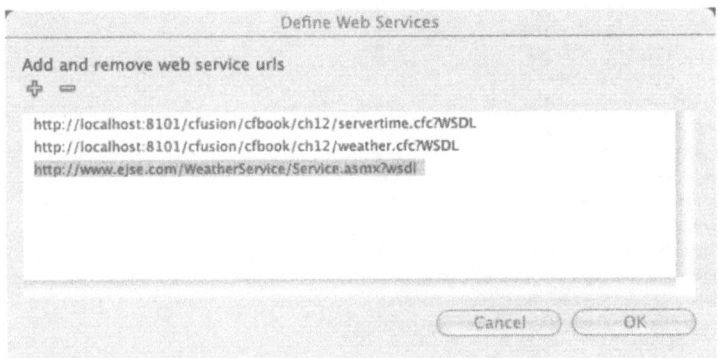

Figure 12-18: Adding the WeatherService web service

Then drill down to the GetWeatherInfo method and expose its parameters and values, as Figure 12-19 shows.

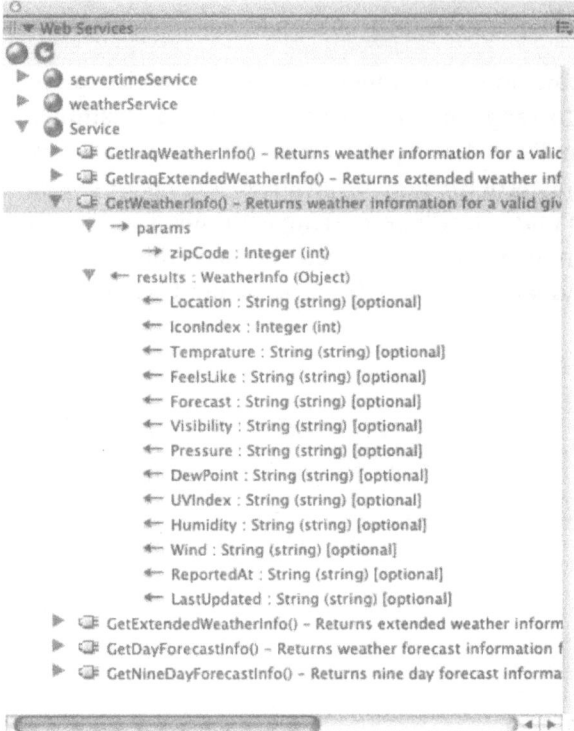

Figure 12-19: Examine the GetWeatherInfo *method.*

As you can see, this web service has many methods, but the one we are interested in here is the GetWeatherInfo method, which takes one argument, zipCode, and returns weather data specific to that zip code. Now that you know what the service expects and the object and that object's properties that will be returned, it is time to set up a CFC to handle the consumption of the web service.

Creating the ColdFusion Consumer

Setting aside weather.fla for the moment, open Dreamweaver, create a new CFC file called weather.cfc within the /cfbook/ch12/ folder, and enter the following code:

```
<cfcomponent>
<cffunction name="getWeatherReport" access="remote" returntype="struct"➡
  output="false">
  <cfargument name="zipCode" type="numeric" required="true">
  <cfset Var weather = "" >
  <cfset Var returnStruct = StructNew() >
```

```
<cfinvoke method = "GetWeatherInfo" returnvariable = "weather"➡
  webservice = "http://www.ejse.com/WeatherService/Service.asmx?wsdl">
  <cfinvokeargument name="zipCode" value="#Arguments.ZipCode#">
</cfinvoke>
<cfscript>
  returnStruct.location = weather.getLocation();
  returnStruct.temperature = weather.getTemprature();
  returnStruct.feelsLike = weather.getFeelsLike();
  returnStruct.forecast = weather.getForecast();
  returnStruct.visibility = weather.getVisibility();
  returnStruct.pressure = weather.getPressure();
  returnStruct.dewPoint = weather.getDewPoint();
  returnStruct.UVIndex = weather.getUVIndex();
  returnStruct.humidity = weather.getHumidity();
  returnStruct.wind = weather.getWind();
  returnStruct.reportedAt = weather.getReportedAt();
  returnStruct.lastUpdated = weather.getLastUpdated();
</cfscript>
<cfreturn returnStruct >
</cffunction>
</cfcomponent>
```

Notice that the component currently has one function, #getWeatherReport()#. This function takes in a single argument, #zipCode#. As you have probably guessed, the argument takes a U.S. zip code and returns the weather report for that area.

For this example, we are using a web service from http://www.ejse.com. This web service offers weather reports only for the U.S. region. To check out a large listing of different web services, go to http://www.xmethods.net.

Going through the rest of the CFC, we can see two local variables: #weather# and #returnStruct#. The #returnStruct# variable will contain the location, temperature, forecast, and a few other values returned by the remote web service. Within the <cfinvoke> tag, we pass the #Arguments.ZipCode# variable to the remote web service. Within the <cfscript> tag, we set the variables that we want to pass back to the Flash movie. Finally, we return the #returnStruct# to the calling page. In this case, it will be our Flash movie.

Before closing Dreamweaver, make a ColdFusion file to test this component. Create a file named test_weather.cfm within the /cfbook/ch12/ directory and type in the following code:

```
<cfinvoke component="cfbook.ch12.weather" method="getWeatherReport"➥
  returnvariable="weatherInfo">
  <cfinvokeargument name="zipCode" value="91792">
</cfinvoke>

<cfdump var="#weatherInfo#">
```

Save this file and press F12 to view the results—you should see an output similar to Figure 12-20.

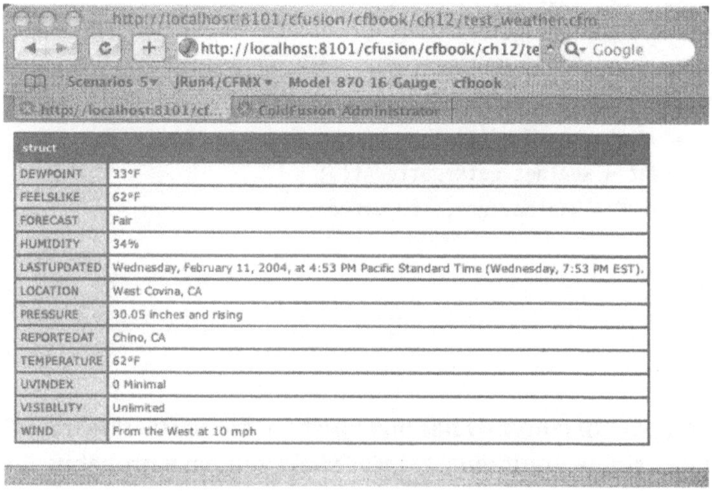

Figure 12-20. The test results displayed in a browser window

If the test file didn't work and you received an error rather than results like these, then quickly look through the test_weather.cfm file and make sure that the path to your CFC is correct and the files are named properly. Also make sure that you are testing with a valid U.S. zip code. Finally, this service is hosted on someone else's server, so the response time maybe slow. Sit it out for a few seconds before assuming that something is wrong.

Describing Web Service Data in Flash

In our previous example, we created a web service to return a simple value, the server time. However, in this example we are returning a complex object that has many properties. Unfortunately, we need to take some time telling

Flash what this object will look like so we can bind the components. To further illustrate, go back to weather.fla and create a new web service in the Web Services panel by using a URL that is appropriate for your server setup, such as http://localhost:8101/cfusion/cfbook/ch12/weather.cfc?WSDL.

Now look at the weatherService web service in the Web Services panel. It should look like Figure 12-21.

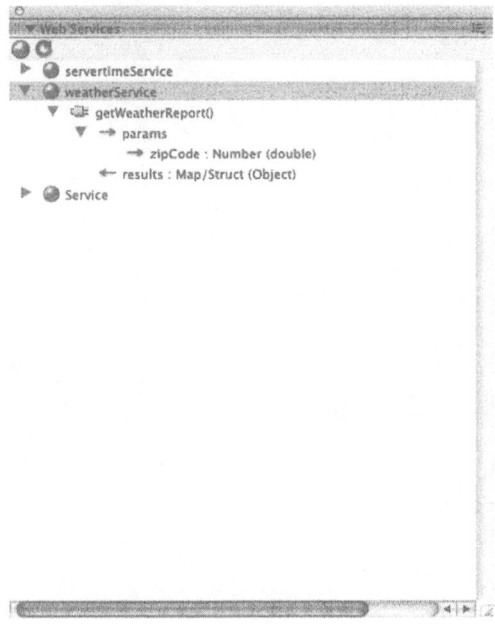

Figure 12-21: weatherService exposed in the Web Services panel

As you can see, the results node shows an object, but not what is within that object. This makes the data result(s) impossible to bind to Flash user interface components. To fix this, we need to tell Flash what to expect from the web service.

To start dictating to Flash the description of the object returned by the weatherService web service, we need to have a WebServiceConnector component on a form to work with. So first, rename the default form1 form to weather_form, as in Figure 12-22.

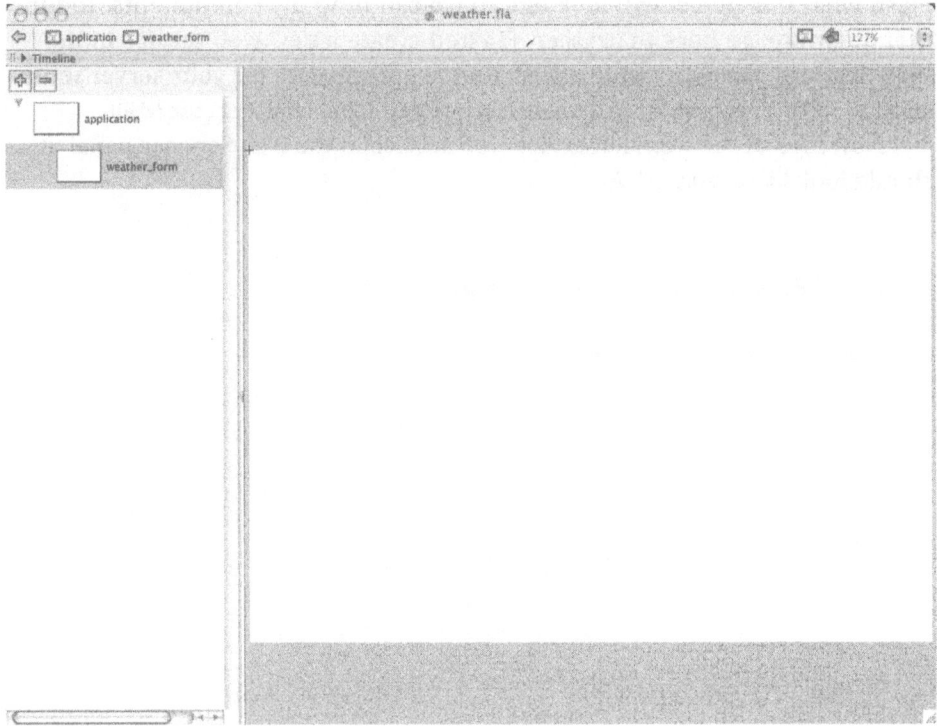

Figure 12-22: form1 *renamed as* weather_form

Next, add a WebServiceConnector component specifically for the weatherService getWeatherReport method by selecting Add Method Call from the Web Services panel while both the weather_form form and the getWeatherReport node are selected. By doing this, a WebServiceConnector component will be added to the form with all of the properties already filled out. See Figure 12-23.

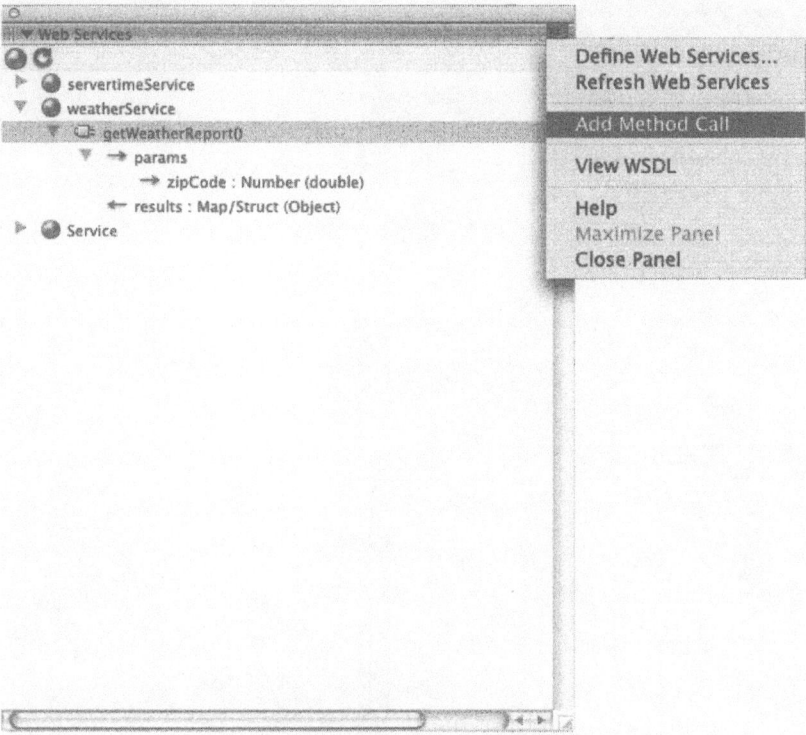

Figure 12-23: Using the Add Method Call shortcut

Then name the newly created `WebServiceConnector` **component** `weather_wsc`.
The resulting component should have properties similar to Figure 12-24.

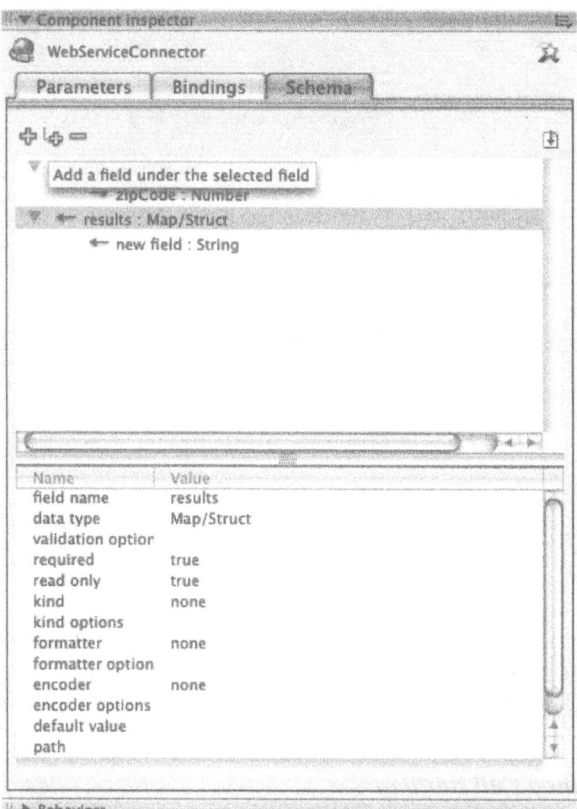

Figure 12-24: Viewing the properties from weather_wsc

At this point the WebServiceConnector component weather_wsc is ready to be "told" what to expect from the getWeatherInfo web service method. This is done by describing the returned object in the Component Inspector panel. To do this, select weather_wsc and click on the Schema tab; you will see the basic description as you already know it, as shown in Figure 12-25.

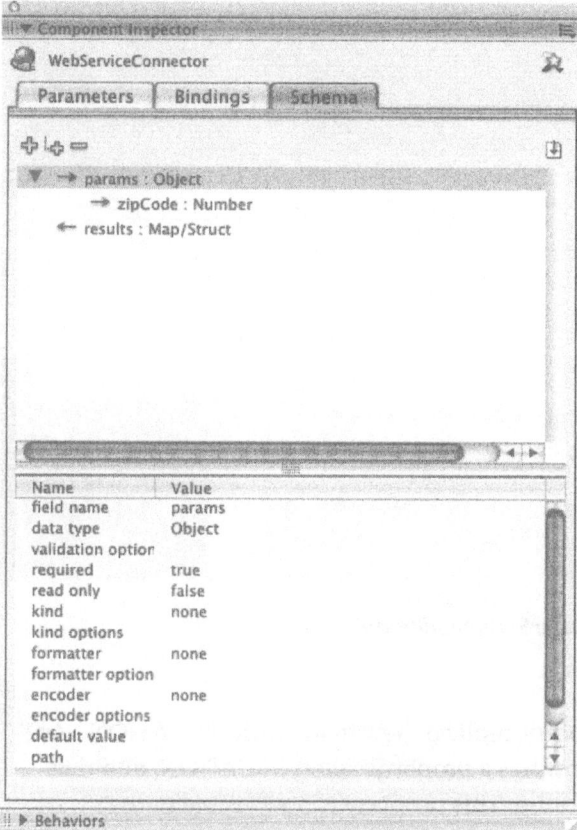

Figure 12-25: Component Inspector view of the weatherService schema

You need to add properties to the return struct that will describe all of the properties within that struct so that they can be bound to the user interface components. To do this select the results : Map/Struct node and click the smaller plus icon to add a field under the selected field, as Figure 12-26 shows.

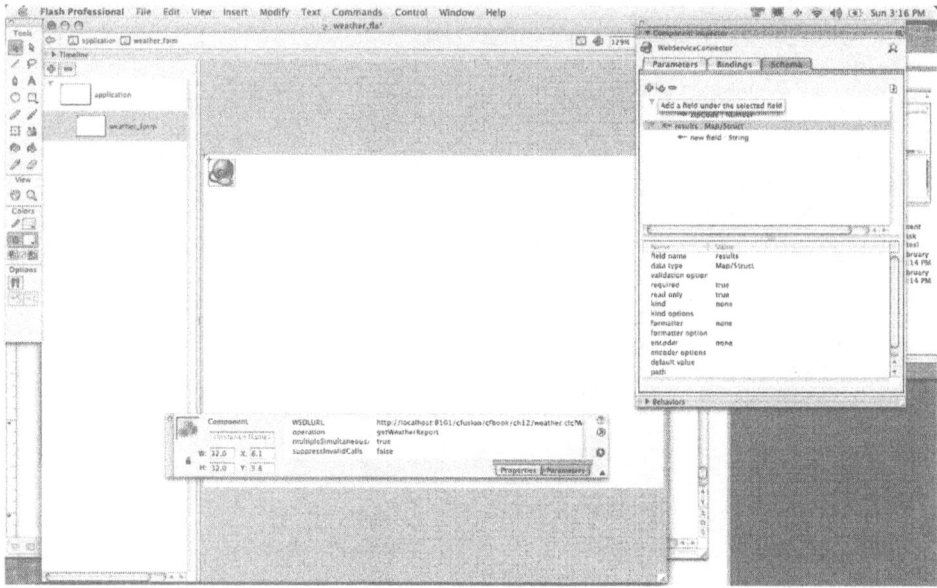

Figure 12-26: Modifying the weatherService schema

Next, in the field name property, replace "new field" with "LOCATION". As you can see, the results struct now has a property called LOCATION, and that property can now be properly bound. This property is now visible to the Component Inspector and will create a reference to the same named property that is in the resulting object. Repeat these last two steps for all of the properties so that your Component Inspector panel looks like Figure 12-27.

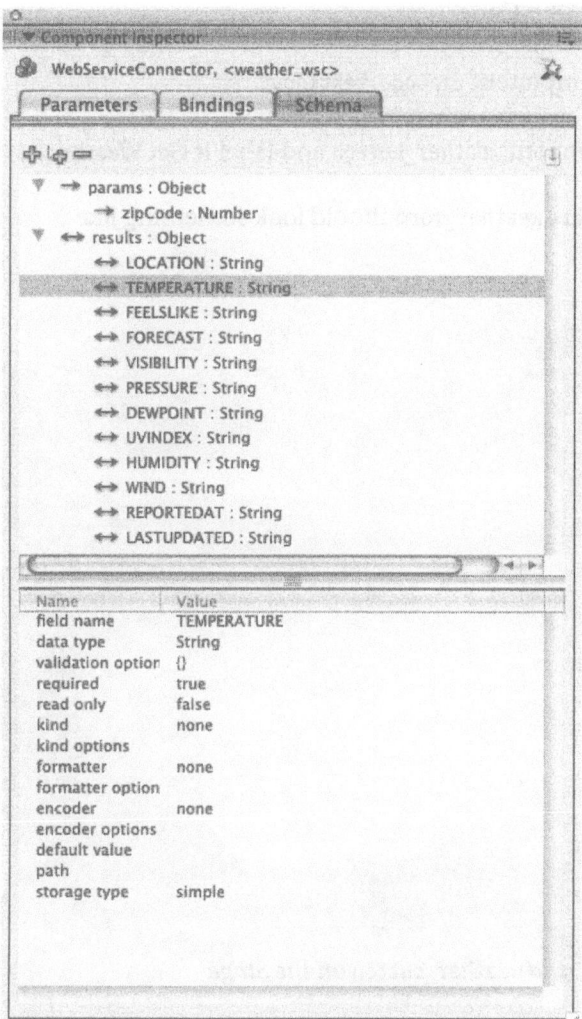

Figure 12-27: weatherService schema fully defined

Creating the `weather.fla` *GUI*

Now that the data has been defined for Flash, you will need to create the interface to display that data. As you have already learned, the user interface components are easy to use and can be bound to data coming into Flash. In this example you will bind data to outgoing and incoming data.

The `getWeatherReport` method takes in one parameter, `zipCode`. To get the `zipCode` input from a user, you will use a `TextInput` control from the user interface components group. Build the interface by using the following components:

1. Fill in the text label as "Zip Code."

2. Name the TextInput component zipCode_textInput.

3. Name the Button component weather_button and label it Get Weather.

At this point your weather.fla weather_form should look something like Figure 12-28.

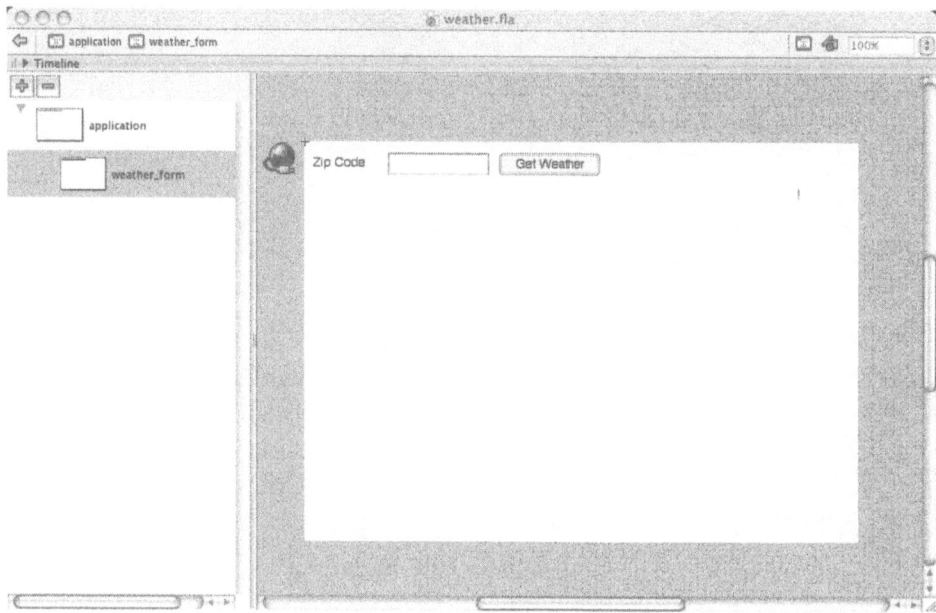

Figure 12-28: zipCode_textInput *and* weather_button *on the Stage*

Binding the zipCode_textInput Component

To bind the zipCode_textInput component to the zipCode parameter for the getWeatherReport method, select the weather_wsc component on the Stage, then the Bindings tab in the Component Inspector. Next click the plus icon to add a binding, select zipCode in the Add Binding dialog, and click on OK. That's it. At this point, when the weather_wsc component is triggered, it will look for a value from zipCode_textInput and pass it to the getWeatherReport method.

Triggering weather_wsc

As with the get server time example you will need to set up a class and associate that class to the form that the WebServiceConnector component is on. For this example, the form is weather_form and the class you will create is WeatherForm.as. To start, create a new ActionScript file and save it as WeatherForm.as in the same directory as weather.fla.

Add import statements to import class definitions for the components that you will be using.

```
import mx.screens.Form;
import mx.controls.Button;
import mx.controls.TextInput;
```

Then create the class definition as follows:

```
import mx.screens.Form;
import mx.controls.Button;
import mx.controls.TextInput;
class WeatherForm extends Form {    static var symbolOwner:Object = WeatherForm;
    static var symbolName:String = "WeatherForm";
    var className:String = "WeatherForm";
}
```

Next declare references to the components placed on the weather_form:

```
import mx.screens.Form;
import mx.controls.Button;
import mx.controls.TextInput;

class WeatherForm extends Form {
    static var symbolOwner:Object = WeatherForm;
    static var symbolName:String = "WeatherForm";
    var className:String = "WeatherForm";

    /* declare a reference to the
    weather_wsc Web Service Connector */
    private var weather_wsc;
    /* declare a reference to the
    weather_button Button*/
    private var weather_button:Button;
    /* declare a reference to the
    zipCode_textInput TextInput*/
    private var zipCode_textInput:TextInput;
}
```

Finally, add the onLoad method and register a listener to weather_button's click event to trigger the weather_wsc component.

```
import mx.screens.Form;
import mx.controls.Button;
import mx.controls.TextInput;

class WeatherForm extends Form {

    static var symbolOwner:Object = WeatherForm;
    static var symbolName:String = "WeatherForm";
    var className:String = "WeatherForm";

    /* declare a reference to the
    weather_wsc Web Service Connector */
    private var weather_wsc;
    /* declare a reference to the
    weather_button Button*/
    private var weather_button:Button;
    /* declare a reference to the
    zipCode_textInput TextInput*/
    private var zipCode_textInput:TextInput;

    function onLoad() {
        var obj = this;
        var weatherButtonListener = new Object();
        weatherButtonListener.click = function() {
            /* when button  is clicked
            trigger the Web Service Connector */
            obj.weather_wsc.trigger();
        }
        weather_button.addEventListener("click", weatherButtonListener);

        // add data restrictions
        zipCode_textInput.maxChars = 5;
        zipCode_textInput.restrict = "0-9";

    }
}
```

The application is now set up to call the getWeatherReport method and pass a zip code for the value.

Showing the Weather Report

Essentially, all that is needed to display the results is two Label components for each property of the returned object from the getWeatherReport method: one

Label component to identify (label) the property and the second to display the actual return value for that property. Drag and drop Label components onto weather_form to look like Figure 12-29.

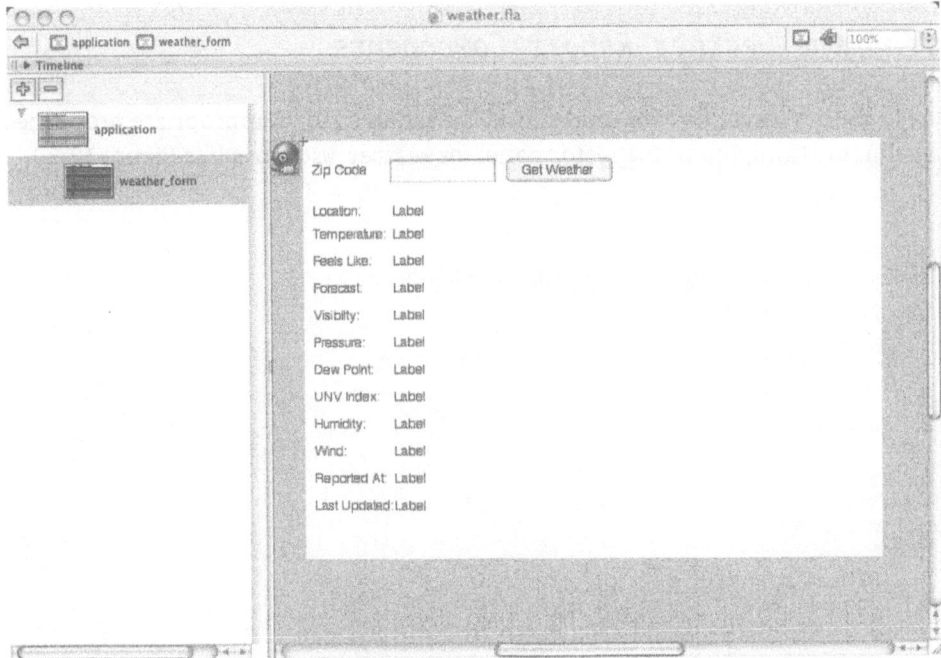

Figure 12-29: weather_form *complete*

Then name the labels on the right-hand side of the descriptive labels appropriately:

```
location_label
temperature_label
feelsLike_label
forecast_label
visibility_label
pressure_label
dewPoint_label
unvIndex_label
humidity_label
wind_label
reportedAt_label
lastUpdated_label
```

> **NOTE** *You may wish to make the labels that hold the return values wider than their default size to show all of the information. You can do this simply by setting the width property in the Properties panel to the desired value.*

Bind the Weather Report Components

As in the get server time example, bind the labels to their appropriate properties so that the Component Inspector panel for weather_wsc looks like Figure 12-30.

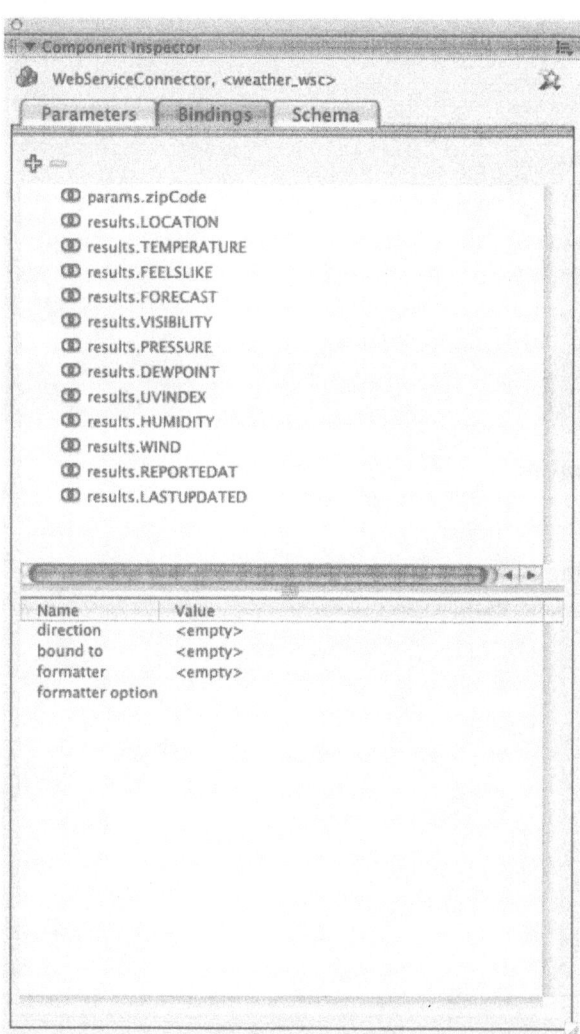

Figure 12-30: All of the components bound to weather_wsc

Testing the Weather Report

Run the weather.fla application. Once the application is running, enter a valid U.S. zip code and click the Get Weather button. Your results should display something similar to Figure 12-31.

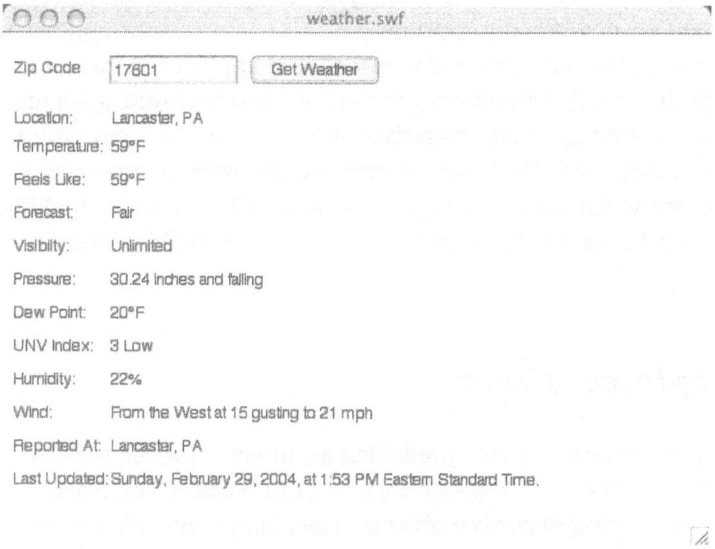

Figure 12-31: Test results from the weather application

The End Result

Many times we have come across an API that that has not been well defined or documented and have had to do the work that should have been done in the first place. Without the flexibility of the Component Inspector, we may not be able to use web services that were not defined correctly. This exercise was intended to show how to take a web service and add additional descriptions of the data to enable Flash to use the Component Inspector panel to bind components to the data. Of the many web services available for use, many were not written by the developers who access them; therefore, having the ability to step outside of the definition and be able to modify that definition is a powerful feature that will prove useful in future web services development.

Web Services Classes

This chapter has shown examples that take advantage of rapid development tools like component binding through the Component Inspector panel, setting properties through the Properties panel, and using graphical components like the WebServiceConnector component to act as the connection between Flash and ColdFusion through web services. These are great and powerful tools that you should take advantage of when appropriate.

There may come a time when you need to put a lot of application logic and flexibility into the application that these components are not accounting for, or maybe you just prefer to code applications rather than use the GUI components and panels. For these cases, Flash Professional provides the web service classes. These classes are located in the mx.services package and will be used for making SOAP calls. We are going to explore the web services classes by building an employee viewer.

Building an Employee Viewer

This example has many similarities to the preceding example. However, here we will retrieve values from a database (CompanyInfo) using ColdFusion, and learn how to pass them to Flash using Recordset objects instead of passing structures. We will bind RecordSets to a ComboBox component. Finally, we will retrieve a single (details) record from a Recordset without having to execute another query.

Passing a Recordset to Flash Using a CFC

We start by writing a CFC that will return a Recordset to a Flash movie.

In Dreamweaver, create a new CFC file in the /cfbook/ch12/ folder and name it employee.cfc. Open the file and add the following code into the document window:

NOTE *The data source* CompanyInfo *used in the following code is set up by default when ColdFusion is installed.*

```
<cfcomponent>
  <cffunction access="remote" name="getEmployees" output="false"➥
    returntype="query">
  <cfset var returnQuery = "" >
    <cfquery name="returnQuery" datasource="CompanyInfo">
    SELECT
      E.*
    FROM
      Employee E
    ORDER BY
      E.LastName ASC,
      E.FirstName ASC
    </cfquery>
    <cfreturn returnQuery >
  </cffunction>
</cfcomponent>
```

This is a simple CFC with only one function returning a single query. The access attribute is set to remote so that you can invoke the function from Flash.

Before opening Flash, create a ColdFusion file called test_employee.cfm in the same directory and add the following code:

```
<cfinvoke component="cfbook.ch12.employee" method="getEmployees"➥
  returnvariable="employee_rs" />

<cfdump var="#employee_rs#">
```

As with the earlier examples, we will test the CFC before trying to consume the web service in Flash. Save this file and press F12 in Dreamweaver to view the results in a web browser. You should see output similar to Figure 12-32.

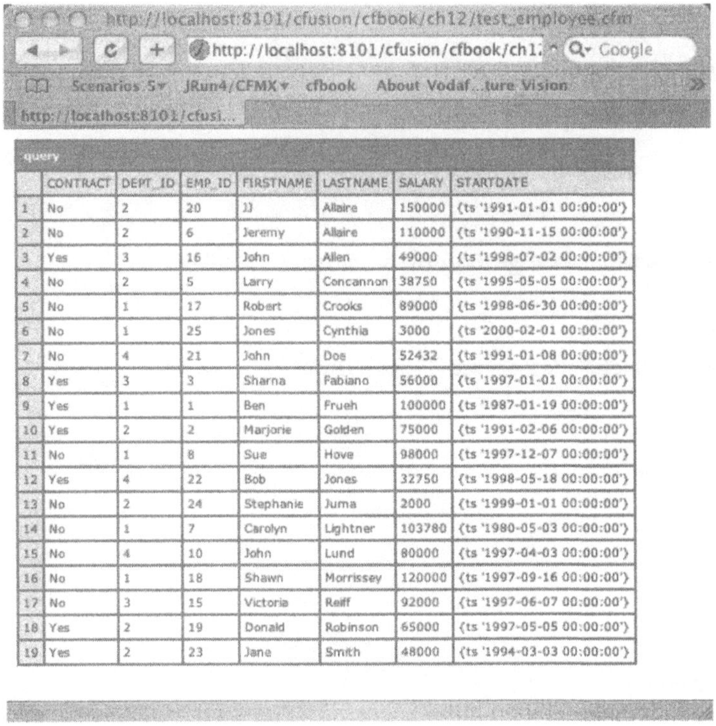

query

	CONTRACT	DEPT_ID	EMP_ID	FIRSTNAME	LASTNAME	SALARY	STARTDATE
1	No	2	20	JJ	Allaire	150000	{ts '1991-01-01 00:00:00'}
2	No	2	6	Jeremy	Allaire	110000	{ts '1990-11-15 00:00:00'}
3	Yes	3	16	John	Allen	49000	{ts '1998-07-02 00:00:00'}
4	No	2	5	Larry	Concannon	38750	{ts '1995-05-05 00:00:00'}
5	No	1	17	Robert	Crooks	89000	{ts '1998-06-30 00:00:00'}
6	No	1	25	Jones	Cynthia	3000	{ts '2000-02-01 00:00:00'}
7	No	4	21	John	Doe	52432	{ts '1991-01-08 00:00:00'}
8	Yes	3	3	Sharna	Fabiano	56000	{ts '1997-01-01 00:00:00'}
9	Yes	1	1	Ben	Frueh	100000	{ts '1987-01-19 00:00:00'}
10	Yes	2	2	Marjorie	Golden	75000	{ts '1991-02-06 00:00:00'}
11	No	1	8	Sue	Hove	98000	{ts '1997-12-07 00:00:00'}
12	Yes	4	22	Bob	Jones	32750	{ts '1998-05-18 00:00:00'}
13	No	2	24	Stephanie	Juma	2000	{ts '1999-01-01 00:00:00'}
14	No	1	7	Carolyn	Lightner	103780	{ts '1980-05-03 00:00:00'}
15	No	4	10	John	Lund	80000	{ts '1997-04-03 00:00:00'}
16	No	1	18	Shawn	Morrissey	120000	{ts '1997-09-16 00:00:00'}
17	No	3	15	Victoria	Reiff	92000	{ts '1997-06-07 00:00:00'}
18	Yes	2	19	Donald	Robinson	65000	{ts '1997-05-05 00:00:00'}
19	Yes	2	23	Jane	Smith	48000	{ts '1994-03-03 00:00:00'}

Figure 12-32: Test results from `test_employee.cfm`

Displaying the Results in Flash

As in our previous examples, you need to create a Flash Form Application. This time save it as `employee.fla`, then rename the `form1` Form to `employee_form`. Next, create a new ActionScript file, name it `EmployeeForm.as`, and save it in the same directory as `employee.fla`. Then in `EmployeeForm.as`, define the class with the following code:

```
import mx.screens.Form;

class EmployeeForm extends Form {
    static var symbolOwner:Object = EmployeeForm;
    static var symbolName:String = "EmployeeForm";
    var className:String = "EmployeeForm";
}
```

As a last step in setting up the `EmployeeForm.as` class file with the `employee_form`, select the `employee_form` in the form tree, then in the Properties panel, replace the Class name property `mx.screen.Form` with `EmployeeForm`. This now associates the `EmployeeForm` class with the `employee_form` in the Flash development environment.

Adding the Web Services Classes

The first operation we need to do is add the web services classes to our `employee.fla` application. Go to Window ➤ Other Panels ➤ Common Libraries ➤ Classes, as Figure 12-33 shows.

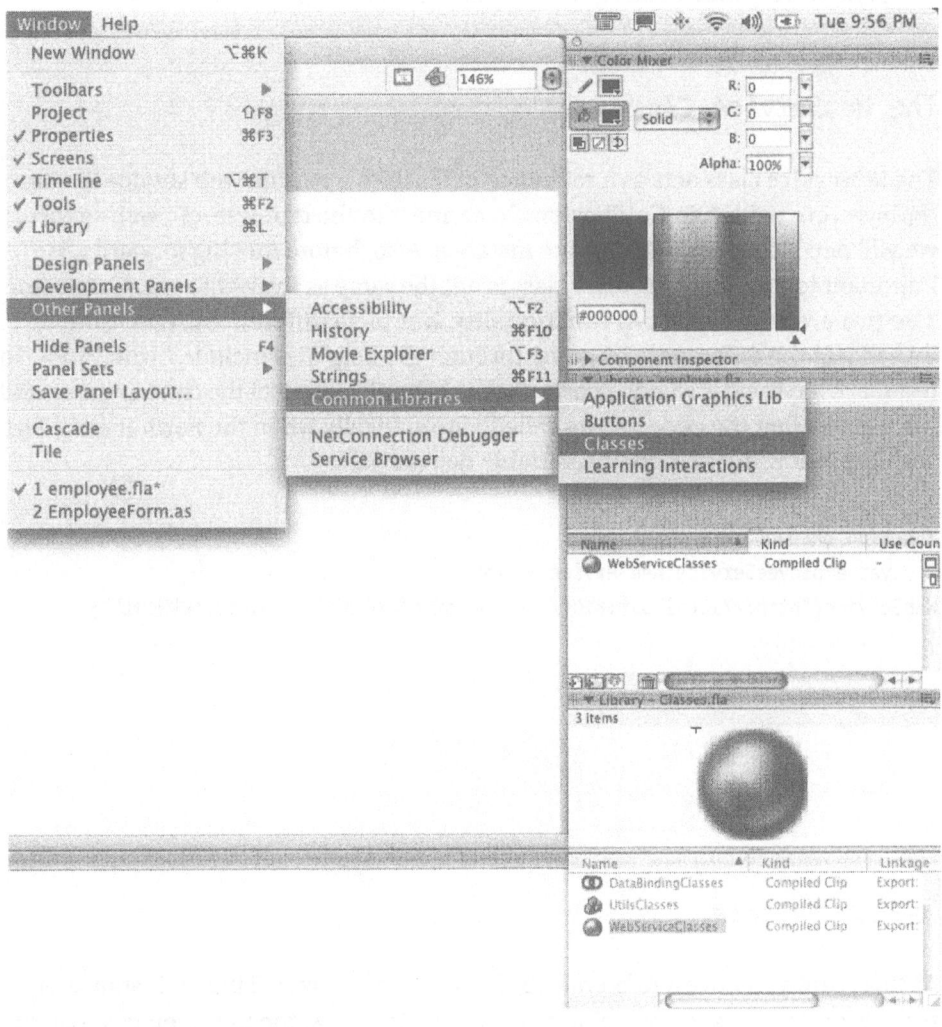

Figure 12-33: Manually adding the web services classes

After selecting the Classes library, a Library panel will open and display three options; the one we want is the WebServicesClasses. Drag this object to the Stage, then feel free to delete it from the Stage. Doing this just adds those classes to the library used by our application; there is no need for the web services classes to remain on the Stage.

Next, the code must be able to reference the classes within the web services classes package, so you will need to add an import statement to your EmployeeForm.as class at the top of the file as you have done in previous examples.

```
import mx.services.*;
```

Now you are able to start making references to web services classes.

The WebService *Class*

The WebService class acts as a reference in Flash to a remote web service like the employee.cfc written in ColdFusion. To connect to the employee.cfc web service, we will need to create a WebService instance. Also, before moving forward it is important to note the WebService class is not the same as the WebServiceConnector. The two are very similar in functionality, but have differences. Take time to investigate the differences by going through the help files included with Flash. To test that everything is working correctly, begin by placing all of the code in the onLoad function so that the code will be called automatically when the Form loads. Start with the following method and variable declaration:

```
function onLoad() {
    var employeeService:WebService = new
WebService("http://localhost:8101/cfusion/cfbook/ch12/employee.cfc?wsdl");
}
```

NOTE   *By declaring the* employeeService *within a function, the scope accessibility to that variable is only within the function itself.*

PendingCall *Class*

At this point you have a reference to the web service by making an instance of the WebService class in a variable employeeService. Now, the next step is to call the getEmployees method of the employee CFC. When this method is called through the WebService object, a PendingCall object is returned. This object will raise one of two events, onResult or onFault. When all goes well and the expected data is returned, the onResult method is raised. When a problem occurs, the onFault method is raised and an error object is returned. In both cases, these events must be handled.

In these next lines of code, you will need to define the method call to getEmployees, assign the PendingCall to a variable, and define the event handlers to handle the result of the method call. Within the onLoad function, enter the following code under the employeeService declaration:

```
var employeeCall:PendingCall = employeeService.getEmployees();
employeeCall.onResult = function(result) {
trace("good call");
}
employeeCall.onFault = function(fault) {
    trace(fault.faultCode + " : " + fault.faultString);
}
```

Testing the Call

Because you wrote all of this code in the onLoad function, you can run employee.fla to test whether your application is working. Run employee.fla and verify that the output window displays "good call."

Populating the Employee Combo Box

Now that you have verified that the getEmployees() method call is working, you will need to display the data in the employee_form. To do this drag a ComboBox component from the user interface components set and drop it on the form. Name the ComboBox employees_combo and set its width equal to 200. Next, go back to the .as file and add some code to get the data into employees_combo.

Add an import statement to reference the ComboBox class:

```
import mx.controls.ComboBox;
```

Next define a reference to employees_combo:

```
// controls
private var employees_combo:ComboBox;
```

You will need a reference to the Employee form to use within the `PendingCall` event handlers. This reference will be used to point to the `employees_combo`. Modify the `onLoad` function to include a reference to the EmployeesForm:

```
function onLoad() {
    var obj = this;
    ...
```

Lastly, change the `onResult` event handler for the `employeeCall` `PendingCall` object:

```
obj.employees_combo.dataProvider = result;
```

Your class should now look like this:

```
import mx.screens.Form;
import mx.services.*;
import mx.controls.ComboBox;

class EmployeeForm extends Form {
    static var symbolOwner:Object = EmployeeForm;
    static var symbolName:String = "EmployeeForm";
    var className:String = "EmployeeForm";

    // controls
    private var employees_combo:ComboBox;

    function onLoad() {
        var obj = this;
        var employeeService:WebService = new
WebService("http://localhost:8101/cfusion/cfbook/ch12/employee.cfc?wsdl");
        var employeeCall:PendingCall = employeeService.getEmployees();
        employeeCall.onResult = function(result) {
            obj.employees_combo.dataProvider = result;          }
        employeeCall.onFault = function(fault) {
            trace(fault.faultCode + " : " + fault.faultString);
        }

    }
}
```

You have not only added a ComboBox component, but also have set its dataProvider property equal to the recordset returned by the getEmployees method call. Flash user interface components that support the dataProvider property will except many formats, in this case a recordset. When this property is set, the ComboBox will automatically populate itself with the values of the recordset. Run the application, and your screen should look similar to Figure 12-34.

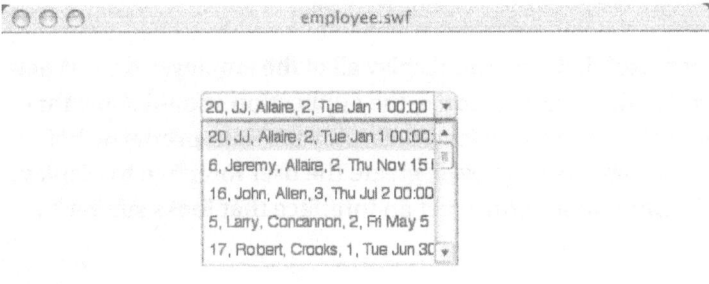

Figure 12-34: Test results showing employees in a ComboBox

Formatting the Result

For this example, you will want to see only the employees' first and last names in the employees_combo ComboBox. To do this, change the structure of the data provider by using the following code:

```
employeeCall.onResult = function(result) {
    var employeesDP = new Array();
    obj.employees_combo.dataProvider = employeesDP;
    for (var i = 0; i < result.length; i++) {
        var record = result[i];
        employeesDP.addItem({
            label: record.LASTNAME + ", " +record.FIRSTNAME,
            data:  record });
    }
}
```

By recreating the data provider, the `employees_combo` will display the name in the correct format, and it will store the rest of the employee information in the data property. This will become useful in the next steps for this example.

Showing All of the Data

To make this application useful, it needs to display all of the employee data. When the user selects a name in the `employee_combo`, the application should show that employee's data that is stored in the selected employee's data property. Before going into the code to display the employee, create the user interface to display the data. Using Label components, construct an interface that looks similar to Figure 12-35.

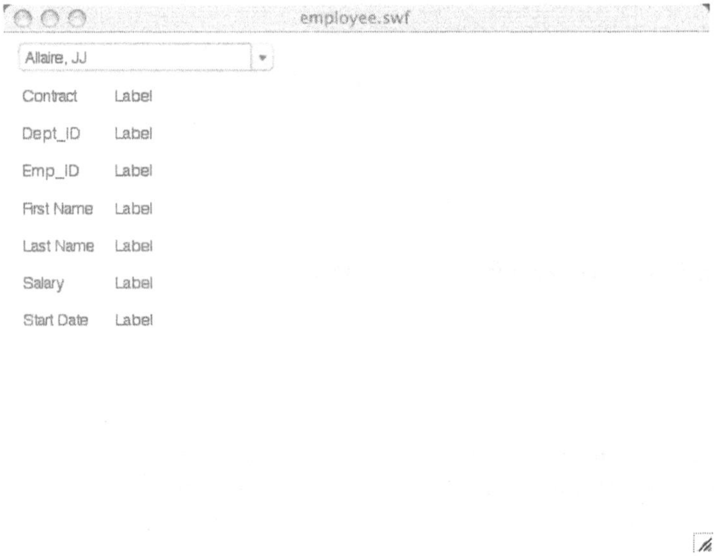

Figure 12-35: Designing the interface to show all of the employee data

Name each Label component in the right-hand component appropriately:

```
contract_label
deptId_label
empId_label
firstName_label
lastName_label
salary_label
startDate_label
```

In the `EmployeeForm` class, add the following import statement to access the Label class:

```
import mx.controls.Label;
```

Now make references to each label in the `EmployeeForm` class:

```
private var contract_label:Label;
private var deptId_label:Label;
private var empId_label:Label;
private var firstName_label:Label;
private var lastName_label:Label;
private var salary_label:Label;
private var startDate_label:Label;
```

The employee_combo needs to have a listener registered to the change event that is fired when an item in the list has been selected. When the change event is called, it will call the function showEmployee, which you will write right after adding these lines of code:

```
var comboListener = new Object();
comboListener.change = function(evnt) {
obj.showEmployee();
}
employees_combo.addEventListener("change", comboListener);
```

The showEmployee method takes the currently selected item, grabs the object from the data property, and uses that object to populate the Label components defined earlier. Create the new function:

```
function showEmployee() {
  var emp = employees_combo.selectedItem.data;
  contract_label.text = emp.CONTRACT;
  deptId_label.text = emp.DEPT_ID;
  empId_label.text = emp.EMP_ID;
  firstName_label.text = emp.FIRSTNAME;
  lastName_label.text = emp.LASTNAME;
  salary_label.text = emp.SALARY;
  startDate_label.text = emp.STARTDATE;
}
```

Now run the application. The output should look similar to Figure 12-36.

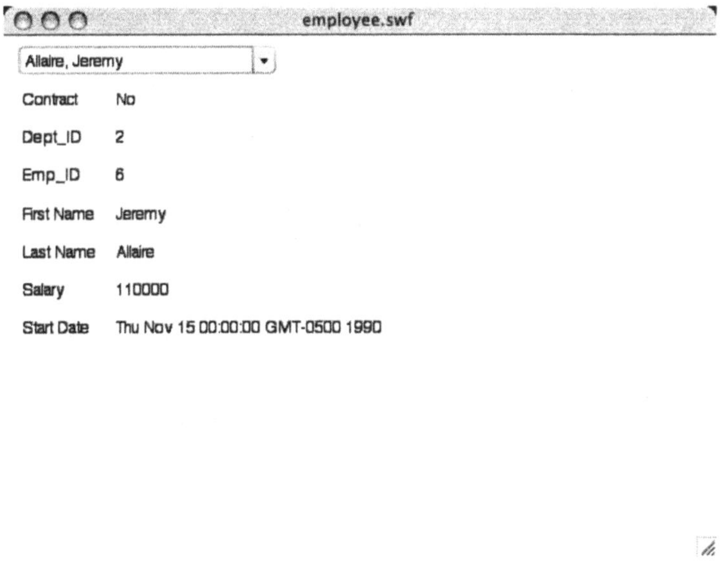

Figure 12-36: Test results from the employee application

Test the application by selecting different employees from the `employee_combo` ComboBox. As each item is selected, the data is pulled from that item's data property and used to populate the screen. All of this was done by coding rather than by using the components and panels discussed in previous examples.

Summary

The combination of Flash, ColdFusion, and web services gives you a powerful solution that is quick enough to develop for small applications and robust enough for highly visible enterprise applications. Flash has gone from a simple web animation tool to a very robust web application development environment that is able to compete with any other client-side technology, including traditional desktop application technologies such as Visual Basic. By gaining a mastery of how ColdFusion can be used to produce web services, you can not only use Flash applications to communicate with those services, but with other technologies as well. It is pretty incredible to think that all of these applications are able to pass such large amounts of very well-defined data among each other with little effort and no requirements other than support for the SOAP protocol. This ability eliminates proprietary technologies and helps push the growth and potential of application development on the web. Also, as you have seen from these examples, the SOAP parser hides all of the details from you the developer so that you can concentrate on using the data rather than parsing it. It really makes you wonder how we ever did without it.

Case Study: A Complete ColdFusion-Based Web Site

IN THIS CASE STUDY, we explore the planning, design, and implementation stages of an entire web site by using code, concepts, and techniques that we've described throughout this book. This web site will incorporate some of the most common web site features:

- An image gallery

- Member and administrator login/logout

- A blog

- Reviews and ratings

We can customize these modules to our specific needs. We will also build a system, comprising the following components, that allows us to control and update the site easily:

- Administration manager

- Member manager

- Content manager

- Banner engine

Running the Example Site

Before we go any further, we will include a very brief summary on how to get the example site up and running quickly—it will aid your learning enormously if you are able to actually view the site as you go through the explanations in this chapter!

First, take the code from the code download and place it so that the root of the site is at C:\CFusionMX\wwwroot\cfbook\casestudy. Now you need to set up a data source to access the casestudy.mdb database contained within the db folder in the site's root. Refer to the "Setting Up a Data Source" section of Chapter 2 for more information on this.

You also need to enable client storage for the database. You do this by logging into your ColdFusion Administrator, clicking the Client Variables link on the left-hand menu, selecting your data source, and hitting the Add button. You can find more on Client scope variables in the "Client Variables" section of Chapter 7.

Now, assuming you've got your ColdFusion server running, when you browse to http://localhost:8500/cfbook/casestudy/index.cfm, you should be presented with the front page of our example site.

Planning a Web Site

Before getting started on a web site, you need to make several considerations. Brainstorming is important at this time. Not only will it probably generate a lot of new ideas for the web site, but you will also gain a clearer idea of all the work that must be done and how you should do it. The next section of this chapter will include some plans and an outline of what will be built for this case study. Here are some general guidelines for planning sites.

First, lay out the goals of the project. Ask yourself the following questions:

- Who is this site for?

- What does this site need to communicate?

- What is the time frame?

We need to figure out who makes up the primary audience that will view our web site. After determining a target audience, we can tailor the site to suit them better. This goes beyond content alone. By figuring out the demographics of this audience, we can design our site to better suit the technology that these users are likely to have on their computers, such as what browser software and Internet connections they may use. Another consideration is what language and locales the user is using.

After we have a solid idea of who our audience is, we can decide what tools are best for building our web site. Make a list of the technologies and tools that you could use to construct the web site, then trim it down until you are left with a suitable set. For example, you may be considering technologies that require plug-ins or high-speed connections—these would be unsuitable for an audience comprising mostly people who have access only to slow dial-up connections.

Constructing a Flowchart

Flowcharts are extremely useful even when we are designing a relatively small web site. Flowcharts allow us to plan a web site visually before taking the time and effort to construct the actual site. Flowcharts vary according the level of detail and depth, and also the software used to create them. There are simple and economical programs like basic versions of SmartDraw (http://www.smartdraw.com), or more expensive, more powerful solutions such as Microsoft Visio 2002 Professional. Visio 2002 even has a new feature that prompts you to enter a URL, after which it returns a flowchart of the web site at that address.

We can create several different kinds of flowchart to depict how a web site works. A typical kind is the org (organizational) chart, which provides a detailed layout of a web site in a branching format, similar to the one shown in Figure 13-1.

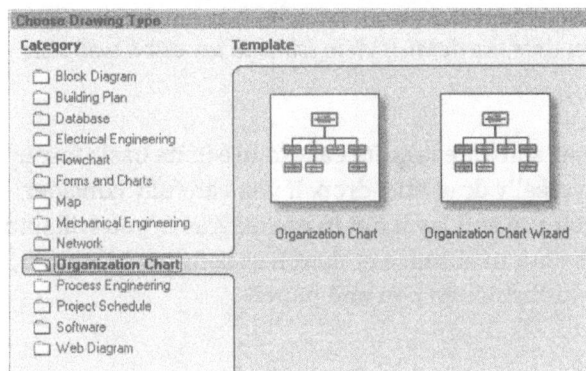

Figure 13-1. Organizational charts are commonly used to lay out web sites.

Visio 2002 also has what is called a conceptual web site chart, with specialized flowcharts specifically for web sites, as shown in Figure 13-2.

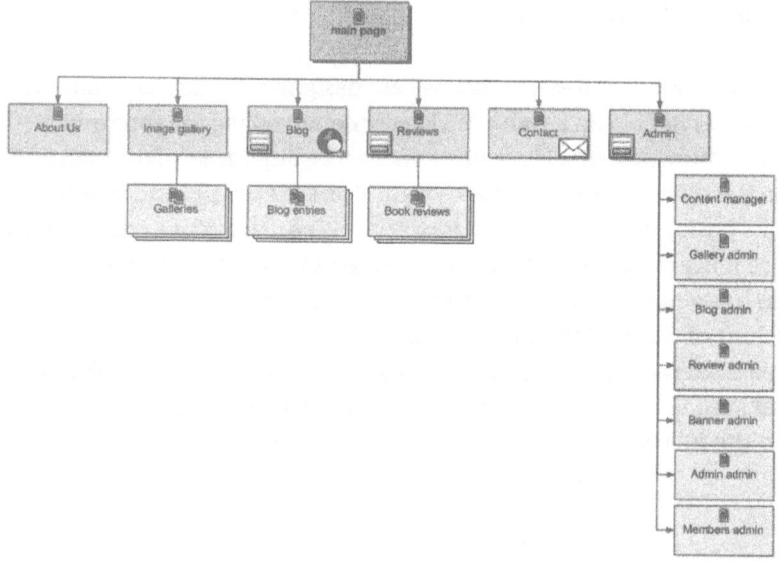

Figure 13-2. This simple diagram uses the default Visio icons to lay out a web site.

Generally speaking, flowchart software is quite easy to use in its basic form. Applications such as Visio are typically drag-and-drop. If you carefully consider all the different areas of your web site and lay it out in the diagrams, you will find it much easier to plan your site's flow. In absence of flowchart software, of course, you can always resort to good old-fashioned pen and paper!

Mock-Ups

Mock-ups, sometimes also referred to as blueprints, prototypes, or storyboards, are drawings on paper or compositions on a computer that are meant to plan the layout of a web site. Even if you are not a graphic designer, or even close to being one, you can easily lay out a web site by using simple sketches. Or, you could use an image editor such as Photoshop to lay out the basic construction of your pages.

Try to create simple mock-ups for each page in the site that will have a different layout, particularly if you don't already have splash screens made by a designer. By using simple shapes, lines, and colors, we can roughly lay out where the images, logos, fields or text blocks will be placed on the page. This helps us construct the functionality, navigation, and flow of our site before actually writing the code that will put it all together.

Planning the Case Study Web Site

For this case study, we have assumed that you have reasonable experience of using Dreamweaver to create web sites. We will not go over mocking up and designing the layout of all the pages—check out the complete code for the site, available in the code download for this book, for inspiration on designing your own pages.

What we will examine and explain is the CFML and logic behind the site's different components. For some components, we have chosen to write our own code rather than use Dreamweaver-generated code. This is because sometimes we need to create more complex queries to retrieve data from the database, or we need perform very specific actions. When you get to a more advanced level, you will find that Dreamweaver cannot provide the answers for everything.

In Figure 13-3 you can see the basic layout for the front-end of the web site, which contains a rotating Flash banner, breadcrumb navigation, a random quote, and a simple content management system.

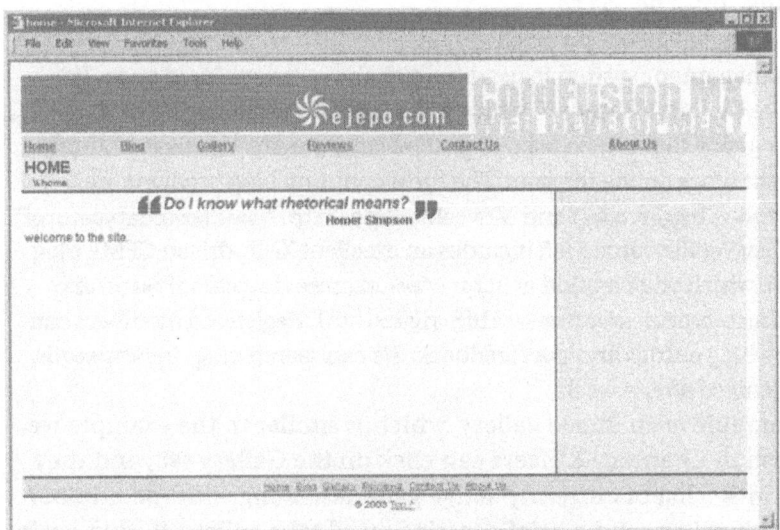

Figure 13-3. The basic layout of the web site's front-end

In the next section, we provide an overview of the site's main elements. The site was mostly built by using the Design View in Dreamweaver to build the general layout, and then it was tweaked by hand to line up all the elements. The rest of the code was created either by hand or by using some of Dreamweaver's prebuilt server behaviors and the Recordset dialog box. Queries were later modified to use the <cfqueryparam> tag to ensure that fields were the correct data type.

At the time of writing, the code for the website consisted of about 110 different files, so this chapter focuses only on snippets from different pages and discuss some of the logic behind the code and why certain decisions were made.

Case Study Overview

Before writing a single line of code, we planned the site and decided which modules would be part of the site. We had a rough idea of how we wanted to present those modules. In a real-world scenario, the requirements analysis phase of development is oftentimes immediately followed by a database design and implementation phase, but in our case the database is already supplied. This case study incorporates several different modules, such as a content manager that allows administrators to change most of the text within the site without having to open any .cfm pages.

Main Sections of the Site

The content management system is used on just about every single page. It is the same one we built in Chapter 7, with only a few minor changes.

The site has a blog that can be used to post news to the site. You have undoubtedly seen different blogs on the Internet. The most common blog products are Blogger (http://www.blogger.com/) and Moveable Type (http://www.movabletype.org/). Macromedia's DevNet Resource Kit 5 includes an excellent XML-driven CFML blog called Blog Man, which you can find at http://www.macromedia.com/software/drk/productinfo/product_overview/volume5/coldfusionmx.html. Registered members can comment on the blog entries and post feedback. We can search blogs for keywords, and blogs are archived after a week.

The next module is an image gallery, which is similar to the example we built using Flash in Chapter 12. Users can click on the Gallery tab, and they are presented with a list of currently active galleries, along with the number of images in each gallery and a brief description of each gallery. Within each gallery, the user can click on different images, view full-sized images along with thumbnails, and also read brief descriptions of each image. The gallery is built using ColdFusion—users will be able to see four thumbnails per page, and a first/previous/next/last navigation system. This is accomplished by using Dreamweaver's Recordset paging server behaviors.

A reviews module allows users to post their comments and a rating (from 1 to 5) on a particular item. In this case study, registered members are allowed to review and rate books that have been entered into the site by an administrator. This is just a basic model, so other users are not allowed to create categories for items to review, or to add new items; they are allowed only to review items existing on the site. This example could easily be extended to accommodate items other than books to review.

We also will build functionality into this part of the site to calculate a particular book's average rating. We do this by adding all the ratings, calculating the average, and rounding to the closest half number. This way, all the average ratings will be nice easily manageable numbers, and we could easily create images for 1.0, 1.5, 2.0, 2.5, etc., and show the average score with images instead of just text. Members must be logged in before they can post reviews to the site.

> **TIP** *By forcing people to log in, we can make sure that a member reviews a certain item only once. However, it won't prevent that user from re-registering with the site under a different username and posting another review.*

Another benefit of forcing members to log in before adding content is that we always know who is posting what. So, if we want to allow users to be able to modify their comments or reviews at a later date, we can include edit buttons beside the entries (we can code it so that, for any logged in user, edit buttons are shown only against the items they created).

The final major component for this site is the contact/feedback page. This form allows visitors to type in comments and send them to the site administrator by using a simple form and <cfmail>. Although it is a basic component to add, it makes it very easy for users to report errors and send comments and suggestions. Often it is this kind of feedback that causes web sites to improve.

Minor Parts of the Site

Several minor components will be built for the site, too.

A quote of the day (qotd) is included on the home page and provides a more dynamic feel to the site.

Breadcrumb navigation allows users to identify where they are within the web site easily. A breadcrumb trail is like a directory path through the web site. Users always have a link back to the home page, as well as to any page between the home page and their current location.

A dynamic right-hand column for additional content lets us easily separate content and provides a consistent feel to the site. In the blog module, the right-hand column is used to hold a calendar and some additional navigational links for intuitive blog navigation, as shown in Figure 13-4.

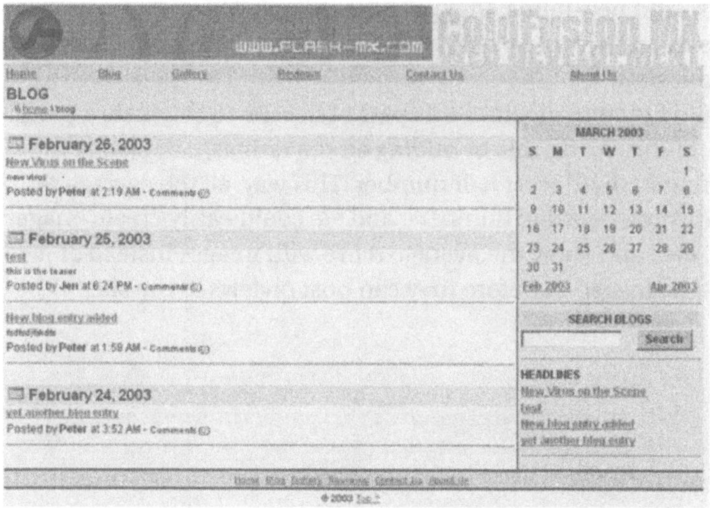

Figure 13-4. On the blog page, the dynamic right-hand column holds a calendar.

Underneath the calendar, a series of anchored hyperlinks that users can click on allows them to move straight to the desired blog entry within the current document. The blog section also has a small keyword search form in the right-hand column, where users can type a word or phrase they want to find in blog titles, teasers, and descriptions. Other sections of the site use the side column for login forms, additional comments, and notes.

We'll also include a rotating banner engine. By designing the banner engine around Flash, we can easily refresh banners on the page without having to reload the entire document. A table in the database for banners includes a column called BannerInterval, which determines how many seconds a banner displays before a new banner is requested. Also, because this banner engine is Flash-based, it has the ability to load static banners (JPEG images) or animated banners (created in Flash). Remember that Flash cannot load GIF images on the fly. In addition, if the Flash banners are interactive (such as mini-games with buttons and clickable regions), they may not work properly, because whenever the banner is clicked, we direct the user to a new URL.

Each of the modules and components we've mentioned so far was designed and planned long before Dreamweaver was even opened. The planning stage is the most important part of any project. If a site is well planned, we can build it more quickly because we have a target in mind. If we rush the planning stage and don't map out the components and business rules properly, we will often have to revisit many pages as we change functionality or add/remove features. A site is rarely ever built completely to specification. Changes are inevitable, but a good plan significantly reduces the amount of rewriting necessary.

Planning and Implementation: The Next Step

The next step in the planning phase is to chart out how we want our site to work and where each module will fit within the site and on each page. This is important because it will help us slice up tables and images to fit within our site's layout. At this stage, it is likely that you'll uncover some of the places where your design limits the ability of your site. For example, you could realize that the right-hand column is too narrow, so it is not able to hold a calendar or search form.

Once the site's layout has been drafted, it is easy to see which modules are consistent throughout the site and how everything will fit together. The next step after this is to code the site's framework, lay out the inner tables, and figure out how the content fits together in a basic HTML mockup. Then we will discuss how we approached this process when we originally designed the site.

After we were satisfied with the look and feel of the site, we converted the basic framework into a header and footer file that would be included on each page. This helped keep the sizing and design consistent throughout the entire site.

Building separate headers and footers allows us to vastly simplify the site and quickly add new pages, instead of having to duplicate the contents of the header.cfm and footer.cfm on each page. We are able to reduce the code down to about eight lines for a basic page by calling the header and footer as custom tags. The entire code for the About Us page is as follows:

```
<cfscript>
  Variables.breadCrumbs = "home|#Request.WebRoot#home/;about us";
  Variables.header = "about us";
</cfscript>
<cfmodule template="#Request.CFRoot#header.cfm" ➥
  breadCrumbs="#Variables.breadCrumbs#" header="#Variables.header#">
  <table width="100%" border="0" cellpadding="1" cellspacing="0">
  <tr>
    <td class="text"><cfoutput>#GetPageContent("aboutus_intro")#</cfoutput></td>
  </tr>
  </table>
<cfmodule template="#Request.CFRoot#footer.cfm" ➥
  rightColumn="#Request.CFRoot#aboutus/address.cfm">
```

The first few lines of code are responsible for setting variables that will be passed into the header custom tag. The Variables.breadCrumbs variable is a string that will be looped over and turned into the breadcrumb trail that appears below the main navigation and header. The second variable, Variables.header, is used for both the title of the window and the text that appears above the breadcrumb trail.

Next we call the header custom tag by using the <cfmodule> tag and pass in the two variables that we created earlier. The header and footer were turned into custom tags so that it would be easier to pass variables into them, plus it keeps all the code nicely separated and reduces the chance of having variables within our header conflict with variables in our page.

The nested table between the header and footer is the content that will appear in the main content area of the site. This table can be as simple or complex as we want, and it can be different on each page depending on what we want to display. In the preceding code, we are calling a function declared in the Application.cfm file (see later). The function calls the content management system and embeds text into the page.

Finally, we call the footer custom tag by using <cfmodule> and include the bottom navigation links and the right content column. Notice that we pass a variable called rightColumn to the footer custom tag, which points to a file within the site. Our custom tag will include any file (or files) listed here and embed them in the right-hand column. In this example, the footer will <cfinclude> a file called address.cfm from the aboutus folder and display a mailing address.

The styles in the site are defined by using a Cascading Style Sheet (CSS) page, styles.css, found in the root of the site. So, if we want to change the site's layout and style in the future, we just need to modify the styles in the CSS file and tweak the header and footer—simple!

Getting Started

At the time of writing, the case study consisted of roughly 95 .cfm pages and 15 .cfc files. We don't have the space in this chapter to go over each page and step through the code, but we will try to look at the more integral parts of the code and explain them.

Application.cfm

Because the Application.cfm page is executed each time a page is requested, it is the natural choice for any of our site-wide settings. Within the Application.cfm file (in the root of the site) you will see the following block of code at the top:

```
<cfscript>
  Request.WebRoot = "/";
  Request.CFRoot = "/casestudy/";
  Request.CFCRoot = "casestudy.";
  Request.CFPath = "C:\Inetpub\sites\cfbook.coldfusion-mx.com\";
  Request.AdminRoot = Request.WebRoot & "admin/";
  Request.AdminCFRoot = Request.CFRoot & "admin/";
  Request.DSN = "cfbook_casestudy";
</cfscript>
```

These variables are all stored in the Request scope, which means that they are available to any page whether it is a CFC, CFM, or a custom tag. Not all of these variables will match every web site configuration exactly, and therefore many of these variables will differ depending on how your server is set up.

#Request.WebRoot# holds the base URL for our web site. The URL of our case study is http://localhost:8500/cfbook/casestudy/, but we've removed the domain so that it is slightly shorter and more readable. Using this variable allows us to reference images in the images folder without having to use relative paths such as ../../images/logo.gif. No matter where we are within the site, we have an absolute URL to the root folder in the web site, so even if we move a page to a different folder, the paths shouldn't need to be changed.

#Request.CFRoot# is similar to the WebRoot, except that this is the path that we will use with ColdFusion when we use the <cfinclude> and <cfmodule> tags we saw previously. We'll discuss how to set up ColdFusion mappings later in this section.

The next variable we use is #Request.CFCRoot#, which is similar to #Request.CFRoot#, except that it is used with ColdFusion components. The #Request.AdminRoot# variable is the URL to the administration area of this site. We created a shortcut to this URL in case we want to move the admin site to a different URL later. For example, this way we don't have to update all the links within our admin site when we move it from /cfbook/casestudy/admin/ to http://admin.mysite.com/. The #Request.AdminCFRoot# variable is used with the <cfmodule> tag to call the header and footer custom tags.

#Request.CFPath# is used when we want to upload files by using the <cffile> tag and need to know the root directory of our application.

The final variable in this section is #Request.DSN#, which is the name of the data source that we're using for this site. Because you have so many pages within this site, it is easier to create a single variable that holds the name of the data source name instead of declaring it at the start of *every* page. This allows us to duplicate this site easily, copy the database, change variables, and have an entirely new site in minutes!

The next part of the Application.cfm sets up the application using the <cfapplication> tag and another new tag that we haven't discussed yet, <cfsetting>:

```
<cfapplication name="casestudy" sessionmanagement="Yes"➡
   sessiontimeout="#CreateTimeSpan(0,0,15,0)#" clientmanagement="Yes"➡
   clientstorage="#Request.DSN#">
<cfsetting showdebugoutput="No">
```

In this code, we give the application a name and enable both client and session management. We use Session variables for the front-end, and Client variables for the administration part of the site. The next tag, <cfsetting>, is used to control how pages are processed. This tag has a few options, as shown in the following list:

- enablecfoutputonly: Suppresses any output generated by ColdFusion that is not explicitly within a `<cfoutput>` tag. This helps to eliminate unneeded white space.

- requesttimeout: Tells ColdFusion how long it should wait for this page to complete before considering it an unresponsive thread and generating an error. Previous versions of ColdFusion used a URL variable of the same name to perform this function.

- showdebugoutput: Controls whether or not ColdFusion should display debug output at the bottom of the current page.

In this application, we only use the last option, showdebugoutput, and explicitly set it to No. This way, even if debugging has been enabled in the ColdFusion Administrator and the current user's IP address is set to receive debug info, all debugging info will be suppressed. Sometimes the debugging info at the bottom of the page affects the page layout, so it is difficult to work out if the page looks how we want it to. Turning off all debugging info by using this tag can simplify the process greatly.

Most of the remaining code within the Application.cfm page deals with the content management system that we looked at in previous chapters. Two new functions at the bottom of this page are used heavily throughout the site:

```
<cfset Request.crlf = Chr(13) & Chr(10) >
<cffunction name="ParaFormat" returntype="string" output="false">
  <cfargument name="Str" required="Yes" type="string">
  <cfset Var returnString = Replace( Arguments.Str, Request.crlf, "<br>", "ALL" ) >
  <cfreturn Trim( returnString ) >
</cffunction>
<cffunction name="getPageContent" returntype="string" output="false">
  <cfargument name="PageName" required="true" type="string">
  <cfset Var returnString = "" >
  <cfif StructKeyExists( Request.ContentManager, Arguments.PageName ) >
    <cfset returnString = Replace( Request.ContentManager[ Arguments.PageName ],
      Request.crlf, "<br>", "ALL" ) >
  </cfif>
  <cfreturn Trim( returnString ) >
</cffunction>
```

The first function, #ParaFormat()#, is a UDF used to display text with line breaks in it. We create our own UDF instead of using the built-in #ParagraphFormat()# function, because #ParagraphFormat()# embeds `<p>` tags, which could potentially interfere with styles in the stylesheet. Like the #ParagraphFormat()# function, the UDF takes in a single parameter, the string to format, and the function replaces any carriage returns/line feeds with the <br /> tag. It also trims any leading and trailing white space from the string and returns the value back to the page.

We already used the second function, #getPageContent()#, in the code for the About Us page. This function is responsible for retrieving and formatting content from the content management system and returning it to our page. Using this function to grab the content, we can put all the complex code in one location. Now we only have to call a single function from any page within the site to retrieve content instead of having to duplicate the logic on a large number of pages.

Creating a Mapping in ColdFusion

ColdFusion mappings are used by the <cfinclude> and <cfmodule> tags, and you can use them to reference files not within the web server's Web-root. To create a ColdFusion mapping, open a web browser, go to the ColdFusion Administration site (http://localhost:8500/CFIDE/administrator/), and log in. Click on the Mappings link under the SERVER SETTINGS heading.

Notice that one active ColdFusion mapping already exists, pointing to ColdFusion's Web-root directory. The reason we are already able to use the mapping of /cfbook/casestudy/ is that ColdFusion automatically uses this existing mapping by default.

To create a new mapping that points directly to the casestudy directory, we first add the name of the mapping in the Logical Path text field—give it the name of /casestudy. Next, click on the Browse Server button and navigate to the following directory: C:\CFusionMX\wwwroot\cfbook\casestudy. Click the Apply button to return to the previous page. Your Add / Edit ColdFusion Mappings section will now look like Figure 13-5.

Once finished, click the Update Mapping button to create the mapping. To use this new mapping instead of the one currently defined in the Application.cfm file, change

Figure 13-5. Adding/editing ColdFusion mappings

```
Request.CFRoot = "/cfbook/casestudy/";
```

to

```
Request.CFRoot = "/casestudy/";
```

That's it—ColdFusion will now use the new mapping instead of the default mapping that already existed in the Administrator.

> **NOTE** *This mapping is used for only ColdFusion. It does not modify the URL path used to access your site from a web browser.*

You can now go back to the site, and the header and footer should still be included using the new mapping.

Building Breadcrumb Navigation

We have simple breadcrumb trails on almost every page on the front-end to help users navigate through the site. You saw part of the code earlier in this chapter when we looked at the About Us page. We create the breadcrumb value within the requested page and pass the value into our header.

```
<cfscript>
  Variables.breadCrumbs = "home|#Request.WebRoot#home/;about us";
  Variables.header = "about us";
</cfscript>
<cfmodule template="#Request.CFRoot#header.cfm"➥
  breadCrumbs="#Variables.breadCrumbs#" header="#Variables.header#">
```

The `#Variables.breadCrumbs#` variable is a list that we parse out within the header and turn into separate links and text. The preceding code splits up links using the pipe character (|) and semicolon (;), like a list within a list. While looping over the list in the header, we will parse out the values by using both the pipe and semicolon as delimiters and determine which breadcrumbs should be hyperlinked and which should remain text.

The following code is from the `header.cfm` file. It parses out the breadcrumb list and turns it into a new variable, which is displayed on the screen later within the header:

```
<cfset Variables.breadCrumbs = "\">
<cfloop list="#Attributes.breadCrumbs#" index="thisCrumb" delimiters=";">
  <cfif ListLen( thisCrumb, "|") EQ 2>
    <cfset Variables.breadCrumbs = Variables.breadCrumbs & '\ <a href="' &➥
      ListLast(thisCrumb, "|") & '" class="smalllink">' &➥
      ListFirst(thisCrumb, "|") & '</a> '>
  <cfelse>
```

```
    <cfset Variables.breadCrumbs = Variables.breadCrumbs & '\ ' &➡
      ListFirst(thisCrumb, "|") & ' '>
  </cfif>
</cfloop>
```

The first line of code sets the initial value for the #Variables.breadCrumbs# variable to a single backslash. Next, we loop through the #Attributes.breadCrumbs# variable within the header by using the semicolon as a delimiter. The first time through the loop, the value of #thisCrumb# will be home|#Request.WebRoot#home/, and the second time through the loop, its value will be about us. Within the loop, we are checking to see how many items in the list use the #ListLen()# function using the pipe as a delimiter. If two items are within the list, the <cfif> code block executes, and we append a hyperlinked breadcrumb onto the existing value of #Variables.breadCrumbs#. However, if something other than two items is in the list, we simply display the first item within the #thisCrumb# list (again, using the pipe character as the delimiter), unhyperlinked.

In the About Me page example, there are two items in the #thisCrumb# list the first time through the loop. The first item in the #thisCrumb# list is home and the second item is #Request.WebRoot#home/, which we use as the URL to redirect users to when they click on the hyperlink. The text for the hyperlink is taken from the first item in the list, which was home. The second time through the loop, the value of #thisCrumb# is about us, so the <cfelse> block is executed and we simply append this string onto the end of the #Variables.breadCrumbs# variable.

That is all there is to creating breadcrumb navigation—it is just a series of nested loops. Whenever two items are present, we create a hyperlink; otherwise, we just display text. This is used throughout the site, and later in the "Building the Blog" and "Building the Review Section" sections, we append the blog name to the end of the breadcrumb trail. We output the breadcrumb navigation later on in the header.cfm page by simply outputting the #Variables.breadcrumbs# variable within the document.

The source code for this part of the web site can be found within the header.cfm page.

Creating the Dynamic Right-Hand Column

In the About Us page earlier in this chapter we defined which pages to include within the right-hand column by adding the rightColumn attribute to the call made to the footer.cfm custom tag. Using the following code, we were able to include the address.cfm page into the right-hand side of the layout:

```
<cfmodule template="#Request.CFRoot#footer.cfm"➡
  rightColumn="#Request.CFRoot#aboutus/address.cfm">
```

The code within the footer.cfm page that actually handles including these files is shown here:

```
<cfif IsDefined("Attributes.rightColumn")>
  <cfloop list="#Attributes.rightColumn#" index="thisTemplate" delimiters=";">
    <cftry>
      <cfinclude template="#thisTemplate#">
      <cfcatch type="missinginclude" />
    </cftry>
  </cfloop>
<cfelse>
   
</cfif>
```

First we check to see if the #Attributes.rightColumn# variable is defined. If the variable isn't defined, we simply put a space into the <td> so that the cell isn't empty. We could also write code that would hide the right-hand column altogether if no content is entered into the column. However, doing so may lead to an inconsistent look throughout the site if the right column disappears on every other page. If the #Attributes.rightColumn# is defined, then we loop over the list and use the semicolon (;) as a delimiter. This allows us to include multiple files by looping through the list and attaching each file in the same order they were specified. Also notice that we've wrapped the <cfinclude> tag within a try/catch block so that if the file is not found, we can trap the error and handle it gracefully.

We can modify this code and use the <cfparam> tag to set a default value if this variable isn't already present. If we set the default value to an empty string and if no value was defined previously, the right-hand column would be blank. Instead, we want to set a default page to display in the right-hand column if no previous value was defined, so we simply add the following code to the top of the footer.cfm:

```
<cfparam name="Attributes.rightColumn"
default="#Request.WebRoot#blog/calendar.cfm">
```

Now if a value for #rightColumn# is not passed to the page, we display a mini-calendar that links to the blog instead. We could even write other modules to use within the right-hand column, such as polls, Flash image galleries, featured books, mini-banners, or login forms. We could even incorporate the Flash weather service we built in Chapter 12 into the right-hand column so members can receive a weather forecast for their area.

The source code for this part of the web site can be found within the footer.cfm page.

Building the Main Areas of the Site

The following sections walk you through some of the most important code sections of the front-end and the administration web site.

Building the Blog

Thousands of blogs on the Web concern almost any subject you can imagine, technical or nontechnical. Blogs are a way to share news within communities and let people stay current with issues that interest them. Our case study includes a basic blog system allowing us to post news to be displayed on the front-end of the site and lets users page through the archive by using either the search feature or the calendar. Registered members can post comments on a blog and even edit their posts later.

The main content area shows the blogs for a single week (starting on Sunday and going until the following Saturday). Blogs are sorted in descending order by date posted. This way, the most current blog entries always appear at the top of the page so users don't have to scroll to see if new content has been posted. The blog page contains three small modules in the right-hand column:

- A blog calendar that hyperlinks days where blog entries were posted

- A blog search form that lets users search by a keyword that can appear within the title, teaser, or details of the blog

- Headlines for the blogs that appear within the current page

These headlines are all internal links that allow users to click on a headline within the right-hand column and immediately jump to that posting. Therefore, users who are interested is a single blog entry don't have to scroll to hunt for it, and can instead jump straight to it. We could also create a new module for the right-hand column that shows the ten most recent blog entries, or even the five blog entries with the most comments posted by users. Another option for extending this module would be to allow members to decide how many days' worth of blogs they want to display at once rather than seeing only whatever value is hard-coded into the page.

When a user searches blogs for a keyword, the results are displayed in the main content area, and the blog title is hyperlinked to the blog details page, where users can read the entire blog entry (up to 4,000 characters long) and view other users' comments on the entry.

Notice that we've also added the recordset navigation code that Dreamweaver automatically generates. We have also included the Recordset navigation bar, so we can limit the search results to ten results per page. This way, if the search returns a large result set, the user will not have to deal with one enormous page. This nod to user-friendliness will also benefit users who are still on dial-up or otherwise slow connections and don't appreciate the slowdowns caused by returning a huge amount of data to their browsers all at once. By returning ten records at a time, we are able to keep the total number of bytes returned to the user relatively low.

When you click on the title for any of these blogs, you're taken to a details page where we display the entire text of the blog and comments that have been posted by site members. There is also a section in the Administration web site where site administrators can log in and delete any comments posted by other users, or even select a series of comments to all delete at once. Once an administrator has deleted a member's message, that member is no longer able to modify the message, and other users will see a red "Comment Deleted" message. A red message indicates that users must log in to the site before they can post new comments, and a login form is handily provided in the right-hand column. After users log in, the red text prompting them to log in is replaced by a large text area where they can enter their comments.

The source files for this part of the web site can be found within the blog folder.

Building the ColdFusion Gallery

The gallery tab in this web site is where users can view any of the recent photos we've uploaded. We can have multiple galleries. Users will be able to read the general gallery content management text at the top of the page. They can read brief descriptions of what images are in each gallery, and they can see how many images are within a given gallery so they will know if any new ones have been added since their last visit.

When users click on a gallery's title, they are taken to the viewGallery.cfm page, where they can see the gallery description at the top, the thumbnails at the left of the page, and the large image in the center. Notice that we show only four images per page. We use the Recordset Navigation Bar and Recordset Navigation Status behaviors from Dreamweaver to allow users to page through the images in the gallery, as shown in Figure 13-6.

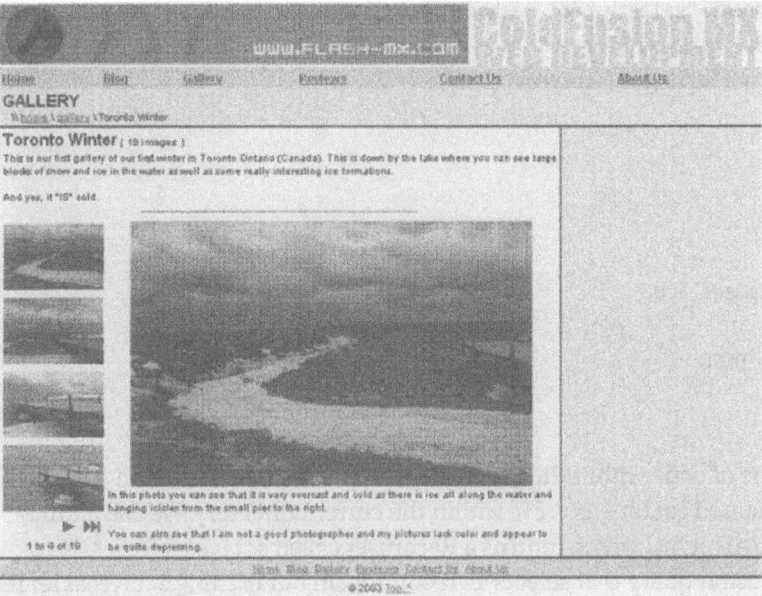

Figure 13-6. Inside an image gallery

The left-hand side of the page has the thumbnails and navigation for the gallery. When users press a thumbnail, the page is refreshed, and the large image and descriptive text below change. We could extend this module by adding the comment code from the blog module so members can post feedback on each image or even rate each one. We could then show the highest-rated thumbnail from each gallery next to each gallery's description on the gallery index page, or have featured galleries and images within the site's right-hand column. We could also use the meta refresh tag to keep loading the next image within the gallery, stopping once the current image number is the same as the number of images within the Recordset. Users could then sit back and have the gallery cycle through all the images without making the effort of clicking constantly.

When building a gallery module, we need to be careful that we don't show empty galleries. The Galleries table in the database has a GalleryActive column, which controls whether the gallery is shown on the front-end or not (only active galleries are displayed to users). We can either enforce a rule that says a gallery cannot be active if there isn't at least one image within the gallery, or else write a query to not display empty galleries.

The case study code included for this chapter filters out empty galleries by using ColdFusion's QueryOfQueries feature to filter out any records in the Recordset with zero images. The code for filtering empty galleries is as follows:

```
<cfinvoke component="gallery_cfc" method="getGalleries"➥
  returnvariable="activeGalleries" />
<cfquery name="getGalleries" dbtype="query">
  SELECT
    *
  FROM
    activeGalleries
  WHERE
    NumGalleryImages > 0
  ORDER BY
    GalleryDate DESC
</cfquery>
```

The first line of code within the preceding snippet invokes a method within a component named gallery_cfc.cfc within the current directory. We call a function named getGalleries, which returns a Recordset called activeGalleries. Next we call a ColdFusion query that selects all records from our existing activeGalleries query and returns only records in which the NumGalleryImages column has a value greater than zero. In the preceding code, note that when performing a query on an existing query, we don't need to define the data source attribute; instead, we set the dbtype attribute to query and then use an existing query name with the FROM keyword instead of a table name. We also could have modified the getGalleries() function to return active or inactive galleries based on a supplied argument.

The source files for this part of the web site can be found within the gallery folder.

Building the Review Section

The next major module we built was the review section. The review section allows users to review products that have already been added to the site. For the case study, we built a module for book reviews, but the code is portable enough that you should be able to add other categories without having to do much coding. Because books are a somewhat specific topic, we created tables within the database containing columns exclusive to books (such as publisher and ISBN). If you wanted to review car stereos, you could create new tables with suitable columns such as manufacturer names, wattage, and so on.

The main page of the review section is a listing of the different areas users can review. Currently, only one category exists: books. However, if we wanted to add different categories, we could add new links and descriptions to this page.

If you click on the Books link, you are taken to the book review section of the site. When you click on the book category, you are taken to a list of books that an administrator has already added to the site.

The links are presented in a simple list and also display the book's publisher Clicking on the book's title brings up the book review details page, which lists average ratings, publisher name and URL, ISBN, and the publication date, as shown in Figure 3-7.

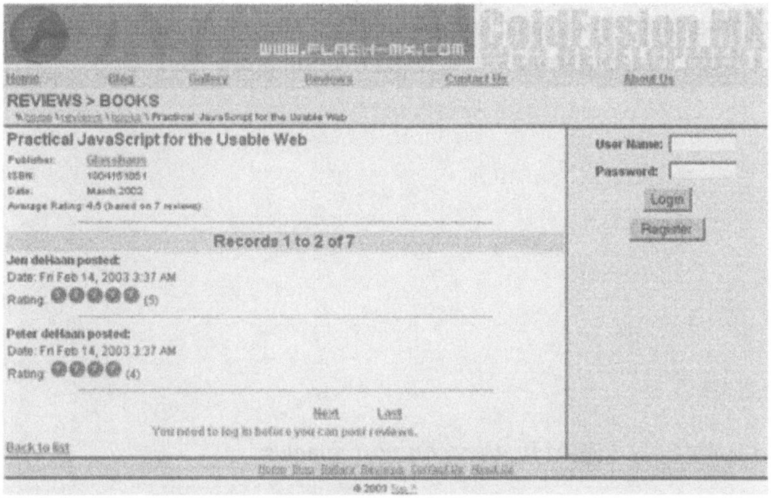

Figure 13-7. The book details page

Members must be logged in before they can post a review for this book, and then they are allowed to post only one. This way, we can be sure that members are allowed to review a book only once and cannot skew the overall rating. We are again using Dreamweaver's Recordset Navigation Bar and Recordset Navigation Status behaviors to limit the number of reviews displayed on the page at one time. Although it isn't readily apparent in Figure 13-7, the ratings are also rounded to the closest half number, like on Amazon.com.

Figure 13-7 also demonstrates how we're using the breadcrumb navigation in this site. Notice how the user is able to go back to the home page, review main page, and book review page all in a single click. Users can also see the book name in the breadcrumb trail. This name hasn't been hyperlinked, because it is the current page. The breadcrumb code for this page is as follows:

```
<cfscript>
  Variables.breadCrumbs =
  "home|#Request.WebRoot#home/;
  reviews|#Request.WebRoot#reviews/;
  books|#Request.WebRoot#reviews/books/;
  #getBookByBookID.BookTitle#";
</cfscript>
```

You can see that we are using the semicolon as a delimiter (just like in our previous examples) and that we have four list items for this page, three of which are linked. Our first link is home, followed by reviews and books, and finally we list the book title that the user is viewing currently.

Once users log in to the web site, the notice saying that they must log in before being able to post a review disappears. They are then presented with a large text area in which they can add comments, and a drop-down menu of ratings to choose from, ranging from 1 to 5, as shown in Figure 13-8.

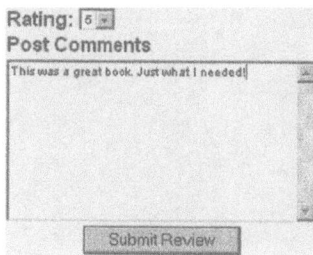

Figure 13-8. After users have logged in, they can post reviews.

The source files for this part of the web site can be found within the reviews and reviews/books folders.

Creating the Feedback Form

The feedback form is a simple three-field form in which users can send comments, errata, or any other feedback to the webmaster. Once users has filled in their comments, they press the Send Comments button at the bottom of the page, as shown in Figure 13-9. The comments will be sent using the <cfmail> tag, and users will be redirected to the Contact Us page and shown a little thank-you message to confirm that their comments were sent successfully.

The text below the confirmation message is taken from the content management system and can be changed to add a more user-friendly message that thanks users for visiting the site and providing some feedback.

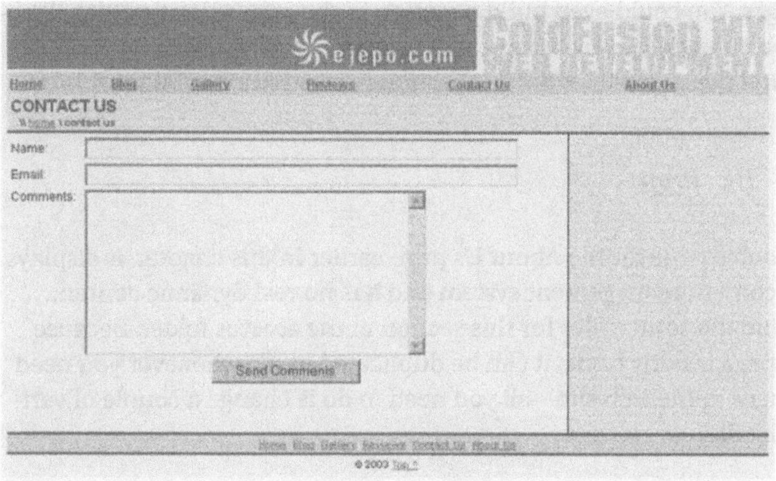

Figure 13-9. The Contact Us feedback form

The code for sending the feedback using the `<cfmail>` tag is as follows:

```
<cfmail from="admin@yoursite.com" to="admin@yoursite.com" ➥
  subject="feedback from the cfbook site.">
#Form.Name# (#Form.Email#) says:

#Form.Comments#
-----------------------------------------------------------------
IP: #CGI.REMOTE_ADDR#
</cfmail>
<cflocation url="index.cfm?success=1">
```

Depending on how your particular server is configured, you may need to provide more attributes than those shown in the preceding `<cfmail>` tag. This code assumes that you've defined a mail server within the ColdFusion Administrator; if this is not the case, you will have to define the outgoing mail server within the `<cfmail>` tag itself. You can see in this code that the e-mail displays the user's name, e-mail address, and comments supplied in the Contact Us form. It also adds the IP address of the user's computer at the very bottom of the e-mail by using the `#CGI.REMOTE_ADDR#` variable.

After the `<cfmail>` tag has sent the outgoing mail to the Spool folder (where it will be queued and sent within a few seconds), ColdFusion redirects the user back to the `index.cfm` page and passes a variable that is used in the `index.cfm` page to determine whether we should display the thank-you message. Instead of using the `<cfmail>` tag, you could modify this code to store all messages sent to the webmaster in a database and build a mini "call center" to store and search e-mail messages. You could even build a section in the administration site allowing you to reply to messages by using a web interface.

You can find the source files for this section in the contactus folder.

The About Us Page

You saw the source code for the About Us page earlier in this chapter. It displays text from the content management system and has no real dynamic content.

You can find the source files for this section in the aboutus folder. Because the About Us page is fairly basic, it can be duplicated easily whenever you need to add new pages to the web site—all you need to do is change a couple of variables within the file.

Creating the Login System

The case study's login system had to be flexible enough to be included within several different modules throughout the web site's front-end. The basic framework of the login system comprises six pages that handle logging in, logging out, and registering new members. The main page in this folder is the loginform.cfm page, which is about 23 lines of code, most of which handles the HTML table and layout. The first two lines of code are responsible for setting default URL variables if they are not already present:

```
<cfparam name="URL.UserName" default="" type="string">
<cfparam name="URL.redirectURL" default="#CGI.SCRIPT_NAME#?#CGI.QUERY_STRING#">
```

The first variable, #URL.UserName#, is the username that the user entered into the form. If this is the first time the user is looking at the form, then the value won't be present and it will default to an empty field. If the user has been to the login form before and logged in unsuccessfully, the URL variable will be present and we can automatically fill the form for the user. Likewise, if the user has come from the registration form, ColdFusion will pass the user's username via a URL variable and fill in the user name field automatically.

The #URL.redirectURL# variable defaults to the current URL (with the Querystring appended to the end). By using this method, we can redirect the user back to the page being viewed before the user had to log in. The only other alternative to this would be to always force the user to return to the home page of the site after logging in or registering with the site. In this scenario, the user would have to navigate all the way back to the blog entry or book review being viewed, which would be time-consuming and frustrating.

The loginform.cfm page has only the most basic formatting, and doesn't call the header and footer pages or need any breadcrumb navigation. This is because it is included only in other pages or within the right-hand side column. The login/index.cfm page also includes the basic login form and is responsible for calling the header and footer code:

```
<cfparam name="URL.redirectURL" default="#Request.WebRoot#">
cfscript>
  Variables.breadCrumbs = "home|#Request.WebRoot#home/;login";
  Variables.header = "login";
</cfscript>
<cfmodule template="#Request.CFRoot#header.cfm"➡
  breadCrumbs="#Variables.breadCrumbs#" header="#Variables.header#">
<br />
<cfif IsDefined("URL.invalid")>
  <p class="error" align="center">Invalid User Name/Password. Please try
again.</p>
<cfelse>
  <p class="bold"> </p>
</cfif>
<cfinclude template="loginform.cfm">
<cfmodule template="#Request.CFRoot#footer.cfm"➡
  rightColumn="#Request.CFRoot#blog/calendar.cfm;➡
  #Request.CFRoot#blog/headlines.cfm">
```

The first line of the preceding code sets the #URL.redirectURL# variable if it hasn't already been defined. This is a very important step because it allows us to override the <cfparam> tag that tries to set the same variable within the loginform.cfm page. The code within the loginform.cfm page that we saw in the previous listing sets the #URL.redirectURL# variable to the current page and Querystring. If we did not override the #URL.redirectURL# variable in this index.cfm, whenever users successfully log in to the web site from the login/index.cfm page, they would be redirected back to the same page even though they are already logged in. This can be very confusing and nonintuitive.

The next step is to set the breadcrumb navigation and header variable, and then pass them to the site's header file. When users unsuccessfully log in to the site, they are redirected back to the login/index.cfm page. On this page, they are shown an Invalid User Name/Password message and are prompted to try again. Next we display the included login form.

When a user presses the Login button, the login form is submitted to the dologin.cfm page, verifying that the supplied username and password are valid, and the current user is active and hasn't been disabled by an administrator. If the user's account is valid, it will update the member's record in the database with the user's last login date and save the user's database record into a Session variable. Whenever we need to access the current user's MemberID or MemberName, we simply have to create a <cflock> around the Session variable and output the value. Finally, we redirect the user back to the value of the #redirectURL# variable.

If the user wasn't found in the database, or was marked as inactive by the site administrator, the user is redirected back to the login page. We then pass the value of the #Form.UserName# variable back to the login form so that we can automatically fill the form and display an error message prompting the user to try again. Notice that we pass back the original #redirectURL# variable to the page so even a user who didn't log in successfully the first time is redirected to the original page being viewed.

The login folder also contains the registration form, allowing new users to register on our site. This registration form has four fields that collect the user's name, e-mail address, username, and password. Here we use Dreamweaver's Check New Username server behavior to make sure that a username isn't already being used by another member. If no other members have this username, we then use the Insert Record server behavior to insert the new member into the Members database table.

If the username is already present, we redirect the user back to the registration form, automatically fill the member's name, e-mail address, and requested username, and prompt the user to try again. Once the new member is successfully created, we redirect the user to the login form and pass the new username as a URL variable to fill the username field in the login form automatically.

A single CFC is included in the login form. It has two functions, checkLoggedIn() and getMemberID(), as shown here:

```
<cfcomponent>
<cffunction name="checkLoggedIn" returntype="boolean" output="No"
access="public">
  <cfset Var isLoggedIn = FALSE >
  <cflock type="READONLY" name="session_userrecord" timeout="10">
    <cfset isLoggedIn = IsDefined("Session.UserRecord") >
  </cflock>
  <cfreturn isLoggedIn >
</cffunction>
<cffunction name="getMemberID" returntype="numeric" output="No" access="public">
  <cfset Var memberID = 0 >
  <cfif checkLoggedIn() >
    <cflock type="READONLY" name="session_userrecord" timeout="10">
      <cfset memberID = Session.UserRecord.MemberID >
    </cflock>
  </cfif>
  <cfreturn memberID >
</cffunction>
</cfcomponent>
```

The first function within the component checks whether the current user is already logged in to the web site. Once a user has logged in to the web site, a variable called `#Session.UserRecord#` is created, which contains the member's record from the Members table in the database. Because this variable is stored in the `#Session#` scope, we have to be careful to lock access to the variable before accessing it. If the `Session` variable is currently defined, the local function variable `#isLoggedIn#` evaluates to `true`; otherwise, its value evaluates to `false`. Finally, the value is returned to the page that called the function, where it can be used to hide or show content as necessary. This function is used within the application to hide the book review form unless a member is already logged in. It could also be used to replace the login form with a logout form if the user is already logged in to the site.

The second function, `#getMemberID()#`, returns the current user's `MemberID` so that we can identify the currently logged in user. It is often preferable to create functions or custom tags to perform these tasks rather than duplicating the code throughout the different parts of the site (such as the blog comment form and book review forms).

To change the `Session` variables to `client` variables in the future, we need to modify only this CFC and the `dologin.cfm` and `dologout.cfm` pages. Because it is built this way, we avoid having to search and replace the entire site's code for the occurrence of "session," which could result in conflicts throughout the site.

The source files for this section are in the `login` folder.

The Administration Site

The heart of any site often lies within the administration functionality. It is not uncommon to find that as little as 20 percent of your development time on a CFML application is spent on the public front-end, while the bulk of your time is spent developing screens and functionality to manage the data in the database (which ultimately drives the public site content). If the administration site isn't intuitively laid out, or is confusing, the clients are less likely to make updates or add new content. In drastic circumstances, clients will almost completely abandon the web site and either give up on having an online presence or else go back to the drawing board and have a different developer create a new site for them.

This is why you should carefully plan the functionality and structure of your administration sites. Notice in Figure 13-10 that our admin site has a fairly simple, intuitive navigation scheme. To access the administrator, you would simply navigate to the `index.cfm` file within the admin folder. We have included a default admin login of username "admin" and password "user."

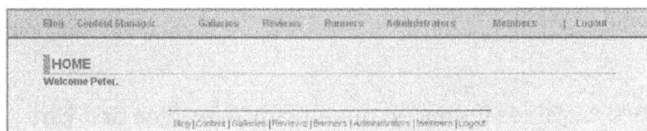

Figure 13-10. The basic case study administration site layout

The main navigation, which is fairly intuitive, has been duplicated on the top and bottom of the page. If the content within the pages gets too long, users can navigate between different parts of the administrator without having to scroll all the way to the top of the page just to click a link. Also, the headings are easy to find and clearly describe what functions they perform.

When you first navigate to the admin site, you are greeted with a basic login form asking for a username and password, similar to the front-end. There are a few different methods we can use here though. The code within the case study allows us to assign different usernames and passwords to different administrators so that they don't all have to share a single login account. To use only a single username/password combination, we could hardcode the username/password into our doLogin.cfm page and check the values entered into the form against these values, although this method can be very limiting in the long run.

One benefit of storing all the usernames and passwords in the database is that we can customize the admin site to whichever user is currently logged in. We could add a few more tables to the case study example database to store the links that appear at the top and bottom of the page. We could store which administrators have access to which tabs so that only certain administrators can perform particular actions. This can be useful when, for example, we want to add an administrator, but only want that administrator to be able to add blog entries but not touch the content management system. Currently, once an administrator logs in to the back-end of the site, they have full access and can add or delete whatever they wish.

Logging In to the Administrator

By default, every page within the admin site requires us to log in before we can view it. The login pages are the only pages within the administration site where we would want to override this behavior (for obvious reasons!). In our admin site, the code that checks whether a user is logged in is placed within the header.cfm custom tag. You can see the first few lines of this file:

```
<cfparam name="Attributes.showMenu" default="true" type="boolean">
<cfparam name="Attributes.checkLoggedIn" default="true" type="boolean">
<cfif Attributes.checkLoggedIn >
  <cfif NOT IsDefined( "Client.AdminID" ) >
    <cfset Client.redirectURL = CGI.SCRIPT_NAME &"?"& CGI.QUERY_STRING >
    <cflocation url="#Request.AdminRoot#login/index.cfm">
  </cfif>
</cfif>
```

By default, we create two variables if they do not already exist. The first variable, #Attributes.showMenu#, determines whether the main admin site's navigation menu will be displayed. If a user hasn't logged into the site, we use this variable to hide the navigation in case these users aren't supposed to have access to the admin web site. We don't want random users to be able to view any part of our administration web site and know what components (and their filenames) we have. They could try and gain access to the back-end if we haven't properly secured it.

The second variable, #Attributes.checkLoggedIn#, is responsible for checking whether the user needs to be logged in before viewing the current page. Both these variables are set only on the login page (to override the login requirement) and can be ignored otherwise. This is because their defaults are usually the best option. By default, the header will require that the user is logged in before being able to view any pages.

The next block of code in the preceding listing does the actual checking of the user's login status. The admin web site uses client variables. If the #Client.AdminID# variable isn't defined, we know the user hasn't been logged in yet, so we set a client variable on the page the user was trying to access and redirect the user to the login form. This is fairly similar to how the front-end login mechanism worked. The rest of the header file sets up the layout of the admin site and displays the menu if the value of #Attributes.showMenu# is true.

The footer.cfm custom tag is similar to the header.cfm file, except that it closes the necessary tables and displays the main navigation at the bottom of the page if the #Attributes.showMenu# variable is true.

The admin/login/index.cfm page has the following code snippet at the top of the file:

```
<cfparam name="URL.UserName" default="" type="string">
<cfmodule template="#Request.AdminCFRoot#layout/header.cfm"➥
   checkLoggedIn="false"➥
   showMenu="false">
<cfoutput>
<cfif IsDefined( "Client.errorMessage" ) >
   <p class="error" align="center">#Client.errorMessage#</p>
   <cfset DeleteClientVariable( "errorMessage" ) >
</cfif>
```

If the UserName variable is present in the Querystring, we use the existing value; otherwise, we set the default username to an empty string. Next, we call the header.cfm custom tag and set our two attributes to false so that the menu isn't displayed to the user until the user has log in. We don't want to check whether the user is currently logged in, because the user is at the login form.

Next, we check whether the client variable named #errorMessage# is defined. If it is, then the user has probably attempted to log in and was unsuccessful. In this case, we display the error message from the client scope and then delete the client variable. The remaining code in this page creates the login form and provides basic <cfform> validation to make sure that the user fills out both form fields.

Once the user clicks the Login button, the user is redirected to the doLogin.cfm page:

```
<cfparam name="Form.UserName" type="string">
<cfparam name="Form.Password" type="string">
<cfinvoke component="#Request.CFCRoot#admin.login.login_cfc"➥
  method="checkUserNamePassword" returnvariable="getAdmin">
  <cfinvokeargument name="UserName" value="#Trim( Form.UserName )#">
  <cfinvokeargument name="Password" value="#Trim( Form.Password )#">
</cfinvoke>
<cfif getAdmin.RecordCount GT 0>
  <cfset Client.AdminID = getAdmin.AdminID >
  <cfset Client.AdminName = getAdmin.AdminName >
  <cfif IsDefined( "Client.redirectURL" ) >
    <cfset Variables.redirectURL = Client.redirectURL >
    <cfset DeleteClientVariable( "redirectURL" ) >
    <cflocation url="#Variables.redirectURL#">
  <cfelse>
    <cflocation url="#Request.AdminRoot#index.cfm">
  </cfif>
<cfelse>
  <cfset Client.errorMessage = "Invalid UserName/Password. Please try again." >
  <cflocation url="index.cfm?UserName=#URLEncodedFormat( Form.UserName )#">
</cfif>
```

At the very beginning of the page, we make sure that both the #Form.UserName# and #Form.Password# variables are present. Then we pass the user-supplied UserName and Password values to the login_cfc component and try and match the values against the database. The #checkUserNamePassword()# function in the database will never return more than one record, so if a match was found, the <cfif> block is then executed. Here we set the values for #Client.AdminID# and #Client.AdminName# to the values from the database. If a variable called #Client.redirectURL# already exists, we set a local variable to the value of #Client.redirectURL#, delete the client variable by using the #DeleteClientVariable()# function, and redirect the user to the value of the #Variables.redirectURL# variable.

If a #Client.redirectURL# variable is not found, the user is redirected to the root admin page, which has a personalized welcome message for the user. If no matches were found in the database, we set the value of the variable #Client.errorMessage# we looked at earlier in this section and redirect the user back to the login form, pass the username, and automatically fill in the appropriate fields. Whew!

> **TIP** *Never automatically fill out the password field, pass it along the Querystring, or store it in a cookie. The plain text password will be visible in the address bar of the browser or in the cookie text file, and users can view a password field's contents by selecting View Source in the browser and looking for the value of the password text field.*

The contents of the `doLogout.cfm` page are as follows:

```
<cfloop list="#getClientVariablesList( )#" index="thisClientVar">
  <cfset DeleteClientVariable( thisClientVar ) >
</cfloop>
<cflocation url="#Request.AdminRoot#">
```

These four lines of code loop through each `client` variable and makes sure they are deleted. Once all the variables have been deleted, the user is redirected back to the root admin page.

The source files for this section are in the `admin/login` folder.

Blog Administrator

The first tab in the top navigation of the admin site is the Blog tab. The blog area is where we can add, edit, and delete blogs on the site and post our daily comments. From the Blog index page we can browse blogs by month, search blogs for a certain keyword (similar to how it worked on the front-end), and add a new blog entry.

If you select a date from the Date drop-down menu under BROWSE BLOGS (as shown in Figure 13-11), you will see a listing of days for the selected month. All dates with blog entries are highlighted and hyperlinked. Click on a hyperlinked date to see a list of blog entries for that specific date at the bottom of the page.

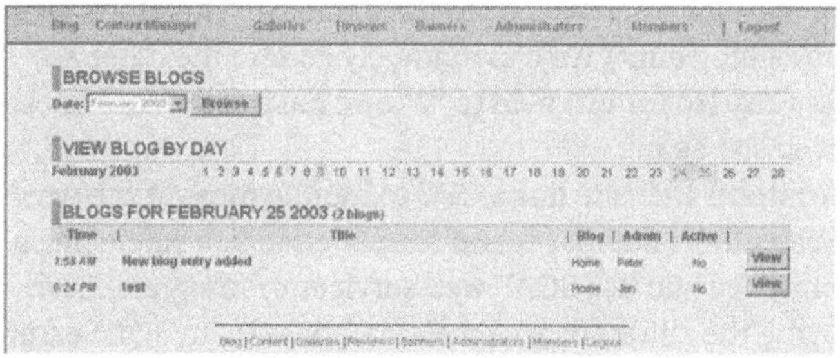

Figure 13-11. The Blog admin page

We can change the month at any point by changing the value in the drop-down menu and clicking the Browse button. We can view a blog entry by clicking the View button, which brings up a detailed page for that blog showing the blog's title, link, teaser, date, full blog text, and the name of the administrator who created the blog. The bottom of the page also has buttons to edit the current blog, delete the current blog, view comments for the current blog, and a Back button that takes us back to the index page.

Notice that the button used to delete the current blog uses red text. If the user presses the button, a JavaScript confirmation dialog box pops up to confirm if the user wants to delete the blog entry. This reduces the chance of an administrator deleting a blog entry by mistake.

> **TIP**   *In cases like this, it is OK to rely on JavaScript if you set the system requirements for the administrative users to include JavaScript.*

Although the pop-up dialog box tells users that the deletion cannot be undone, it is a little misleading. For most tables in the database, there is an option to set the object to be active or inactive. Only active items are shown on the front-end. Inactive items are shown only in the back-end and are used when an administrator wants to hide that item until they are ready for it to be displayed on the front-end.

An example of this would be the photo gallery section of the web site. It's best to leave the galleries inactive until you are completely finished adding and ordering images, and have assigned a text description to each. You wouldn't want users viewing the gallery when you are in the middle of doing this.

Once an item is deleted by way of the web site, another bit field within the table is changed. Almost every table within the database also allows you to set a Deleted flag that hides the item from the site's front-end and back-end. This lets the admin site users believe that the content has actually been removed from the database, but allows the developer to still view the content and not lose any information until the developer manually purges it from the database. Therefore, even if a user accidentally deletes a blog entry, we can manually go into the database and set the BlogEntryDeleted Yes/No (or bit) field to "0" and have the record show up in the administration web site again.

Each folder within the admin web site has a CFC to handle most of the work as well. This allows us to keep all the databases and similar code in a single place, and extend our application so we can use SOAP web services or integrate Flash Remoting. If you were moving the site from an Access database to an SQL Server database so you could take advantage of Stored Procedures or Views, and you would be able to see all the queries for that folder in a single file. The blog_cfc.cfc page in the admin/blogs folder contains a total of 11 functions:

- getBlogs(): returns all blog categories within the database

- searchBlogsByKeyword(): searches all blog entries for a particular keyword

- getBlogMonths(): returns month/year combinations, which contain blog entries

- getBlogMonthDays(): returns the days which have blog entries in a given month

- getBlogEntriesByDate(): returns every blog entry for a given date

- getBlogByBlogEntryID(): returns a specific blog entry based on the supplied BlogEntryID

- insertBlogEntry(): inserts a blog entry into the database

- updateBlogEntry(): updates an existing blog entry in the database

- deleteBlogEntry(): marks a existing blog entry as "deleted" within the database

- getBlogCommentsByBlogEntryID(): retrieves user comments for a particular blog entry

- deleteBlogComments(): deletes a single blog comment or group of blog comments from the database

Some of these function names are long and cumbersome to type. Adding intuitive names to functions and variables goes a long way toward easing your task when debugging your application or modifying it in the future. Each of the other modules within the admin site share similar functions that perform the basic tasks, such as select all records, select a single record, insert a new record, update an existing record, and mark an existing record as deleted.

The horizontal calendar navigation for the VIEW BLOG BY DAY section is generated by running a query that grabs every distinct day having a blog entry within a given month. The code for this is found in the #getBlogMonthDays()# function that resides within the blog_cfc.cfc page in the admin/blog folder. This function returns the Recordset back to the blogsByDate.cfm page. Here the query is converted into a list by using the handy #ValueList()# function. This function takes in a single parameter, query name, and column name, and returns every value from that query's column as a comma-delimited list. Here is an example:

```
<cfparam name="URL.date" default="#Now()#" type="date">
<cfobject name="blog_cfc" component="blog_cfc" type="component">
<cfset getBlogDays = blog_cfc.getBlogMonthDays( URL.date ) >
<cfset blogDayList = ValueList( getBlogDays.BlogEntryDay ) >
```

We first create an object within ColdFusion for the CFC. This enables us to easily call multiple functions within this CFC without having to invoke functions constantly by using a tag-based syntax. Now, by passing a date to the #getBlogMonthDays()# function, the #getBlogDays# variable will be made to hold a query containing a single column of the days in a certain month that contains blog entries.

We convert this query of day numbers into a comma-separated list by using the #ValueList()# function, which tells the function which query and column we want to convert to a list. The comma-delimited list of days is now stored in a variable called #blogDayList#; this is used when looping through each day of the current month and hyperlinking any day that appears within this list, as follows:

```
<cfloop from="1" to="#DaysInMonth( URL.date )#" index="thisDay">
  <cfif ListFind( blogDayList, thisDay )>
    <td class="smalltext" bgcolor="##DDDDDD">
      <a href="blogsbydate.cfm?date=#DateFormat( CreateDate( Year(URL.date),➡
        Month(URL.date), thisDay ),"mm/dd/yyyy" )#" class="smalllink">#thisDay#➡
      </a>
    </td>
  <cfelse>
    <td class="smalltext">#thisDay#</td>
  </cfif>
</cfloop>
```

This code loops from 1 to the number of days in the specified month and, if the previously created list of days contains the same value as the current day, we highlight that cell and hyperlink the day. Otherwise, the date is displayed without being linked. By linking only days with actual blog entries, the user won't have to click on each day of the month to check whether an entry was posted on that date.

Within the VIEW BLOG page we looked at previously, click on the Edit button to open the edit form shown in Figure 13-12.

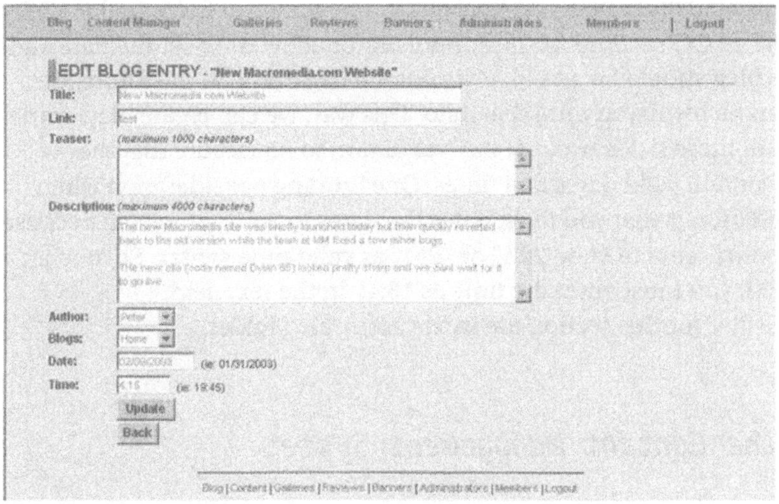

Figure 13-12. The Edit Blog Entry form

Notice that for the text fields, we have included the maximum number of characters that the database column will accept. Because text fields don't have a built-in maximum length attribute, we must ensure that the user hasn't entered more characters than the database will accept. If the user has, errors will be thrown when we try and insert/update that record. Within the form we could create a small text field that reports the number of characters the user has already entered—once the user reaches the maximum allowance, no more characters would be accepted. While this is probably the most user-friendly approach, it won't work if the user has disabled JavaScript in the browser.

The other option is to simply trim the data before it is entered into the database, so if the user entered 1,200 characters and your database will only accept 1,000, we could trim the last 200 characters by using the following snippet:

```
<cfset Variables.trimmedTeaser = Left( Form.BlogEntryTeaser, 1000 ) >
```

If using this approach, you have a couple of options to choose from. You could display a message to the end-user warning of the impending truncation before inserting the trimmed data into the database, thereby giving the user a chance to go back and modify the text. Or, you could trim the data before inserting it and notify the user afterward that the text had to be cropped.

You can also see an Author drop-down menu in Figure 13-12. This menu contains the names of each site administrator. If we add a new blog entry, the Author menu will default to the currently logged in user.

There is also a drop-down menu for the blog. This system is designed so that if we want to add multiple blogs to a site, we can easily modify the existing code and create additional blogs with minimal effort. The final two fields in the ADD BLOG and EDIT BLOG sections of the administrator allow us to set the date and time when the blog should be added. If we enter a date/time in the future, the blog entry won't be displayed until that date. This way, we can create blog entries in advance! Both these fields use `<cfform>` validation to make sure that they're filled out and contain valid dates and times. One limiting consideration when using time validation is that you must enter the dates in 24-hour format because ColdFusion doesn't seem to view "AM" or "PM" as valid time syntax. So, to post a blog at 6:45PM, you must enter the time as 18:45 in the text field.

The source files for this section are in the `admin/blog` folder.

Building the Content Management System

The content management system is one of the more basic modules in the admin site. Administrators are presented with a drop-down menu of available pages to edit, and a button to add new pages as required, as shown in Figure 13-13.

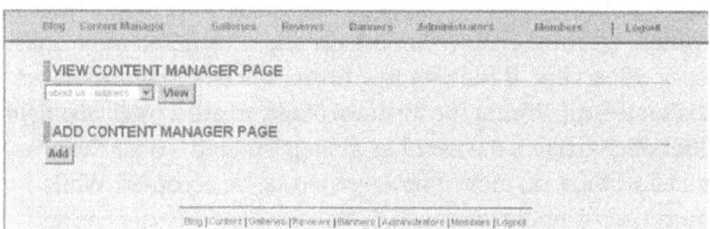

Figure 13-13. The Content Manager home page

In a similar fashion to the Blog administrator, clicking on the View button on the main page brings up a details page. Here the user can see the page name, the title of the page (more on this in a moment), the text that will appear on the front-end, and the date and time when the content was last modified. Currently, the date the content was last updated is shown only in the administration section, but we can easily add it to the front-end and include a last-modified date so users will be able to tell how current the site's content is (see Figure 13-14).

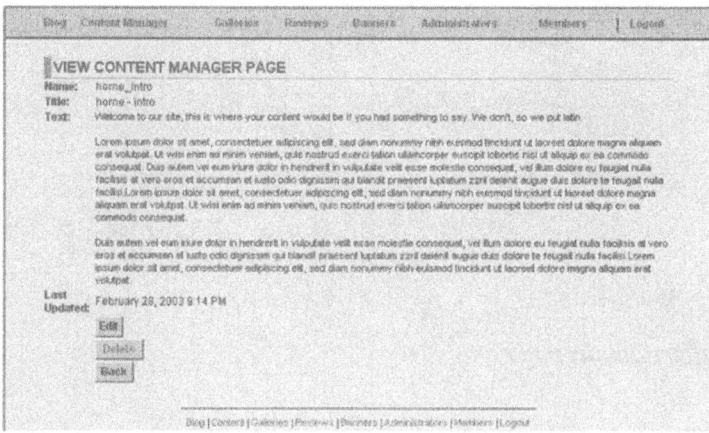

Figure 13-14. The Content Manager details page

You can see from Figure 13-14 that there is both a page name and a page title in the content management system. The page name is how the content is referred to in the front-end. You saw earlier in this chapter that we used the following code when calling the content management system on the About Us page.

```
<cfoutput>#GetPageContent("aboutus_intro")#</cfoutput>
```

The page title is used only in the administration portion of the site and should ideally be a more "human readable" form. Instead of trying to remember the difference between aboutus_intro, aboutus_address, and aboutus_footer, give these pages a more descriptive title so that you can easily distinguish between each entry.

The rest of the content management system is similar to the blog admin we saw earlier in the chapter. There is an add page, edit page, delete page, and appropriate "back" buttons, which allow users return to the previous screen without committing any changes.

The source files for this section are in the admin/contentmanager folder.

Building the Gallery Administrator

The gallery administrator shows a list of galleries with View buttons beside each record. These buttons allow us to view the details of the image gallery, similar to the previous two sections within the administrator. From the details page we can click a button and edit the gallery name, description, date, and set the gallery to active or inactive. There are also buttons to delete the gallery, or view all the images within the current gallery, as shown in Figure 13-15.

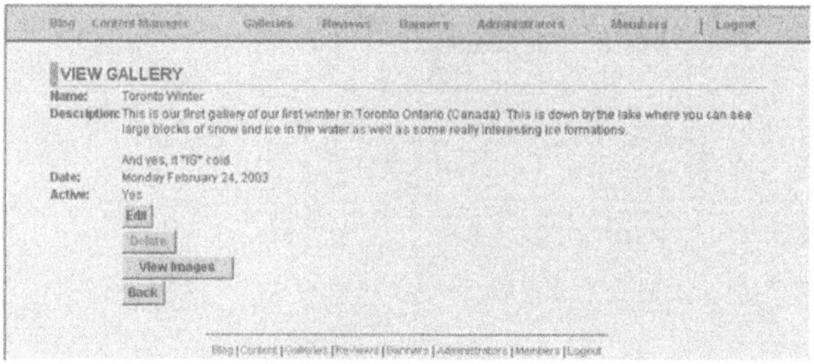

Figure 13-15. The Gallery details page

Clicking on the View Images button brings up a page that lets us reorder the images within the gallery, or add a new image to the current gallery.

Above each gallery image is a text box where we can reorder the images by assigning each image a number, then clicking the Update Gallery Images button. ColdFusion will loop through each text field and update the corresponding record in the database, and it will sort the images in the order we specified. To modify an image, we click on the thumbnail to bring up the EDIT GALLERY IMAGE page, where we can assign the image to a different gallery, change the image, modify the description, or delete the image altogether.

The code to reorder the images within the gallery is as follows:

```
<!--- doUpdateGalleryImageOrders.cfm --->
<cfparam name="Form.GalleryID" type="numeric">
<cfparam name="Form.GalleryImageIDList" type="string">
<cfset Variables.GalleryImageIDArray = ListToArray( Form.GalleryImageIDList ) >
<cfloop from="1" to="#ArrayLen( Variables.GalleryImageIDArray )#" index="index">
  <cfset Variables.thisGalleryImageID = Variables.GalleryImageIDArray[ index ] >
  <cfif IsNumeric( Variables.thisGalleryImageID ) >
    <cfquery datasource="#Request.DSN#">
      UPDATE
        GalleryImages
      SET
        GalleryImageOrder = <cfqueryparam value="#Val( Form[ "GalleryImageOrder_" &➥
        Variables.thisGalleryImageID ] )#" cfsqltype="CF_SQL_INTEGER">
      WHERE
        GalleryImageID = <cfqueryparam value="#Variables.thisGalleryImageID#">
    </cfquery>
  </cfif>
</cfloop>
<cflocation url="viewGalleryImages.cfm?GalleryID=#Form.GalleryID#">
```

Within the doUpdateGalleryImageOrders.cfm page, we first check that two variables exist before we try to use them: #Form.GalleryID# and

#Form.GalleryImageIDList#. The second variable is a comma-separated list of the GalleryImageID for each image on the viewGalleryImages.cfm page. This value is passed from viewGalleryImages.cfm as a hidden value:

```
<input type="hidden" name="GalleryImageIDList" ➡
  value="#ValueList(getGalleryImages.GalleryImageID)#">
```

The #ValueList()# function returns a comma-separated list of values based on a query column. We pass that to the doUpdateGalleryImageOrders.cfm page as a hidden variable, which is then converted to an array by using ColdFusion's #ListToArray()# function. Often it is easier to convert values back and forth from lists to arrays when we need to perform certain tasks. In this case it is easier to access values within the array by using array notation than it is to use the #ListGetAt()# function repeatedly to grab certain items from a list. We loop from 1 to the number of items within the array and set a local variable called thisGalleryImageID, which represents the current GalleryImageID within the array.

For each gallery image, we will update the GalleryImages table and set the order to the value that was passed in the text box. We only update that specific gallery image with the new order. Once ColdFusion has finished updating each image in the gallery, the administrator is redirected back to the viewGalleryImages.cfm page, and the images should now be in the desired order.

The source files for this section are in the admin/galleries folder.

Building the Book Review Administrator

This section is very similar to the blog administrator, except that it has a little less navigation. The books are displayed as a simple list (similar to the Galleries section) rather than having a search feature and calendar to locate a record. Books must be entered by a site administrator before they are visible and can be reviewed by members. Each book has a title, a unique ISBN and publisher, and can be marked as active or inactive depending on whether we want it to be shown on the front-end.

By clicking on the View button, we are able to see the book's overall ratings and the number of reviews it has received. Unlike the front-end, the administration site shows the real average rating, which isn't rounded to the closest half digit.

When a book is deleted, it still remains in the database, but the record is flagged as deleted and isn't shown on the front-end or back-end. This also means that all the reviews stay intact, so if we want to create reports later on which books were the highest rated or most reviewed, we haven't lost any historical data. To actually remove these items and reviews from the database, we would need to delete them manually or create a page that will allow us to remove them from the database for good.

The source files for this section are in the admin/reviews/books folder.

Creating the Banner Engine

The banner engine is built primarily in Flash, but uses Flash Remoting and a CFC to retrieve a list of available banners from the server. Currently, the banner engine is flexible enough to accept both JPEGs and SWF files, and we can specify how many seconds the banner should stay visible before refreshing. Future banner engine upgrades could include logging how many times the banner was displayed and clicked by users, and building simple charts to show how many times the banners were clicked within a certain period of time.

The screenshot in Figure 13-16 shows three currently active banners in the site, and each banner is a JPEG image.

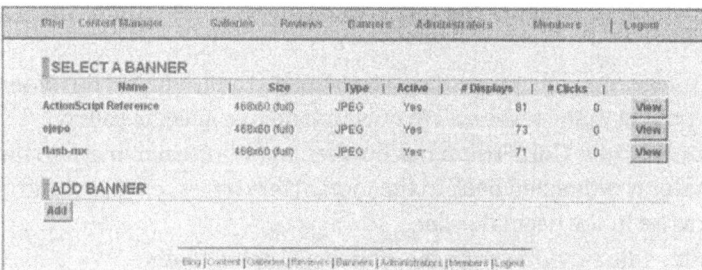

Figure 13-16. The main banner admin page

Clicking on the View button brings up the details page, as shown in Figure 13-17.

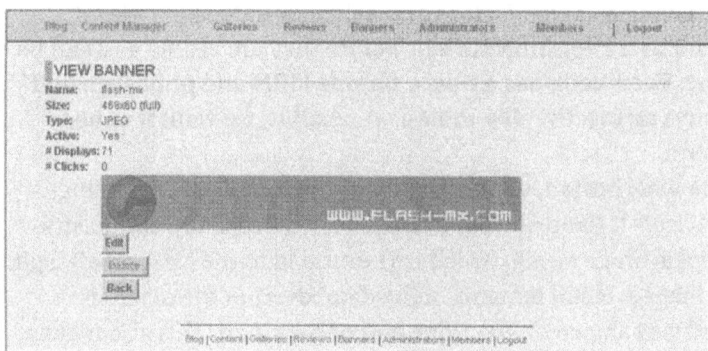

Figure 13-17. The banner details page

The source files for this section are in the admin/banners folder.

Building the Administrator and Member Modules

The remaining two sections of the admin web site are very similar. The Administrator tab allows us to select from a list of administrators or add a new one. The only information currently being saved to a database on administrators is their name, e-mail address, username, password, and whether they are active. Much like members on the front-end of the web site, if an administrator is inactive or has been deleted, that administrator can no longer log in to the web site; another administrator must mark this user as active before the user is able to log in again.

To limit the tabs that each administrator has access to, we would need to create a page with each section of the administrator (such as Blog, Content Manager, Galleries, Reviews, etc.). Each menu item would have a checkbox beside it that controls whether the administrator has access to that page. We could even extend this security model further by trying to limit the actions that an administrator can take within a section, or organize administrators into groups and assign group privileges similar to Windows security, via a few extra database tables. For example, we could limit a certain administrator to only the Members tab, and within that the administrator would be allowed only to add a new user but not modify or delete any existing users.

The final section, Members, allows administrators to modify a user's settings, change passwords, e-mail a member (assuming the member used a valid e-mail address) and inactivate/delete current users. Similar to the blog calendar navigation, the Members section uses letter-based navigation and only hyperlinks the appropriate letters of the alphabet that contain users. Administrators can also click the ALL button within the navigation and page through all members of the site ten at a time.

The administration site also displays the date the users were created on, how many days they have been members, and when the users last logged in. We could take this further and log the most recent IP address that the users connected from, or create a script to delete members who haven't logged in within the last 90 days.

The add/edit member forms also contain code that prevents administrators from creating two members with the same username. If you try creating a new user account with a password that is already in use, a message displays, prompting you to try a new username.

The source files for this section are in the admin/administrators and admin/members folders.

This has been a fairly fast-paced look at a complete working application. We could extend the modules shown in this chapter in almost an infinite number of ways. Other ideas include creating a syndicated XML feed of our blog, letting users rate and comment on gallery images, allowing members to have their own journals/blogs within the site, and letting users customize how many days of blog entries they want to display at a time. We could even integrate more

Flash Remoting into this application and convert our existing images galleries into a Flash gallery, similar to the Flash banner engine included here, or the image gallery we built in Chapter 12.

If you are using SQL Server or Oracle, you could convert your queries to Stored Procedures and use Views to simplify many of the queries.

Summary

This chapter has walked you through the process of building a complete web site and a few of the design/programming considerations to keep in mind when building an application. We also saw a few more tags and functions, and how several of the techniques described throughout the book work together to build modules and perform calculations.

Although this book is not a completely exhaustive reference, we are confident that we have provided you with enough knowledge to start producing great dynamic ColdFusion applications using Dreamweaver MX. Dozens of excellent resources are available to help you learn more about ColdFusion. Some of the best places to meet other ColdFusion developers are on mailing lists such as:

- ColdFusion Developers Journal (CFDJ) mailing list: http://www.sys-con.com/coldfusion/list.cfm

- House of Fusion: http://www.houseoffusion.com/cf_lists/ (currently has 21 different mailing lists ranging from ColdFusion, Dreamweaver, and SQL, to ColdFusion Job Boards)

- Macromedia LiveDocs site: http://livedocs.macromedia.com/ (contains comprehensive documentation on ColdFusion and Flash Remoting)

- Macromedia's DevNet: http://www.macromedia.com/devnet/ (features development centers for ColdFusion, Dreamweaver, Flash, Flash Remoting and a handful of other Macromedia products)

- CFLib.org: http://www.cflib.org/ (has an excellent collection of UDFs)

- CFStandards.org: http://www.cfstandards.org/ (a site devoted to defining CFML code and architecture best practices, and free distribution of modules for "dropping" functionality into CFML applications)

- DevMX: http://www.devmx.com/ (boasts excellent tutorials and fantastic forums on most of the Macromedia product line, as well as mailing lists that heavily favor ColdFusion/Flash integration)

Index

forums.apress.com

FOR PROFESSIONALS BY PROFESSIONALS™

JOIN THE APRESS FORUMS AND BE PART OF OUR COMMUNITY. You'll find discussions that cover topics of interest to IT professionals, programmers, and enthusiasts just like you. If you post a query to one of our forums, you can expect that some of the best minds in the business—especially Apress authors, who all write with *The Expert's Voice*™—will chime in to help you. Why not aim to become one of our most valuable participants (MVPs) and win cool stuff? Here's a sampling of what you'll find:

DATABASES
Data drives everything.

Share information, exchange ideas, and discuss any database programming or administration issues.

INTERNET TECHNOLOGIES AND NETWORKING
Try living without plumbing (and eventually IPv6).

Talk about networking topics including protocols, design, administration, wireless, wired, storage, backup, certifications, trends, and new technologies.

JAVA
We've come a long way from the old Oak tree.

Hang out and discuss Java in whatever flavor you choose: J2SE, J2EE, J2ME, Jakarta, and so on.

MAC OS X
All about the Zen of OS X.

OS X is both the present and the future for Mac apps. Make suggestions, offer up ideas, or boast about your new hardware.

OPEN SOURCE
Source code is good; understanding (open) source is better.

Discuss open source technologies and related topics such as PHP, MySQL, Linux, Perl, Apache, Python, and more.

PROGRAMMING/BUSINESS
Unfortunately, it is.

Talk about the Apress line of books that cover software methodology, best practices, and how programmers interact with the "suits."

WEB DEVELOPMENT/DESIGN
Ugly doesn't cut it anymore, and CGI is absurd.

Help is in sight for your site. Find design solutions for your projects and get ideas for building an interactive Web site.

SECURITY
Lots of bad guys out there—the good guys need help.

Discuss computer and network security issues here. Just don't let anyone else know the answers!

TECHNOLOGY IN ACTION
Cool things. Fun things.

It's after hours. It's time to play. Whether you're into LEGO® MINDSTORMS™ or turning an old PC into a DVR, this is where technology turns into fun.

WINDOWS
No defenestration here.

Ask questions about all aspects of Windows programming, get help on Microsoft technologies covered in Apress books, or provide feedback on any Apress Windows book.

HOW TO PARTICIPATE:
Go to the Apress Forums site at **http://forums.apress.com/**
Click the New User link.